Access to International Justice

There is much debate about the scope of international law, its compatibility with individual state practice, its enforceability and the recent and limited degree to which it is institutionalized.

This collection of essays seeks to address the issue of access to justice, the related element of domestic rule of law which does not yet figure significantly in debates about international rule of law. Even in cases in which laws are passed, institutions are present and key players are ethically committed to the rule of law, those whom the laws are intended to protect may be unable to secure protection. This is an issue in most domestic jurisdictions but also one which poses severe problems for international justice worldwide.

The book will be of interest to academics and practitioners of international law, environmental law, transitional justice, international development, human rights, ethics, international relations and political theory.

Patrick Keyzer is Head of School and Chair of Law and Public Policy, La Trobe University, Melbourne, Australia.

Vesselin Popovski is Senior Academic Programme Officer at the United Nations University, Tokyo, Japan.

Charles Sampford is Director of the Institute for Ethics, Governance and Law, a joint initiative with the United Nations University, Griffith, QUT, ANU, Jindal Global University and the Center for Asian Integrity.

Routledge/Challenges of Globalisation
Edited by Charles Sampford and Carmel Connors
Griffith University, Australia

This series seeks to make systematic contributions to international debates over two intimately related issues:

- The values that should inform the governance of modern states and the globalizing world in which they are increasingly enmeshed, in particular whether the liberal democratic values that sought to civilize the sovereign state need to be reconceived as global values.
- The institutions that are needed to realize those values, be they local, national, regional, international, transnational or global.

1 **Globalisation and Equality**
Edited by Keith Horton and Haig Patapan

2 **Globalisation and the Rule of Law**
Edited by Spencer Zifcak

3 **Environmental Values in a Globalising World**
Nature, justice and governance
Edited by Jouni Paavola and Ian Lowe

4 **Globalisation and Citizenship**
The transnational challenge
Edited by Wayne Hudson and Steven Slaughter

5 **Global Democracy and its Difficulties**
Edited by Anthony J. Langlois and Karol Edward Soltan

6 **New Visions for Market Governance**
Crisis and renewal
Edited by Kate MacDonald, Shelley Marshall and Sanjay Pinto

7 **Shifting Global Powers and International Law**
Challenges and opportunities
Edited by Rowena Maguire, Bridget Lewis and Charles Sampford

8 **Institutional Supports for the International Rule of Law**
Edited by Charles Sampford and Ramesh Thakur

9 **Access to International Justice**
Edited by Patrick Keyzer, Vesselin Popovski and Charles Sampford

Access to International Justice

Edited by Patrick Keyzer,
Vesselin Popovski and
Charles Sampford

Routledge
Taylor & Francis Group
LONDON AND NEW YORK

First published 2015
by Routledge
2 Park Square, Milton Park, Abingdon, Oxfordshire OX14 4RN

and by Routledge
711 Third Avenue, New York, NY 10017

First issued in paperback 2016

Routledge is an imprint of the Taylor & Francis Group, an informa business

British Library Cataloguing in Publication Data
A catalogue record for this book is available from the British Library

Library of Congress Cataloging in Publication Data
Access to international justice/edited by Charles Sampford, Patrick Keyzer, Vesselin Popovski.
pages cm. – (Challenges of globalisation)
Includes bibliographical references and index.
1. International law. 2. International courts. 3. International law and human rights. I. Sampford, C. J. G. (Charles J. G.) editor. II. Keyzer, Patrick, editor. III. Popovski, Vesselin, editor.
KZ3410.A282 2015
341–dc23 2014022475

ISBN 13: 978-1-138-23824-4 (pbk)

ISBN 13: 978-1-138-78733-9 (hbk)

Typeset in Times New Roman
by Wearset Ltd, Boldon, Tyne and Wear

Contents

Contributors

Afshin Akhtarkhavari is Associate Professor and Reader in Law, Griffith University. He researches and writes from a range of perspectives to critique and study conceptions of nature in the context of global politics and law. His first book, *Global Governance of the Environment: Environmental Principles and Change in International Law and Politics*, sought to explore epistemological issues around the nature of change in international environmental law and politics.

Dan Banik is a visiting scholar at both CDDRL and the Center for the Study of Poverty and Inequality (SCSPI). He is an Associate Professor and Research Director of the Centre for Development and Environment at the University of Oslo, Norway. Dr Banik's research interests include development theory, democracy, inequality, human rights, legal empowerment of the poor, policy studies and implementation, development ethics, under-nutrition and famine, civil service reform and media in developing countries.

Edwin Bikundo is a Lecturer at the Griffith Law School. He has teaching and research interests in international and comparative law, international criminal law, international humanitarian law, the law of evidence and critical legal theory. His current research focuses on the role of the international criminal trial in preventing the reoccurrence of violence.

Simon Chesterman is Dean of the National University of Singapore Faculty of Law. He is also Editor of the *Asian Journal of International Law*. Chesterman is the author or editor of twelve books, including *One Nation Under Surveillance* (OUP, 2011); *Law and Practice of the United Nations* (with Thomas M. Franck and David M. Malone, OUP, 2008); *You, The People* (OUP, 2004); and *Just War or Just Peace?* (OUP, 2001).

David P. Forsythe is University Professor and Charles J. Mach Distinguished Professor of Political Science, Emeritus, University of Nebraska. His work focuses on international human rights, international law and organization, American foreign policy, and international relations.

Patrick Keyzer is Head of School, Chair of Law and Public Policy, La Trobe Law School, Australia. Patrick has teaching and research interests in constitutional law, human rights law and disability, and risk management in a variety of contexts. Patrick is a barrister who has appeared as counsel in the High Court of Australia and represented fellow Australians in the United Nations Human Rights Committees.

Susan Lamb is Professor and Vice Dean, Executive Director, Centre for International Criminal Justice and International Humanitarian Law at O.P. Jindal Global University. Susan Lamb joined the Jindal Global Law School in July 2013 following a fifteen-year career with various United Nations justice responses to atrocity crimes in the former Yugoslavia, Rwanda and Cambodia. Between 2009 and 2013, she was the Senior Judicial Coordinator to the United Nations Assistance to the Khmer Rouge Trials (UNAKRT) and the Senior Legal Officer to the Trial Chamber of the Extraordinary Chambers in the Courts of Cambodia (ECCC).

Brendan Mackey is Director of the Griffith Climate Change Response Program. He has a PhD in ecology from the Australian National University. He is a member of the international Council for the International Union for Conservation of Nature (IUCN) and co-chairs the Earth Charter International Council. Brendan serves on various governmental advisory bodies including the science advisory group to the Climate Change Commission.

Rahmat Mohamad read law at the Institut Teknologi MARA, Malaysia, pursued his LLM at Bristol University, England, and earned his Doctor of Philosophy (PhD) at the University of Aberystwyth, United Kingdom. Currently H.E. Professor, Dr Rahmat Mohamad is the Secretary-General of the Asian-African Legal Consultative Organization (AALCO) where he was appointed in 2008 and then re-appointed in 2012. His work with AALCO has seen him bring the weight of the opinions and collective voices of developing countries in the Asian–African region to bear in various international forums, particularly with regards to providing a third-world perspective on the progressive development of international law, as well as the dissemination of international law in Asian–African countries.

Darren O'Donovan is Associate Professor, Faculty of Law, Bond University. Darren completed his PhD thesis on equality, multiculturalism and housing rights at University College Cork in Ireland in 2009. He worked at UCC as a lecturer for three years before joining Bond in January 2012.

Mirinda O'Gorman, BBus (Finance) and LLB, is a recent graduate of the Queensland University of Technology. Mirinda graduated with first-class honours and was the recipient of a University Medal. During 2011, she worked as an intern at the Delhi Office of the South Asia Human Rights Document Centre and at the International Criminal Court, The Hague.

Vesselin Popovski is Senior Academic Programme Officer, United Nations University, Tokyo. He undertakes research and postgraduate teaching and supervision in the field of international relations, peace and security, international law, human rights, international criminal justice and governance.

Nicole Rogers is a Senior Lecturer in the School of Law and Justice at Southern Cross University, NSW. Nicole's research interests include the intersection of performance studies theory and law and climate change law, with a particular emphasis on climate change litigation.

Charles Sampford is Director of the Institute for Ethics, Governance and Law, a joint initiative with the United Nations University, Griffith, QUT, ANU, Jindal Global University and the Center for Asian Integrity in Manila. He is Professor of Law and Research Professor in Ethics, Griffith University and Adjunct Professor, QUT and York.

Ramesh Thakur is Director of the Centre for Nuclear Non-proliferation and Disarmament (CNND) in the Crawford School, Australian National University. The author or editor of over thirty books and 300 articles and book chapters, he also writes regularly for quality national and international newspapers around the world. He serves on the international advisory boards of institutes in Africa, Asia, Europe and North America.

Yasunobu Sato is an advisor at Nagashima Ohno and Tsunematsu and is a Professor at the University of Tokyo, Graduate School of Arts and Sciences, Graduate Program on Human Security and Visiting Fellow of The Australian National University. Professor Sato has practised law in Japan, the United States and Europe and worked for refugee protection, peacekeeping/-building and law and judicial reform as a legal official with international organizations.

Acknowledgements

This research was supported under an Australian Research Council (ARC) Linkage Grant: Building the Rule of Law in International Affairs. The views expressed herein are those of the authors and are not necessarily those of the Australian Research Council.

The editors also wish to acknowledge the generous support and substantial funding provided by the Centre for International Governance Innovation (CIGI), as well as the support provided by the UN Rule of Law Unit and the United Nations University.

Abbreviations

AAP	Aam Admi Party
ACABQ	Advisory Committee on Administrative and Budgetary Questions
ACT	Australian Capital Territory
ADR	Alternative Dispute Resolution
AICHR	Intergovernmental Commission on Human Rights
ARC	American Red Cross
ASEAN	Association of Southeast Asian Nations
BRICS	Brazil, Russia, India, China and South Africa
CARE	Cooperative for Assistance and Relief Everywhere
CEM	Chamber for Environmental Matters
CIA	Central Intelligence Agency
CLEP	Commission on Legal Empowerment of the Poor
CSC	Convention on Supplementary Compensation for Nuclear Damage
DFID	Department of International Development
DRC	Democratic Republic of the Congo
DSB	Dispute Settlement Body
ECC	European Criminal Court
ECCC	Extraordinary Chambers in the Courts of Cambodia
ECHR	European Convention on Human Rights
ECtHR	European Court of Human Rights
EFP	Exempted Fishing Permit
EIA	environmental impact assessment
FAO	Food and Agriculture Organization of the United Nations
G8	Canada, France, Germany, Italy, Japan, Russia, UK and USA
G-20	The Group of Twenty Finance Ministers and Central Bank Governors
GATT	General Agreement on Trade and Tariffs
GDP	gross domestic product
GE	General Electric
HRBA	Human Rights-Based Approach to Development
HRC	Human Rights Committee
IAEA	International Atomic Energy Agency

IAHCR	Inter-American Commission on Human Rights
ICANN	Internet Corporation for Assigned Names and Numbers
ICC	International Criminal Court
ICCPR	International Covenant on Civil and Political Rights
ICJ	International Court of Justice
ICRC	International Committee of the Red Cross
ICSID	International Centre for Settlement of Investment Disputes
ICTR	International Criminal Tribunal for Rwanda
ICTY	International Criminal Tribunal for the Former Yugoslavia
IFPRI	International Food Policy Research Institute
IHL	International Humanitarian Law
IHRL	International Human Rights Law
ILC	International Law Commission
IMF	International Monetary Fund
IMO	International Maritime Organization
IMT	International Military Tribunal
IPCC	Intergovernmental Panel on Climate Change
ISAF	International Security Assistance Force
ISO	International Organization for Standardization
ITLOS	International Tribunal for the Law of the Sea
L20	The Leaders 20 is not intended as a replacement for the G-20, as the G-20 is a meeting of Finance Ministers, while the proposed L20 would include the Leaders from member countries.
LEP	Legal Empowerment of the Poor
MINT	Mexico, Indonesia, Nigeria and Turkey
MSF	Médecins Sans Frontières (Doctors Without Borders)
NATO	North Atlantic Treaty Organization
NFSB	National Food Security Bill
NGO	Non-Government Organization
OAS	Organization of American States
OAU	Organization of African Unity
OECD	Organisation for Economic Co-operation and Development
OHCHR	Office of the UN High Commissioner for Human Rights
OPCAT	Optional Protocol on the Convention against Torture
OTP	Office of the Prosecutor
PCA	Permanent Court of Arbitration
PIL	Public Interest Litigation
PUCL	People's Union of Civil Liberties
S-21	Security Prison 21
SADC	Southern African Development Community
SCSL	Special Court for Sierra Leone
TEPCO	Tokyo Electric Power Company
UAV	Unmanned Aerial Vehicles
UK	United Kingdom
UN	United Nations

UNCLOS	UN Convention on the Law of the Sea
UNDP	United Nations Development Programme
UNFCCC	United Nations Framework Convention on Climate Change
UNGA	United Nations General Assembly
UNICEF	United Nations Children's Emergency Fund
UNSC	United Nations Security Council
UPR	Universal Periodic Review
USA	United States of America
VSS	Victims Support Section
WHO	World Health Organization
WTO	World Trade Organization
WWI	First World War
WWII	Second World War

1 What is 'access to international justice' and what does it require?

Patrick Keyzer, Vesselin Popovski and Charles Sampford

Justice is a notion as old as humanity. Nomadic peoples had procedures for distributing the foods they hunted and gathered – as well as for dealing with those who breached their norms. In the ancient Greek poem *Iliad*, justice is equal with revenge: the king of Sparta, Menelaus, furious after the abduction of his wife Helen by Paris, prince of Troy, asks his brother Agamemnon to bring justice by destroying Troy. Aristotle (384–322 BC) regards justice as a tool to restore a 'proper balance'. He makes the distinction between 'involuntary justice' in criminal prosecutions and 'voluntary justice' in trade transactions and they both restore the balance, damaged because one person has taken an unfair advantage over another person.[1] In contrast with legal philosophers, who simplify justice to a framework of legal rights within which citizens can be remedied, Aristotle believes that just society is one that empowers and enables citizens to realize their virtue and take what they deserve. Justice as a restoration of a 'proper balance', fits with the idea of the 'golden mean', the desirable middle between two extremes, which can be found in other long-standing cultures and traditions. Confucianism regards justice as proper and just relations between the individual, family, community and the state.[2] Justice (in Chinese *Yi*) is the harmony between heaven, earth and humanity; it is not an abstract, but a result of the emperor's rule and realization of harmony and reciprocity. Confucianism inherits the ancient idea of 'mandate of heaven', whereby rulers who bring peace and prosperity possess divine justice; whereas unjust rulers who do not fulfil their obligations to society fall upon personal or political misfortune, losing the 'mandate of heaven'.

The idea that justice is not only a societal balance, but also a principle guiding judges in legal process, is also ancient – the Code of Hammurabi (1772 BC)[3] offers aggrieved citizens the chance to seek redress and pursue their arguments in court, using lawyers, trained as such. The Code requires the prosecutor to substantiate the accusations and gives the accused the right to respond – an incredibly sophisticated remedial process for such an early stage in human history, containing not only procedures for the parties and their witnesses to give evidence, but even to be punished for giving false evidence.

In modern times, John Rawls in *The Theory of Justice* distinguishes between concept of justice, conception of justice, and sense of justice. The concept of justice, is a minimal ('thin') understanding of justice, prescribing that 'institutions are just when no arbitrary distinctions are made between persons in the assigning of basic rights and duties and when the rules determine a proper balance between competing claims to the advantages of social life'.[4] The conception of justice is similar to what Aristotle and others describe as 'proper balance' and the sense of justice is 'the capacity to understand, to apply, and to act from principles of justice'.[5] Rawls and Confucius, for example, have different conceptions of justice, but they share the concept of justice and the belief that all humans have a capacity for a sense of justice. Rawls also establishes two principles of justice: the first symbolizes the equal right to liberty; whereas the second – and central for our book – prescribes that:

> social and economic inequalities are to be arranged so that: (a) they are to be of the greatest benefit to the least-advantaged members of society, consistent with the just savings principle; (b) offices and positions must be open to everyone under conditions of fair equality of opportunity.[6]

Justice, therefore, could be seen as divine, but also could be manufactured and institutionalized. It could be a majestic formula enshrined in eternal monuments, but it could also be a banal everyday reference. Justice is not the same as the law, in fact some may seek extrajudicial justice exactly when the strict letter of the law may not satisfy the sense of justice. Law is a set of rules, a system defining the institutionalized and formalized right and wrong, the legal and the illegal, the guilty and the innocent and, more prosaically and more frequently, the valid and the invalid. Justice is often seen as a concept forming the basis of a legal system and lawyers are frequently sworn to promote 'justice according to law'.[7]

Amartya Sen in *The Idea of Justice*[8] agrees that social justice can be an ideal, an intellectual construction, but also emphasizes that the idea of justice can play a real role in how people live. He criticizes the theory of social justice that, in its grip on social and political thinking, has left practical realities behind. People of different persuasions can reasonably see clear and straightforward resolutions to questions of justice; but these resolutions might be completely different. Sen appeals to us to respect these reasoned differences and advocates a comparative perspective that can guide the choice between alternatives. In addition to creating theories of justice, it is crucial to enhance people's capacity to address injustices, what Martha Nussbaum defines as a 'capabilities approach' to justice,[9] also central for our book.

The legal process for aggrieved citizens to seek justice has developed over many centuries in many domestic jurisdictions. The evolution of citizens' access to justice in domestic courts has been millennia long, whereas the access to mechanisms of international justice – the subject of this book – by individual citizens has been only recent. In a previous edited volume focusing on international rule of law, we demonstrated in a similar way how the:

> rule of law has followed a long evolutionary tract from being a normative idea in ancient times to its codification in modern liberal constitutions.

> Throughout this historical voyage the crystallization of the rule of law at the domestic level has evolved significantly, whereas at the international level it is still in its infancy.[10]

The focus of this edited volume is to present and debate the evolution of the notion of access to justice from a domestic level to an international level, including both the normative developments and the acceptance of international rules and standards, and the institutional developments and the establishment of international arbitrations and tribunals.

The Nuremburg Charter and the UN Charter in 1945 became the first global agreements, pronouncing the access to international justice not only a human ideal or desire, but also a practical feasibility. The Nuremburg Tribunal was created 'for the just and prompt trial and punishment of the major war criminals of the European Axis'[11] and it delivered justice (although often criticized as 'victor's justice') for millions of victims of the Nazi aggression, war crimes and crimes against humanity. If the Nuremburg Charter makes individuals directly responsible and punishable in international law, the UN Charter mandates (but does not enforce) the protection of individuals from violation of human rights. Justice is mentioned in the Preamble, expressing the strong determination 'to establish conditions under which justice and respect for the obligations arising from treaties and other sources of international law can be maintained' and 'to employ international machinery for the promotion of the economic and social advancement of all people'.[12] The *Universal Declaration of Human Rights*, adopted in December 1948, pointed out that the 'recognition of the inherent dignity and of the equal and inalienable rights of all members of the human family is the foundation of freedom, justice and peace'.[13] It listed a comprehensive list of specific human rights and fundamental freedoms, among them the right of every person 'to an effective remedy by the competent national tribunals for acts violating the fundamental rights granted him by the constitution or by law',[14] and the 'a fair and public hearing by an independent and impartial tribunal, in the determination of his rights and obligations and of any criminal charge against him'.[15] The access to justice has evolved from being a recognized right in domestic law (from the time of the Code of Hammurabi) into an obligation in international law, further specified and codified in 1966 with the adoption of the two International Covenants on Civil and Political Rights, and on Economic, Social and Cultural rights. The adoption of the European Convention of Human Rights in 1950 and the establishment of the European Court for Human Rights in Strasbourg offered individuals for the first time in history direct access to international justice, where victims of violations of their rights, if all domestic remedies have been exhausted, can file an application and obtain judges' decisions with mandatory effect on domestic authorities. While this is only available for citizens of signatory European states, it is an example for other regions, several of which have made tentative starts.[16] It does provide hope for a greater recognition of justice and the rule of law in international affairs and a greater willingness to provide access to that justice without which justice is merely a word, and possibly a misleading one.

This edited volume is the fourth in a series on Building the Rule of Law in International Affairs (funded by the Australian Research Council and the Centre for International Governance Innovation in conjunction with the United Nations University and the United Nations Rule of Law Unit). Three books were based around a workshop and one around a pair of conferences. This book is the product of a workshop convened by the Institute for Ethics, Governance and Law (a joint initiative of the United Nations University, Griffith University, Queensland University of Technology, Australian National University and OP Jindal Global University) and the Centre for Law, Governance and Public Policy at Bond University where the workshop was held. The first two workshops/edited collections looked at the ethical and institutional supports for the international rule of law, using the ethical and institutional supports found in strong domestic legal systems as a starting point to consider whether similar or substitute supports might be found in international affairs.[17] The third book looked at various conceptions of justice at the international level, considering similarities and differences to the conceptions of justice found domestically,[18] in particular Sampford's 'Is justice the first virtue of international institutions', which considers the many forms of justice at the domestic level and whether these translate to the international level – concluding that the first virtue of international institutions has, for a long time, been stability and the preservation of the peace rather than justice: but that justice can and must become the first virtue of international institutions.

This volume considers the extent to which individuals have access to international justice, recognizing that access to justice is a problem in all legal systems and even more so in the relatively undeveloped international legal systems. As in the other volumes, we consider domestic comparators and examine ways in which access to justice has developed from a largely domestic issue to an international one – albeit to a limited extent and with state perpetrators blocking attempts to seek such access. The workshop and its essayists considered a number of questions: Can national legal systems provide effective protection of international human rights? Can international courts and institutions support the realization of international justice within countries? What can be done when nation states act with impunity, tolerating or even participating in injustices? How should we measure justice? Should national interest be our yardstick? Should human rights be our sole focus or even our principal focus, or should we now expand our focus to consequential, distributive, retributive, intergenerational or ecological justice? Should we concentrate on the development of administrative rules that do not rely on formal legal sanctions for their effectiveness, or should we focus on the development of legal systems that use sanctions to secure compliance? Should we work on our international institutions, our national institutions, or both? In one article Cappelletti and Garth wrote:

> The words 'access to justice' are admittedly not easily defined, but they serve to focus on two basic purposes of the legal system – the system by which people may vindicate their rights and/or resolve their disputes under

> the general auspices of the state. First, the system must be equally accessible to all; second, it must lead to results that are individually and socially just.[19]

Justice is deeper and wider than law, requiring not only just rules and systems but just results. The chapters in this volume probe our international systems and rules in order to determine whether we are achieving (the human right of) equal access to justice (not only individual and social justice), but also many other varieties of ecological justice. Exploring our achievements and failures in diverse contexts, the contributors to this volume demand that we closely interrogate the fundamentals of both 'access' and 'international justice'.

There could hardly be a better place to start our consideration of the utility of international justice than to consider whether our rules and systems can ensure that starving children are fed. India accounts for one-third of the world's undernourished children. One in three women in India is undernourished, and over 50 per cent are anaemic. Dan Banik, in his chapter 'Walking the talk: human rights, access to justice and the fight against poverty', explores how the concepts of 'legal empowerment of the poor' and a 'human rights-based approach' to the advancement of economic and social rights have been utilized by the Indian People's Union of Civil Liberties and the Human Rights Law Network to advance public-interest test-case litigation in the Supreme Court of India championing the international human right to food. Legal empowerment of the poor is an approach to human rights practice that emphasises the provision of legal institutional tools to people experiencing poverty so that they can be active agents of change rather than passive recipients of assistance. It is concerned with the provision of access to legal remedies that will enable people to achieve their rights by ensuring the accountability of institutions with the power to ensure the realization or progressive realization of their rights. The human rights-based approach to economic and social rights emphasises the importance of advancing development and aid (for example, basic life-sustaining requirements of food, water and shelter) within a human rights framework.

Legal empowerment of the poor and the human rights-based approach to economic and social rights have been criticized as approaches that lack conceptual rigour and belie the complex challenges that thwart the realization of basic human rights for people living in poverty. Evaluation of the utility of these approaches should account for the gap between international human rights instruments and discourse, on the one hand, and (the politics of) practical results in national settings, on the other. This is, of course, one of the fundamental issues that vex the achievement of distributive justice.

Banik identifies how civil society organisations in India have been able to utilize legal empowerment of the poor and a human rights-based approach to yield positive results. A series of petitions made to the Indian judiciary in the last thirty years has brought national attention to persistent hunger and starvation deaths in that country, and drawn attention to the role and duties of regional and national governments to assist. While governments largely ignored early court orders mandating the development and implementation of just solutions to the problem, recent court orders have produced significant, positive changes in food policy and programmes in that country. As a direct result of the ongoing right to food case in the Supreme Court, and following decades of civil society organization and judicial interest in food security, the Indian parliament passed national food security legislation in 2013.

While the litigation campaign to advance the right to food has been particularly prominent in India, other public interest litigation has advanced rights to health, medical care, education, housing, and clean and healthy environments. Banik argues that so long as the orders of the judiciary are respected and implemented, legal empowerment of the poor and a human rights-based approach hold very considerable promise for the realization of international justice.

Rahmat Mohamad shares Banik's enthusiasm for the potential of using national institutions to advance international justice. In 'Access to international justice: the role of the International Criminal Court in aiding national prosecutions of international crimes', Mohamad explores the potential for the expansion of the role of the International Criminal Court (ICC) in aiding national prosecutions of international crimes. Domestic national tribunals and processes remain the primary locus for combating impunity, but by applying William W. Burke-White's principle of 'proactive complementarity', Rahmat Mohamad outlines a number of ways that the ICC could assist national judicial systems with the prosecution of international crimes. Mohamad first outlines the historical events and international law-making activities leading to the establishment of the ICC. He notes that international prosecutions by the ICC represent a direct and significant contribution to the fight against impunity for international crimes. However, international justice mechanisms are not intended to supplant states where they have organized criminal justice systems which are willing and able to ensure that there is accountability for international crimes.

Rahmat Mohamad then provides a number of examples of how the International Criminal Court could assist national institutions in their efforts to prosecute international crimes. The ICC could take up a case where it determines that a national judicial system has been unable to investigate or prosecute because of a lack of resources or expertise. In post-conflict societies where national governments are unwilling to prosecute international crimes, the Office of the Prosecutor of the ICC could undertake its own investigations and prosecutions. The ICC could also strengthen the judicial capacity of states, and train local judges, investigators and prosecutors. It could share its expertise in matters ranging from investigation techniques, international law research or victim protection issues. By offering its resources and expertise during joint investigations, the ICC could relieve financial pressure on domestic judicial and investigative offices. With the consent of a government, the ICC could conduct joint investigations and prosecutions, offering technical and logistical support, increasing the likelihood of effective prosecutions. The ICC could also help national prosecutions with arrests by providing information to justify warrants, and information that would help identify and locate suspects. The ICC would also be able to assist governments with issuing arrest warrants for some categories of offenders that are beyond the reach of national judiciaries, such as those protected by official immunity or by statutes of limitations in national courts.

The ICC is the first international criminal tribunal offering victims direct access to justice as a party in the litigation, not just indirect participation via the prosecutor. This is a significant step in the advancement of access to justice internationally. Importantly, when domestic courts are empowered to address international crimes, victims have access to international standards of justice. The ICC has a major role in enabling domestic jurisdictions to rise up to international standards of due process and the rights of defendants.

Mirinda O'Gorman and Charles Sampford are also very interested in the greater access to justice potentially available by the ICC (and also domestic courts exercising Rome Statute jurisdiction). However, they consider the obstacles to that access generated by the consent principle in international affairs – in particular its iteration in *Monetary Gold Removed from Rome in 1943*. Despite the agreement to define the crime of aggression and include it within the ICC's jurisdiction, *Monetary Gold* may significantly limit the ICC's jurisdiction by preventing consideration of issues that might involve reference to the conduct of non-signatory states. The authors consider whether the *Monetary Gold* principle applies solely to the International Court of Justice (ICJ), or if can it be applied to other international bodies and if so, with what force and to what effect. To provide substantive answers to these two important questions the authors offer an outline of a 'strong' view and a 'weak' view of the content and effect of *Monetary Gold* in international criminal law.

Using case law and commentary the authors present a 'strong' view of the applicability of the *Monetary Gold* principle to the crime of aggression, preventing any consideration of the behaviour of any state that has not consented to the Court's jurisdiction for the crime of aggression. This would mean that members of the armed forces of a signatory defending the territory of another state from the aggression of a non-signatory state would not be able to argue self-defence because it would invite findings about the non-signatory's aggression. This limiting of jurisdiction based on consent is strongly entrenched in international law, highlighting the difference between the nature of domestic and international law. The 'weak' view of *Monetary Gold* is based on the differences between criminal law and civil law and the absence of consent in the much shorter history of international criminal law. It is suggested that the 'weak' view on the applicability of the *Monetary Gold* principle is the direction to which international law should proceed. This view presents an interweaving of international and domestic law, the relationships between law and principles at the domestic and international levels, the role of international courts and the implications of all for access to justice.

Like Banik and Rahmat, Vesselin Popovski is encouraged by recent developments towards access to justice, but reminds us of an important threshold; whether or not a state is willing to investigate and compensate victims of human rights violations. When states fail to deliver remedies domestically, victims should have access to international justice. Popovski illustrates this by reflecting on some achievements and some shortcomings in the practice of the European Court of Human Rights (ECtHR) through the prism of three cases: *Kalashnikov v. Russia*, *Budayeva v. Russia*, and *Bankovic v. NATO*. Kalashnikov, a bank official convicted of embezzlement, filed a complaint with the ECtHR regarding unsanitary conditions in overcrowded cells and the failure of the prison authorities to provide proper medical treatment. Russia, defending the case, pointed out that many detention centres were in similar conditions, and there was nothing prejudicial in their treatment of Kalashnikov. The judges, however, ruled that finding of purpose, or intention to humiliate Kalashnikov, is applicable to 'torture', but not to 'inhuman or degrading treatment' – a strong message that Russia should improve the conditions in pre-trial detention. Inspired by *Kalashnikov* many others later filed similar cases in ECtHR and as a result Russia adopted in 2002 a new Criminal Procedure Code, aligning its standards to international norms. The access to international justice of one person, Popovski argues, can give hope to 'millions of victims suffering in similar conditions'.

In *Budayeva v. Russia*, the applicant's husband and parents were killed in a mudslide that was predicted by meteorologists, but government officials failed to provide warnings to potential victims. Claims were rejected in domestic courts on the basis that little can be done to stop natural disasters and that the local population had been informed of the risk by the media. Budayeva went to the ECtHR, and its decision became the first precedent in an international court of establishing violations of human rights for state negligence both before and after natural disasters. Popovski demonstrates how *Budayeva* opened the door for other similar claims and court rulings (*Kolyadenko v. Russia*) crystallizing states' responsibility for mitigating suffering from natural disasters in substance and procedure.

Finally, *Bankovic v. NATO* was filed by the relatives of victims of the NATO bombing of a Serbian television station in May 1999, who first approached the International Criminal Tribunal for Former Yugoslavia, and after failing there, went to the ECtHR. The judges, sadly, could not establish a jurisdictional link between the victims and the member states of NATO. They opined that if Bankovic had died on a NATO country territory, the case would be admissible, but she was unlucky to die from NATO bombs on Serbian territory. Popovski questions why the ECtHR did not determine whether the victims were within the jurisdiction of the respondent NATO states by virtue of an extraterritorial act, but decided to define such extraterritoriality depending on the effective control of the relevant territory as a consequence of military occupation or through the consent, invitation or acquiescence of the government. In an incredible irony as NATO bombed Yugoslavia without the consent of Yugoslavia, *Bankovic* had no jurisdiction and the case was inadmissible. Notwithstanding this, Popovski argues that access to justice is important no matter whether all cases will be successfully litigated. Individuals being denied justice domestically can challenge states, even big ones such as Russia and NATO members, for violations of human rights and therefore open chances for others suffering from similar violations to file applications and receive remedies.

The lacuna identified by Popovski in his analysis of *Bankovic* emerges prominently in the chapter by Ramesh Thakur. In 'Drone strikes and human rights: balancing national security, individual rights and international justice', Thakur examines the loosening of rule of law restraints on the use of remote-controlled aerial vehicles and asks whether targeted killing by drones represents an extraterritorial extension of the normative authority of the state to cover gaps in the existing legal order, or is a covert attempt to breach the limits of the legal competence of a state over conduct in foreign jurisdictions. Drones hold out the promise of 'war on the cheap' and provide a means for killing the enemy without risking your own soldiers. However, while militarily expedient, it is not thereby lawful or morally permissible. Drone strikes have replaced war with murder. The pursuit of national interest by sovereign states is being privileged over justice at the national and international levels. Laws and procedures for bringing perpetrators of drone strikes to justice are missing. Eighty-four per cent of the deaths by US drone strikes in Pakistan were during the Obama presidency. Drones are a potent, unnerving symbol of unchecked American power and as Thakur observes, given the memorable record of the US intelligence community on the 'slam dunk' evidence proving Saddam Hussein's pursuit of weapons of mass destruction, one cannot but be troubled by the substitution of secretive determinations of guilt and imposition of capital punishment by intelligence-bureaucratic processes instead of open and contested judicial trials.

Thakur recommends that a 'balance of interests' approach be adopted to achieve justice in this context. He rejects the normative framework adopted by the United States in advocating the use of drones, arguing that 'the national interest' is a category that is empty of substantive content. By contrast, a 'balance of interests' approach would be equally applicable to all international actors and would allow an assessment of the diverse interests, values, short- and long-term effects, and different policy options. The US government has adopted the rhetoric of a nation at war to justify strikes that violate the territorial sovereignty of another nation, unable or unwilling to deal effectively with a threat to the United States. Thakur reminds us of the Attorney General Eric Holder's argument that while the US Constitution guarantees due process, it does not guarantee judicial process. The result is that an opaque executive process is applied, where there is no genuine balancing of interests, and drone strikes are used ostensibly as a weapon of war but in fact as a technique of murder.

The limitations that beset the capacity of international institutions to provide justice are explored by Susan Lamb in her chapter on international criminal tribunals. Although such tribunals, alongside the International Criminal Court, represent significant breakthroughs in the quest to end impunity for atrocity crimes, Lamb identifies a number of impediments to access to international justice in these forums. The first impediment is resources. A well-functioning domestic legal system ensures that all instances of crime are tried and punished. But the struggle to obtain sufficient and consistent funding means that the international system cannot meet this expectation. Most international criminal tribunals have a limited jurisdictional reach; set up to prosecute particular crimes at a particular time. This means that only a fraction of victims will see perpetrators punished. In addition, the focus of international criminal tribunals on senior leaders, while understandable, means that many wicked mid-level or lower-level perpetrators go unpunished. This reflects practical considerations such as funding issues but also the principle of complementarity. It does, however, result in incomplete achievement of justice.

A second impediment is one of institutional design, though steps have been taken to ameliorate it. Criminal courts in the common law tradition are designed to punish, and have historically been limited in their capacity to provide reparation to victims. Civil party participation in criminal matters by victims, a feature of civil law systems and the European Criminal Court (ECC), is now emerging as a procedure in international criminal law. Civil party participants – commonly victims – can individually request investigations, file motions, question witnesses and seek reparation. While this development is in its infancy, Lamb detects a number of problems reflected in the early experience of the ECC with direct victim participation, including, amongst other things, the administrative burden of processing thousands of victim applicants, the difficulty of achieving rights without legal assistance, the increased participation of lawyers, difficulties with the enforcement of reparation, and the length and complexity of criminal proceedings. In addition, Lamb argues that the involvement of victim applicants in international criminal tribunal proceedings may raise expectations and delay achievement of core objectives. While Lamb argues that the success of international criminal tribunals can be measured in terms of their efforts to provide redress, build national capacity, create an historical record and promote national reconciliation, these institutions cannot accomplish these objectives single-handedly. For this reason, international criminal tribunals should be seen as one measure amongst many to deal with the consequences of atrocity crimes.

In 'Access to justice for victims of the use of force in international affairs: individual civil responsibility for aggression', Edwin Bikundo focuses on the function and symbolic role of the international criminal trial in preventing injustice. Bikundo charts the historical development of the public international law prohibition on the use of force and explores whether the International Criminal Court could be accessed to *prevent* acts of aggression, rather than merely being used to bring perpetrators of international crimes to justice after the fact. Bikundo concludes that the ICC has made 'slow progress' in invoking jurisdiction over the crime of aggression, and that victims of the crime of aggression 'would be better served under the current regime of state responsibility'.

A stark contrast between the European system and the Australian approach to international human rights is evident from the chapter written by Darren O'Donovan and Patrick Keyzer. In 'Visions of a distant millennium? The effectiveness of the UN Human Rights Petition System', O'Donovan and Keyzer examine a particularly challenging subset of the human rights implementation problem: What can be done when a country that has been identified as abusing human rights, and has the capacity to implement those human rights, simply refuses to do so? O'Donovan and Keyzer demonstrate that even rich, developed, liberal democracies can pursue a policy of deliberate and persistent non-compliance. This approach renders access to international justice meaningless.

O'Donovan and Keyzer's chapter examines the patterns of Australia's non-compliance with the International Covenant on Civil and Political Rights (ICCPR) through the prism of two international human rights communications (*Fardon v. Australia* and *Tillman v. Australia*), with the objective of identifying where the pressure points for greater compliance lie. Fardon and Tillman were prisoners incarcerated under laws of Australian states that authorise the detention of people in prison for dangerousness, even though they had committed no fresh crime and were not found guilty of any such crime before they were re-imprisoned. Australia is unusual in that it does not have a national constitutional or legislative bill of rights. This means that, remarkably, Australians have very limited options for challenging legislative or executive action on human rights grounds.

Australia rejected communications made by Fardon and Tillman to the United Nations Human Rights Committee, and rejected the findings of the Committee that Australia had violated the prohibition on arbitrary detention. The upshot, domestically, is that Australian governments are failing to comply with their obligation to rehabilitate under the International Covenant on Civil and Political Rights, but are instead expanding their use of prisons as warehouses for people who have not been convicted of crime. Australia, in its response to the decision of the United Nations Human Rights Committee that it had violated the ICCPR, adopted an extraordinarily constricted vision of how international legal obligations are to be translated to concrete circumstances. Effectively rejecting the UN Committee's views, Australia concluded its correspondence with the Committee on the matter by saying that it now regards both communications as finalized, even though it has done nothing to implement the decisions. It is difficult not to characterize this approach as a repudiation of obligations.

David Forsythe provides an alternative and perhaps, to lawyers, confronting approach to access to international justice in his chapter, 'The International Committee of the Red Cross and access to international justice: a carefully considered paradox'. Arguing that access to international justice extends beyond solely individual access to courts, Forsythe writes that those in legal circles who think of access to international justice might want to rethink their assumptions, taking into account that some humanitarian organizations as well as many of the victims they represent or support might prioritize a more pressing need for social justice. While the International Committee of the Red Cross (ICRC) is certainly attentive to law and legal justice, including international criminal justice, it pursues legal justice in a way that does not jeopardize social justice.

Outlining the history of the ICRC, Forsythe demonstrates how, while focusing on the basic human needs of sick, wounded or detained combatants and civilians, it can help create laws and institutions to get others to meet those needs. Social justice precedes legal justice. Applying this approach, the ICRC has the largest and most systematic prison visit programme on earth, guided by what is equitable or morally appropriate in the context, with law providing only one reference point. Forsythe asks: 'What good is legal justice, especially in the form of ex post facto criminal justice, if one in the meantime has died from hypothermia or malnutrition or dysentery or torture?' The answer, as Forsythe indicated in the title to his chapter, is the ICRC's posture – a carefully considered paradox. So, while the ICRC has made a significant contribution to the development of international humanitarian law, it is unwilling to testify in national and international investigative or judicial proceedings. By relying on legal normative structures without being a participant in legal action, it can engage in discreet humanitarianism and deliver social justice.

In 'Convergence, fragmentation and sustainability in access to international justice', Simon Chesterman considers how we conceive of the access to international justice in extrajudicial forums through the lens of accountability and governance deficits. Chesterman is particularly interested in procedures and normative standards for regulatory decision-making that fall outside domestic legal structures and yet are not properly covered by public international law. Chesterman utilizes the notion of global administrative law to describe a variety of measures emerging internationally to moderate governance and ensure accountability. These regulatory decisions take place in treaty-based organizations such as the United Nations and the World Trade Organization, but also networks of government officials such as the Basel Committee of national bank regulators, committees of experts such as the International Organization for Standardization (ISO), and less formal networks of organizations calling for fair trade in coffee, dolphin-friendly tuna, and the like.

The standards that are being imported into this new sphere of regulatory activity draw upon administrative law principles common in many jurisdictions, such as transparency, participation and review. The common theme of these developments is to make more reasoned decisions. Chesterman describes these phenomena, and then makes the case for consolidation of an emerging body of norms, which would improve both the quality of decision-making and the ability of those affected by decisions to protect their legitimate rights and interests. He charts a range of accountability mechanisms across the political and legal spectrum, arguing that while legal claims of right, which require 'the creation of institutions, the elaboration of standards, and the potential for sanctions', have traditionally been regarded as necessary for the realization of rights, many other forms of accountability can produce similar results, and our thinking about accountability should extend well beyond judicial review. While global administrative law is not proposed as a comprehensive problem to governance deficits, the procedures will improve the quality of decision-making and responsiveness to those affected by decisions. Chesterman concludes that the intention is not to make such decision-making structures more democratic, but to make the decisions themselves more reasoned.

The remaining chapters in this volume explore different dimensions of ecological justice. Afshin Akhtarkhavari is critical of the 'fragmented' approach of international law to claims for ecological justice and outlines the growing recognition of environmental concerns in international justice, showing how institutions such as the International Court of Justice, the dispute settlement body of the World Trade Organization, the UN Convention on the Law of the Sea dispute resolution mechanisms, the Investor State Arbitrations and Permanent Court of Arbitration have raised important points of international environmental law. However the focus of this jurisprudence has been humans and *their* environment (thus, 'environmental law') rather than the advancement of ecological justice or the *justness* of the relationship that humans have with the natural world.

Akhtarkhavari uses Edvard Munch's painting *The Scream of Nature* as a point of departure for the recognition of a new philosophical approach to nature in the Anthropocene epoch. He argues that Munch's work portrays our anthropocentric tendencies that describe nature only in terms of the effect that it has on us, and at the same time representing nature 'through the metaphor of the unnatural state it is in, which indicates the hurt and harm it is experiencing'. Akhtarkhavari argues that 'however we conceptualize nature and our relationship to it, humanity is capable of responding to its cry and scream'. Invoking the ecological thinking of Michael Serres, Akhtarkhavari develops the idea of a reciprocal or symbiotic partnership with nature as a foundation for a theory of ecological justice. In *The Natural Contract*, Serres writes that this was possible, but our contemporary contractual relationships exclude planet earth. We are not at the centre of nature:

> The Earth existed without our unimaginable ancestors, could well exist without us, will exist tomorrow or later still, without any of our possible descendants, whereas we cannot exist without it. Thus we must indeed place things in the center and us at the periphery, or better still, things all around us and us within them like parasites.[20]

To achieve ecological justice we must become 'sages' and construct a harmonious relationship between science and culture: 'we have to better understand our own capacities to engage with nature as reciprocal partners in a world where ours as well as the natural world's existence depend on it'.[21]

Tackling climate change requires urgent and effective global action. Attempts to use domestic legal regimes to advance claims for climate justice, such as the claim by the Inuit of Kivalina (who will have to abandon their village as a consequence of erosion caused by the melting of sea ice) or the claim of Ioane Teitiota in Kiribati (who unsuccessfully sought asylum in New Zealand due to the fact that her home is rapidly becoming uninhabitable due to climate change), have failed due to the inadequacy of our legal systems to provide climate justice. In 'Climate justice and the distribution of rights to emit carbon', Brendan Mackey and Nicole Rogers explore the varieties of justice – procedural, deontological, consequential, distributive, retributive, intergenerational, ecological – that are implicated in the quest for a genuine solution to the need to mitigate greenhouse gas emissions in order to control runaway climate change.

Focusing on justice issues arising in the context of the international negotiations on climate change, Mackey and Rogers argue that at its core, climate justice is concerned with consequential justice measured in utilitarian terms, and consequential justice can only be served when climate change is avoided or minimized. In this context, the 'contraction and convergence' approach developed by Aubrey Mayer is pragmatic and has the potential to settle the justice balance. Contraction refers to the reduction in global emissions necessary to achieve a safe level, and convergence refers to each nation's per capita emissions converging to the same annual rate on an agreed date. This would require successful international negotiations determining the size of the global carbon budget, the total amount of permissible emissions to be allocated among the world's nations, and then the allocation of emissions on a per capita basis. Emissions could be decreased by switching from fossil fuels to renewable energy. Mackey and Rogers explore the challenges associated with this approach, but conclude that it offers the best chance of progress because 'the reality' is 'that no [carbon emission] allocation principle can deliver a perfectly just outcome with respect to all forms of justice' and that 'the greatest injustice will result from a failure on the part of the world community to mitigate emissions'.

Finally, in 'Nuclear power and human security: lessons from the Fukushima Daiichi nuclear power plant accident', Yasunobu Sato argues that the absence of an effective international legal regime for the assistance and compensation of victims of the Hiroshima and Nagasaki bombings has meant that the victims of the disastrous meltdown of the Fukushima Daiichi power plant in 2011 have had no international legal recourse for their complaints. Sato expresses concern about the absence of a national and international legal regime to govern the safety risks associated with nuclear technology. Normally, product liability rules would apply if a product was unsafe, but Japanese law and international law provides immunity for manufacturers of nuclear plant technology. Criminal complaints lodged against senior officials in TEPCO (the operator of the Fukushima plant) and senior regulatory officials are fraught with difficulties relating to proving causation, and the penalties that might be imposed are disproportionately small. While significant civil compensation payouts are expected from TEPCO under the new Nuclear Damage Compensation Law, that law has the dual objective of compensating victims but also promoting the nuclear power industry by providing immunity for nuclear power operators for the damage caused by disasters. Furthermore, failure of regulatory oversight before Fukushima has not been repaired by the creation of a new regulation agency, set under the Ministry of Environment, which is showing signs of the same regulatory capture that preceded the accident.

International rules on compensation for nuclear damage lack teeth, and are also pro-nuclear. They limit compensation to national jurisdictions, which is inconsistent with the way radioactivity spreads by wind and water, and with demands for ecological justice in a global age. The UN Guiding Principles on Internal Displacement adopted by the UN Commission on Human Rights in 1998 could be applied to the displaced people from the nuclear disaster in

Fukushima, however Sato detects a significant legal and ethical gap: there is no international instrument to protect people who cross national borders to escape a natural disaster. The Fukushima incident has reminded us that we have not yet solved the problem of nuclear waste, the cost and risk of which appears to have been forgotten. Sato advocates global governance based on the precautionary principle due to the risk presented to all people and creatures by a nuclear disaster. Sato concludes:

> [We are] leaving future generations a huge burden and significant safety and security risks. No international law addresses these significant issues. Access to international justice for future generations should be seriously considered to prevent further humanitarian disasters such as the Fukushima disaster.

Notes

1 Aristotle, 'Politics' (350 BC), http://classics.mit.edu/Aristotle/politics.5.five.html.
2 Confucius, 'Analects', www.britannica.com/EBchecked/topic/132184/Confucius.
3 Set of laws carved in stone in ancient Babylon.
4 Rawls (1971: 76).
5 Rawls (1971: 85).
6 Rawls (1971: 60–61).
7 As to whether law does form a system, especially one based on the content of its laws (especially one based on justice) is a matter for considerable debate. See, for example, Sampford 1989.
8 Sen 2009.
9 Nussbaum 2009.
10 Popovski (ed.) (2014: 10).
11 International Military Tribunal, 'Charter of the International Military Tribunal', (London 8 August 1945), Art. 1.
12 United Nations, 'Charter of the United Nations', (24 October 1945), Preamble.
13 United Nations General Assembly, 'Universal Declaration of Human Rights', (10 December 1948).
14 'Universal Declaration of Human Rights', (10 December 1948), Art. 8.
15 'Universal Declaration of Human Rights', Art. 10.
16 Organization of American States (OAS), *American Convention on Human Rights, 'Pact of San Jose',* Costa Rica, 22 November 1969 (entered into force 18 July 1978). OAS has the Inter-American Commission on Human Rights (IACHR). 1978 *Inter-American Court of Human Rights* was also established. AU (African Union) – *African Charter on Human and Peoples' Rights* (adopted 27 June 1981, OAU Doc. CAB/LEG/67/3 rev. 5, 21 I.L.M. 58 (1982), entered into force 21 October 1986) and *African Commission on Human and Peoples' Rights*. ASEAN – has an Intergovernmental Commission on Human Rights and a Human Rights Declaration – adopted November 2012.
17 Sampford *et al.* 2014.
18 Sampford 2014, Ch 2.
19 Cappelletti and Garth 1978.
20 Serres 1995.
21 Akhtarkhavari, this volume.

References

Aristotle. 'Politics'. Book V, (350 BC). Online. Available at http://classics.mit.edu/Aristotle/politics.5.five.html (accessed 5 June 2014).

Cappelletti, Mauro, and Garth, Bryant. 'Access to Justice: The Newest Wave in the Worldwide Movement to Make Rights Effective'. *Buffalo Law Review* 27 (1978): 181–292.

Confucius. 'Analects'. *Encyclopaedia Britannica Academic Edition (principal contributor Roger T. Ames)*. Online. Available at www.britannica.com/EBchecked/topic/132184/Confucius (accessed 5 June 2014).

International Military Tribunal. 'Charter of the International Military Tribunal'. London, 8 August 1945.

Nussbaum, Martha. *Frontiers of Justice*. Cambridge, MA: Harvard University Press, 2009.

Popovski, Vesselin, (ed.) *International Rule of Law and Professional Ethics*. Surrey: Ashgate, 2014.

Rawls, John. *The Theory of Justice*. Cambridge, MA: Belknap Press of Harvard University Press, 1971.

Sampford, Charles. *The Disorder of Law: A Critique of Legal Theory*. Oxford: Blackwell, 1989.

Sampford, Charles. 'Is Justice the First Virtue of International Institutions?'. In *Rethinking International Law and Justice*, Charles Sampford, Spencer Zifcak and Derya Aydin Oku, (eds). Farnham, Surrey: Ashgate Publishing, 2014.

Sampford, Charles and Thakur, Ramesh, (eds). *Institutional Supports for The International Rule of Law*. Oxford: Routledge, 2014.

Sampford, Charles, Zifcak, Spencer and Oku, Derya Aydin, (eds). *Rethinking International Law and Justice*. Farnham, Surrey: Ashgate Publishing, 2014.

Sen, Amartya. 'The Idea of Justice'. Cambridge, MA: Belknap Press of Harvard University Press, 2009.

Serres, Michael. *The Natural Contract* (trans. Elizabeth Macarthur and William Paulson). Ann Arbor: University of Michigan Press, 1995: 33.

United Nations. 'Charter of the United Nations'. 24 October 1945.

United Nations General Assembly. 'Universal Declaration of Human Rights'. 10 December 1948.

2 Walking the talk

Human rights, access to justice and the fight against poverty

Dan Banik

Introduction

The past couple of decades have witnessed growing interest in linking poverty reduction efforts with improved access to justice. With the UN Millennium Declaration (2000), world leaders appeared to endorse the idea that the abolition of poverty was in reality a matter of international redistributive justice. And 189 countries reaffirmed their commitment to do their utmost to help individuals and groups facing 'the abject and dehumanizing conditions of extreme poverty' and committed themselves 'to making the right to development a reality for everyone and to freeing the entire human race from want'.[1] Thus, numerous scholars, international agencies and aid practitioners began to advocate in the 1990s for a closer linkage between human rights and economic development. They claimed that a human rights focus ensures that the developmental process is correct, both morally and legally, and helps build stronger national and local institutions based on genuine social mobilization and accountability. Some argued that the human rights-development linkage forces development practitioners to confront the tough questions of their work: matters of power and politics, exclusion and discrimination, structure and policy.[2] Others argued that the astonishingly high levels of global poverty required revisiting its root causes, including the role of affluent nations. Accordingly, the existence of poverty in a world of plenty, they argued, should be viewed as a 'violation of human rights'.[3]

Two approaches in particular – the human rights-based approach to development (HRBA) and the legal empowerment of the poor (LEP) – have been promoted and applied by a set of international, national and local organizations in their attempt to promote development and combat poverty. These approaches aim at reforming conventional (needs-based) developmental efforts, which are criticized for treating the poor as passive receipts of welfare rather than active participants and agents of change. With an emphasis on respecting, protecting and promoting the human rights of people living in poverty, these approaches have focused attention on the actual *process* and *means* of development, which proponents argue should aim to empower marginalized individuals and groups to participate in decision-making and holding power-holders to account. By comparison, they argue, conventional development strategies have failed to substantially reduce poverty as they have been excessively concerned only with the end results.

Despite their obvious merits, both HRBA and LEP have been labelled by their critics as appealing buzzwords that give the impression of radical change but deliver very little in practice. The increased frequency and ease with which HRBA and LEP have been used by various agencies has also been criticized for betraying the complex challenges that thwart the realization of basic human rights for people living in poverty. And the constant desire to introduce new terms and approaches has not only flooded the development discourse with jargon that is difficult, if not impossible, to operationalize, but scholars and activists around the world also worry that there is limited empirical evidence available to suggest that such concepts are being rigorously applied by those who are responsible for designing and implementing aid-driven development programmes. Critics thus argue that behind the scenes lie a multitude of voices, interests and perspectives that draw upon very different conceptual understandings of poverty, rights and the relationship between the two.

I begin this essay by briefly and critically discussing the main features of the HRBA and LEP approaches in relation to development and poverty reduction. There is now a growing volume of literature on the difficulties of operationalizing these approaches. My aim is the opposite. I wish to identify and highlight a set of efforts by a wide range of actors at national and local levels using key elements of the HRBA and LEP that yielded numerous positive results. Thus the empirical focus here is on various initiatives that are aimed to promote the right to food in India. These include a series of petitions handled by the Indian judiciary starting in the mid-1980s that brought national attention to the persistence of extreme hunger and starvation deaths in many parts of the country, and the role and duties of national and regional governments to provide adequate assistance to households vulnerable to hunger. While the initial verdicts by the courts in the late 1980s and early 1990s generated considerable media interest on the issue of under-nutrition and starvation, the ensuing recommendations of the judiciary were largely ignored by the political and administrative leadership at both central and state levels. By comparison, I also examine the basic conceptual frameworks of the LEP and HRBA approaches in light of an ongoing case on the right to food in the Indian judicial system, which has been championed by civil society organizations and that – despite the awaited final verdict – has resulted in significant and positive changes in policies and programmes on food policy in the country. The overall aim of this essay is to identify the conditions under which human rights-based and legal empowerment approaches can be useful in promoting the access to justice of people living in poverty.

Human rights and legal empowerment for poverty reduction

The development discourse in the past couple of decades has witnessed growing interest in viewing poverty through a human rights lens. This has largely corresponded with the increased frustration and impatience over the inability of conventional 'needs-based' or 'economic growth-based' developmental approaches to deliver quick and long-lasting impacts on poverty reduction in large parts of the globe. Since the 1990s, various attempts have been made to articulate what a human rights-based approach to development (HRBA) actually means. Given the involvement of a wide variety of development actors, organizations and academic disciplines, the HRBA has appeared to be a broad collection of ideas and practice centred on a set of core human rights principles. These include participation of the poor in decision-making, and ensuring that state and non-state actors are aware of the importance of, and practice, social inclusion, non-discrimination and enhanced accountability of power-holders in the discharge of their duties. Hence, there is now general acceptance of the idea that conceptually the HRBA entails a process of human development that is normatively based on international human rights standards and operationally aimed at promoting and protecting human rights (OHCHR 2006).[4] The main value added of the HRBA, according to its supporters, is that the approach creates claims and not charity[5] and that it promotes the sustainability of development work by empowering marginalized peoples with the ability to 'participate in policy formulations and to hold accountable those who have a duty to act'.[6] At the same time, the universality of human rights is highlighted, in addition to the principle of 'progressive realization' of rights in development, which means that given resource constraints, not all problems of all people must be tackled at once.

One of the early supporters of the HRBA, and a former senior official of UNICEF, argues that human rights are important (and differ from conventional need-based approaches) because they represent specific relationships between individuals (who have valid claims) and others (for example, individuals, groups or institutions) that possess the duty to respect, protect and fulfil human rights.[7] And '[e]xcept for very young children, all individuals have both valid claims (rights) and duties'.[8] By comparison, development approaches that emphasize basic needs do not recognize the idea of a duty-bearer, with the result that no one has a clear-cut responsibility to meet the needs of the poor and protect their rights. Within the HRBA framework, the poor do not lose their rights when they are incapable of claiming them (fulfilment of rights may be compromised), as human rights are considered universal, inviolable and inalienable. The HRBA consequently emphasizes the principle of equality in that community resources must be shared equally, ensuring that access to various services is enjoyed by all. By comparison, the basic needs approach often tends to place greater emphasis on acquiring additional resources to improve the access that marginalized groups in the population have to various basic services. Thus, while conventional development approaches do not necessarily recognize 'wilful or historical marginalization, a human rights approach aims directly at overcoming such marginalization' by getting more actively involved in the political discourse on such issues.[9]

When examined in relation to conventional need-based approaches, the HRBA also differs with respect to its emphasis on the *process* of development and the manner in which development policies are implemented. In other words, 'the means, the processes, are different, even if many of the goals remain the same'.[10] While basic needs can often be met through 'benevolent and charitable actions', the HRBA is based on 'legal and moral obligations to carry out a duty that will permit a subject to enjoy her or his right'.[11] And this implies that a duty-bearer must *accept* the responsibility of taking rightful action and be motivated by a desire to promote justice, features that are negated by the basic needs approach's emphasis on charity and benevolence.[12]

Based on the above two sets of issues, the Office of the High Commissioner for Human Rights[13] argues that human rights 'contribute to human development by guaranteeing a protected space where the elite cannot monopolize development processes, policies and programmes'. Moreover, by linking human rights to development, development practitioners are in a better position to confront and address issues of unequal power relations in local society, and the politics and practice of exclusion and discrimination.[14] Others have argued that the continuation of world poverty should be viewed as a violation of human rights, and by doing so public action can be mobilized against the governments of democratic countries for the adoption of more pro-poor policies.[15] In practice, the HRBA has been variously used by international agencies and civil society organizations. These include: as a set of normative tools on which development strategies are based; as a set of instruments with which to develop assessments, checklists and indicators against which interventions can be assessed; as a component to be integrated into programming; and as the underlying justification for interventions aimed at strengthening governance and institutions.[16]

Although the HRBA was gathering some momentum in the 1990s and the early 2000s, its popularity was restricted to a handful of UN agencies (for example, UNICEF, UNDP), bilateral aid agencies (for example, Norwegian Norad, British DFID) and international organizations (for example, ActionAid, CARE). The claim that poverty persists partly because the poor do not enjoy legal rights (and that over three billion people currently live without legal protection) popularized the legal empowerment approach that evolved parallel to the HRBA discourse. And considerable momentum was generated with the establishment of the Commission on Legal Empowerment of the Poor (CLEP) in 2005. The informal sector suddenly returned to being the focus of research and policy attention again, including the range of problems faced by the poor who are often confined to, and operate within, the informal economy. Thus the LEP approach began highlighting: the local complexities and nuances of land reforms and peasants' rights; how 'formalization' (including enforcement of property rights in the informal economy, providing legal identities and titles of ownership) can benefit the poorest of the poor and marginalized groups, particularly women; the role and status of certain unique and flexible traditions of collective rights among indigenous groups; and the capacity of the formal judicial system to live alongside customary law, promote socio-economic equity and prevent elite capture.

The international discourse on the relationship between law and development was, for many decades, largely centred on improvements of the content of laws, the working conditions and facilities available to lawyers and strengthening the capacity of state institutions. The World Bank and other organizations continue to believe that rule of law is directly related to per capita GDP and that citizens will benefit from economic growth when their governments uphold the rule of law. Numerous critics of this emphasis on the rule of law[17] highlight the uncertainty of economic and political benefits (for example, democracy) that result from improvements in the rule of law. The LEP approach, in contrast, has emphasized the provision of, and access to, legal and institutional tools by the poor. An influential report by the Commission on Legal Empowerment of the Poor (hereafter CLEP report) defined LEP as 'the process of systemic change through which the poor and excluded become able to use the law, the legal system and legal services, to protect and advance their rights and interests as citizens and economic actors'.[18] Rather than simply providing advice, lawyers were encouraged to view the poor as partners, so as to encourage people to participate directly in influencing public policy and priorities. Legal empowerment also places emphasis on the use of non-judicial strategies, which may in certain situations be better able to address the concerns of the poor. Laws in many poor countries typically work against the poor, and hence the LEP approach advocates a better integration of law into a broader package of development-related activities[19] by placing emphasis on the 'use of legal services and related development activities to increase disadvantaged populations' control over their lives'.[20]

The CLEP report, which proposed a framework of legal empowerment based on four pillars – access to justice and rule of law, property rights, labour rights and business rights – argued that the main goal of a LEP approach is to protect poor people from injustice (for example, wrongful eviction, expropriation, extortion and exploitation) and offer them 'equal opportunity to access local, national, and international markets'.[21] Not surprisingly, the pillar pertaining to access to justice and the rule of law was considered to be the most important, providing an enabling framework for the remaining three pillars. Accordingly, the LEP approach claims that large parts of the developing world must implement reforms aimed at ensuring the right to legal identity (for example, registration at birth), repealing or modifying discriminatory laws, strengthening the work of civil society organizations, supporting alternative dispute resolution mechanisms, supporting paralegals, improving the workings of the police force, creating accessible judicial and land administration systems that recognize and integrate customary and informal legal procedures and focusing on the legal empowerment of specific groups such as women, refugees, indigenous populations and internally displaced persons.[22]

There are many benefits of pursuing HRBA and LEP in the fight against poverty. These approaches highlight the distinct character and normative force of law, the equal manner in which legal standards are applicable to all actors, the potential use of codified international legal standards to criticize government action or inaction and the ability to recognize the state as the primary duty-bearer in promoting human development. The HRBA and LEP approaches have been the subject of substantial praise as well as strong criticism. I have discussed these in detail elsewhere.[23] In the context of this essay, two broad sets of criticisms appear particularly relevant.

The first set of issues relate to the allegation by several scholars and development practitioners (especially at country levels) that these approaches are mainly rhetorical (rights and empowerment are proclaimed) rather than forwarding concrete advice for the practical implementation of development policies.[24] Related to this is the claim that the approaches lack conceptual rigour and virtually all current efforts can be loosely labelled as 'rights-based' or aimed at promoting empowerment of people living in poverty. As Darrow and Tomas[25] observe, 'continued credibility of rights-based approaches demands a higher degree of conceptual rigor and clarity than has prevailed in the past, along with a frank appraisal of their relative strengths and limitations'. Many development practitioners, including the staff of NGOs and UN agencies believe that the human rights community is preoccupied with events taking place in UN headquarters and donor country capitals, where good intentions and appealing buzzwords are reiterated without there being appreciation for ground-level realities. Developing country governments often pay lip service to human rights language, include binding obligations, and are reluctant or unwilling to push for adoption and closer integration of internationally ratified human rights instruments into national law and policymaking. Others point to the obsession of the international community to propose new buzzwords, rather than concentrating on how established approaches can be improved. Hence Sengupta[26] argues that the LEP approach builds on human rights principles and will have most impact if it is viewed as a subset of the HRBA, rather than an independent set of strategies for developing countries to pursue.

The second broad set of criticisms relate to the challenge of translating global theory into national and local practice. These mainly relate to the lack of conceptual clarity of both approaches at programmatic levels – where anti-poverty policies are implemented. There are concerns that HRBA and LEP do not provide adequate tools for the actual design and implementation of required programmes and projects. In spite of their theoretical underpinnings, the HRBA and LEP have proved difficult to operationalize in practice, particularly in relation to socio-economic rights such as those related to food, water and health. This is because, as Alston[27] argues, HRBA criteria are much too often 'expressed at a level of abstraction and generality that is not uncharacteristic of some human rights discourse but that is likely to seem abstract, untargeted, and untested to the community of development economists'. Consequently, policymakers and those implementing public policy do not believe that the HRBA provides concrete advice and guidance on how to address complex challenges and trade-offs on the ground. A crucial step to understanding and thereby evaluating the impact that the HRBA and the LEP can have in relation to specific socio-economic rights is to understand the factors that explain the considerable gap between the international human rights discourse and instruments on the one hand and the politics of incorporating the same discourse in national settings on the other. And both HRBA and LEP tend to underestimate the ability of political actors to ignore, bypass or selectively implement judicial recommendations and verdicts.

Despite the obvious merits of the above criticisms, and I have often been critical of both approaches in my previous work, there is emerging evidence to suggest that HRBA and LEP can indeed be usefully applied in the fight against poverty. Using the case of the social and judicial activism on the right to food in India, I aim to illustrate some concrete successes that have been achieved using a combination of the strategies advocated by HRBA and LEP.

Social and judicial activism on the right to food in India

While there is a widespread belief that the home of the malnourished child is sub-Saharan Africa, all available data clearly show that the worst affected region is South Asia. The enormity of the problem is borne out by the fact that India accounts for one-third of the world's undernourished children, every third woman in the country is undernourished, and 55.3 per cent of Indian women are anaemic. Moreover, an intergenerational cycle of under-nutrition is perpetuated when 22 per cent of children are born underweight and thus susceptible to numerous infections. Although there has been some progress in reducing undernourishment, from 240 million in 1990 to 217 million in 2012,[28] India ranked sixty-fifth among seventy-nine countries in a recent Global Hunger Index; with an estimated 19 per cent of the population that is undernourished,[29] the country is far from meeting its Millennium Development Goal targets scheduled for 2015. Indeed, improvements in nutritional status have not kept pace with the country's impressive economic growth in the past decade. This stark reality prompted the Indian prime minister to admit in January 2012 that 'the problem of malnutrition is a matter of national shame' and that the country has not managed to reduce hunger 'fast enough'.[30]

The daily presence of food insecurity (difficulties in accessing and consuming adequate amounts of good-quality food) facing large groups in the Indian population – and the more sensational media reports of 'starvation deaths' in various parts of the country amidst large amounts of food rotting in storage houses – has been an issue that has attracted the attention and interest of the media, civil society organizations, political parties and, in particular, the Indian judiciary. A main catalyst for litigating economic, social and cultural rights in India has been the series of radical changes undertaken by the Supreme Court since the 1980s, which popularized so-called public interest litigation (PIL). These initiatives not only pre-date the legal empowerment approach, but also allow lawyers, civil society organizations or any other organization to petition the court in order to protect and promote universal human rights. And not only have the requirements of standing been widened to allow anyone to litigate in the public interest, but fact-finding initiatives by the court have been institutionalized, and the judiciary has assumed supervisory powers to monitor the implementation of its own orders. The courts in India have thus experienced a radical transformation of their roles in safeguarding human rights, especially the right to life.[31] The result has been hundreds of cases concerning the enforcement of economic, social and cultural rights through the use of PIL. In addition to food, the rights to health, medical care, education, housing and clean and healthy environment have also been addressed by the courts through PIL cases.[32] Despite the ever-increasing number of PILs handled by courts in India, one particular case – related to the right to food – has not only received much national and international attention but has also achieved concrete policy outcomes. This is the focus of the ensuing sections of this essay and illustrates the operationalization of the HRBA and LEP in practice.

Judicial activism on hunger and starvation deaths: 1980s–1990s

The Indian courts have a long history of intervening on matters related to food security and drought relief. In the mid-1980s, the media began reporting on the drastic rise of starvation deaths and related suffering such as forced migration and child sales. The eastern state of Orissa was particularly singled out in such reports, with one particular district in Orissa – Kalahandi (literally meaning 'black pot') – receiving the most media and political attention. Two social workers from Kalahandi district filed a PIL in the Supreme Court in October 1985 and drew attention to large groups of people facing destitution and starvation as a result of recurrent droughts and resulting food shortages.[33] The petition claimed that anti-poverty programmes implemented by the Orissa government had failed to deliver benefits and that large groups of people in the district were facing starvation and destitution. A similar PIL was filed in the Supreme Court in 1987 by the Indian People's Front (a breakaway faction of the Communist Party of India), which alleged that destitution and starvation deaths had become a regular feature of Kalahandi and neighbouring districts due to the callous attitude and negligence of the Orissa government.[34] It requested the Court to investigate the Orissa government's inaction in these districts highly vulnerable to starvation. Upon receipt of the two petitions, the Supreme Court appointed a district judge to conduct an inquiry. The ensuing report, submitted to the Court in 1988, did not establish any cause to criticize the Orissa government's efforts, and the judge concluded that no starvation deaths had taken place. This conclusion, however, was highly criticized by the petitioners and the media, and even the Supreme Court distanced itself from the report, concluding in 1989 that there was considerable evidence the starvation deaths had indeed occurred in Kalahandi, and the Orissa government was instructed to be more active and responsive to the needs of households vulnerable to extreme poverty and hunger.[35]

Through the late 1980s, similar PILs were filed in the Orissa High Court, highlighting cases of bonded labour, forced migration of large groups of people fleeing from starvation, child sales, and exploitation of indigenous groups by village elites.[36] In early 1992, the High Court passed its final ruling on these cases and concluded that its own investigation had established several cases of starvation deaths, and hence the Orissa government was directed to pay compensation to the families of the deceased. The Court was highly critical of the implementation of social welfare programmes and held two senior civil servants accountable for failing to take quick and appropriate action to prevent human suffering in Kalahandi and adjoining areas.

The immediate impact of the judicial interventions was a drastic increase in media attention on Kalahandi and pressure on the Orissa government to react. Indeed, the Orissa High Court's ruling was the first time in history that a public authority in Orissa had concluded that starvation deaths in Kalahandi had actually occurred. Successive ruling parties since 1985 had denied all such claims. The adverse publicity on the state of governance in Orissa that followed the Court rulings that began in the late 1980s appeared to also have an impact in the elections, with the ruling (Congress) party being voted out of office in 1990. However, when the Orissa High Court confirmed starvation deaths in Kalahandi in 1992, the new government formed by the Janata Dal party began blaming the previous government for its failures instead of initiating radical change to address vulnerability to hunger in starvation-prone areas. And despite the fact that reports of starvation deaths in Kalahandi and other districts in Orissa continued to appear in local and national dailies right throughout the period this government was in office, the major political actors in charge of the state largely ignored judicial recommendations to radically reformulate guidelines for improving administrative responses to starvation.[37] Although a handful of civil society organizations and concerned citizens kept the starvation deaths issue alive in the media, in addition to petitioning the courts and quasi-judicial organizations such as the National Human Rights Commission, the Orissa government showed little interest in making drastic changes to its social welfare and drought relief policies. Thus, although there was considerable media interest in the stories of starvation deaths taking place in Kalahandi, and the highest levels of the judiciary were mobilized by civil society organizations and other well-meaning local actors, the direct impact of these actions on people vulnerable to starvation was negligible.

Social movements and litigation on the human right to food in India

The 1990s witnessed a growing interest in extreme poverty and food-related deprivation in the media and political discourse. When major national newspapers began to publish news articles on starvation deaths in many parts of the country despite an abundance of food available in government storage houses, the People's Union of Civil Liberties (PUCL) – a coalition of fifty-six civil society organizations – became actively involved in seeking judicial redress on behalf of households facing destitution and starvation. Using the language of the HRBA, the Rajasthan branch of PUCL submitted a PIL to the Supreme Court in April 2001 questioning whether the right to life guaranteed under Article 21 of the Indian constitution also included the right to food.[38] The petition requested the Court to intervene to prevent starvation deaths that were taking place despite surplus food stocks in possession with the central and state governments. It further asked:

> Does not the right to food which has been upheld by the apex Court imply that the state has a duty to provide food especially in situations of drought to people who are drought-affected and … not in a position to purchase food?[39]

Using the human rights language of duty-bearers who must act to respect, protect and fulfil the rights of the poor, PUCL identified central and state governments in India as the main duty-bearers with the obligation to protect the right to food. It further argued that these duty-bearers must be held to account for their failure to assist individuals and households facing acute hunger and starvation while large stocks of food remained hoarded in government storage houses. The petition also requested the Court to push the government to address the implementation shortcomings of the country's main social security programmes such as the Public Distribution System (that provides subsidized food and other items to poor households), and ensure that vulnerable groups in the population (for example, impoverished women, children and the aged) were adequately covered and targeted by public policy.

The Supreme Court is yet to award a final verdict in the case, but since 2001 it has held hearings at regular intervals and issued over 100 very detailed 'interim orders' that are considered applicable as law until the case is closed. While the PIL was initially brought against the government of Rajasthan, thanks to civil society activism and mobilization, it now applies to all state governments in India. Further, the case does not only address the problem of hunger but also issues of food insecurity, urban destitution, right to work, transparency and accountability in government and the implementation of social security programmes.

The case is currently coordinated, on behalf of the petitioners, by the Human Rights Law Network – an organization of lawyers and social activists working to use the legal system to advance human rights.[40] Despite hundreds of PILs filed every year, this particular case has been the Indian judiciary's most prominent attempt to make economic, social and cultural rights justiciable. In the process the case has received widespread attention both at home and abroad. In the following sections I will discuss four main categories of impact that this ongoing case in the Supreme Court has had, followed by a separate section on the recently enacted National Food Security Bill.[41]

First, some of the most important anti-poverty programmes in the country were converted into legal entitlements, i.e. the government could not stop or make major changes to these without the approval of the Supreme Court. For example, the Court delivered a landmark judgment in November 2001 on eight specific programmes or schemes with a food component. Among its recommendations, the Court ordered full implementation of the Public Distribution System, which offers subsidized food to below poverty-line households, converted a previously voluntary programme (Mid-Day Meal Scheme) to provide cooked meals at schools to an obligation on the part of all states, and ordered improved implementation of the Integrated Child Development Services, which provides assistance to children and pregnant and nursing women, and other programmes aimed at helping impoverished families whose primary breadwinner has died. With this particular order, the Court converted the benefits of the eight programmes into legal entitlements and hence provided all programme beneficiaries with the ability to claim benefits as a matter of right and seek judicial redress if such rights were violated.[42] This particular order together with previous and subsequent interim orders have thus given rise to a set of 'umbrella orders' (applicable to all relevant social programmes) and more specific orders relating to the functioning of specific social protection programmes. These umbrella orders cover numerous issues, including the identification of agents or agencies with responsibility for compliance (mainly chief secretaries in the various states) and village councils (or Gram Sabhas) that can demand accountability by accessing all relevant information, monitoring the functioning of government programmes and investigating misuse of funds.[43]

Second, various levels of government in India have quite regularly been held to account by the Supreme Court. For example, the highest civil servant in each state (the chief secretary) is now required to be present during certain hearings in order to put forward the government's views on food security. And the Court has established a new mechanism for ensuring compliance with, and the monitoring of, its orders by appointing two commissioners in 2002 to monitor and report on the implementation of a whole range of public welfare programmes. The commissioners were given the power to investigate potential violations of the interim orders and to demand redress from the political and administrative leadership, with the full backing of the Supreme Court.[44] In addition to providing periodic reports to the Court, the commissioners are authorized to seek responses from state governments, investigate complaints from civil society organizations and set up relevant enquiry committees.[45] A major impact of these initiatives has been the gradual increase in the amount of funds allocated by state governments for improving coverage of social security programmes within their territories.[46]

Third, essential services provided by the government are now becoming legal rights as a result of this ongoing case. The impact is not only confined to the right to food, but there have been important spillover effects in relation to other social and economic rights including the right to education and the right to work. Thus, the orders issued by the Supreme Court on the right to food case so far have catalysed the Indian government to enact some very progressive legislation on other socio-economic rights.

Fourth, the actions of the Supreme Court and the ensuing interim orders have encouraged regional (state) governments in India to enact legislation of their own in order to improve service delivery. One prominent example is Chhattisgarh, a state which ranks low among other Indian states in relation to human development, where the government successfully enacted the Chhattisgarh Food Security Act in December 2012 with the aim of ensuring 'access to adequate quantity of food and other requirements of good nutrition to the people of the State, at affordable prices, at all times to live a life of dignity'. With several innovative features related to targeting of vulnerable food-insecure households, availability and distribution of various types of food, and speedier mechanisms for service delivery, this piece of legislation has been hailed as a major success story amidst the general reluctance of state and national governments in India to abide by the directions of the central government and the courts that are aimed at improving food security.

One of the most important impacts of the right to food movements has been the recent enactment of national legislation on food security, which was a direct result of the growth and popularity of a human rights-based approach to development in the national political discourse.

Human rights-based policy intervention: the National Food Security Bill

As a direct result of the ongoing right to food case in the Supreme Court, and following decades of civil society and judicial interest in food security, the Indian parliament finally passed the National Food Security Bill (hereafter NFSB) in August 2013. This was the culmination of a series of promises by the central government in New Delhi, led by the United Progressive Alliance, since being voted back to power in 2009 and concerted efforts by civil society organizations to legislate a bill specifically focused on food security. The NFSB was also the product of several years of deliberation, often at the prodding of the National Advisory Council headed by the president of the Congress Party, Sonia Gandhi, and consisting of several well-known academics and civil society activists working on food- and nutrition-related issues.

Despite the delays in enacting the legislation, and the innumerable compromises in the final draft, the NFSB has been hailed by many societal and political actors as a watershed. Some of the features of the Bill include the ambitious goal of providing up to 75 per cent of the rural population's and up to 50 per cent of the urban population's monthly foodgrains per person or per household. There is a focus on exclusive breastfeeding of children below six months, while for children between six months and six years, the Bill provides for a free age-appropriate hot, cooked meal. And for children aged six to fourteen, one free midday meal every day (except on school holidays) will be provided in all government and government-aided schools up to eighth grade. Similarly, pregnant women and nursing mothers are entitled to a free meal every day during pregnancy and six months after childbirth, and there are provisions for basic maternity benefits. Another progressive feature aimed at promoting empowerment of women entails that women of eighteen years of age or above will be considered to be the household head when 'ration cards' (that serve as proof of identity and status as programme beneficiary) for subsidized food programmes are issued. A relatively new feature to the Indian system of social protection – inspired by the conditional cash transfer models successfully implemented in Brazil and Mexico – is the right to receive food security allowance (or cash transfers) in situations when 'the entitled quantities of foodgrains or meals to entitled persons' are not available.[47]

The main responsibility for the implementation of the NFSB provisions belongs, however, to state governments, 'in accordance with the guidelines, including cost sharing, between the Central Government and the State Governments in such manner as may be prescribed by the Central Government'.[48] In addition, state governments are expected to constitute a seven-member State Food Commission for monitoring and reviewing the implementation process, with at least two women members and one member each from traditionally disadvantaged communities (Scheduled Caste and Scheduled Tribe communities). The NFSB also provides for the redress of complaints and grievances, including call centres and help lines.

From a HRBA perspective, the most important step forward is the recognition in the Bill of explicit duties or 'obligations' of various levels of government for the promotion of food security. Thus, the main obligation of the central government is to provide foodgrains (or adequate funds) to state governments at specified prices. State governments, however, have the main duty to implement the provisions of the Bill together with local government institutions and may extend the level of benefits with additional resources from their own coffers.

Despite the obvious benefits of legislating the right to food and guaranteeing access to food to large sections of the population, the NSFB has been heavily criticized by opposition political parties and other societal actors, including PUCL. These include the following: lack of focus on nutritional rights; ambiguity in terms of identifying food-insecure households; the enormous costs associated with covering the very large group of proposed eligible beneficiaries; the persistence with flawed social protection programmes (such as the Public Distribution System) without undertaking major reforms; the reluctance of state governments to bear additional costs and be accountable to the central government for implementation failures; and fears that the central government will discriminate against states controlled by opposition parties. Despite these very valid concerns, the NFSB appears to be a step in the right direction, and if properly implemented, can make a major impact in improving economic, social and cultural rights for hundreds of millions of people in India.

Concluding remarks

The Indian case provides a useful prism to test the added value of applying a human rights and legal empowerment lens to addressing the pressing concern of chronic and acute hunger that affect large sections of the global population. Although the rulings of the Indian Supreme Court and lower-level courts in the 1980s and 1990s helped to focus considerable media attention on certain starvation-hit areas of India and put several state governments on the defensive, there was very little political and administrative commitment to follow up the judicial recommendations. It is now widely recognized that simply a focus on law and judicial institutions is inadequate for fostering and promoting economic development and well-being. In addition to legal empowerment, there is also need for genuine political empowerment where citizens are not only aware of their rights but also in a position to successfully claim them.

The added values to pursuing a HRBA in relation to human development are numerous and include a focus away from viewing development as charity and a specific outcome or achievement to one where development interventions are evaluated on the process by which they empower the poor. The right to food movements in India (but also elsewhere, such as Brazil and South Africa) have indeed documented some impressive results, particularly in terms of concrete policy outcomes. And although numerous challenges remain, the Indian experience provides some useful insight into the conditions under which a focus on rights and empowerment can actually be successful in fighting poverty.

An important criterion for success is when people living in poverty are better identified and targeted by public policy. Undertaking this task in a country as large and diverse as India is not an easy task, as previous experiences with social protection programmes have shown. Nonetheless, the ongoing right to food case shows that civil society and the judiciary have provided valuable suggestions and recommendations to administrators and political leaders regarding the use of alternative methods for identification and targeting of beneficiaries. Many of these suggestions now form an integral part of the NFSB, which include recognizing the status of women as household heads and the use of identity cards (increasingly with biometric information) for providing food rations or cash transfers and checking the abuse of resources. The challenges that continue to exist include extending coverage to remote areas of the country and limiting political clientelism where politicians take undue credit for distributing resources. Moreover, greater awareness is required among all groups in society on what it means to be a right holder and a duty-bearer, and how one can effectively claim one's rights and carry out one's duties.

Another criterion of successful rights and empowerment-based approaches is when public policies focus on daily vulnerabilities, rather than being emergency-oriented responses. The traditional Indian response to past food shortages and allegations of starvation deaths has usually been crisis induced. The political leadership is quite successful in mobilizing efficient administrative responses to clearly visible and substantially large crises such as those resulting from floods and cyclones. In contrast, the less visible impacts of recurrent droughts and hidden hunger do generate the same type of urgent political-administrative response. This is where the NFSB, if implemented well, can make a major difference by addressing the problems of chronic hunger by guaranteeing individuals and households access to basic amounts of food and essential commodities either for free or at affordable prices.

Another key ingredient to the NFSB's success will be how well its provisions and goals are understood and implemented by civil servants. The successful application of a HRBA requires that the attitudes and practices of civil servants change from arrogance to one of genuine commitment and service to those they serve. This is easier said than done, and some of the major social protection programmes implemented in India would work even better if corruption and leakages were kept in check and officials were more motivated in their jobs and better understood their functions as duty-bearers. What, then, does it mean to be a duty-bearer? The evidence from India shows that politicians and bureaucrats resort to a considerable amount of blame-gaming whenever they are criticized for programme failures. Moreover, most power-holders in India or other developing countries do not understand the concept of duty-bearer in the human rights sense. The general attitude remains one of providing charity to the masses in the form of handouts, which are distributed for gaining popularity and votes before elections. The problems of under-nutrition and starvation in many Indian states (for example, in Orissa and Madhya Pradesh) are highly prevalent among indigenous groups (often referred to as 'tribals'), who are often the targets of social, economic and political discrimination, exclusion and marginalization.

A frequent criticism of development programmes is that they are often heavy top-down in character, decided by power-holders far removed from ground-level realities and without consultations with intended beneficiaries. While the right to food movement in India did not involve a mass mobilization of the poor, it is nonetheless a good example of civil society organizations pooling their resources and organizational skills to garner support and attention on the failure of public policy. Here, the role of lawyers working for the rights and empowerment of the poor has been crucial, as exemplified by the active contribution of members of the Human Rights Law Network, who have represented the petitioners of the right to food case in the Supreme Court and have been credited for pioneering work in the field of public interest litigation in India.

In the past few years, India has witnessed a growth in social movements that have initially focussed on specific topics (for example, corruption) and later metamorphosed into political entities. The Aam Admi Party (AAP) that started off as an anti-corruption movement, and which has recently formed the government in Delhi, is a good example of a movement that has exerted considerable political influence with the backing of India's middle class. It remains to be seen whether and to what extent the AAP can exert political influence and continue to champion the rights of the poor. The sad reality is that in many parts of the developing world, including India, opposition political parties have simply performed an adversarial function in order to gain power and then largely ignored these very same causes when they have assumed positions of authority. The HRBA and LEP approaches require that in addition to media and civil society organizations, political parties must revamp their organizational and incentive structures and work towards promoting increased answerability and accountability of state institutions. In other words, governments must be forced to prioritize development efforts in, and resource allocation to, regions irrespective of personal and political ties.

Similarly, the functioning and influence of oversight agencies such as the Ombudsman and Human Rights Commission are crucial. The provisions in the NFSB for food commissions with the power to address complaints and abuse of resources at local levels will only have a major impact if these institutions and their office bearers are given adequate resources and are able to work independent of political interference. While the judiciary can hold authorities to account for failing to protect the rights of the poor, the verdicts of the courts must have teeth. Public interest legal representation on the right to food in India, Brazil and South Africa show that the use of the legal system has not only advanced the right to food in these countries but also strengthened other economic, social and cultural rights. However, for judicial interventions to have a major impact, the actions and recommendations of the courts must be taken seriously by the political and administrative leadership. There are often no strict sanctions for non-compliance, and many governments around the world routinely ignore or sidestep court orders.

Rhetorical statements and appealing buzzwords are increasingly commonplace in development and policy circles. The urgency of world poverty requires not just talk, but genuine political commitment and concrete action.

Cases

A.C. Pradhan v. State of Orissa. Case No. 525/89 filed in 1989.
Bhawani Mund v. State of Orissa. Case No. 3517/88 filed on 17 October 1988.
Kishan Pattnayak and Another v. the state of Orissa, Paragraph 1 (quoted in Currie 1998: 423).
Nagbhushan Patnaik v. State of Orissa, Writ Petition (Civil) No. 1081 of 1987.
PUCL v. Union of India and others (Writ Petition [Civil] No. 196 of 2001).

Notes

1 UN General Assembly 2000.
2 Uvin 2004.
3 Pogge 2005; Sengupta 2005.
4 OHCHR 2006.
5 Uvin 2004: 129.
6 OHCHR 2006
7 Jonsson 2003.
8 Ibid., 16.
9 Ibid., 20.
10 Uvin 2004: 129.
11 Jonsson 2003: 20.
12 Ibid., 20, 21.
13 OHCHR 2006.
14 Uvin 2004.
15 Pogge 2005; Sengupta 2008.
16 Nyamu-Musembi and Cornwall 2004.
17 Carothers 2003; Golub 2003.
18 CLEP 2008: 3.
19 Golub 2003: 3–4.
20 Ibid.
21 CLEP 2008: 28.
22 Ibid., 5–6, 31–34.
23 Banik 2009, 2010.
24 Banik 2010; Eide 2006.
25 Darrow and Tomas 2005: 537.
26 Sengupta 2008.
27 Alston 2010: 802.
28 Food and Agriculture Organization of the United Nations (FAO) 2012.
29 International Food Policy Research Institute (IFPRI) 2012.

30 Full text of PM's speech at the release of the HUNGaMA Report see Singh 2012.
31 Fredman 2008: 124.
32 Banerjee *et al.* 2005: 111–138; Gonzalves 2008.
33 PIL Writ Petition (Civil) No. 12847 of 1985, *Kishan Pattnayak and Another v. the state of Orissa*, Paragraph 1 (quoted in Currie 1998: 423).
34 Writ Petition (Civil) No. 1081 of 1987, the Indian People's Front through its chairman, *Nagbhushan Patnaik v. State of Orissa.*
35 Order, Supreme Court of India 1989, Paragraph 7.
36 Case No. 3517/88 filed on 17 October 1988, *Bhawani Mund v. State of Orissa*; Case No. 525/89 filed in 1989, *A.C. Pradhan v. State of Orissa.*
37 Banik 2007.
38 Writ Petition (civil) 196 of 2001, submitted in April 2001.
39 'PUCL Petitions Supreme Court on Starvation Deaths', *PUCL Bulletin*, July 2001.
40 The case is technically known as *PUCL v. Union of India and others* (Writ Petition [Civil] No. 196 of 2001).
41 This section has benefited from personal communication with Kavita Srivastava, the national general secretary of the People's Union for Civil Liberties (PUCL), during her visit to Stanford University in November 2013.
42 Right to Food Campaign Secretariat 2005: 10.
43 Interim order, Supreme Court, 8 May 2002.
44 Interim order, Supreme Court, 29 October 2002.
45 Right to Food Campaign Secretariat 2005: 7–8.
46 Right to Food Campaign Secretariat 2012.
47 Government of India, National Food Security Bill (2013), Sec. 13.
48 Government of India, National Food Security Bill (2013), Sec. 7.

References

Alston, Philip. 'Report of the Special Rapporteur on Extrajudicial, Summary or Arbitrary Executions, Addendum, Study on Targeted Killings'. Geneva: OHCHR, A/HRC/14/24/Add.6, 28 May 2010.

Banerjee, U.D., Naidoo, V. and Gonsalves, C. 'The Right to Food Campaign in India: A Case Study of Entitlement-Oriented Rights-Based Strategies Used to Reclaim the Right to Food for Vulnerable and Marginalized Groups'. In *Lessons Learned from Rights-Based Approaches in the Asia-Pacific Region*, edited by U.D. Banerjee. Bangkok: UNDP and OHCHR, 2005: 111–138.

Banik, D. *Starvation and India's Democracy*. London: Routledge, 2007.

Banik, D. 'Legal Empowerment as a Conceptual and Operational Tool in Fighting Poverty'. *Hague Journal on the Rule of Law* 1, No. 1 (2009): 117–131.

Banik, D. *Poverty and Elusive Development*. Oslo: Scandinavian University Press, 2010.

Carothers, T. *Promoting the Rule of Law Abroad: The Problem of Knowledge*. Washington DC: Rule of Law Series working paper, Democracy and Rule of Law project, Carnegie Endowment for International Peace, 2003.

CLEP. *Making the Law Work for Everyone*. New York: Commission on Legal Empowerment of the Poor, UNDP, 2008.

Currie, B. 'Laws for the rich and flaws for the poor? Legal action and food insecurity in the Kalahandi case'. In *A World Without Famine: New Approaches to Aid and Development*, edited by H. O' Neill and J. Toye. Basingstoke: Macmillan, 1998: 423.

Darrow, M. and Tomas, A. 'Power, Capture, and Conflict: A Call for Human Rights Accountability in Development Cooperation'. *Human Rights Quarterly* 27 (2005): 471–538.

Eide, A. 'Human Rights-Based Development in the Age of Economic Globalization: Background and Prospects'. In *Development as a Human Right: Legal, Political, and Economic Dimensions*, edited by B.A. Andreassen and S.P. Marks, Chapter 11. Cambridge, MA: Harvard University Press, 2006.

FAO. *State of Food Insecurity in the World 2012*. Rome: Food and Agricultural Organization of the United Nations, 2012.

Fredman, S. *Human Rights Transformed: Positive Rights and Positive Duties*. Oxford: Oxford University Press, 2008.

Golub, S. *Beyond Rule of Law Orthodoxy: The Legal Empowerment Alternative*. Washington DC: Rule of Law Series, Carnegie Endowment for International Peace, 2003.

Gonzalves, C. 'The Indian Supreme Court, Esc Rights and the Right to Food 2008'. In *Human Rights and Extreme Poverty Conference on 'Eradicating Poverty: Development and Empowerment of the Poor'*. Kolkata: Food and Agriculture Organization of the United Nations in Bangladesh, 2008.

Government of India, National Food Security Bill, 2013.

IFPRI. *Global Hunger Index 2011: The Challenge of Hunger – Taming Price Spikes and Excessive Food Volatility*. Washington DC: International Food Policy Research Institute, 2012.

Jonsson, U. *A Human Rights-Based Approach to Programming (HRBAP)*. New York: Human Rights-Based Programming Unit, UNICEF, 2003.

Nyamu-Musembi, C. and Cornwall, A. *What Is the 'Rights-Based Approach' All About? Perspectives from International Development Agencies*. Brighton: University of Sussex Institute for Development Studies, 2004.

OHCHR. *Frequently Asked Questions on a Human Rights-Based Approach to Development Cooperation*. Geneva: United Nations, Office of the High Commissioner for Human Rights, 2006.

Pogge, T. 'World Poverty and Human Rights'. *Ethics and International Affairs* 19, No. 1 (2005): 1–7.

'PUCL Petitions Supreme Court on Starvation Deaths'. *PUCL Bulletin*, July 2001. Online. Available at www.pucl.org/reports/Rajasthan/2001/starvation_death.htm (accessed 10 September 2010).

Right to Food Campaign Secretariat. 'Supreme Court Orders on the Right to Food: A Tool for Action'. Delhi: Right to Food Campaign Secretariat, 2005.

Right to Food Campaign Secretariat. 'Right to Food Campaign's Critique of the National Food Security Bill 2011'. Delhi: Right to Food Campaign Secretariat, 2012.

Sengupta, A. *Human Rights and Extreme Poverty: Report of the UN Independent Expert on the Question of Human Rights and Extreme Poverty*. Geneva: Economic and Social Council, E/CN.4/2005/49, 2005.

Sengupta, A. 'The Political Economy of Legal Empowerment of the Poor'. In *Rights and Legal Empowerment in Eradicating Poverty*, edited by D. Banik. Farnham: Ashgate, 2008: 31–46.

Singh, Manmohan. 'HUNGaMA Report Speech'. *NDTV*, 10 January 2012. Online. Available at www.ndtv.com/article/india/full-text-of-pm-s-speech-at-the-release-of-the-hungama-report-165450 (accessed 1 September 2012).

UN General Assembly. 'United Nations Millennium Declaration, Resolution Adopted by the General Assembly'. A/RES/55/2, 18 September 2000. Online. Available at www.un.org/millennium/declaration/ares552e.htm (accessed 9 April 2014).

Uvin, P. *Human Rights and Development*. Bloomfield, Conn.: Kumarian Press, 2004.

3 Access to international justice

The role of the International Criminal Court in aiding national prosecutions of international crimes

Rahmat Mohamad

Introduction

The establishment of the International Criminal Court (ICC or the Court) represents a major milestone in the fight against impunity at the international level and towards achieving international justice. One of the essential components of the rule of law at the international level is the struggle to end impunity for international crimes. International criminal justice has recently emerged as a powerful, resonant and effective voice in this new age of accountability.

International prosecution by the ICC represents a direct contribution to the fight against impunity for international crimes under the Rome Statute regime. However, international justice mechanisms, whether permanent or ad hoc, are not intended to supplant states where they have organized criminal justice systems which are willing and able to ensure that there is accountability for the crimes concerned. Indeed, pursuant to the principle of complementarity, the Rome Statute provides ample room not only for the exercise of national jurisdiction, but also for the development of international criminal law at the national level.

National prosecution of international crimes under the ICC has assumed critical importance in the current juncture for two reasons. First, the rapid development of international criminal law and the demand to put an end to the culture of impunity has led to an increase in the prosecution of international crimes. In recent times, while prosecutions have often been carried out by ad hoc tribunals, special courts and the ICC, some countries have carried out prosecutions through their national courts. Second, if prosecution of those responsible for large-scale human rights abuses is the rule rather than the exception, the ICC surely needs to go beyond complementarity and systematically integrate assistance to national authorities/judiciaries into its work when appropriate.

Against this background, and given the fact that the success of the ICC is predicated on state parties' compliance with their obligations under the treaty, this chapter explores the various avenues open to the parties to the Rome Statute to undertake domestic prosecutions of ICC offences of crimes against humanity, war crimes, genocide and the crime of aggression. With this objective, the chapter is structured in the following manner.

First, it will dwell on the important efforts undertaken on the road to the adoption of the ICC. In order to assess the role of domestic courts in prosecuting international crimes, some preliminary observations concerning the International Criminal Court and its background and salient features are considered necessary.

Second, it will move on to explore the notion of national prosecution of international crimes in general, and the role of the ICC in this endeavour. Specifically, it will deal with the various avenues that are available under the ICC that could be used by states to prosecute international crimes.

Lastly, in the light of these analyses, it will offer some final observations.

The long road to Rome

International criminal courts are a relatively recent development. The modern history of international criminal law began after the First World War (WWI). After the war, the Allies established a commission to determine who was responsible for starting the war and committing various violations of the laws of war. The commission recommended that a special tribunal be established to try persons for violations of the laws of war and humanity. Although the Treaty of Versailles includes provisions for prosecutions, none of these provisions were ultimately utilized.

After the Second World War (WWII), the Allies established the Nuremberg International Military Tribunal (Nuremberg IMT) and the International Military Tribunal for the Far East (Tokyo IMT) to try persons for crimes against peace, war crimes and crimes against humanity committed during the war. The Nuremberg and Tokyo tribunals had established the principle that individual leaders could be held responsible for crimes against the peace, war crimes and crimes against humanity. These tribunals laid the foundation for the establishment of the International Criminal Tribunal for Former Yugoslavia (ICTY) and the International Criminal Tribunal for Rwanda (ICTR), and, later, other hybrid international courts and a permanent institution, the International Criminal Court.

With the end of bipolar hostilities in the early 1990s, though, ethnic tensions, which had been quelled in certain parts of the world during the hegemonic post-war years, came to the forefront. In the former Yugoslavia, and in Rwanda, these tensions exploded into 'ethnic cleansing' and genocide. These conflicts, which had involved gross human rights violations, demanded an immediate response from the international community. The United Nations (UN) Security Council, triggered as it was by these events, created two ad hoc tribunals acting under Chapter VII of the UN Charter. These two tribunals, namely the ICTY and the ICTR, which provided the impetus for the International Law Commission (ILC) to adopt its draft statute for the proposed International Criminal Court, showed that international criminal justice was a practical possibility.

The ILC completed the draft in 1994 and forwarded it to the General Assembly for consideration. The General Assembly in turn established a Preparatory Committee to prepare a consolidated draft statute that would serve as the basis for negotiations at a diplomatic conference in Rome in 1998. After intense negotiations, the Rome Statute of the International Criminal Court was signed on 17 July 1998 at the United Nations Diplomatic Conference of Plenipotentiaries. The ICC came into force – far sooner than even the most optimistic observers had imagined – in 2002, and to date has secured 139 signatories form state parties with 118 ratifications. Whereas the two institutional precursors to the ICC, the ad hoc tribunals for the former Yugoslavia and Rwanda, were established by the UN Security Council and operate as subsidiary organs of the Security Council, the ICC is an independent treaty-based international organization.

Apart from the two ad hoc international criminal tribunals mentioned above, the UN has inspired, sponsored or supported the establishment of various hybrid criminal tribunals around the world. The Special Court for Sierra Leone (SCSL) was jointly established by the Sierra Leonean government and the UN to prosecute those responsible for crimes against humanity, war crimes, and other serious violations of international humanitarian law and Sierra Leonean law committed in the territory of Sierra Leone since 30 November 1996. A similar approach was also adopted in responding to the variety of crimes committed from May 1998 to June 1999 in the course of the armed conflict between Kosovo separatists and the forces of the Federal Republic of Yugoslavia with the establishment of special panels within the Kosovo legal system composed of a mix of international and national judges and prosecutors.

The primary difference between the ad hoc tribunals and hybrid tribunals lies in the fact that hybrid tribunals have both international and domestic elements. For instance, hybrid tribunals frequently use local judges or institutions in their proceedings. Precisely because they have national components, these tribunals are 'often regarded as giving more deference to state sovereignty than [international criminal] tribunals'.[1]

The ICC, which represents an important milestone in the advancement of the international criminal justice system, represents the beacon of a new era of global justice, unfettered by national boundaries. The purpose of the ICC is three-fold:

- to punish individuals responsible for extremely serious crimes;
- to bring justice to victims; and
- over time, to deter perpetrators and create a Culture of Accountability.

The core mission of the ICC was aptly captured by the UN Secretary-General's 2004 'Report on the Rule of Law and Transitional Justice in Conflict and Post Conflict Societies' which observed that the ICC 'offers new hope for a permanent reduction in the phenomenon of impunity'.[2]

After giving a brief overview of the developments leading up to the adoption of the ICC, the salient features of the ICC are discussed below.

Salient features of the ICC system

Jurisdiction

Temporal jurisdiction

The ICC Statute came into force on 1 July 2002. The Court's jurisdiction only extends to crimes committed after that date.

For a state which ratifies after 1 July 2002, the Court's jurisdiction only applies to that state from the date of its ratification. However, such a state may, by declaration, accept the Court's jurisdiction from an earlier time. The Court can never exercise jurisdiction over offences occurring prior to 1 July 2002.

Substantive jurisdiction

The jurisdiction of the International Criminal Court is limited to the most serious crimes of concern to the international community as a whole. It has jurisdiction over:

- genocide;
- crimes against humanity;
- war crimes; and
- aggression (from 2017).

Personal jurisdiction

The Court has jurisdiction only over individuals and not states.

The Court's jurisdiction is not universal. It is clearly limited. The Court has jurisdiction only over offences committed:

- by a national of a state party; and
- on the territory of a state party.

In addition, the Court will have jurisdiction over situations referred to the Court by the Security Council in exercise of its power to restore or maintain international peace and security. The Security Council no longer has to establish expensive ad hoc tribunals as in Yugoslavia and Rwanda. Instead, it can refer situations to the ICC, something that it has already done in relation to Darfur.

Complementarity

Another key feature of the Rome Statute is the principle of complementarity that involves the relationship between the jurisdiction of the Court and the jurisdiction of states. Under this principle, the Court does not intervene if a domestic system is carrying out its responsibilities. A case is not admissible if it is being or has been investigated or prosecuted by a state with jurisdiction. The ICC will act only if a state is unwilling or unable genuinely to carry out an investigation or prosecution. The ICC's role as an institution complementary to domestic courts proved to be so fundamental to the Court's purpose that state parties included three references to it in the Rome Statute – in the Preamble, Article 1 and Article 17.

Even as complementarity was entrenched in the Statute, the Court was given the ultimate power to decide when it could admit a case to its docket. In other words, the Court itself would make the final determination as to whether a country is 'unwilling' or 'unable' to prosecute a case:

- In order to determine inability of a state to bring transgressors to justice, the Court will consider whether a state's national judicial system has partially or totally collapsed or is unavailable.
- In order to determine unwillingness, the ICC will examine whether a state has acted in such a way so as to try to shield an accused from criminal responsibility.

State cooperation

The enforcement regime/capabilities of the ICC rely heavily on states and not on the Court. The ICC does not have its own police force, much less an army. The cooperation of states is, therefore, absolutely crucial in obtaining the arrest and surrender of persons wanted by the Court. Cooperation is also essential in other areas, such as in providing evidence, relocating witnesses and enforcing the Court's sentences. It is for this reason that Judge Philippe Kirsch, the first president of the ICC stated: The Rome Statute of the ICC is a two-pillar system – a judicial pillar represented by the Court, and an enforcement pillar represented by the States – which undertake a legal obligation to cooperate with the Court through the Statute.[3] In this regard, the main challenge to the success of the Court will be ensuring sufficient cooperation.

National prosecution of international crimes

It needs to be underlined here that national prosecutions for international crimes could take place through a variety of ways. For example, crimes against humanity, genocide, war crimes and piracy may in principle be tried by the normal criminal courts of any country under the principle of universal jurisdiction. This principle has long been part of international law. When prosecuting on this basis, the courts of one country act in the general interest of all (law-abiding) states. Some countries' legal systems make it relatively easy to bring such prosecutions; others make it difficult unless their own nationals are involved. The precise conditions under which a state may do so, however, remain highly controversial.

Be that as it may, this chapter only focuses on the various ways through which domestic jurisdictions could prosecute international crimes with the aid of the ICC. The responsibility of states to comply with their obligations to end impunity and to prosecute those responsible for the most serious crimes is established firmly. The need to have domestic mechanisms, in addition to the international criminal justice mechanisms, to create a dent on the culture of impunity arises for a number of reasons:

- First, international justice mechanisms, whether permanent or ad hoc, are not intended to supplant states where they have organized criminal justice systems which are willing and able to ensure that there is accountability for the crimes concerned.
- Second, they are not substitutes for national mechanisms. Thus it could be seen that, within the Statutes of the international criminal courts and tribunals, there is ample room for the exercise of national jurisdiction.
- Third, the primary role of national jurisdictions in the prosecution of crimes has been thrown into greater relief as international justice has evolved and as the ICC in particular has become operational. The principle of complementarity is the bedrock of international criminal justice.

To put it differently, no matter how well the ICC performs its tasks, national prosecutions will always be essential to the fight against impunity. The ICC Statute's complementarity provisions recognize the importance of national trials, in both its complementarity rule and its provisions which allow the court to help local judiciaries.

This provision has given rise to what has been called the 'Principle of Proactive Complementarity'.[4] It recognizes that the ICC can and should encourage, and perhaps even assist, national governments to prosecute international crimes. Proactive complementarity builds on the fact that the Rome Statute does far more than merely define the limits of the Court's power. The Statute creates a system of judicial enforcement for the prosecution of the most serious international crimes at both the domestic and international levels of governance.[5] The Statute also affirms the duties and rights of both national governments and the ICC to prosecute such crimes.[6] Furthermore, it also reifies the obligation of states to assist the ICC in its own investigations and prosecutions.[7]

Simply, under the ICC prerogative, both the domestic and international levels of governance have interrelated international legal duties to provide accountability for international crimes. This interplay between the ICC and the national mechanisms/actors can take numerous forms. The following part of the chapter would focus on ways through which the ICC can engage national authorities in the enforcement of international criminal law.

Where states are willing, but unable, to prosecute

Though the ICC is a court of last resort, the Court has been given the ultimate power to decide when it could admit a case to its docket. When a state in question finds it difficult to undertake investigations or prosecutions of international crimes, the ICC has an important role to play. The inability of states to undertake domestic prosecutions can stem from a number of reasons that include, inter alia, civil war, the collapse of domestic institutions, or a lack of resources and expertise. Furthermore, in the aftermath of a war or an extremely divisive and disruptive armed conflict, many national judicial systems may lack the wherewithal to conduct adequate proceedings. With outside help, however, countries in transition can regain the capacity to prosecute war crimes fairly and effectively. Practitioners in countries in transition have suggested that the ICC could help greatly in these situations by providing logistical support and sharing its expertise.[8]

The ICC can take up a case where it determines that a national judicial system has substantially collapsed. The question in such instances is purely one of capacity and not of willingness to prosecute. Hence, if there are significant benefits to local prosecutions, then the ICC should work to rebuild the capacities of the ailing national judicial system. In cases where the local government is simply unable to prosecute war crimes by itself, the ICC should not take cases to The Hague, but instead work with the government to enforce international criminal law locally.

In the area of strengthening the judicial capacity of states which are *unable* to prosecute international crimes, a number of avenues are open to the ICC. To start with, the Office of the Prosecutor (OTP) should carefully consider the reasons behind that inability and determine whether it can alter the ability of a state to investigate and prosecute. Such a determination again requires a careful balancing of the OTP's limited resources with the likely impact that international assistance will have. In some circumstances, efforts by the OTP to enhance domestic judicial capacity will be appropriate. In other circumstances, the resources required to enhance the ability of a national judiciary to prosecute will be far too great to justify ICC assistance.

At the most basic level, the Court could help by training local judges, investigators and prosecutors. It could also offer to share its expertise in matters ranging from investigation techniques to international law research to victim protection issues.[9] It would be well beyond the Court's mandate to provide basic material resources that state judiciaries might lack, but the collaboration of ICC officials with local authorities is likely to raise awareness of these needs among international donors. Furthermore, by offering its resources and expertise during joint investigations with local authorities, the ICC could also relieve financial pressure on domestic judicial and investigative offices.

With the consent of the national government, the ICC could provide more than logistical support and training to domestic authorities. Its officers could perform joint investigations and prosecutions on the ground. When a request is made by a member state, the ICC can cooperate with that state's authorities in investigating offences within the jurisdiction of the Court, or even offences that constitute 'a serious crime under the national law of the requesting State'.[10] Under certain conditions, the Court may also provide assistance to states that are not parties to the Rome Statute.[11] The types of cooperation and assistance explicitly authorized by the Statute include the transmission of evidence obtained by the Court and the questioning of persons detained by the order of the Court.[12] This cooperation can even occur on the territory of the state where the crime was committed. The Statute allows the Court to 'exercise its functions and powers ... on the territory of any State Party and, by special agreement, on the territory of any other State'.[13]

The ICC should actively promote such cooperation arrangements. Joint investigations harness the advantages of local prosecutions, even where the local criminal justice system is not fully capable of conducting such prosecutions by itself. By providing technical and logistical support to local authorities, this arrangement also increases the likelihood of effective prosecutions. Effective prosecutions, in turn, increase public respect for the legal system and thus promote the rule of law over the long run. Finally, the collaboration between national and international investigators and prosecutors also has the potential to spur a productive dialogue about the substance and procedure of prosecutions for international crimes.

Where states are unwilling to prosecute their nationals

This relates to a situation where a state is unwilling to undertake its own prosecutions despite the fact that it has the capacity to do so. Needless to say, the apathy to exercise criminal jurisdiction could be the result of political calculation on the part of national officials of a government, who might feel that inaction is politically preferable to the exercise of domestic jurisdiction.

This situation might very well occur in post-conflict societies wherein national governments might be unwilling to prosecute international crimes themselves and also refuse to allow the ICC to join in on prosecutions and trials. Even in the face of such reluctance, the Court might be able to obtain custody of suspects with the help of third-party states or of international peacekeeping forces. In those instances, the Court could take up cases in The Hague, as stated by the current admissibility provisions.

In such situations, the ICC should first attempt to motivate the state to undertake its own investigations and prosecutions and then, only if these efforts are unsuccessful, undertake its own investigation and prosecution. In this regard, the role of the Office of the Prosecutor (OTP) is critical. One of the means available to motivate an unwilling state to act is to threaten international intervention should the state concerned continue to abstain from undertaking its own investigations and prosecutions. When this is done, the message is clearly sent that international prosecution is a meaningful possibility. This might force the Country concerned to go for the far more palatable alternative of domestic prosecutions.

The OTP could also engage in dialogue with states that are unwilling to investigate or prosecute crimes themselves. By using the modalities established in the Rome Statute to communicate with states that were previously unwilling to prosecute, the OTP may be able to cajole those states into prosecuting crimes domestically. Such communication may focus states' attention on their obligations to prosecute international crimes, may provide a form of acculturation through which accountability becomes a norm of state conduct, and may allow states to recognize their own interests in domestic prosecutions.

The normative basis for such dialogue/communication could be found in a number of provisions of the Rome Statute. The Prosecutor's assessment of a potential situation under Article 15, the initial determination of admissibility under Article 17, the process of informing states of a possible investigation under Article 18(1), the reports to the Prosecutor with respect to a deferred investigation under Article 18(5), and the Prosecutor's decision to initiate or terminate an investigation under Articles 53(1) and 53(2) all foresee communications between the OTP and states and the provision of information to the OTP with respect to investigations and prosecutions undertaken by national judiciaries. The powers of OTP, which clearly envisage such communications, and which are fully consistent with the Rome Statute, have the capability to put states on notice of the potential for international prosecution, and could pressure them to exercise domestic jurisdiction.[14]

Arrests

The ICC could best help national prosecutions with arrests by providing information to justify warrants, and information that would help to identify and locate suspects. Although under certain provisions a person arrested pursuant to a Court warrant could be transferred for a national prosecution, these provisions are extremely limited.[15] As with evidentiary assistance, the ICC's help in apprehending individuals is technically possible, but ultimately will depend on the political will of other states to help it and its own willingness to share the information.

The ICC has broad powers to issue arrest warrants on the application of the Prosecutor to the pre-trial chamber.[16] A warrant may be issued for any of several reasons, including the existence of reasonable grounds to believe the person has committed a crime within the ICC's mandate, or in order to ensure the person's appearance at trial, prevent the obstruction of the investigation or court proceedings, or prevent the continuing commission of crimes under investigation by the Prosecutor.[17] The ICC's ability to have these warrants executed is of great benefit to a national prosecution, even if the arrestees are not subsequently handed over to the national effort. Initially, if arrestees are obstructing the ICC prosecution, it is likely that they are also wielding influence over the domestic effort. If they are instrumental for the ICC prosecution, they are likely to have valuable information that the local prosecutors could access via interrogations.

The ICC will be able to arrest some categories of offenders beyond the reach of national judiciaries, such as those protected by official immunity or a statute of limitations in the national court. Under the Statute, a defendant's official capacity does not exempt him from criminal responsibility, and no statute of limitations applies. The ICC, however, has no police force, and its ability to execute warrants is circumscribed by its reliance on domestic authorities for enforcement.

After having highlighted the various ways through which the ICC could influence national authorities/domestic prosecutions, final remarks on this issue are offered.

Final remarks

The ICC's ability to help national prosecutions, as with its own ability to prosecute, depends largely on states, and how much those states are willing to let it or help it perform those functions. But – as we have seen – the ICC Statute specifically authorizes many ways of providing assistance, and there are many other ways that fit within the existing framework. To maximize these opportunities, the Court should integrate assistance to national prosecutions into the core of its work, especially hiring, investigation, witness protection, and arrest activities. Such assistance will help the ICC to be more responsive to the conditions of its target countries, and it will support the judiciaries in a difficult process of transition while they come to terms with the past. Most important, providing assistance to national judiciaries is allegedly the only way that the world will have accountability for the majority of crimes under the ICC's mandate.

As a strategy for encouraging national governments to undertake their own prosecutions of international crimes, proactive complementarity would allow the Court to catalyse national judiciaries to fulfil their own obligations to prosecute international crimes. Even when we explore the possibility of aiding the national authorities to undertake prosecutions for international crimes, we need to be mindful of a number of factors. These include the development of useable tactics of political influence, the practical difficulties of coordinating with national governments, and the legal dangers around compromising a case's subsequent admissibility before the ICC. The need to develop a cautious and carefully tailored strategy to be used by the OTP remains compelling. This would make sure that such strategies achieve maximum benefits and to the maximum possible extent minimize the potential hazards.

The need to persuade the states to undertake domestic prosecutions can also be hardly exaggerated. The fact that it is in the self-interest of the individual states to be in a position to prosecute international crimes to at least the same extent as the ICC needs to be understood. This does not only give meaning to the concept of the primary punishment of international crimes by national courts, but it also takes into account the states' interests in national sovereignty. After all, the states parties to the ICC must recognize that the ICC is not the primary locus for combating impunity. Domestic national tribunals and processes constitute the primary and lasting solutions to impunity and that by actively assisting the Court the state parties could indeed create a dent in the culture of impunity.

Notes

1 Bernaz and Prouvèze 2010: 293–294.

2 United Nations Secretary-General, 'Report of the Secretary-General on the Rule of

Law and Transitional Justice in Conflict and Post Conflict Societies', (UN Doc. S/2004/616, 23 August 1994:1), delivered to the Security Council and General Assembly.

3 Judge Philippe Kirsch (President of the International Criminal Court), *Opening Remarks at the Fifth Session of the Assembly of States Parties* (ICC, 23 November 2006):

> In establishing the ICC, States set up a system designed on two pillars. The Court itself is the judicial pillar. The enforcement pillar belongs to States. In national systems, the two pillars are intertwined. Courts rely automatically on the enforcement powers of the State. In the case of the ICC, the two have been separated. The Court depends on the cooperation of States Parties. With the support and cooperation of States Parties, the Court will continue to be a strong, credible judicial institution.

4 Burke-White 2008: 68–70.

5 Burke-White 2008: 56.

6 UN General Assembly, 'Rome Statute of the International Criminal Court (Last Amended 2010)', (ICC, 17 July 1998), Preamble: '[I]t is the duty of every State to exercise its criminal jurisdiction over those responsible for international crimes' and 'the most serious crimes of concern to the international community as a whole must not go unpunished and ... their effective prosecution must be ensured by taking measures at the national level and by enhancing international cooperation'.

7 See, 'Rome Statute of the International Criminal Court (Last Amended 2010)', (ICC, 17 July 1998), Articles 86–99.

8 Concannon 2002: 234.

9 Ibid., 240–244.

10 UN General Assembly, 'Rome Statute of the International Criminal Court (Last Amended 2010)', Art. 93(10)(a).

11 'Rome Statute of the International Criminal Court (Last Amended 2010)', Art. 93(10)(c).

12 'Rome Statute of the International Criminal Court (Last Amended 2010)', Art. 93(10)(b).

13 'Rome Statute of the International Criminal Court (Last Amended 2010)', Art. 4(2).

14 The potential for dialogue with national governments to encourage domestic prosecutions is illustrated by the ICC's influence on Colombia's hesitancy to hold paramilitary groups accountable for their crimes. In an effort to bring paramilitary groups out of the jungle, the Colombian government offered very generous terms for paramilitaries willing to join the peace process. Specifically, Colombia's Peace and Justice Law, passed in late June 2005, limited accountability for the perpetration of crimes within the jurisdiction of the ICC by allowing paramilitaries to confess and face relatively light sentences. The confessions, investigations and sentences were designed to cover any crimes an individual may have committed and did not offer guarantees of transparency or judicial process. At the very least, the scope of accountability that the law would provide was questionable. Nonetheless, the judicial process enabled by the law might have deemed a national investigation sufficient, under Articles 17 and 20 of the Rome Statute, to limit the admissibility of those cases before the ICC. Even though the ICC had not opened an investigation in Colombia, senior officials in the OTP, concerned by the lack of accountability for potential crimes within the Court's jurisdiction, addressed a letter to the government of Colombia in 2005 alerting them to the nature of the crimes to which the law applied and informing them of the Court's potential interest in the situation. Subsequently, the Colombian Constitutional Court struck down the law, modifying it to remove certain amnesty provisions and to better address various human rights concerns. Senior Colombian officials have attributed this change, at least in part, to fear of ICC involvement. Through dialogue with the Colombian government, the ICC was able to help preserve the possibility of full accountability in domestic courts.

15 UN General Assembly, 'Rome Statute of the International Criminal Court (Last Amended 2010)', Art. 90.
16 'Rome Statute of the International Criminal Court (Last Amended 2010)', Art. 58.
17 'Rome Statute of the International Criminal Court (Last Amended 2010)', Art. 58(1).

References

Bernaz, Nadia, and Prouvèze, Rémy. 'International and Domestic Prosecutions'. In *The Pursuit of International Criminal Justice: A World Study on Conflicts, Victimization and Post-Conflict*, edited by M. Cherif Bassiouni. Mortsel, Belgium: Intersentia, 2010: 269–298.

Burke-White, William W. 'Proactive Complementarity: The International Criminal Court and National Courts in the Rome System of International Justice'. *Harvard International Law Journal* 49, No. 1 (2008): 53–108.

Concannon Jr., Brian. 'Beyond Complementarity: The International Criminal Court and National Prosecutions, a View from Haiti'. *Columbia Human Rights Law Review* 32 (2002): 201–250.

Kirsch (President of the International Criminal Court), Judge Philippe. *Opening Remarks at the Fifth Session of the Assembly of States Parties*. ICC, 23 November 2006. Online. Available at www.icc-cpi.int/iccdocs/asp_docs/library/organs/presidency/PK_20061123_en.pdf (accessed 6 August 2014).

UN General Assembly. 'Rome Statute of the International Criminal Court (Last Amended 2010)'. ICC, 17 July 1998.

United Nations Secretary-General. 'Report of the Secretary-General on the Rule of Law and Transitional Justice in Conflict and Post Conflict Societies'. UN Doc. S/2004/616, 23 August 1994.

4 Aggression and *Monetary Gold* quo vadis?

Mirinda O'Gorman and Charles Sampford

Introduction

No lawyer should object to Jackson's statement. Indeed, to deny it is to not only deny the international rule of law but, for many, the concept of law itself. It would also ignore the only strong (and it was strong) legal foundation for the trials – the Pact of Paris[1] – which was signed by the nations sitting in judgment and those whose citizens were judged. The only objection that might be made is that its force might be confined to mere utility.

Yet it is a trite reflection that what Robert Jackson thought was clear was denied institutional expression for the following half century and has been making only slow and uneven progress since. It is beyond the scope of this chapter to list, let alone determine, the reasons why the powers that established the Nuremberg and Tokyo war crimes trials institutionally ignored the laws they had so loudly proclaimed and thereby retrospectively denied the legitimacy of the trials they had established.[2] Despite the enormous progress made by the states parties at the Review Conference of the Rome Statute in Kampala[3] in activating the jurisdiction over crimes of aggression when it is ratified by the required 30 states, there will be many obstacles to its implementation, even within those states that ratify the changes.

One of the more intriguing potential obstacles is provided by the *Monetary Gold* principle that arose from *Monetary Gold Removed from Rome in 1943* (*Monetary Gold Case*)[4] heard by the International Court of Justice (ICJ) soon after Nuremberg. It applies a strong form of consent theory to prevent the court making any finding (positive or negative) about a party that has not agreed to the court's jurisdiction. This raises two questions for the crime of aggression. First, does the *Monetary Gold* principle apply solely to the ICJ, or can it be applied to other international bodies? Second, we need to consider the way the crime of aggression introduces issues of consent to the International Criminal Court (ICC). If applied in its strongest form it would not only limit who might be prosecuted but what defences could be run. Mirinda O'Gorman did extensive research in the lead-up, and during an internship at the International Criminal Court in 2011. She developed a powerful argument, grounded in case law and legal commentary, that *Monetary Gold* applies to the crime of aggression, preventing any consideration of the behaviour of an alleged victim-state who has not consented to the Court's jurisdiction for the crime of aggression. This argument, based on a strong view of the principle of consent enshrined in international law, had considerable support among lawyers at the ICC but less support among the international lawyers present at the workshop. The authors do not seek to affirm either as the better view and/or the view most likely to be adopted by a court of competent jurisdiction. We seek to outline the 'strong view' (of the content and effect of *Monetary Gold* in international criminal law) and a 'weak view' and consider some of the potential implications for each. We argue that the strong view reflects much about past approaches to international law, differences between the international public law and (domestic) public law as well as differences between international and domestic criminal law. We will argue that international law can and should move in the direction of the weaker view of *Monetary Gold*. In doing so, we get some purchase on some more general issues about including the relationship between public international law and international criminal law, the extent to which domestic law principles influence international law principles, the relationship between various international courts and related issues of impunity and access to justice – the principle concern of this book.

The strong argument – applying *Monetary Gold* to international tribunals

The crime of aggression

The crime of aggression under the amended Rome Statue defines the individual crime of aggression as the planning, preparation, initiation or execution by a person in a leadership position of an act of aggression, where that the act of aggression constitutes a manifest violation of the Charter of the United Nations. An act of aggression is the use of armed force by a state against the sovereignty, territorial integrity or political independence of another state, or in any other manner inconsistent with the Charter of the United Nations.[5]

The crime of aggression is the least developed crime in international law[6] and assesses state responsibility to a far greater degree.[7] It is these distinguishing features that form the basis of the primary legal question this chapter seeks to address: Will the ICC violate the *Monetary Gold* principle when deciding cases that involve a victim-state that is either not a state party or is a state party that has not consented to the Court's jurisdiction for the crime of aggression?

The Monetary Gold *principle and the ICJ*

The ICJ *Monetary Gold Case* involved a number of states laying claim to gold that went missing during the Second World War. Italy's claim to the gold was based on its assertion that Albania had committed an international wrong against Italy requiring her to pay Italy compensation. Albania, however, was not a party to the ICJ dispute and had not consented to the jurisdiction of the Court. The ICJ found that they could not determine the dispute without the consent of Albania and thus established the *Monetary Gold* principle. The ICJ stated that:

> To adjudicate upon the international responsibility of Albania without her consent would run counter to a well-established principle of international law embodied in the Court's Statute, namely, that the Court can only exercise jurisdiction over a State with its consent.[8]

The ICJ stated that the limitation of their jurisdiction was at the point that 'Albania's legal interests would not only be affected by a decision, but would form the very subject-matter of the decision'.[9] This test has been repeated and followed in a number of ICJ decisions.[10]

The Monetary Gold *principle and other international bodies*

The *Monetary Gold Case* refers to the ICJ's Statute when reaching its conclusion regarding the principle. It is thus important to note that the *Monetary Gold* principle has also been applied in other international law bodies such as the World Trade Organization[11] and Permanent Court of Arbitration.[12] In addition, the International Law Commission's commentary to Article 16 on its Articles on State Responsibility highlights the general applicability of the principle when it states that 'the *Monetary Gold* Principle is concerned with the admissibility of claims in international judicial proceedings'.[13]

In the Permanent Court of Arbitration case, *Larsen v. Hawaiian Kingdom*,[14] the parties argued that the *Monetary Gold* principle should be confined to the ICJ.[15] The Permanent Court of Arbitration, when refuting this contention and applying the principle to the arbitration, explained the applicability of the ICJ jurisprudence by stating 'it is the consent of the parties which brings [a] tribunal into existence'[16] concluding that 'an international tribunal may not exercise jurisdiction over a State unless that State has given its consent to the exercise of jurisdiction'.[17] This highlights that the principle's application is not confined to international law disputes governed by the ICJ Statute, but rather, finds its basis in the importance of consent for the existence of an international tribunal.

Issues of consent: judicial guidance

There is little judicial guidance as to whether the *Monetary Gold* principle should apply to international criminal law: the ad hoc criminal law tribunals of the former Yugoslavia,[18] Rwanda,[19] Sierra Leone,[20] along with the ICC's consideration of the situations of Darfur, Sudan and Libya received delegated jurisdiction as a result of Security Council referral.[21] The ad hoc criminal tribunals of Lebanon[22] and Cambodia,[23] along with the situations of Congo, Uganda, and the Central African Republic in the ICC all involve states that requested the criminal tribunals[24] and the situation of Kenya in the ICC involves a consenting state.[25]

As a result, the issue of a criminal tribunal considering a situation involving a non-consenting state has not yet arisen, thus offering no jurisprudence as to whether the *Monetary Gold* principle should apply to the ICC.[26] Further, the crime of aggression has not yet been considered by a court since the Nuremberg and Tokyo Tribunals. When the Rome Statute[27] entered into force in 2002, no agreement was reached on the definition for the crime of aggression.[28] Article 5 provided for the Court to exercise jurisdiction over the crime of aggression sometime in the future.[29] In 2010 at the Rome Statute Review Conference in Kampala the Assembly of State Parties agreed on a definition of the crime of aggression.[30] States are not scheduled to make a decision regarding the inclusion of the definition into the Rome Statute until 2017,[31] giving the international community ample time to discuss any uncertainties they have about the definition.

The Court will, no doubt, be called upon to assess the merits of applying the *Monetary Gold* principle once it begins to consider the crime of aggression. This issue is likely to arise as: the Court's consideration of the crime will involve more than one state party; the definition of the crime does not require the victim-state to have consented to the Court; and the Court will be required to make a determination about state actions that is the 'very subject matter' of the case.

The crime, by definition, involves more than one state party

Resolution RC/Res 6 distinguishes between the 'crime of aggression'[32] and the 'act of aggression'.[33] The 'act of aggression' is defined in accordance with General Assembly resolution 3314 (XXIX) of 14 December 1974.[34] This definition stipulates that an 'act of aggression means the use of armed force by a State against the sovereignty, territorial integrity or political independence of another'[35] and thus requires the involvement of two states. This enhances the chance that the Court will have to consider a situation that involves a state that has not consented to its jurisdiction.

The jurisdictional limits established by the resolution do not require the victim-state to have given consent

The Resolution details how the ICC may gain jurisdiction over a situation, and the situations in which their jurisdiction will be limited. In doing so, it helps ensure consent to a degree.

The Resolution provides that jurisdiction over the crime of aggression may be conferred on the Court by state referral or the prosecutor acting *proprio motu* under Article 15*bis*, or as a result of a referral from the Security Council under Article 15*ter*. If the Court receives its jurisdiction as a result of a referral from the Security Council, it receives the 'delegated universal jurisdiction' from the Security Council[36] so is not limited to the states that have consented to the Court.[37] However under Article 15*bis*, the Court must have *ratione materiae* jurisdiction,[38] *ratione temporis* jurisdiction,[39] *ratione tertiis* jurisdiction[40] and *ratione personae* jurisdiction[41] to prosecute. This is a higher level than is required for the other crimes under the Rome Statute, which, while still needing *ratione materiae*[42] and *ratione temporis* jurisdiction,[43] requires only one of either *ratione tertiis*[44] or *ratione personae* jurisdiction.[45] This is significant as the Court only has *ratione tertiis* and *ratione personae* jurisdiction if the state party on whose territory the action occurred, or of which the accused is a national, has consented to the Court's jurisdiction. Therefore, the crime of aggression requires a higher level of consent than the other crimes within the jurisdiction of the ICC.

This consent is again heightened by the Resolution's inclusion of Article 15*bis*(4), which allows for states that are party to the Rome Statute to lodge a declaration with the Registrar stating that it does not accept the jurisdiction of the Court derived from Article 15*bis*.[46] This has been termed the 'opt-out' clause.[47] As a result of this clause, the Court cannot have *ratione personae* jurisdiction over a national from a state that has opted out; however, the Court does still retain jurisdiction over that state's territory.[48]

The requirement for *ratione tertiis* jurisdiction ensures that the territory where the act of aggression occurred involves a state who has consented to the Rome Statute. Similarly, the *ratione personae* jurisdiction ensures that the accused is a national of a state party who has consented to the crime of aggression. However, in a case where the act of aggression occurs somewhere other than on the territory of the victim-state's, these current requirements for jurisdiction do not require the victim-state to have consented to the jurisdiction of the Court. As a result, the Court would have jurisdiction over a situation that involves a non-consenting victim-state, that is, a victim-state that is not a state party to the Rome Statute (non-state party) or who has opted out of the crime of aggression.

An example of such a situation, if the Court currently had jurisdiction over the crime of aggression,[49] can be hypothesized by examining the recent deployment of 100 American military advisers to Uganda.[50] Uganda is a state party to the Rome Statute,[51] however America is not. If a Ugandan national acting as a leader of the state was indicted for a crime of aggression allegedly committed on Ugandan territory against the American forces,[52] the Court would have jurisdiction over the situation as the national and territory is a consenting state party.[53] If the Ugandan national argued in defence of the allegation that there was no act of aggression as Uganda was acting in self-defence of American use of force in their state, the Court would need to determine whether America's actions were lawful or whether such actions by Uganda amounted to a manifest violation of the UN Charter. The Court's consideration of a non-consenting victim-state's actions is bound to result in resistance and disapproval from states.[54]

This is therefore the second reason why the *Monetary Gold* principle is likely to be important for the ICC application of the crime of aggression – it will probably be called upon to determine a case that involves a victim-state that has not consented to the jurisdiction of the Court.[55]

The ICC is required to make determinations on state responsibility that are the 'very subject' of the decision

The *Monetary Gold* principle protects states from an international tribunal making determinations about the state's international responsibility without her consent. However the test for when this principle applies is that the 'legal interests would not only be affected by a decision, but would form the very subject matter of the decision'.[56] This strong argument sees the ICC, when determining an individual's culpability for the crime of aggression, make a determination on state responsibility and this determination is the 'very subject' of the decision (as we shall see later, the alternative argument sees the very subject of the decision to be the guilt or innocence of the accused and whether the accused's belief in the alleged aggression of a state provides a reason not to convict).

Determinations on state responsibility

The *Monetary Gold* principle protects third-party states from international tribunals adjudicating upon their international responsibility without their consent.[57] The argument has thus been raised that because the ICC is determining an individual's culpability, it does not determine state responsibility, or if it does, its finding is *obiter dictum* at best.[58] Judge Tomka of the International Criminal Tribunal for the former Yugoslavia commented:

> The ICTY has to determine the personal guilt and individual criminal responsibility of those indicted for the crime of genocide, crimes against humanity and war crimes. It has no jurisdiction over States as such and thus cannot make any pronouncement on the responsibility of States for the many serious atrocities committed during the Balkan wars since 1991.[59]

While it is true that, like the ICTY, the ICC's purpose is to determine personal guilt, it is important to note that the ICTY does not include within its jurisdiction the crime of aggression. The definition of genocide, crimes against humanity and war crimes do not necessarily involve a dispute between states, rather, the definitions restrict these crimes to actions of individuals against people.[60]

Unlike the other crimes currently within the Court's jurisdiction, the crime of aggression definition specifically refers to the actions of the state and requires the Court to determine the legality of the state's actions.[61] The *crime* of aggression involves an individual planning, preparing, initiating or executing an act of aggression.[62] The *act* of aggression is the use of armed force by a state against the sovereignty, territorial integrity or political independence of another state.[63] The elements of the crime of aggression that provide the Court guidance as to how the definition should be interpreted[64] specify that for a state's action to be considered an act of aggression in accordance with the definition, it needs to be in manifest[65] violation of the UN Charter.[66] Thus the Court needs to consider the actions of the state and determine whether, according to their gravity, character and scale, they are in manifest violation of the UN Charter.[67] In the ICJ case of *Gabcikovo-Nagymaros Project*, the Court stated that 'when a State has committed an international wrongful act, its international responsibility is likely to be involved whatever the nature of the obligation it has failed to respect'.[68] Thus for the Court to determine whether the victim-state committed an international wrongful act so as to justify the aggressor state acting in self-defence, the Court will be determining the victim-state's responsibility.[69] The crime of aggression thus requires the Court to judge the victim-, and aggressor-, states' responsibility when determining an individual's culpability.

Victim-state's interests go to the very subject matter of the case

It has been argued that, as the ICC's role is to judge an individual's guilt, the 'very subject matter' of the decision cannot be the action of a state, but rather, those of the individual.[70] While this may be true for the current crimes within the Court's jurisdiction, it is this chapter's contention that this is not so for the crime of aggression.

The elements of the crime of aggression ensure that there can be no finding of an individual planning, preparing, initiating or executing an act of aggression, if the Court believes the alleged aggressor-state's actions do not amount to an act of aggression under international law.[71] This requires the Court to consider the actions of the victim-state to determine if there was any reason why the aggressor-state's actions, which are *prima facie* acts of aggression, are not in manifest violation of the UN Charter. The Court's determination of the victim-state's responsibility is a prerequisite for the decision of the case.[72] A comparison can be made to the ICJ cases of *Monetary Gold Case*[73] and the *East Timor Case.*[74] In both cases, before the court could proceed to determine other matters, the Court would have had to make a determination about the third-party state's interest. As a result, the ICJ applied the *Monetary Gold* principle and did not exercise jurisdiction over the cases.[75] In contrast, in the *Nauru*[76] and *Nicaragua* case,[77] the Court held that a decision in the proceedings may *affect* the third-party state's interests, but the third-party state's interests were not the 'very subject matter' of the Court's decision.[78] It is clear that the aforementioned situation goes beyond merely affecting the interests of the victim-state as the ICC is required to determine the lawfulness of the state's actions before continuing on to decide the individual's culpability.

Accordingly, the strong argument concludes that the ICC determines state responsibility when determining whether the alleged acts committed by the aggressor-state amount to an act of aggression in manifest violation of the UN Charter. This determination is a prerequisite for the Court being able to determine the individual's culpability and thus can be said to be the 'very subject matter' of the decision. Accordingly, on the strong argument, the ICC should apply the *Monetary Gold* principle to ensure that it does not judge a victim-state's responsibility without her consent.

Ramification of non-application of the Monetary Gold *principle: consent required to enforce the consent principle to ensure legitimacy and powers of the court*

It may be argued that because the ICC, unlike the ICJ,[79] does not have the power to bind states by its decision[80] there is no need to apply the *Monetary Gold* principle to protect non-consenting states.[81] However, while the ICJ's decision is binding on consenting state parties, Article 59 of the ICJ Statute ensures that non-consenting states are not bound by the decisions. It can thus be said that the absent third-party state in both an ICJ decision and ICC decision are equally affected by the Court's decision. Thus as the ICC is required to make determinations on state responsibility, the *Monetary Gold* principle should apply for the same reasons it applies to the ICJ – to ensure compliance with the consent principle. This argument is further supported by consideration of advisory opinions by the ICJ. These opinions are not binding on the state parties, however in the *Western Sahara Advisory Opinion*, the ICJ stated that 'the lack of consent of an interested State may render the giving of an advisory opinion incompatible with the Court's judicial character'.[82] Thus it can be seen that international law requires tribunals to respect the consent principle, even when states are not bound by the decision.

Accordingly the *Monetary Gold* principle should be applied to the ICC as 'to adjudicate upon the international responsibility of [a non-consenting victim-state] without her consent would run counter to a well-established principle of international law'.[83] Indeed, the supporters of the strong argument might argue that, if the Court was to not apply the *Monetary Gold* principle, it is disregarding the protection of the consent principle, and, thus, a misalignment with international law would diminish the Court's legitimacy.[84] Further, it might be argued that the Court's powers depend on the consent of states,[85] meaning it is in the Court's interest to ensure that it applies principles that highlight, and protect, consent. (On the alternative argument set out in the next section, the ICC should look to the states that have ratified the Rome Statute and they certainly do not want their soldiers, or those on their territory with their consent, being accused of aggression when acting in self-defence against the aggression of non-signatory states.)

Ramifications continued: avoiding individual acquittal due to a non-consenting state's refusal to cooperate

The non-application of the *Monetary Gold* principle could result in detrimental ramifications for international criminal justice. If the *Monetary Gold* principle is not applied, there will be no reason to limit the Court's jurisdiction based on a non-consenting victim-state.[86] The Court will thus proceed to hear the case regarding an individual's culpability. The Court will need to be satisfied beyond a reasonable doubt that the crime of aggression has occurred.[87] If the issue of the victim-state's actions is raised in support of the proposition that the alleged aggressor-state's actions were not in manifest violation, the Prosecutor will be required to present enough evidence to prove to the Court, beyond reasonable doubt, that the victim-state did not act unlawfully.[88] Considering the victim-state has not consented to the Court's jurisdiction it is not unreasonable to suggest that the victim-state, not bound by the obligations to cooperate with the Rome Statute,[89] will not participate with the Prosecutor[90] especially as 'States would have reason to be more concerned about the political impact of adjudications before an international court than before an individual State's courts'.[91]

This proposition is supported once it is considered that the Prosecutor would likely require access to information regarding the victim-state's military actions to be able to prove that the state did not use force, or did not even threaten force.[92] It is unlikely that a state that has refused to consent to the ICC's jurisdiction would give such sensitive information.[93] The problem this will create is highlighted by consideration of the ICJ case *Nicaragua.* In that case the Court had to determine whether the United States' use of force was in self-defence of actions of Nicaragua. In its judgment, the ICJ commented on the difficulty of the task of finding enough evidence to support one state's claim over another.[94] It is highly likely, therefore, that if the ICC hears a case that involves a non-consenting victim-state, the Court will have evidential difficulties proving, beyond reasonable doubt whether the state committed an act of aggression, or, for example, was acting in self-defence of the actions of the victim-state. It will be detrimental if the ICC acquits an individual for the 'supreme international crime'[95] due to a non-consenting state's lack of cooperation. It is imperative, to ensure the ICC's legitimacy and support by states, that an acquittal of an individual is a sign of criminal justice prevailing, rather than signifying the lack of power of the ICC. If the *Monetary Gold* principle is applied, the Court would prevent a situation where a non-consenting state can limit the powers of the Court.

There is thus also a policy reason for the ICC to consider the application of the *Monetary Gold* principle as its application would ensure the protection of the consent principle in international law, but also would ensure the legitimacy of the ICC. Tokyo claimed self-defence against US because of sanctions. In fact the latter were blatant acts of war which were justified by Japanese aggression in China for nearly a decade. Interestingly enough, the immediate trigger was the occupation of French Indochina with the apparent acquiescence of the Vichy government which may not have met the definition of aggression.

Concluding the strong case

The Kampala Conference has introduced an exciting time for the International Criminal Court, a definition for the crime of aggression was decided upon by state parties and the ICC is one step closer to having the crime of aggression within its jurisdiction. Once the crime is within the Court's jurisdiction, the Court will need to analyse its role with states and consider whether the *Monetary Gold* principle should apply in its proceedings. This is likely to become an issue for the ICC quickly as the definition drafted at the Review Conference does not require the victim-state party to have consented to the jurisdiction of the Court. The crime of aggression is a contentious addition to the Court's jurisdiction and there may be a number of conflicting views about whether the Court's determination about the legality of the victim-state and aggressor-state's alleged actions could ever be the 'very subject matter' of an individual's criminal proceedings. It is this chapter's view, however, that the crime of aggression should not be forced to fit the mould of the previous crimes. The Court should recognize that the judgment of a crime of aggression involves a determination on a state's actions, and its responsibility, to a far greater degree than its previous crimes. In response to this recognition, the Court should ensure that it does not exercise jurisdiction over a non-consenting state regarding its responsibilities in accordance with the *Monetary Gold* principle. This principle should be applied even if the state is not the alleged aggressor-state. The Court depends on states' consent and this should be reflected in the Court protecting the principle of consent. The consent principle has been recognized in international law by a number of different bodies and the ICC should adhere to this precedent. The application of the principle ensures that the Court's powers are not limited by a non-consenting state party. Ultimately, it may be argued that if the Court does not apply this principle, and thus does not protect the principle of consent, it risks its legitimacy and power.

Counter-point: criminal law is different

While *Monetary Gold* is an important precedent within the ICJ and is rooted in the consent principle of classic public international law, there is a real question of how applicable it is to international criminal law and the institutions which enforce it. There are important differences between domestic criminal law and domestic civil law, and extensive differences between international criminal law which is directed at individuals and international public law which is agreed by states.

ICJ, ICC and consent

The first question is whether a principle developed in the ICJ should be applied by the ICC. This reflects the problem that international courts are not linked in an appeal structure as they are in most domestic legal systems. Most state jurisdictions have an ultimate appellate court. Even if it cannot hear all appeals (for example, the US Supreme Court cannot hear appeals on state law from state supreme courts) there are other unifying factors. One example is the way that the US Bill of Rights and the fourteenth amendment give the US Supreme Court extensive application to substantive law within the states. Another is the widespread use of persuasive authorities from other State Supreme Courts and the long-standing efforts to establish model codes. Under these circumstances decisions by the ICJ are at best persuasive authority even if the relevant law and facts are the same.

Of course, *Monetary Gold* is rooted in the consent of the parties. This consent principle has long been at the core of public international law and its core institutions – starting with independent arbiters –[96] moving international arbitration panels to the Permanent Court of International Justice[97] which metamorphosed into the International Court of Justice. This consent has seemed central to international law because international courts had no power to compel the parties to appear or to enforce their judgment. Unlike domestic courts, international courts were entirely dependent on the parties' good will and compliance to even have the opportunity to give judgment, let alone the prospect of compliance. It is quite appropriate that *Monetary Gold* is applied to other international arbitral tribunals such as the WTO and the Permanent Court of Arbitration which operate in the arbitral milieu from which the ICC emerged.[98]

However, international criminal law and international criminal jurisdiction are not so tied to consent. It is a much more recent phenomenon, but its short history commenced with an institution that was not based on consent. While the German and Japanese governments had signed the Pact of Paris[99] and the prosecuting powers agreed among themselves, Germany had not consented to the establishment of, and jurisdiction of, the court, let alone the individual trials. The individual defendants had definitely not consented and any objections to the jurisdiction were dismissed. Other institutions of international criminal law have similarly ignored the issue of state or individual consent – including ad hoc international tribunals like the International Criminal Tribunal for the Former Yugoslavia (ICTY). Other tribunals have had the consent of the state concerned (Cambodia and Rwanda) – though the consent was to try predecessors who had been overthrown by force. Neither universal jurisdiction nor specific war crimes legislation rely on the consent of the defendants or the states they served. Before the ICC, consent of the states which employ them is generally, but not always, required (for example, war crimes committed on the territory of a signatory, war crimes investigated by the pre-trial procedure and investigations ordered by the UNSC).

This reflects differences within domestic courts. While civil jurisdiction is conferred by the state in which the court operates and can be invoked by either party to a dispute, the matter can generally be terminated by an agreement between the parties. Criminal jurisdiction is very different. The prosecution is not a party so much as an official or an office following its institutional and legal duty. The defendant is a party, indeed the Nuremberg trials provide an example of international legal personality being conferred on individuals for the first time.[100] But the defendant cannot merely reach a settlement and end proceedings as they can in domestic civil courts, arbitration panels and the ICJ.

Like Nuremberg, the ICC has jurisdiction over individuals, not states.[101] Just as Nuremberg concentrated on individuals, so will the ICC. Unlike Nuremberg, the ICC does consider state consent to be relevant to jurisdiction but does not consider it as determinative as the ICJ. In any case, like all courts, the ICC should look to the statute that founds its jurisdiction rather than the precedents from other courts with a different history and a different jurisdiction.

How broad was Monetary Gold *at the time it was decided?*

While we are in favour of a restrictive interpretation of the *Monetary Gold* principle, it is not clear to us that it would have been expected to extend to international criminal law at the time. The *Monetary Gold Case* was decided in 1954, not long after the conclusion of the international war crimes trials. One wonders how the argument would have been handled if it had been raised at Nuremberg or Tokyo.

At Nuremberg, the court did not address the issue but the American prosecutor, Robert Jackson, did address the suggestion that Germany acted in self-defence (as they had laughably claimed that they had invaded Poland on the basis of border violations and the persecution of German-speaking Polish citizens).

> It is not necessary to examine the validity of an abstract principle which does not apply to the facts of our case. I do not doubt that if a nation arrived at a judgment that it must resort to war in self-defense, because of conditions affording reasonable grounds for such an honest judgment, any tribunal would accord it great and perhaps conclusive weight, even if later events proved that judgment mistaken. But the facts in this case call for no such deference to honest judgment because no such judgment was ever pretended much less honestly made.[102]

Jackson is not addressing the question of whether the alleged aggressor had consented to the jurisdiction – consent was irrelevant. But he is addressing the case where the defendant mistakenly but honestly believed he was acting in self-defence. This would require an acquittal of the defendant without a presumption of guilt on the part of those against whom he believed he was acting in self-defence. The leeway suggested by Jackson implies that a serious argument should be entertained by the court – and, indeed, by the prosecutor.

Accordingly, it would seem extremely unlikely that the Nuremberg or Tokyo tribunals, the precursors to the ICC, would have applied *Monetary Gold.* This might mean that the 1954 ICJ had a totally different view to the ICC precursors. But we doubt it. If the ICJ had been asked whether their *Monetary Gold* principle applied to Nuremberg, we would have been very surprised if they had.

State responsibility and jus ad bellum *crimes*

Of course, there is a stronger link between the individual defendants and states in the crime of aggression. Unlike *jus in bello* crimes, *jus ad bellum* crimes are generally conceived as crimes by the states themselves.[103] If the quintessential act of state is the making of war and peace, then a war of aggression is a crime by the state. The UNGA Resolution 29 of 1974 on the definition of aggression makes this clear.[104] There are two counter-points to be made. First, all states have abjured aggressive war and signed the UN Charter. Second, it is quite clear that those who can be charged with aggressive war are individuals. One could say that, as states have forsworn aggressive war, then any attempt by its officials to engage in aggressive war is beyond the power of a state and involves the officials on a 'frolic of their own'. Alternatively, one could accuse states who sign the Rome Statute of leaving the individuals to 'carry the can'. But if we apply a domestic analogy, we could point out that criminal liability normally lies with individuals. The employees, managers or directors of corporations may be charged with murder or manslaughter but corporations are only guilty of corporate manslaughter by specific legislative provision. In the absence of such provision, they cannot be charged. The same is true in the international sphere. It may be unfair that states allow individuals to be charged for crimes committed in their name. But it is not a reason to restrict the words of the Rome Statute. If both individual and state are guilty, that is no reason not to prosecute the individual guilty parties. We might want greater access to justice against states, but that is no reason for complicit individuals to go free.

Burden and standard of proof

The *Monetary Gold* issue raised here is not about the trial of non-signatory states but the defences available to individual defendants from signatory states. To be guilty of the crime of aggression, the use of force must be in 'manifest violation of the UN Charter'.[105] If the use of force is in self-defence against an act of aggression of another state[106] then it is clearly not in breach of the Rome Statute. The argument concerns whether the ICC must ignore such pleas because the aggression claimed in self-defence is by a non-signatory.

However, the ICC does not need to make such a finding against the other state – or whether the alleged aggression is by the relevant state or its rogue elements. The Court only needs to go so far as to conclude that it cannot be proved beyond a reasonable doubt that the act of aggression was in manifest violation of the UN Charter or that, given the evidence, it would be unsafe for the Court to convict them of a violation of the UN Charter, let alone a 'manifest violation'. The evidence required to prove that the aggressor-state *may* have been acting in self-defence is less than the evidence to prove the victim-state acted unlawfully.[107] Apart from the fact that the ICC cannot make a finding against a state, acquittal of the official of one state does not constitute a finding against a state.

This is where a domestic criminal analogy might be useful. If someone is engaged in a barroom brawl and is acquitted because the court considers there is a possibility that another person struck first and the accused was acting in self-defence, it does not mean that the court has found the other person guilty. The fact that the other party is not in court (because they are not within the jurisdiction or because they have unwaived diplomatic immunity)[108] does not prevent the defendant from raising the argument. Of course, if the other party were prepared to attend court and give evidence, they would be able to tell their own side of the story and adverse inferences would be less likely to be made. However, the refusal to turn up does not mean that rights of the defendant should be compromised. Where states have subjected their leaders and soldiers to the possibility of prosecution for aggressive war, their rights to a fair trial and their right to lead arguments that would justify their actions should not be compromised because of the unwillingness of others to do so.

These distinctions go to whether the tribunal is making 'a decision at the core of which was a determination of the legality or illegality of the conduct of a non-party'.[109] Or whether there is an inextricable link between the 'very subject matter' of the case and the legal rights of a non-party. We agree with Akande that 'a finding of aggression by the ICC will result in significant pressure on the State concerned, and that the State would subsequently face an uphill battle in arguing that its use of force was not unlawful under international law'.[110]

But the ICC would not be making a finding of aggression by a non-signatory state. It would merely be saying that there was no manifest violation of the UN Charter by those charged. This might make it a little more difficult for the non-party states to argue that the war was not a war of aggression. However, the US and the UK had great difficulties arguing that the Kosovo and Iraq wars were legal even though there was no ICC trial or acquittal. The basic problem faced by the US and UK was that the arguments they deployed varied from the weak to the pathetic to the downright dishonest. If they had had good arguments, they could have let them run in the ICC when given the opportunity.[111] The fact that they did not take up that opportunity and sought to avoid that opportunity supports the presumption that their arguments were as bad as the vast majority of international lawyers.

In which court is the issue likely to be first raised?

Much of the argument is over what the ICC would decide if the aggression of a non-signatory state was raised as a defence to a charge of aggression made against officials of a signatory state or operating within a signatory state. However, as Rahmat Mohamad reminded us in the previous workshop in this series, the Rome Statute puts the obligation on signatory states to prosecute their own, with the ICC only getting involved if signatory states fail in their primary duty. We do not see signatory states who charge their own officials preventing those officials from pleading self-defence or their prosecutors leaving out such arguments in their prosecution. While the ICC is the ultimate interpreter of the Rome Statute, they would be cautious in finding that a signatory had failed to adequately prosecute a defendant because they had allowed him to plead self-defence. If the ICC did so, they might find the signatory state withdrawing from the Rome Statute. So caution might operate against a strong interpretation of the *Monetary Gold* principle and its extension to international criminal law.

Legitimacy

International courts have to take much greater care about their perceived legitimacy than domestic courts because they have no way of enforcing their decisions on states that do not accept the legitimacy of their actions. However, with the

Rome Statute, the key issue of legitimacy is for the signatory states that have to try their own officials or offer them up to the ICC. If it difficult for the Court to please those who do not want it to exist and wish to preserve the ability to wage what most international lawyers would consider aggressive wars, then there is only so far that one can go to accommodate spoilers.

Ultimately courts do have to determine questions about their jurisdiction in interpreting the instruments that give them jurisdiction and whether to import, extend or limit principles found in other jurisdictions. The ultimate question is whether those who give them jurisdiction will respond to clarify the matter (very difficult here) or refuse to cooperate with the court. Will it increase support of states parties? Will it attract more states parties – either by giving them confidence to join or creating difficulties for those who stay out?

If courts do reject a strong version of *Monetary Gold*, what would happen? It may be seen as illegitimate. But the court may be able to secure legitimacy through the way it is done, the way it is argued, and the fact that they are seen as taking action. Ultimately it depends on how others react – peoples and states. If the objections of the latter are muted and the support of the former is great, they will not only 'get away with it' but grow in stature and standing. Given that this is likely to be first tested by a domestic court within a signatory state, it is likely to get much support if it allows members of their own armed forces to defend themselves than by convicting them because they are not allowed to plead criminality by other non-signatory states.

Reflections – two directions for international law

Extend or restrict Monetary Gold *– and jurisdiction generally?*

In the longer term, one would hope that, with the strengthening of the rule of law in international affairs, consent would be given more generally and required less often.[112] Indeed, the rule of law is based on the application of the law to all – and its acceptance by those in power. We know we are a long way from that point and the Australian Research Council project we have been conducting over the last five years is designed to look at ways of strengthening the rule of law.

Rather than extending the consent principle from the ICJ to the ICC, we would like to see as strong a case put to the ICC that it should not be. The ICC should emphasize the individual personality of the defendants and the irrelevance of their consent. Of course, the jurisdiction of the ICC is established by the states who have signed up to it. But unlike the ICJ, they are not parties before the ICC.

The caution with which international courts consider jurisdiction is natural. Domestic courts are dependent on the state in which they operate for their effectiveness. International courts depend on litigant states for their effectiveness. This means that domestic courts are relatively happy to assume jurisdiction and international courts are very cautious about asserting it. If the international rule of law can be strengthened, then international courts may start acting more like domestic courts and assert jurisdiction when they can. As they do, they will absorb more of the long developed principles and approaches found with the domestic law of signatory states. Fifteen years ago, Charles Sampford suggested that lines in international public law and domestic public law (generally just called 'public law') are likely to blur, and more and more constitutional and administrative law principles would be incorporated into international jurisprudence. This is happening gradually. He suggests that the same process will apply in international criminal law – and probably much more quickly. The need to provide access to justice for victims needs to be matched by the access by the accused to defend themselves. These matters have been long discussed and debated. While they will never be finally resolved, there is much jurisprudence on it and the ICC is bound to be affected more by that domestic jurisprudence than the other way around – especially as most cases will probably be heard at state level and few will migrate to the ICC. The ICC will give states with an interest in the matters argued by defendants greater scope to make their point (cf. in domestic criminal law, they would merely be called as hostile defence witnesses). But they should not give them a veto as to whether defendants can claim self-defence against their conduct.

There is, of course, a choice. Some writers think international law and its institutions will head in the direction of *Monetary Gold*, others in the opposite direction.[113] Our hopes, and predictions, are with the latter.

Access, impunity and legitimacy

In both domestic and international spheres, impunity from prosecution generates genuine and justified outrage. Impunity is the opposite of access to justice for the victims of the worst international crimes. Courts should not read *Monetary Gold* any more expansively than they must. However, *Monetary Gold* also raises issues of access to justice for the accused. The ICC (and domestic courts exercising primary jurisdiction) face a stark choice. If *Monetary Gold* does not apply, then non-signatories may be accused of aggression by would-be defendants alleging self-defence – the mischief identified very clearly in the previous section. But if *Monetary Gold* applies, the defendant is precluded from seeking to make a case of self-defence against an alleged aggressor who is not a signatory. This could have one of two perverse effects. If the preclusion from arguing self-defence results in a conviction, then this is very unfair to leaders of signatories attacked by non-signatories. If this is seen as unfair the alternative might be to acquit because the defendant cannot argue his defence. However, this might lead to the equally perverse result that the flimsiest of claims could be made for self-defence. The first would deny access to justice to the accused. The latter denies access to justice for the victims.

Legitimacy and enforcement

All courts are dependent on others to enforce their decisions. It is taken for granted in most strong states subject to the rule of law that state agencies will enforce decisions but even then it will not be universally true. In other states, enforcement against officials, crime lords, oligarchs and billionaires (and especially when potential defendants are more than one of the aforementioned) cannot be taken for granted and courts may avoid judgment. This reticence does nothing for their legitimacy even if it does do much for their self-preservation. International courts are not at such risk (despite the threat to invade The Hague incorporated into US legislation).[114] If an international court bows to an over-mighty subject of international law, it will lose legitimacy. If it does not, it will gain respect and it is the legitimacy of the state defying it that will come into question.

Like other matters of international affairs (for example, the rejection of the principle that sovereignty in international law is bound on the prior successful use of force,[115] we are engaged in a long game. Judges of international courts cannot get too far ahead of the game but should be part of it and push it along when it can. International courts can give precision to the conscience of mankind which is offended by the crimes prosecuted at Nuremberg and listed in the Rome Statute. In this matter, they might do better to quote Jackson than *Monetary Gold*. In doing so, they invite the prosecuting nations at Nuremberg to act with integrity rather than transparent hypocrisy that radically undermines states that could be international leaders provided they followed the lead provided by their finest.

Cases

Application of the Convention on the Prevention and Punishment of the Crime of Genocide (Bosnia and Herzegovina v. Serbia and Montenegro) (Merits) (2007) ICJ Rep 310, 351 (Judge Tomka).

Certain Phosphate Lands in Nauru (Nauru v. Australia) (Preliminary Objections) (1992) ICJ Reports 240.

Continental Shelf (Libyan Arab Jarnahiriyu/Malta) (Application for Permission to Intervene) (1984) ICJ Reports 3.

East Timor (Portugal v. Australia) (Judgment) (1995) ICJ Rep 90.

Frontier Dispute (Burkina Faso/Republic of Mali) (Judgment) (1986) ICJ Reports 554, 579.

Gabčikovo-Nagymaros (Hungary v. Slovakia) (Judgment) (1997) ICJ Rep 7.

Judgment of the International Military Tribunal (IMT) for the Trial of German Major War Criminals in Nuremberg 30 September and 1 October, Miscellaneous No. 12 (1946) 13.

Land, Island and Maritime Frontier Dispute (El Salvador v. Honduras) (Application by Nicaragua for Permission to Intervene) (1990) ICJ Reports 92, 116.

Larsen v. Hawaiian Kingdom (2001) 119 ILR 566.

Military and Paramilitary Activities in and Against Nicaragua (Nicaragua v. United States of America) (Jurisdiction of the Court and Admissibility of the Application) (1984) ICJ Reports 392, 431.

Military and Paramilitary Activities in and against Nicaragua (Nicaragua v. United States of America) (Merits) (1986) ICJ Rep 14.

Monetary Gold Case (Italy v. France) (Preliminary Questions) (1954) ICJ Rep 19.

Prosecutor v. Blaskic (Judgment on the Request of the Republic of Croatia for Review of the Decision of Trial Chamber II of 18 July 1997) (International Criminal Tribunal for the Former Yugoslavia, Appeals Chamber, Case No. IT-95–14, 29 October 1997) (reversing a Trial Chamber decision of 18 July 1997 to issue a *subpoena ducestecum* against Croatia).

Western Sahara (Advisory Opinion) (1975) ICJ Rep 12.

Notes

1 The Kellogg-Briand Pact (the Pact of Paris) formally known as General Treaty for Renunciation of War as an Instrument of National Policy. Signed at Paris, 27 August 1928. No. 2137, League of Nations. See Kellogg and Briand 1928.

2 While the wars of aggression by those powers have been relatively few and of much more limited extent, there has, of course, been much interference in the internal affairs of other countries, particularly in the form of the support for insurgents and juntas.

3 International Criminal Court, 'Review Conference of the Rome Statute of the International Criminal Court'" (Resolution ICC-ASP/8/Res 6, 31 May–11 June (2010a)).

4 *(Italy v. France) (Preliminary Questions)* (1954) ICJ Rep 19.

5 See, International Criminal Court, 'Review Conference of the Rome Statute of the International Criminal Court', Art. 8*bis*. ICC jurisdiction commences when at least 30 states parties have ratified or accepted the amendments; and a decision is taken by two-thirds of states parties to activate the jurisdiction at any time after 1 January 2017.

6 Kacker 2010: 74; Glennon 2010.

7 Cf. UN General Assembly, 'Rome Statute of the International Criminal Court', (2187 UNTS 3, Art. 83(2) (entered into force 1 July 2002), 17 July 1998), Art. 6–8. See also, 'Definition of Aggression', (UNGA Resolution 3314 (XXIX)14 December 1974); Glennon 2010: 72; Meron 2001: 3.

8 ICJ, *Monetary Gold Case* at 32.

9 Ibid.

10 *Military and Paramilitary Activities in and Against Nicaragua (Nicaragua v. United States of America) (Jurisdiction of the Court and Admissibility of the Application)* (1984) ICJ Reports 392, 431 [88]; *Land, Island and Maritime Frontier Dispute (El Salvador v. Honduras) (Application by Nicaragua for Permission to Intervene)* (1990) ICJ Reports 92, 116 [56]; *Certain Phosphate Lands in Nauru (Nauru v. Australia) (Preliminary Objections)* (1992) ICJ Reports 240, 258–262 [48]–[55]; *East Timor (Portugal v. Australia) (Judgment)* (1995) ICJ Reports 90, 102–105 [28]–[35]. *Continental Shelf (Libyan Arab Jarnahiriyu/Malta)(Application for Permission to Intervene)* (1984) ICJ Reports 3, 25 [40]; *Frontier Dispute (Burkina Faso/ Republic of Mali) (Judgment)* (1986) ICJ Reports 554, 579 [49].

11 World Trade Organization, 'Turkey – Restrictions on Imports of Textile and Clothing Products: Report of the Panel', (WT/DS34/R (99–2081), 31 May 1999), para 9.10.

12 See *Larsen v. Hawaiian Kingdom*, (2001), 119 ILR 566.

13 International Law Commission, 'Commentary to Art. 16', (2001), [11].

14 *Larsen v. Hawaiian Kingdom*, (2001), 119 ILR 566.

15 Ibid. [11.17].
16 Ibid.
17 Ibid.
18 International Criminal Tribunal for the Former Yugoslavia (ICTY).
19 International Criminal Tribunal for Rwanda (ICTR).
20 Special Court for Sierra Leone (SCSL).
21 UN Security Council, 'Statute of the International Criminal Tribunal for the Former Yugoslavia (ICTY)', (SC Res 827, UN SCOR 48th Sess, 3217 Mtg, 1993). As amended by 'Security Council Resolution 1877 (2009) [on Extension of the Terms of Office of Permanent and Ad Litem Judges to the International Criminal Tribunal for the Former Yugoslavia (ICTY) and on Amending Article 14 of the Statute of the International Tribunal]', (S/RES/1877, 7 July 2009). Special Court for Sierra Leone was created by 'Security Council Resolution 1315 (2000) [on Establishment of a Special Court for Sierra Leone]', (S/RES/1315, 14 August 2000). Libya was referred by 'Security Council Resolution 1970 (Libya)', (S/RES/1970, 26 February 2011).
22 Special Tribunal for Lebanon.
23 Extraordinary Chambers in the Courts of Cambodia.
24 The Special Tribunal for Lebanon was requested by Lebanon to the Security Council. After the agreement was not ratified, the Security Council passed SC Res 1757. See, UN Security Council, 'Security Council Resolution 1757 [on the Establishment of a Special Tribunal for Lebanon]', (S/RES/1757 30 May 2007). The Extraordinary Chambers in the Courts of Cambodia was requested by the then co-prime ministers in June 2007. The UN responded in UN General Assembly, 'Situation of Human Rights in Cambodia', (UN Doc A/RES/52/135, Agenda Item 2 27 February 1998). The ICC received a letter from the president of the Democratic Republic of Congo requesting investigation, see International Criminal Court, 'Press Release: Prosecutor Receives Referral of the Situation in the Democratic Republic of Congo', (ICC Doc ICC-OTP-20040419–50, 2004b). The president of Uganda referred the situation of Uganda, 'Press Release: President of Uganda Refers Situation Concerning the Lord's Resistance Army (LRA) to the ICC', (ICC Doc No ICC-20040129–44, 2004a). See also, 'Press Release: Prosecutor Receives Referral Concerning Central African Republic', (The Hague: ICC-OTP-20050107–86-En, 7 January 2005).
25 Kenya became a member to the Rome Statute on 1 June 2005 thus consenting to the ICC's jurisdiction; see also: *Understanding the International Criminal Court* (International Criminal Court, 2010b).
26 Akande 2011: paper 10; Abass 2006.
27 UN General Assembly, 'Rome Statute of the International Criminal Court'.
28 'Rome Statute of the International Criminal Court', Art. 5, para 1; Lavers 2008: 301; Peirce 2001: 281.
29 UN General Assembly, 'Rome Statute of the International Criminal Court', Art. 121, 23. See Kress 2007: 854.
30 International Criminal Court, 'Review Conference of the Rome Statute of the International Criminal Court', ICC-ASP/8/Res 6.
31 'Review Conference of the Rome Statute of the International Criminal Court', ICC-ASP/8/Res 6, Arts 15*bis*(3), 15*ter*(3).
32 'Review Conference of the Rome Statute of the International Criminal Court', ICC-ASP/8/Res 6, Art. 8*bis*(1), annex II Art. 8*bis* elements 1 and 2.
33 'Review Conference of the Rome Statute of the International Criminal Court', elements 3 and 5.
34 UN General Assembly 1974.
35 Ibid., Art. 1.
36 Bekou and Cryer 2007: 51. See, for example, Olasolo 2005: 128–129.
37 International Criminal Court, 'Review Conference of the Rome Statute of the International Criminal Court', ICC-ASP/8/Res 6, Art. 15*ter*.

38 'Review Conference of the Rome Statute of the International Criminal Court', Art. 15; UN General Assembly 1998 Art. 5.
39 International Criminal Court, 'Review Conference of the Rome Statute of the International Criminal Court', Art. 15*bis*(2).
40 'Review Conference of the Rome Statute of the International Criminal Court', Art. 15*bis*(5).
41 'Review Conference of the Rome Statute of the International Criminal Court', Art. 15*bis*(5), Art. 15*bis*(4).
42 UN General Assembly 1998 Art. 5.
43 'Rome Statute of the International Criminal Court', Arts 11, 22, 24.
44 'Rome Statute of the International Criminal Court', Art. 12.(2)(a).
45 'Rome Statute of the International Criminal Court', Art. 12(2)(b).
46 International Criminal Court, 'Review Conference of the Rome Statute of the International Criminal Court', Art. 15*bis*(4).
47 A term used by David Scheffer in relation to Art. 124 of the Rome Statute: See, 'Statement by David Scheffer in Relation to Art. 124 of the Rome Statute: Developments at the Rome Treaty Conference: Hearing before the Senate Foreign Relations Committee', International Criminal Court, 23 July 1998; Amnesty International 2010.
48 International Criminal Court, 'Review Conference of the Rome Statute of the International Criminal Court', Art. 15*bis*(4).
49 The Court can only exercise jurisdiction over crimes committed one year after ratification or acceptance of the amendments by 30 state parties: 'Review Conference of the Rome Statute of the International Criminal Court', Art. 15*bis*(2), Art. 15*ter*(2). See also 'Review Conference of the Rome Statute of the International Criminal Court', Art. 15*bis*(3), Art. 15*ter*(3).
50 BBC News Online 18 October 2011.
51 Assuming Uganda does not opt out of the crime of aggression jurisdiction: see International Criminal Court, 'Review Conference of the Rome Statute of the International Criminal Court', Art. 15*bis*(4).
52 See, 'Review Conference of the Rome Statute of the International Criminal Court', Art. 8*bis*(2)(d). (An act of aggression is the attack by the armed forces of a state on the land, sea or air forces of another state.)
53 'Review Conference of the Rome Statute of the International Criminal Court', Art. 15*bis*(4), Art. 15*bis*(5).
54 Morris 2001: 26.
55 Examples where force was used between two states on a third-party state's territory include: Korean War; Vietnam War; Soviet war in Afghanistan; Gulf War; First World War; Second World War.
56 *Monetary Gold Case (Italy v France) (Preliminary Questions)* (1954) ICJ Rep 19, 32.
57 Ibid.
58 Triffterer 1996: 346; Megret 2001: 253–254.
59 *Application of the Convention on the Prevention and Punishment of the Crime of Genocide (Bosnia and Herzegovina v. Serbia and Montenegro) (Merits)* (2007) ICJ Rep 310, 351 (Judge Tomka).
60 UN General Assembly 1998 Arts 6–8. See Morris 2001: 25.
61 Wagner 2003: 470. See also UN General Assembly 1998 Arts 6–8.
62 International Criminal Court, 'Review Conference of the Rome Statute of the International Criminal Court', Art. 8*bis*(1).
63 'Review Conference of the Rome Statute of the International Criminal Court', Art. 8*bis*(2).
64 UN General Assembly 1996: 16; International Criminal Court, 'Review Conference of the Rome Statute of the International Criminal Court', amendment to Art. 9(1). See also Wagner 2003: 416.

65 United Nations, *Vienna Convention on the Law of Treaties*, vol. 1155, Treaty Series 1969), Art. 46(2). (A violation can be invoked as manifest 'if it would be objectively evident to any State conducting itself in the matter in accordance with normal practice and in good faith'.) International Criminal Court, 'Report of the Special Working Group on the Crime of Aggression', (ICC-ASP/7/SWGCA/2, 9–13 February 2009), at 4; 'CICC Background Paper on the Crime of Aggression', (ASP 5, Resumed Session, 29 January–1 February 2007).
66 'Review Conference of the Rome Statute of the International Criminal Court', Art. 8*bis*, element 5.
67 'Review Conference of the Rome Statute of the International Criminal Court', Art. 8*bis*(5).
68 *Gabčikovo-Nagymaros (Hungary v. Slovakia) (Judgment)* (1997) ICJ Rep 7, [46]–[47].
69 See Morris 2001: 25; Abass 2006: 379.
70 Triffterer 1996: 346; Megret 2001: 353–354.
71 International Criminal Court, 'Review Conference of the Rome Statute of the International Criminal Court', Art. 8*bis*; Art. 8*bis* (elements).
72 Claus Kreb 2009: 1135.
73 *Monetary Gold Case (Italy v. France) (Preliminary Questions)* (1954) ICJ Rep 19.
74 *East Timor (Portugal v. Australia) (Judgment)* (1995) ICJ Rep 90.
75 See *Monetary Gold Case (Italy v. France) (Preliminary Questions)* (1954) ICJ Rep 19, 102 [28].
76 *Certain Phosphate Lands in Nauru (Nauru v. Australia) (Preliminary Objections)* (1992) ICJ Rep 240.
77 *Military and Paramilitary Activities in and Against Nicaragua (Nicaragua v. United States of America) (Jurisdiction of the Court and Admissibility of the Application)* (1984) ICJ Rep 392.
78 *Military and Paramilitary Activities in and Against Nicaragua (Nicaragua v. United States of America) (Jurisdiction of the Court and Admissibility of the Application)* (1984) ICJ Rep 392, 431 [88]; *Certain Phosphate Lands in Nauru (Nauru v. Australia) (Preliminary Objections)* (1992) ICJ Reports 240, 261–262.
79 International Court of Justice, 'Statute of the International Court of Justice', (United Nations, 26 June 1945), Art. 59.
80 See UN General Assembly 1998 Art. 25(4). (No provision of this Statute relating to criminal responsibility shall affect the responsibility of states under international law.)
81 Megret 2001: 254.
82 *Western Sahara (Advisory Opinion)* (1975) ICJ Rep 12, 25 [33].
83 *Monetary Gold Case (Italy v. France) (Preliminary Questions)* (1954) ICJ Rep 19; *East Timor (Portugal v. Australia) (Judgment)* (1995) ICJ Rep 90.
84 Franck 1990: 183; Solera 2009: 821–822; Murphy 2000: 54, 1149.
85 Dobelle 1998: 367; Swart and Sluiter 1999: 91.
86 International Criminal Court, 'Review Conference of the Rome Statute of the International Criminal Court'.
87 UN General Assembly 1998 Art. 66(3).
88 'Rome Statute of the International Criminal Court', Art. 67. See also Friman 2003.
89 UN General Assembly 1998 Art. 93.
90 Paulus 2009: 1127; Akande 2009; Morris 2001: 17.
91 Morris 2001: 30.
92 The proposition that evidence from a victim-state is used to determine whether an alleged aggressor-state has committed an act of aggression can be adduced from UN Security Council, 'Resolution 387 Adopted by the Security Council at Its 1906th Meeting', (S/RES/387, 31 March 1976). (Where the Security Council, in its Resolution condemning South Africa for its use of force against Angola, stated that it

'*having heard* the statement of the representative of the People's Republic of Angola' (emphasis added); 'Resolution 573 (1985) Adopted by the Security Council at Its 2615th Meeting', (S/RES/573, 4 October 1985). (The Security Council '[h]aving heard the statement by the Minister for Foreign Affairs of Tunisia' proceeded to condemn 'vigorously the act of armed aggression perpetrated by Israel against Tunisian territory'); UN General Assembly, 'Complaint by the Revolutionary Government of Cuba Regarding the Various Plans of Aggression and Acts of Intervention Being Executed by the Government of the United States of America against the Republic of Cuba, Constituting a Manifest Violation of Its Territorial Integrity, Sovereignty and Independence, and a Clear Threat to International Peace and Security', (A/RES/1616, 21 April 1961).

93 See *Prosecutor v. Blaskic (Judgment on the Request of the Republic of Croatia for Review of the Decision of Trial Chamber II of 18 July 1997)* (International Criminal Tribunal for the Former Yugoslavia, Appeals Chamber, Case No. IT-95–14, 29 October 1997) (reversing a Trial Chamber decision of 18 July 1997 to issue a *subpoena ducestecum* against Croatia). See also Friman 2003: 398; Morris 2001: 18.

94 See *Military and Paramilitary Activities in and against Nicaragua (Nicaragua v. United States of America) (Merits)* (1986) ICJ Rep 14, 38.

95 *Judgment of the International Military Tribunal (IMT) for the Trial of German Major War Criminals in Nuremberg 30 September and 1 October*, Miscellaneous No. 12 (1946) 13.

96 For example, the Pope mediating between Spain and Portugal, in the Treaty of Tordesillas (1494) and later, states agreeing to third-party adjudication or mediation in, for example, the Treaty of Amity, Commerce, and Navigation (Jay Treaty) 1794.

97 The PCIJ was detailed in the Covenant of the League of Nations and the Statute of the Permanent Court of International Justice passed in 1920. The International Court of Justice heard its first matter in 1946, replacing the PCIJ.

98 See, for example, the Permanent Court of Arbitration decision in *Larsen v. Hawaiian Kingdom*, (2001) 119 ILR 566.

99 See Kellogg and Briand 1928.

100 See International Committee of The Red Cross (ICRC), 'Charter of the International Military Tribunal Annexed to the Agreement for the Prosecution and Punishment of the Major War Criminals of the European Axis', (30.AJ, 8 August 1945), Art. 6 para (c). As highlighted by Cassidy 2004: 551.

101 See *Application of the Convention on the Prevention and Punishment of the Crime of Genocide (Bosnia and Herzegovina v. Serbia and Montenegro) (Merits)* (2007) ICJ Rep 310, 351 (Judge Tomka).

102 International Conference on Military Trials, 'Report of Robert H. Jackson – United States Representative to the International Conference on Military Trials London 1945', US Department of State 1949: 420–421.

103 Note that hard and fast distinctions between *jus in bello* and *jus ad bellum* crimes may not be watertight. Given the proportionality requirements often read into *jus in bello* crimes, there is a real possibility that courts might be more willing to find actions by invaders disproportionate.

104 UN General Assembly 1974.

105 'Rome Statute of the International Criminal Court', Art. 8*bis*.

106 Or, based on the above, individuals acting outside the authority a state signatory to the UN Charter can give.

107 See International Conference on Military Trials 1949.

108 A reasonable analogy?

109 *Larsen v. Hawaiian Kingdom*, (2001) 119 ILR 566.

110 Akande 2011: 26.

111 Serbia/FRY sought to sue in ICJ and Iraq was seeking to do so but ran up against the fact that the US did not accept ICJ compulsory jurisdiction, UK required the other

Olasolo, Hector. *The Triggering Procedure of the International Criminal Court.* Leiden and Boston: Martinus Nijhoff, 2005.

Orakhelashvili, Alexander. 'The Competence of the International Court of Justice and the Doctrine of the Indispensable Party: From Monetary Gold to East Timor and Beyond'. *Journal of International Dispute Settlement* 2, No. 2 (2011): 373–392.

Paulus, Andreas. 'Second Thoughts on the Crime of Aggression'. *European Journal of International Law* 20, No. 4 (2009): 1117–1128.

Peirce, Rachel. 'Which of the Preparatory Commission's Latest Proposals for the Definition of the Crime of Aggression and the Exercise of Jurisdiction Should Be Approved into the Rome Statute of the International Criminal Court?'. *Brigham Young University Journal of Public Law* 15 (2001): 281–300.

Ronen, Yaël. 'Israel, Palestine and the ICC — Territory Uncharted but Not Unknown'. *Journal of International Criminal Justice* 12 (2014): 7–25.

Sampford, Charles. 'Challenges to the Concept of Sovereignty and Intervention'. In *Human Rights in Philosophy and Practice*, edited by Burton M. Leiser and Tom D. Campbell. Aldershot: Ashgate, 2001, Ch. 16.

Sampford, Charles. 'The Potential for a Post-Westphalian Convergence of "Public Law" and "Public International Law"'. In *Sanctions, Accountability and Governance in a Globalised World*, edited by Jeremy Farrall and Kim Rubenstein. Cambridge: Cambridge University Press, 2009: 53–71.

Solera, Oscar. 'The Definition of the Crime of Aggression: Lessons Not-Learned'. *Case Western: Reserve Journal of International Law* 42 (2009): 801–824.

Swart, Ben and Sluiter, Göran. 'The International Criminal Court and International Criminal Co-Operation'. In *Reflections on the International Criminal Court*, edited by Herman von Hebel, Johan Lammers and Jolien Schukking. The Hague: T.M.C. Asser Press, 1999: 85–112

Triffterer, Otto. 'Prosecution of States for Crimes of State'. *International Review of Penal Law* 67 (1996): 341–364.

United Nations. *Vienna Convention on the Law of Treaties*. Treaty Series. Vol. 1155, New York: United Nations, 23 May 1969.

UN General Assembly. 'Complaint by the Revolutionary Government of Cuba Regarding the Various Plans of Aggression and Acts of Intervention Being Executed by the Government of the United States of America against the Republic of Cuba, Constituting a Manifest Violation of Its Territorial Integrity, Sovereignty and Independence, and a Clear Threat to International Peace and Security'. A/RES/1616, 21 April 1961.

UN General Assembly. 'Definition of Aggression'. UNGA Resolution 3314 (XXIX), 14 December 1974.

UN General Assembly. 'Report of the Preparatory Committee on the Establishment of the International Criminal Court'. UN GAOR, 51st sess, Supp No. 22 UN Doc A/51122, 26 July 1996.

UN General Assembly. 'Situation of Human Rights in Cambodia'. UN Doc A/RES/52/135, Agenda Item 2 27 February 1998.

UN General Assembly. 'Rome Statute of the International Criminal Court'. 2187 UNTS 3, Art. 83(2) (entered into force 1 July 2002), 17 July 1998.

UN Security Council. 'Resolution 387 Adopted by the Security Council at Its 1906th Meeting'. S/RES/387, 31 March 1976.

UN Security Council. 'Resolution 573 (1985) Adopted by the Security Council at Its 2615th Meeting'. S/RES/573, 4 October 1985.

UN Security Council. 'Statute of the International Criminal Tribunal for the Former Yugoslavia (ICTY)'. SC Res 827, UN SCOR 48th Sess, 3217 Mtg, 1993.

UN Security Council. 'Security Council Resolution 1315 (2000) [on Establishment of a Special Court for Sierra Leone]'. S/RES/1315, 14 August 2000.

UN Security Council. 'Security Council Resolution 1757 [on the Establishment of a Special Tribunal for Lebanon]'. S/RES/1757 30 May 2007.

UN Security Council. 'Security Council Resolution 1877 (2009) [on Extension of the Terms of Office of Permanent and Ad Litem Judges to the International Criminal Tribunal for the Former Yugoslavia (ICTY) and on Amending Article 14 of the Statute of the International Tribunal]'. S/RES/1877, 7 July 2009.

UN Security Council. 'Security Council Resolution 1970 (Libya)'. S/RES/1970, 26 February 2011.

Wagner, Markus. 'The ICC and Its Jurisdiction: Myths, Misperceptions and Realities'. *Max Planck Yearbook of United Nations Law* 7 (2003): 409–512.

World Trade Organization. 'Turkey – Restrictions on Imports of Textile and Clothing Products: Report of the Panel'. WT/DS34/R (99–2081), 31 May 1999.

5 Drone strikes and human rights

Balancing national security, individual rights and international justice

Ramesh Thakur

The previous project in this series had examined the institutionalization of the rule of international law. This chapter examines a steady loosening, as a result of the march of technology, of the institutionalized constraints, based in the rule of law, on the use of deadly force against individuals.[1] On 18 August 2012, for example, from 30–50 Afghans were killed in a missile strike in the Chapah Darah district in Kunar on the Afghanistan–Pakistan border. In its press release on the incident, the International Security Assistance Force (ISAF) said:

> During the operation, the Afghan and coalition security force observed a large group of heavily armed insurgents engaging in insurgent activity. After ensuring there were no civilians in the area, the security force engaged the insurgents with a precision airstrike.
>
> After the strike, the security force conducted an initial follow-on assessment and confirmed the strike had not injured any civilians or damaged any civilian property.[2]

The sparse and impersonal account begs many questions:

- What constitutes 'insurgent activity'?
- What constitutes a 'precision airstrike'?
- How did ISAF establish that no civilians were present before the strike nor injured or killed in it?
- How do they prove a dead person is an (un)armed civilian or a Taliban supporter or fighter?
- How thorough was the post-strike inquiry?

An alternative narrative holds that a quarrel leading to someone's death had broken out between families and/or clans in a region where the writ of the Afghan national government is non-existent. Tribal elders called in the Taliban to adjudicate the dispute and mete swift exemplary justice. Spotting known Taliban individuals, ISAF launched a deadly missile strike by remote-controlled unmanned aerial vehicles (UAVs or drones) that killed aggrieved family members, perpetrators of the original killing, and tribal elders, as well as Taliban officials.[3] The incident shows that there are three kinds of victims: alleged Taliban leaders; men of military age participating in hostility; and civilians. Killing of all could be legal or illegal, for in turn there are three kinds of killings: of civilians; mistaken killings, owing to acts of recklessness or carelessness; and collateral killings, allowed under laws of war, but with the possibility of entitlement to redress or reparation.

The Obama administration has so greatly expanded the Bush policy of drone strikes as to leave neutral observers queasy about the legal regime governing the new tools of warfare. Does targeted killing represent an extraterritorial extension of the normative authority of the state to cover gaps in the existing legal order, or is it a covert attempt to breach the limits of the legal competence of a state over conduct in foreign jurisdictions? As in so many other aspects of human life, the march of technology has greatly outpaced the laws and institutions to regulate the behaviour they make possible. The relationship between technology and ethics was explored by Plato in his *Dialogues*. Fearing the destruction of humanity if it gained access to technology without standards for their proper use, Zeus had the knowledge of justice delivered to humans to temper the use of technology.[4] Friedrich Schiller had warned at the end of the eighteenth century of the dehumanizing risks of newly developing battlefield technologies.[5] Today, its high-tech arsenal enables the United States to project military power to the remotest corners of contested areas of the postcolonial world. Such technological prowess holds the seductive promise of 'war on the cheap' with respect to blood and treasure,[6] and 'morality lite' with respect to human conscience.

Military expediency does not compute into moral virtue. Because a new means of killing the enemy without risking one's own soldiers' life and minimizing the risk to innocent civilians is technologically feasible and militarily expedient, it is not also thereby lawful and morally permissible. Human morality cannot be outsourced to robots and machines. Neither can legal accountability for the proper use and consequences of the means of modern warfare be transferred from humans to machines.[7] The task of weighing in the balance the moral choices, as well as the military necessity and expediency and political wisdom, of targeted assassinations by UAVs is a profoundly human calculation. If drone technology enables violated countries to deliver justice *individually* to those who have perpetrated armed attacks against them from remote and physically inaccessible hiding places, it also raises troubling questions with respect to justice for those killed and maimed. How is their individual guilt to be determined and established? How can individuals be held accountable for these life and death decisions?

Structures, laws and procedures for ensuring that wronged individuals have access to justice are missing at the national, regional and global levels. A criminal suspect is entitled to due process. A captured combatant is entitled to treatment as a combatant. Are there categories of people not covered by either set of protection? What can be done about any miscarriage of remote-controlled justice? How can people get redress in the contemporary, fragmented legal order? If mistakes have been made – which is inevitable, given human agency in the decisions and operations – how can the victims of mistaken identity or targets, as well as of collateral injury and death, seek legal redress, remedy or compensation?

A major explanation for the systemic injustice of the outcome is that in the pursuit of the national interest in a system of sovereign states, national security is typically privileged over justice as both a national and international value goal. This chapter embeds the discussion of individuals' access to international justice in a larger exploration of the inappropriateness of 'the national interest' as an analytical framework.[8] In a speech at the National Defense University at Fort McNair on 23 May 2013, President Barack Obama justified the continued use of UAVs in the global war on terror but announced a tightening of the conditions regulating when and against whom the strikes would be directed.[9] Commenting on the speech, the editorial board of *USA Today* concluded that the president had struck a balance between the attractions and 'major downsides' of using drones.[10]

I will argue that 'a balance of interests' is a better analytical framework for comprehending and critiquing the use of drones as a policy tool than the more common but also far more woolly 'the national interest'. The first section asserts that 'a balance of interests' is a more satisfactory descriptor, analytical concept and policy precept than 'the national interest'.[11] The rest of the paper illustrates the conceptual arguments with the American use of targeted assassinations using missile strikes by drones as a case study, focusing on the growing use of drones by Washington, the justification offered by US officials for the policy, and the troubling legal, moral and prudential questions raised by the policy. My overall argument is that from the perspective of the national interest, the defence of US national security leads to the killing of its enemies hiding beyond the reach of US justice with drone strikes. But from the alternative framework, on balance the strikes do more harm than good.

From 'the national interest' to 'a balance of interests'

It is difficult to prove that 'the national interest' exists objectively and independently of policymakers and analysts. Nor, being an exhortation more than a prescription, is it a satisfactory guide to policy. Lacking a clear, unambiguous meaning, 'the national interest' is empty of substantive content.[12] And where do promotion of core political values, ideological principles, a favourable world order, and the long term fit into the scheme? 'The national interest' by itself cannot determine the combination of – or the balance among and between – a state's interests and values in any given situation. It is also limited by being actor-specific in a world in which the numbers and roles of non-state actors have grown dramatically.

By contrast 'a balance of interests' is equally applicable to all international actors. Substituting the word 'a' in 'a balance of interests' for 'the' in 'the national interest' has a threefold significance. It indicates that one particular balance is struck from among several possible options; it indicates human agency: individual people make specific decisions in the name of the entity concerned, be it a state or non-state actor; and it includes the possibility of human fallibility, errors of policy or implementation, and the prospect of course corrections. Moreover, internal policy debates are often the most fiercely contested precisely because the opposing arguments and proponents are so finely balanced. It takes just one extra argument, consideration or policymaker to tip the scales decisively on one side. 'The national interest' fails to do justice to this tipping effect reality. In sum, 'a balance of interests' permits a far better assessment of the diverse interests, values, actors, short- and long-term effects, and different policy options.

The proliferation of drones

Increasingly, the weapon of choice for targeted killing is missiles fired by drones. The buzz of the US fleet of Predator and Reaper drones that at any moment can let loose their deadly arsenal of Hellfire missiles is a familiar terror in the sky for the people of Waziristan in north-western Pakistan. The United States has more than 7,000 UAVs today compared to just 50 a decade ago. The number of strikes jumped from just 1 in 2004 to 122 in 2010 before falling back below the hundred level since (Table 5.1). By the end of 2013 the number of US Air Force pilots 'flying' drones is expected to be more than those actually leaving the ground.[13] China is fast following the US in acquiring a fleet of drones for use in a range of potential contingencies in Asia-Pacific.[14] In addition to the United States, Israel is the other country known to use drones to target-kill its enemies,[15] although around 75 countries possess and more than 50 are building drones. In October 2012, France said that it was sending drones to Mali in the fight against al-Qaeda-backed insurgents,[16] while Britain announced it was doubling the number of drones being used in Afghanistan.[17]

Obama continued and intensified the Bush policy of targeted assassinations and missile strikes.[18] On 30 September 2011, Anwar al-Awlaki, an American of Yemeni descent, was killed by a US drone strike somewhere in Yemen – the first instance of a US citizen being the victim of a targeted assassination.[19] Also killed in the same strike was a Pakistani-American jihadist, Samir Khan. Awlaki's 16-year-old son (that is, a juvenile) was killed in a follow-up strike some weeks later. The hit list of terrorist suspects has grown alarmingly. Fifteen drone strikes hit Yemen in May 2012, equal to the total number during the previous decade. This may be the analogue of the old saying that to someone with a hammer, the world looks like a nail. The New America Foundation estimates that 2,780 people were killed in 357 drone strikes in Pakistan alone from 2004 to the end of June 2013. Of these, only 400–500 were killed in 48 strikes during the Bush years 2004–2009; that is, 84 per cent have been killed during the Obama years (Table 5.1). In addition, from 596–832 people were killed in 71 drone strikes in Yemen.

Drone dependency has grown owing to its convenience. It is faster, less complicated and more expedient to eliminate the enemy terrorist – as with Osama

Table 5.1 Numbers of drone strikes and fatalities in Pakistan, 2004–2012

Year	*No. of Strikes*	*No. of Fatalities*
2004–2007	10	179
2008	36	298
2009	54	549
2010	122	849
2011	73	517
2012	48	306
Total	343	2,698

Source: compiled from: New America Foundation, 'Drone War Pakistan: Analysis 2004–2012'. Available at http://counterterrorism.newamerica.net/drones.

bin Laden in May 2011 – than to arrest and try him. Against scores killed under the Obama administration's targeted assassination policy, only one prisoner has been taken into custody. The senior Republican on the intelligence committee, Senator Saxby Chambliss, admits candidly that '[t]heir policy is to take out high-value targets, versus capturing high-value targets' even though they will not advertise the policy as such.[20]

Drones have greater endurance, cost less and reduce the risk to US soldiers to zero. They can be flown for long hours over treacherous, inhospitable terrain and vast distances. The policy plays well domestically in that it gives the impression of toughness. The degree of US public acceptance of and apathy towards drone strikes was evident also in it not being an issue in the 2012 presidential election.[21] On the plus side of the ledger, they have undoubtedly killed, captured, dispersed and forced into deep hiding many al-Qaeda and Taliban commanders, decapitated the leadership, disrupted the global networks, and so contributed to averting terrorist and insurgent attacks on and away from the battlefield.[22] They facilitate the policy of reducing the size of the US military footprint overseas. In contrast to the strategic bombing of the type that reduced Dresden and Tokyo to rubble during the Second World War, the precision drone strikes minimize collateral civilian casualties. By definition, an 'untargeted killing' is indiscriminate. Comprehensive prohibitions on the use of weaponized drones are unlikely because 'the demonstrated usefulness of the technology is too enticing to resist'.[23]

Drones and a balance of interests

And yet they are not cost free and the very real gains have to be weighed in the balance against the equally real costs. There are several legal, moral and strategic problems with the increasing use of drones to kill the enemy. Justice dispensed by drones cannot easily be reconciled either with the rule of law or with a system of morality. In addition, 'Sir Sherard Cowper-Coles, Britain's former special representative to Afghanistan and Pakistan, is ... adamant that drone attacks are horribly counter-productive because of the hatred they have started to generate'.[24]

According to New American Foundation data, since 2004, only 49 high-value militant leaders have been killed in strikes (accounting for just 2 per cent of all drone killings). The rest have largely been low-level combatants.[25] According to the London-based Bureau of Investigative Journalism, drone strikes have killed between 474–881 Pakistani civilians since 2004, out of 2,562–3,325 total deaths, and injured an additional 1,228–1,362 individuals.[26] Secret documents obtained by the US news agency McClatchy showed that 265 of the 482 people killed by the CIA-operated drone strikes in the 12 months to September 2011 were simply listed as 'unknown extremists'.[27] That is, they were unidentified victims who posed no immediate threat to the US. Indeed at times the CIA targeted and killed people who Pakistan's agencies considered to be their enemies, in exchange for access to Pakistani airspace.[28]

Top legal experts who had eloquently condemned the Bush administration's torture practices have serially defended the Obama administration's targeted killings, starting with White House legal counsel Harold Koh in March 2010,[29] and including the new CIA chief John Brennan. They argue that being at war with al-Qaeda and associated forces gives the United States the legal right, consistent with US laws, the laws of war and the principles of international humanitarian law (IHL), to defend itself by killing those who are plotting to kill Americans. The so-called kill list[30] seems to be causing more anguish to independent commentators than to the president or the administration. Obama presides over the regular Tuesday counterterrorism ('Terror Tuesday') meeting in the White House Situation Room of about two dozen security officials and signs off personally on any additions to the kill list, in the belief that as president 'he should take moral responsibility for such actions' (drone strikes).[31] Obama signed off personally on the Awlaki death sentence by drone.

The Justice Department's Office of Legal Counsel prepared a long memorandum that asserts that the Fifth Amendment's guarantee of due process for a US citizen could be satisfied by internal deliberations in the executive branch.[32] Given the memorable record of the US intelligence community on the 'slam dunk' evidence proving Saddam Hussein's pursuit of weapons of mass destruction, one cannot but be troubled by the substitution of secretive determinations of guilt and imposition of capital punishment by intelligence-bureaucratic processes instead of open and contested judicial trials. Unease over the policy intensified with revelations that the administration had authorized so-called signature strikes,[33] where drones can kill not just identified high-value terrorists but also unknown targets like training camps and suspicious compounds based on patterns of suspicious behaviour observed from drones, electronic surveillance and on-the-ground intelligence sources. But are men loading trucks with fertilizer bomb-makers or farmers? If three people are engaged in a game of jumping jacks, are they in a terrorist training camp or friends enjoying themselves in a time-honoured, innocent pastime? Is someone who opens the gate for an 'operational' terrorist a facilitator of terrorism or just a gatekeeper?

In effect drone technology has blurred the distinction between war and murder. The policy – which is infinitely malleable and expansive in both principle and practice under all future administrations and by foreign governments as they acquire the technology – 'looks like murder in the cause of war', with Obama 'not observing moral distinctions so much as … *inventing* them'. When Israel first adopted such a policy in 2000 and called it 'targeted killing', Washington expressed clear opposition to such 'extrajudicial killings'. And now the administration has redefined due process such that 'a citizen's presence on a kill list [is] *itself* proof that due process had been afforded'.[34] The definition of 'imminent threat' has been broadened from clear and present danger to anyone who seems to be dangerous, while that of 'collateral damage' has been made more restrictive from someone who was not directly targeted to women, the elderly and children.

The most substantial public justification for the administration's policy on drones was provided by Attorney General Eric Holder in a speech at Northwestern University in Chicago on 5 March 2012.[35] He began with a dramatic statement: 'We are a nation at war. And, in this war, we face a nimble and determined enemy'. This is a powerful reminder of the danger of describing the campaign against international terrorists as a war on terror. The label acts as a legal enabling device, allowing the president to claim the powers and authority of a wartime administration. Holder insisted that Washington is mindful of other countries' sovereignty and looks to obtain the consent of the country concerned on the use of force on their territory. But such consent is not required 'if the nation is unable or unwilling to deal effectively with a threat to the United States'.

Moreover, Holder argued, 'citizenship alone does not make such individuals immune from being targeted'. The constitution prohibits the government from killing a citizen without due process of law, but: 'The Constitution guarantees due process, not judicial process'. Especially on national security issues, the Supreme Court

> has applied a *balancing* approach, weighing the private interest that will be affected against the interest the government is trying to protect, and the burdens the government would face in providing additional process. Where national security operations are at stake, due process takes into account the realities of combat [emphasis added].

The decision to use lethal force against a citizen, Holder acknowledged, 'is among the gravest that government leaders can face'. Therefore it will be authorized only if:

1 the US citizen is a senior operational leader of al-Qaeda or associated forces and is actively engaged in planning to kill Americans to the point of posing 'an imminent threat of violent attack';
2 capture is not feasible; and
3 the operation using lethal force is conducted in conformity with applicable law of war principles.

Holder concluded with an explicit use of the balance argument:

> Military and civilian officials must often make real-time decisions that balance the need to act, the existence of alternative options, the possibility of collateral damage, and other judgments – all of which depend on expertise and immediate access to information that only the Executive Branch may possess in real time.

His definition of imminent threat was also couched in the language of balance of interests:

> The evaluation of whether an individual presents an 'imminent threat' incorporates considerations of the relevant window of opportunity to act, the possible harm that missing the window would cause to civilians, and the likelihood of heading off future disastrous attacks against the United States.[36]

This is not a definition of 'imminent' that most scholars of international law would recognize. Nor – because it follows the language and logic of the national interest – does it include a complete calculation of the balance of interests. These silent, terrifying killers from the air 'are a potent, unnerving symbol of unchecked American power'.[37] UAV technology has expanded presidential power enormously relative to Congressional checks and judicial oversight. Keeping the strikes covert enables the administration to avoid court reviews of their constitutionality. Having criticized the Bush administration for the secret practices of surveillance, interrogation and detention, Obama has greatly expanded the practice of secretly putting people on kill lists.[38]

A self-serving, Alice-in-Wonderland definition eases legal and moral concerns. The Obama administration 'in effect counts all military-age males in a [drone] strike zone as combatants … unless there is explicit intelligence posthumously proving them innocent'.[39] This is certainly convenient in claiming minimum loss of innocent civilian lives in the strikes. It also gives the military a perverse incentive to avoid a rigorous and thorough probe into drone strikes that might indeed uncover 'explicit intelligence' proving that any/some/all of the dead were innocent civilians. An honest accounting would include anyone not already identified as a combatant among the civilian casualties. The dishonest attempt at accountability produces its own 'double effect': the low to nil civilian casualty count becomes a justification for a subsequent strike.

Holder did not address some fundamental questions: How is a threat determined? What counts as decisive evidence on determining the status of operational commander? And how do officials conclude that arrest is not feasible? Is targeted killing required for self-defence and permitted by the requirements of proportionality and non-discrimination? Who is an enemy combatant? Who is a non-combatant? Who decides if the target is attempting to surrender or fight? Where does the battle space begin, the zone of combat end, and civilian rules apply? What is the anticipated collateral damage? Who determines if the foreign state is unable or unwilling to arrest and prosecute the target? How – on what evidence and by what rules – do we know the answers to these questions that are troubling morally and legally, not just factually? Where are the *institutional points* of scepticism that put the onus of proof on those advocating the killing against others probing their claims? It is worth noting that in this part of the world, almost every male has a beard, wears a turban and carries an AK–47. This raises doubts about the ability of remote CIA electronic peeping toms to distinguish a Taliban from a non-Taliban.

A legal black hole?

The use of drones to kill alleged enemies of the state in pursuit of US national security must be balanced against two potential downsides. The first is the reputational damage to the US as a state actor if it is perceived to be flouting international law and undermining the principle of a world of laws not states. Second, in the brief unipolar moment after the end of the cold war, Washington seemed prepared to impose and enforce international law on others while exempting itself from the same constraints by 'globalizing' its self-assessment as a uniquely virtuous and exceptional power. But that interlude is passing, even on its own judgment. The US National Intelligence Council's latest quadrennial report on global trends maps the world out to 2030 in the considered view of 16 intelligence agencies.[40] The era of Western ascendancy since 1750 and of US ascendancy known as Pax Americana that began in 1945, the report argues, is coming to an end. By 2030, Asia will be bigger in economic size and strategic weight than Europe and the US combined. In such a shifting global order, it would appear to be in the US interest to consolidate instead of undermining the normative constraints of international law and IHL for regulating the behaviour of the rising powers.

The country most closely associated with targeted assassinations of its enemies in recent decades is Israel. Because of the existential threats it faces, the make-up of its geographical neighbourhood, the virulent rhetoric often directed at it, the unexpiated Western historical guilt over the Holocaust, and the terrorist attacks that it has been subjected to, Westerners unconvinced of the lawfulness or wisdom of the policy have nonetheless managed to live with it. But with the greater US technological sophistication and the global reach of its military, the hard questions can no longer be avoided.

One of the most exhaustive studies of the use, impact and legality of drone strikes was a joint endeavour by the law schools of Stanford and New York universities. It concluded that the US campaign of drone strikes has traumatized and terrorized an entire population on a daily basis. Yet the evidence that they have made the United States safer overall is at best ambiguous.[41] They have undermined respect for the rule of law and international legal protection, and set dangerous precedents for facilitating the recourse to lethal force around the world even as lethal drone technologies are being developed by several countries and export control barriers are softening.

The study provides powerful analysis of the legal issues involved in the programme of drone strikes in Pakistan. First, the strikes constitute a violation of Pakistan's sovereignty under international law. Second, they violate the international humanitarian law (IHL) requirements of distinction, proportionality, humanity, and military necessity. The IHL compliance of individual strikes on mosques, funerals, schools and meetings of elders; of 'signature strikes' based on behaviour patterns; and of 'double' and 'triple tap' strikes on onlookers, rescuers and first responders are particularly troubling. Third, in the absence of armed conflict, only international human rights law (IHRL) is applicable. On the publicly available evidence, targeted killings, because they are intentional and premeditated, do not fulfil the strict legal test of killing only if necessary to protect against a threat to life and no other means such as capture or non-lethal incapacitation is feasible. Fourth and finally, individual strikes could also 'constitute acts of illegal extrajudicial assassination' under US domestic law.[42]

UN concerns

Just as Washington has a broad interest in strengthening the rule of international law, so it has an extended interest in strengthening the United Nations[43] as the cornerstone of global governance – a rules-based world in which norms, laws and institutions collectively provide order, stability and predictability even in the absence of world government.[44] UN officials have become increasingly outspoken in expressing unease about various aspects of drone strikes to kill people in distant lands. UN Special Rapporteur Philip Alston argued that extrajudicial killings using drones pose a challenge to international law and may constitute war crimes. Moreover, 'because operators are based thousands of miles away from the battlefield, and undertake operations entirely through computer screens and remote audio-feed', they risk developing 'a "Playstation mentality" to killing'.[45] The 'displacement of clear legal standards with a vaguely defined licence to kill' has created 'a major accountability vacuum'.[46]

Louise Arbour, a former special prosecutor at The Hague and a Justice of the Supreme Court of Canada, believes that as the use of drones has expanded, accountability for the new form of warfare has declined. She cautions that 'NATO countries ... must carefully weigh the policies and practices for using a weapon that distances them from the human, political, legal, and moral costs of war'.[47] Her successor as UN High Commissioner for Human Rights, Navi Pillay, has also raised serious questions about drone strikes. Because they are conducted 'beyond effective and transparent mechanisms of civilian or military control', they make it difficult to ensure accountability for any failure to comply with international law. And their compliance with IHL, 'in particular the principle of distinction and proportionality', is questionable.[48]

At the Human Rights Council session in June 2012, many countries – including Pakistan where most such strikes have taken place and China and Russia as UN Security Council permanent members – called for an investigation into the use of drones for targeted killings.[49] South African law professor Christof Heyns, the Special Rapporteur on Extrajudicial, Summary and Arbitrary Executions, told a conference in Geneva that the US policy of serial drone strikes was a major challenge to the system of international law that has endured since the Second World War and survived nuclear threats, and that some strikes – such as secondary strikes on rescuers helping those hit in the initial attack – may indeed constitute war crimes.[50] At the same conference, Ben Emmerson, a London-based barrister and the UN Special Rapporteur on Human Rights and Counter-Terrorism, added that it was time to end the 'conspiracy of silence' on drone strikes because they were an attack not just on the victims but on the system of international law itself.[51] In January 2013 he announced an inquiry into 25 drone strikes in Afghanistan, Pakistan, the Palestinian territories, Somalia and Yemen.[52]

Drones and a liberal state of laws and the constitution

What is the proper relationship between military technology, just war and ethical decision-making?[53] As the weaponry of war has become more precise, so the language of warfare has become vaguer and more ambiguous. Targets can be chosen and hit with ever-increasing precision, but the definition of 'terrorist', 'enemy combatant' and 'contingent threat' is inherently vague and subjective and therefore tells us little about the legitimacy of the target. The seductive promise of precision munitions is to neutralize the biggest number of targets at least cost to one's own soldiers and also the least risk to innocent civilians. However, judgments about the status of enemy combatants and terrorists, and therefore about the definition of legitimate targets, are not technological but moral determinations that can be made only by humans, not machines. The capacity to identify and hit high-value targets with precision instruments and munitions must still be subordinate to and guided by social purposes and moral deliberation. In a familiar example, the human instinct of adult soldiers stops them from killing an 11-year-old child being used as a human shield by the enemy who has no compunction about shooting from behind the child.[54] This is a deeply internalized moral prohibition that overrides prudential calculations. A robot will have no such moral compunction. The use of a robot instead of a human soldier to deal with the situation may prove technologically expedient but does not solve the moral dilemma. Nor does it absolve the operator of the robot from the burden of making the moral choice. Machines cannot process context and moral ambiguity: an automated ethical system is a conceptual oxymoron.

Michael Adas concludes that the elision from surgical strike technology to efficient warfare is but the latest iteration of the historical partnership between technology and imperialism,[55] whereby 'the mouthpieces of war machines co-opt the language of ethics and justice'.[56] Technological precision is neutral with respect to the moral distinctions among potential targets. The precision accuracy of strikes is pointless unless accompanied by a matching accuracy of target identification, as otherwise the munitions will be delivered with great accuracy to the wrong target. And therefore precision munitions cannot be delinked, in the chain of moral decision-making, from the intelligence information and assessment behind it. 'Americans' claims that their advanced surveillance systems and the pinpoint accuracy of their futuristic weaponry minimize civilian losses ring false in much of the world.'[57] It also feeds perceptions of Americans as cowards unwilling to back their principles with sacrifice. And it calls into question the morality of the strikes if the information has been collected using torture. That is, the demand for accurate intelligence to underpin the selection of targets in order to use the available technology of precision missiles fired from drones, produces the 'negative externality' of pressures for 'enhanced interrogation techniques' to extract intelligence from captured enemy combatants. There is, therefore, a link between drone strikes and the relaxed, compromised or violated Geneva Convention standards.[58]

Fernando Tesón raises the question of whether the intentional targeting of identified individuals is sufficiently different from the random killing of anonymous enemy soldiers on the battlefield as to be subject to the requirements of law enforcement officers for the use of deadly force.[59] These include standards of proof for establishing that the intended target committed an act of deadly violence or poses an imminent threat, the use of lethal force against him will save many innocent lives, and non-lethal alternatives such as capture are not feasible. Unless such a clear and just social purpose can be established, targeted killing must remain a deeply immoral act for a liberal state. Where the alternative is feasible, capture rather than extrajudicial killing is an ethical requirement, not just the preferred alternative. Legal and moral distinctions do not turn on the mechanics of targeting and the type of weaponry, but on the process of legal deliberation and analysis to establish guilt by due process and the appropriate punishment.

> [C]ustom and morality have confined war, and the license to kill that it entails, to cases where the liberal state faces an organized enemy … the state may not declare war against individuals. [Moreover,] the prohibition against killing anyone without due process … extends to foreigners, even if they have committed crimes.[60]

The moral case for drones emphasizes both their greater precision and their lower collateral casualty rate. On the first point, drone operators can track a target for days, with significantly greater accuracy than either ground troops or pilots who may have to make judgments on 'look-shoot-look' kills in a compressed timeframe under the pressure of battlefield conditions. Drone operators can time their strikes to reduce the likelihood of innocent civilians being in the vicinity and are able to delay, suspend or abort strikes should innocent people stray into the strike zone. On the second point, compared to almost every other mode of warfare as a benchmark, as well as to other theatres of war, drone strikes have a significantly lower collateral casualty rate: the civilian proportion of US drone casualties dropped from 28 to 16 per cent between 2008 and 2011.[61]

But others fear that the convenience of drones might be producing the perverse incentive of lowering the threshold of the resort to lethal violence. Instead of war being the last resort in conventional armed conflict, war by drones becomes a default strategy and targeted killing 'a convenient substitute for capture'.[62] 'By reducing the risks and costs of war, the use of UAV and precision weapons may actually encourage more bellicosity and longer wars.'[63] Because political leaders can escape the agony of putting sons and daughters in harm's way, they can avoid giving decisions on war and peace the due weight accorded it previously in national security deliberations. Citizens not having to bear personal risks frees leaders from having to bear the corresponding political risks. This is the route to lowering the threshold for waging war by other means. The use of drones has never been debated or voted on in Congress in relation to Afghanistan, Pakistan, Yemen or Libya. That is, without a debate in Congress or a national conversation, the Obama administration has set the precedent that war that keeps humans at a safe distance from the battlefield – the new normal with developments in technology – is not subject to the constitutional constraint of Congressional authorization.

Drone technology has helped to consolidate still further the United States as a national security state at the cost of core liberal democratic values. Drones enable – legally as well as materially – the United States to wage war as a matter of executive privilege. Writing that Obama has 'changed a technological capability into a moral imperative', Tom Junod labels his administration the 'Lethal Presidency',[64] while a British columnist dubs Obama the 'Lord High Executioner'.[65] In effect Obama personally hands down death sentences to suspected terrorists all over the world.[66] This greatly stretches the boundaries of the imperial presidency and raises the obvious question: What 'qualifies one person to render alone a decision that twelve could only with difficulty make in good conscience'?[67] Even if Obama should be a wise philosopher-king, the expanded, unchecked power will be available to subsequent administrations.

The use of drones is troubling enough for democracies. It deepens the discomfort level as a policy tool for authoritarian regimes which by definition have 'fewer checks on their use of lethal force'.[68] With about 300 combat drones and reports that it is building a stealth drone capacity, China is second only to the US in this field and reportedly considered using one to eliminate a Myanmar-based drug trafficker, Naw Kham, who has killed several Chinese citizens.[69] If Washington can use drones extensively in the face of domestic and international criticism, might Beijing use them some day against domestic violent protests – which China denounces as terrorism? How might China's leaders 'apply Obama's [drone] doctrines to Tibetan activists holding meetings in Nepal?'[70] What if China eliminated the Dalai Lama in a drone strike?[71] Is the West to be the moral arbiter of the use of and limits to drone strikes both for itself and for others? As the barriers to entry on the production of drones fall and more countries acquire and begin to use them, their choice of targets and extraterritorial sites of strikes will be justified by US precedent, for Washington has signally failed to create a globally relevant legal standard. The seduction of zero risk to one's soldiers, efficiency and lethality of drones, and the lack of international norms distinguishing legitimate from rogue uses mean that by labelling targets as terrorists, Syria and Iran could use it against Syrian rebels, Moscow against Chechens and Georgians, China against Tibetan activists in Nepal, and so on. India has often accused Pakistan of harbouring terrorists who carry out raids across the border. Bearing in mind that both countries are nuclear-armed, the consequences could be very grave indeed if India decided to target alleged terrorists living in Pakistan for deadly strikes by drones.

Balance between counterterrorism and counter-insurgency

In addition to unease over the legal and moral permissibility of drone strikes, there are concerns about their strategic utility and wider political damage. In a now-famous memo on the war on terror on 16 October 2003, Secretary of Defense Donald Rumsfeld had posed the prophetic and critical question: 'Are we capturing, killing or deterring and dissuading more terrorists every day than the madrassas and the radical clerics are recruiting, training and deploying against us?'[72] Echoing that concern, an article in the *New York Times* argued that drone strikes become 'the recruiting tool of choice for militants'.[73] The majority of those killed by US drone strikes had no connection with 9/11. America's Muslim enemies are fighting it because US soldiers are in their lands, not the other way round, with 'drones executing mass destruction on the family and tribal scale'.[74]

Three-quarters of those killed in drone strikes in Pakistan are claimed to have been militants, a figure impossible to verify. Others claim that drone strikes kill seven times as many followers as top-level terrorists[75] – that is, supporters and sympathizers, not 'enemy combatants'. And therefore they create martyrs and act as a recruiting motor for fresh terrorists.[76] Faisal Shahzad, the failed Times Square bomber of May 2010, when asked about potential innocent victims of his plot, replied: 'US drone strikes don't see children, they don't see anybody. They kill women, children; they kill everybody'.[77]

Some of the 'other judgments' that Holder referred to in his Chicago speech in March 2012 would presumably have to include a whole series of balances regarding Pakistan: between Pakistan's needed help in combating insurgency in Afghanistan and its need for strategic depth in Afghanistan against India; between independent and sometimes contradictory demands and signals from the military and civilian authorities as competing centres of authority in Pakistan; between the wish to stiffen Pakistani resolve in fighting the militants and denying them bases and safe refuge inside Pakistan, the fear of nuclear-armed Pakistan collapsing into a failed state under the weight of internal challenges from the militants and external pressures, and concerns that increased US pressure will only deepen and intensify Pakistanis' alienation from their own government and hostility towards the US. The US ambassador to Pakistan, Cameron Munter, lost the internal battle over authority to veto CIA operations that in his judgment would harm long-term US–Pakistan relations.[78]

In this complex and volatile environment, it is hard to see what utility 'the national interest' has either for describing and explaining US policy choices or for prescribing the correct course of action. Washington must balance its national security interest in killing high-value terrorists against its equally compelling national security interest in not losing Pakistan as a valuable ally in the global war on terror, not destabilizing the nuclear-armed state with 175 million Muslims, and not antagonizing the people of Pakistan against the United States and against their own government. According to the Pew Research Center's public opinion poll published on 27 June 2012, only 12 per cent of Pakistanis hold a favourable opinion of the United States, 80 per cent hold an unfavourable opinion, and 74 per cent consider it to be an enemy (up from 64 per cent in 2009). Only 17 per cent backed American drone strikes against leaders of extremist groups 'even if they are conducted in conjunction with the Pakistani government'.[79]

Missile strikes by drones produce civilian casualties. From the point of view of counter-insurgency as distinct from counterterrorism, far from solving the problem, this aggravates the situation. According to Pakistan's ambassador to the US Sherry Rehman, the drone war 'radicalises foot soldiers, tribes and entire villages'.[80] While her objection might be dismissed as self-serving, it is backed by the joint study by Stanford and New York universities: 'It is clear from polling and our research team's interviews that drone strikes breed resentment and discontent toward the US, and there is evidence to suggest that the strikes have aided militant recruitment and motivated terrorist activity'.[81] The promiscuous use of drone strikes thus may have upset the balance between counterterrorism and counter-insurgency. Under the former, every death of a terrorist is a victory against terrorism. From the point of view of the latter, however, if the death of one terrorist leads to the recruitment of another ten, then that one death is self-defeating. And the argument holds that drone strikes in Pakistan and Yemen have enraged, embittered and radicalized many young Muslims into becoming eager recruits into the ranks of the terrorists, sustaining al-Qaeda with an expanded base of sympathizers and territory.[82] Al-Qaeda recruiters reportedly wave photographs of drone-butchered women and children in the faces of Yemeni villagers.[83] Farea al-Muslimi is a 23-year-old Yemeni writer whose village Wessab was struck by drones on 18 April 2013. In powerful testimony to the US Senate on 24 April, he argued that instead of fighting terrorism in Yemen, US drone strikes were fuelling it:

> Instead of first experiencing America through a school or a hospital, most people in Wessab first experienced America through the terror of a drone strike. What radicals had previously failed to achieve in my village, one drone strike accomplished in an instant: there is now an intense anger and growing hatred of America.[84]

Nor is the adverse unintended effect limited to the local theatre. Washington must balance its national security interest in killing high-value terrorists in the

Af-Pak and Yemen theatres of operations against the reputational damage around the world as a law-abiding country that respects the decent opinion of mankind. In former president Jimmy Carter's view, 'instead of making the world safer, America's violation of international human rights [through drone strikes] abets our enemies and alienates our friends'.[85] Public opinion polls show that most Americans support but a majority of almost all other nationals oppose drone strikes. In a 2012 global poll, Americans approved of drone strikes by a 62–28 margin. But Britons opposed it by 47–44; more than half of Germans, Poles, French, Italians, Czechs and Chinese opposed it; and three-quarters and more opposed it in Mexico, Spain, Japan, Brazil, Turkey, Jordan, Egypt and Greece (90 per cent!).[86] Because the drone strikes are completely unilateral and focused on American concerns, they reinforce the widespread perception of the US as a state that acts unilaterally without consideration for the opinion and interests of other countries. In the eyes of many foreign observers, drone strikes 'are all about American domestic politics'.[87]

Legal remedies for the wrongly killed and wounded

On the night of 31 October 2011, a 16-year-old Pakistani boy, named as Muhammad Tariq and Tariq Khan in different news accounts, was killed in a US drone strike in North Waziristan.[88] The accounts agree that he was killed along with his cousin Waheed Khan after he had taken part in a protest demonstration against an earlier drone strike that had killed his teenage cousin Asmar Ullah. The BBC's reporter in Islamabad noted that '[i]f the strike actually killed two young boys – as appears to be the case – it's unlikely anyone will ever be held to account', leading locals to claim that 'the US is getting away with murder'.[89]

As individuals become the subjects and not merely the objects of international law, IHL and IHRL, the obvious challenge that will intensify is: what legal remedies exist or can be provided (1) to punish the perpetrators of violence against individuals; (2) to protect civilians from cross-border state-directed or state-sponsored violence targeting individuals; and (3) to compensate individual victims of illegal attacks by states across borders? If wronged individuals have been at the receiving end of justice meted out by drone strikes, in due course justice demands that they should be able to hold perpetrators, including heads of state and generals under the principle of command responsibility, to account in their own country's courts, in the courts of the country that carried out the strikes, and/or in institutions of international criminal justice. In other words, if individuals who have been wronged by drone strikes are to have access to justice, and justice is to be seen to have been done in their cases, then we need some sort of convergence of the principles of universal justice, command responsibility, individuals as bearers of rights and states as holders of duties, territorially unbounded criminal jurisdictions with international transparency and due process, and the correlative derogation of state sovereignty.

There is little prospect of any US military commander or senior official being called to international criminal account. This reflects inadequacies and imperfections in the existing modalities and institutions of international criminal justice. Perhaps appropriate NGOs and entities could turn their attention to possible amendments to the statute of the International Criminal Court (ICC) to make it possible to hold states to account for state violence in foreign jurisdictions.

What of Pakistan's duty to protect its citizens and prosecute a non-enemy state attacker? Providing adequate law and order and national defence to assure the safety of its people and ensure their security against foreign enemies is an elemental and irreducible function of government in the social compact with citizens. Under IHRL, no state can consent to the killing of its citizens on its own territory by a foreign power. What duties does this claim impose on Pakistan to protect its people from US drone strikes, and to help the victims and the families of those killed and injured in efforts to hold US officials and operatives criminally responsible and accountable and seek legal remedies and compensation? One option is to assist individuals in bringing cases in foreign jurisdictions, or to join with public interest bodies that do so. The charity Reprieve, based in Australia, Britain and the United States, is challenging the drone strikes in the courts of Pakistan, Britain and the US on behalf of non-US citizens.

Conclusion

International law, like all law, is an effort to align power to justice. Where they cannot be aligned, their competing demands and requirements have to be weighed against each other in order to decide where to strike the balance between them. With the increasing use of remote-controlled drone warfare, the United States has to weigh in the balance national security interests in terms of eliminating terrorists and their networks located in foreign lands beyond the reach of US law; military necessity versus due process; risks of death and injury to innocent civilians by accident, error or collateral damage; relations with countries whose sovereignty is violated; the risks of creating new terrorists from among those angered and embittered by the deadly strikes on their families and communities; risks of violating IHL; reputational damage as a law-abiding international citizen-state; and the tension between being an enforcer of IHL as a permanent member of the UN Security Council and putting its own actions outside the jurisdiction of international criminal justice mechanisms.

The 'marginal costs' of the use of missile strikes by drones include collateral damage in the form of dead civilians, violating the sovereignty of a country – Pakistan – with which the United States is not at war and whose parliament has denounced the drone strikes,[90] the destabilization of Pakistan, the deepening antagonism of several Western countries and Islamic peoples towards the US, and the proliferation of drone technology and capacity to other actors. With respect to values, the moral qualms over a president claiming the right to murder foreign and US citizens based on a secret process – with no contestability, checks and balances – have grown and deepened. Perhaps the inflection point of diminishing utility and returns has been reached, and the time has come to tighten targeting standards. Otherwise the US will become a world leader in killing people who had no connection to 9/11, to al-Qaeda or any other terrorist group, and pose no threat to US interests abroad or to the US homeland.[91]

In pursuing 'the national interest', the US administration finds in drone technology a useful tool with which to kill US enemies hiding in inaccessible foreign lands beyond the reach of US law and justice. They contain the least risk of loss of life for US soldiers and for innocent civilians. But when examined from the alternative analytical framework of 'a balance of interests', the net damage turns out to be more substantial than the narrow counterterrorism gains. The strikes fail to satisfy the strict requirements of international law, IHL, IHRL and even US constitutional law. They breach existing normative standards of good international behaviour. They set a dangerous precedent for other governments and future US administrations in the international use of lethal violence by states as newer war technologies are developed. They create perverse incentives to lower the threshold of resort to lethal violence and broaden the definition of combatants/militants. They increase the motivation for twisted and angry young men to take to terrorism against the West and sustain and widen the recruitment, sympathy and support base among peoples for the terrorists. And they point to significant justice deficits for wronged individuals to hold foreign states to criminal account, thereby weakening support for an international order based on the rule of law.

In turn, the UN system, as the custodian of international law, IHL, IHRL and international peace and security, must balance incapacity or unwillingness to enforce IHL and global norms on US behaviour against the deepening perceptions of seriously biased and selective international justice, the failure to protect the sovereignty of the weak against the strong (a cardinal original purpose in setting up the United Nations), the damage to the principle of world affairs being governed by a system of laws, and, in an age that has seen a growing individualization of rights and responsibilities, the rights of victims to seek redress of grievances through international justice mechanisms.

Notes

1 See Kalshoven and Zegveld 2011.
2 International Security Assistance Force 2012.
3 Dreyfuss 2012.
4 Plato 2009: 19.
5 Schiller 2004.
6 Kaag and Kaufman 2009: 604.
7 For an argument on how a command decision can be shifted consistent with the laws of armed conflict more towards – but not completely to – autonomous systems from humans, see Gillespie and West 2010: 1–32.
8 I would like to thank the participants, and in particular Gerry Simpson, in the project workshop held at Bond University in the Gold Coast, Queensland, in October 2012 for the many helpful comments on an earlier draft of the chapter.
9 Obama 2013.
10 'Obama Drone Policy Strikes Right Balance: Our View', *USA Today*, 23 May 2013.
11 See Thakur 2013a: 70–87; Thakur 2013b.
12 Burchill 2005.

13 Mazzetti 2012.
14 Richardson 2012.
15 Lattimer 2012.
16 Hirsch 2012.
17 Hopkins 2012.
18 Cohen 2011; Savage 2011; Smith 2011.
19 'Flight of the Drones', *The Economist*, 8 October 2011; Savage 2011; Smith 2011.
20 Quoted in Becker and Shane 2012.
21 Joyner 2012.
22 Johnston 2012: 47–79.
23 Falk 2012.
24 Oborne 2012.
25 As reported in Bergen and Rowland 2012.
26 Statistics cited in International Human Rights and Conflict Resolution Clinic, *Living under Drones: Death, Injury, and Trauma to Civilians from US Drone Practices in Pakistan* 2012: vi, 45. For a review of the different estimates of militant and civilian casualties, see 125–131.
27 Judd 2013.
28 Mazzetti 2013.
29 Koh 2010.
30 Coates 2012.
31 Becker and Shane 2012.
32 Ibid. In February 2013 the US Department of Justice 'White Paper' justifying the 'targeted killing' of a US citizen was leaked: US Department of Justice, 'Lawfulness of a Lethal Operation Directed against a U.S. Citizen Who Is a Senior Operational Leader of Al-Qa'ida or an Associated Force' 2013.
33 As part of the more restrictive conditions regulating drone strikes announced by Obama on 23 May 2013, 'signature strikes' would end and only 'personality strikes' against identified individuals would continue. In the same speech Obama for the first time publicly admitted that four US citizens had been killed in drone strikes to date, of whom only one – Anwar al-Awlaki – had been intentionally targeted.
34 Junod 2012, emphases in original.
35 Holder 2012.
36 Ibid.
37 Rohde 2012.
38 DeYoung 2011.
39 Becker and Shane 2012.
40 U.S. National Intelligence Council 2012.
41 International Human Rights and Conflict Resolution Clinic 2012: 125.
42 Ibid., Chapter 4, 104–122.
43 See Thakur 2012: 388–396.
44 Weiss and Thakur 2010.
45 Alston 2010: 25, para 84. The ethicist Peter Singer, too, has written of a video-game and voyeuristic approach to warfare by operators controlling drones from remote locations: Singer 2009.
46 Alston 2010: 3, para 3.
47 Arbour 2012. Note the implicit use of the balance metaphor in the word 'weigh'.
48 BBC News 2012. See also Jenks 2010: 649–672; Drummond 2011.
49 Judd 2012.
50 Bowcott 2012.
51 Ibid.
52 BBC News 2013.
53 See Luban 2012.
54 Bellavia and Bruning 2007: 10.

55 Adas 2006, especially 'Epilogue: The Paradox of Technological Supremacy', 385–415.
56 Kaag and Kaufman 2009: 594.
57 Adas 2006: 403.
58 Kaag and Kaufman 2009: 603.
59 Tesón 2012. See also McMahan 2012: 135–155.
60 Tesón 2012.
61 Figures cited in Shane 2012.
62 Ibid.
63 Kreps and Kaag 2012: 282.
64 Junod 2012.
65 Harnden 2012.
66 Klaidman 2012.
67 Bromwich 2012: 42–43.
68 Erickson and Strange 2013.
69 Ibid.
70 Coll 2013. Moss 2013.
71 Gallagher 2013.
72 The full text of the memo was published in Rumsfeld 2005.
73 Becker and Shane 2012.
74 Pfaff 2013.
75 Darnstädt *et al.* 2012
76 Oborne 2012.
77 Quoted in Darnstädt *et al.* 2012.
78 Ignatius 2012.
79 'Pakistani Public Opinion Ever More Critical of U.S.', *PewResearch Global Attitudes* 2012 (emphasis added). Similarly, 'after years of violent action against AQAP [al-Qaeda in the Arabian Peninsula], there are more al Qaeda terrorists in Yemen than ever before'; Foust 2012.
80 Quoted in Jones 2012.
81 International Human Rights and Conflict Resolution Clinic 2012: 132.
82 See Mothana 2012. But for an argument that increased accuracy in hitting terrorists has softened the radicalizing effects among local populations, see Swift 2012.
83 Jenkins 2013.
84 'Yemeni Man Brings the Horror of Drone Strikes Home to US Senate', *The Independent*, 26 April 2013. See also Raghavan 2012.
85 Carter 2012.
86 Pew Research 2012.
87 Cockburn 2012.
88 Laskar 2011; Guerin 2011.
89 Guerin 2011.
90 See O'Connell 2010.
91 Finel 2012.

References

Adas, Michael. *Dominance by Design: Technological Imperatives and America's Civilizing Mission.* Cambridge MA: Belknap Press of Harvard University Press, 2006.

Alston, Philip. 'Report of the Special Rapporteur on Extrajudicial, Summary or Arbitrary Executions, Addendum, Study on Targeted Killings'. Geneva: OHCHR, A/HRC/14/24/Add.6, 28 May 2010. Online. Available at www2.ohchr.org/english/bodies/hrcouncil/docs/14session/A.HRC.14.24.Add6.pdf (accessed 6 June 2010).

Arbour, Louise. 'Unmanned and Dangerous'. *Foreign Policy*, 18 May 2012. Online. Available at www.foreignpolicy.com/articles/2012/05/18/drones_uav_dangerous (accessed 4 August 2014).

BBC News. 'US Drone Strikes "Raise Questions" – Un's Navi Pillay'. 7 June 2012. Online. Available at www.bbc.co.uk/news/world-asia-18363003 (accessed 6 July 2012).

BBC News. 'UN Launches Inquiry into Drone Killings'." 24 January 2013. Online. Available at www.bbc.co.uk/news/world-21176279 (accessed 6 February 2013).

Becker, Jo and Shane, Scott. 'Secret "Kill List" Proves a Test of Obama's Principles and Will'. The *New York Times*, 29 May 2012.

Bellavia, David and Bruning John. *House to House*. New York: Free Press, 2007.

Bergen, Peter and Rowland, Jennifer. 'CIA Drone War in Pakistan in Sharp Decline'. CNN, 28 March 2012. Online. Available at www.cnn.com/2012/03/27/opinion/bergen-drone-decline/index.html (accessed 30 March 2012).

Bowcott, Owen. 'Drone Strikes Threaten 50 Years of International Law, Says UN Rapporteur'. *The Guardian*, 21 June 2012.

Bromwich, David. 'Diary'. *London Review of Books* 34, No. 13 (5 July 2012): 42–43.

Burchill, Scott. *The National Interest in International Relations Theory*. London: Palgrave Macmillan, 2005.

Carter, Jimmy. 'A Cruel and Unusual Record'. The *New York Times*, 24 June 2012.

Coates, Ta-Nehisi. 'The Kill List'. *The Atlantic*, May 2012. Online. Available at www.theatlantic.com/international/archive/2012/05/the-kill-list/257890/ (accessed 4 August 2014).

Cockburn, Patrick. 'America Is Deluded by Its Drone-Warfare Propaganda'. *The Independent*, 10 June 2012.

Cohen, Richard. 'Who Signed Anwar Al-Awlaki's Death Warrant?'. The *Washington Post*, 11 October 2011.

Coll, Steve. 'Remote Control: Our Drone Delusion'. The *New Yorker*, 6 May 2013. Online. Available at www.newyorker.com/arts/critics/books/ (accessed 20 May 2013).

Darnstädt, Thomas, Hujer, Marc and Schmitz, Gregor Peter. 'Are Obama's Efforts to Justify Drone Warfare Aimed at Iran'. *SpiegelOnline*, 15 March 2012, trans. Christopher Sultan. Online. Available at www.spiegel.de/international/world/0,1518,druck-821151,00.html (accessed 20 March 2012).

DeYoung, Karen. 'Secrecy Defines Obama's Drone War'. The *Washington Post*, 20 December 2011.

Dreyfuss, Robert. 'Counterinsurgency or Civilian Slaughter in Afghanistan?'. *The Nation*, 20 August 2012. Online. Available at www.thenation.com/blog/169455/counterinsurgency-or-civilian-slaughter-afghanistan (accessed 9 September 2012).

Drummond, Keith. 'The Legality of America's Program of Targeted Killings by Unmanned Aerial Vehicles'. *e-International Relations*, 18 February 2011. Online. Available at www.e-ir.info/2011/02/18/ (accessed 3 March 2011).

Erickson, Andrew and Strange, Austin. 'China Has Drones. Now What?'. *Foreign Affairs Snapshot*, 23 May 2013. Online. Available at www.foreignaffairs.com/articles/139405/andrew-erickson-and-austin-strange/china-has-drones-now-what (accessed 4 August 2014).

Falk, Richard. 'Plague of Locusts: Our Failure to Regulate Drone Warfare'. *Boston Review*, 14 March 2012. Online. Available at www.bostonreview.net/richard-falk-drone-warfare-international-law (accessed 4 August 2014).

Finel, Bernard. 'Transitioning to a Post-Drone CT Policy'. 5 June 2012 Online. Available at www.bernardfinel.com/?p=2090 (accessed 10 June 2012).

'Flight of the Drones'. *The Economist*, 8 October 2011.

Foust, Joshua. 'What We Misunderstand About Drones'. *The Atlantic*, June 2012. Online. Available at www.theatlantic.com/international/archive/2012/06/what-we-misunderstand-about-drones/257778/ (accessed 3 July 2012).

Gallagher, Tom. 'What If the Chinese Killed the Dalai Lama with a Drone Strike?'. *Common Dreams*, 22 February 2013. Online. Available at www.commondreams.org/views/2013/02/22/what-if-chinese-killed-dalai-lama-drone-strike (accessed 4 August 2014).

Gillespie, Tony and West, Robin. 'Requirements for Autonomous Unmanned Air Systems Set by Legal Issues'. *The International C2 Journal* 4, No. 2 (2010): 1–32.

Guerin, Orla. 'Pakistani Civilian Victims Vent Anger over US Drones'. BBC News, 3 November 2011. Online. Available at www.bbc.co.uk/news/15553761 (accessed 6 November 2011).

Harnden, Toby. 'So Much for That Nobel Peace Prize: How Anti-War Obama Has Become Lord High Executioner'. *Daily Mail*, 6 June 2012.

Hirsch, Afua. 'France to Send Drones to Mali in Fight against Al-Qaida-Backed Insurgents'. *The Guardian*, 22 October 2012.

Holder, Eric. *Attorney General Eric Holder Speaks at Northwestern University School of Law*. Washington DC: Department of Justice, 5 March 2012. Online. Available at www.justice.gov/iso/opa/ag/speeches/2012/ag-speech-1203051.html (accessed 10 March 2012).

Hopkins, Nick. 'UK to Double Number of Drones in Afghanistan'. *The Guardian*, 22 October 2012.

Ignatius, David. 'An Embassy Asks, Drones or Diplomacy?'. The *Washington Post*, 21 June 2012.

International Human Rights and Conflict Resolution Clinic. *Living under Drones: Death, Injury, and Trauma to Civilians from US Drone Practices in Pakistan*. New York: Stanford Law School and Global Justice Clinic, New York University Law School, 2012. Online. Available at http://livingunderdrones.org (accessed 3 October 2012).

International Security Assistance Force. 'ISAF Joint Command Morning Operational Update 2012–08-S-037'. 19 August 2012. Online. Available at www.isaf.nato.int/article/isaf-releases/isaf-joint-command-morning-operational-update-aug.19.html (accessed 3 September 2012).

Jenkins, Simon. 'Drones Are Fool's Gold: They Prolong Wars We Can't Win'. *The Guardian*, 10 January 2013.

Jenks, Chris. 'Law from Above: Unmanned Aerial Systems, Use of Force, and the Law of Armed Conflict'. *North Dakota Law Review* 85, No. 3 (2010): 649–671.

Johnston, Patrick B. 'Does Decapitation Work? Assessing the Effectiveness of Leadership Targeting in Counterinsurgency Campaigns'. *International Security* 36, No. 4 (2012): 47–79.

Jones, Owen. 'Getting Rid of Dubya Wasn't Enough. The US Remains a Bully'. *The Independent*, 23 August 2012.

Joyner, James. 'America's Scandalous Drone War Goes Unmentioned in the Campaign'. *The New Republic*, 26 September 2012. Online. Available at www.newrepublic.com/article/107795/americas-scandalous-drone-war-goes-unmentioned-campaign (accessed 4 August 2014).

Judd, Terri. 'US "Should Hand over Footage of Drone Strikes or Face UN Inquiry"'. *The Independent*, 20 August 2012.

Judd, Terri. 'US Drones Target Low-Level Militants Who Pose No Threat'. *The Independent*, 10 April 2013.

Junod, Tom. 'The Lethal Presidency of Barack Obama'. *Esquire*, August 2012. Online. Available at www.esquire.com/features/obama-lethal-presidency-0812 (accessed 3 September 2012).

Kaag, John and Kaufman, Whitley. 'Military Frameworks: Technological Know-How and the Legitimization of Warfare'. *Cambridge Review of International Affairs* 22, No. 4 (2009/12/01 2009): 585–606.

Kalshoven, Frits and Zegveld, Liesbeth. *Constraints on the Waging of War: An Introduction to International Humanitarian Law*. Fourth edn. Cambridge: Cambridge University Press and the International Committee of the Red Cross, 2011.

Klaidman, Daniel. *Kill or Capture: The War on Terror and the Soul of the Obama Presidency*. New York: Houghton Mifflin Harcourt, 2012.

Koh, Harold. 'The Obama Administration and International Law'. Paper presented at the Annual Meeting of the American Society of International Law, Washington DC, 2010.

Kreps, Sarah and Kaag, John. 'The Use of Unmanned Aerial Vehicles in Contemporary Conflict: A Legal and Ethical Analysis'. *Polity* 44, No. 2 (2012): 260–285.

Laskar, Rezaul H. 'Pak Teen Who Protested US Drone Strikes Killed in Uav Hit'. *Press Trust of India*, 1 November 2011. Online. Available at www.rediff.com/news/report/pak-teen-who-protested-drone-strikes-killed-in-uav-hit/20111101.htm (accessed 6 November 2011).

Lattimer, Connor. 'Flight of the Drone: Geopolitical Analysis of Drone Warfare over the Gaza Strip'. *e-International Relations*, 2012. Online. Available at www.e-ir.info/2012/05/31/ (accessed 5 June 2012).

Luban, David. 'What Would Augustine Do? The President, Drones and Just War Theory'. *Boston Review*, 6 June 2012. Online. Available at www.bostonreview.net/david-luban-the-president-drones-augustine-just-war-theory (accessed 4 August 2014).

Mazzetti, Mark. 'The Drone Zone'. The *New York Times*, 6 July 2012.

Mazzetti, Mark. 'A Secret Deal on Drones, Sealed in Blood'. The *New York Times*, 6 April 2013.

McMahan, Jeff. 'Targeted Killing: Murder, Combat or Law Enforcement?'. In *Targeted Killings: Law and Morality in an Asymmetrical World*, edited by Claire Finkelstein, Jens David Ohlin and Andrew Altman. Oxford: Oxford University Press, 2012: 135–155.

Moss, Trefor. 'Here Come … China's Drones'. *The Diplomat*, 2 March 2013. Online. Available at http://thediplomat.com/2013/03/02/here-comes-chinas-drones/ (accessed 4 April 2013).

Mothana, Ibrahim. 'How Drones Help Al Qaeda'. The *New York Times*, 13 June 2012.

Obama, Barack. 'Remarks by the President at the National Defense University'. Washington DC: The White House Office of the Press Secretary, 23 May 2013. Online. Available at www.whitehouse.gov/the-press-office/2013/05/23/remarks-president-national-defense-university (accessed 25 March 2014).

'Obama Drone Policy Strikes Right Balance: Our View'. *USA Today*, 23 May 2013.

Oborne, Peter. 'It May Seem Painless, but Drone War in Afghanistan Is Destroying the West's Reputation'. *The Telegraph*, 31 May 2012.

O'Connell, Mary Ellen. *Unlawful Killing with Combat Drones: A Case Study of Pakistan, 2004–2009*. Notre Dame, Ind.: Law School, University of Notre Dame, 2010.

'Pakistani Public Opinion Ever More Critical of U.S'. *PewResearch Global Attitudes*, 2012. Online. Available at www.pewglobal.org/2012/06/27/pakistani-public-opinion-ever-more-critical-of-u-s/ (accessed 29 June 2012).

Pew Research. 'Global Opinion of Obama Slips, International Policies Faulted'. In *Global Attitudes Project*. Washington DC: Pew Research Center, 13 June 2012. Online. Available at www.pewglobal.org/2012/06/13/global-opinion-of-obama-slips-international-policies-faulted (accessed 26 March 2014).

Pfaff, William. 'Anonymous Murder from a Safe Distance'. *Japan Times*, 17 April 2013.

Plato. *Protagoras*. Trans C.C.W. Taylor. Oxford: Oxford University Press, 2009.

Raghavan, Sudarshan. 'Villagers Join Al-Qaeda after Deadly US Strike'. *The Age*, 27 December 2012.

Richardson, Michael. 'Drone Race Heats up between U.S. And China'. *Japan Times*, 6 December 2012.

Rohde, David. 'The Obama Doctrine'. *Foreign Policy*, March/April 2012. Online. Available at www.foreignpolicy.com/articles/2012/02/27/the_obama_doctrine? (accessed 5 May 2012).

Rumsfeld, Donald. 'Rumsfeld's War-on-Terror Memo'. *USA Today*, 20 May 2005 Online. Available at www.usatoday.com/news/washington/executive/rumsfeld-memo.htm (accessed 26 March 2014).

Savage, Charlie. 'How U.S. Justified Killing Al-Awlaki'. The *New York Times*, 2011.

Schiller, Friedrich. *Aesthetic Education of Man*. Trans. R. Snell. New York: Courier Publications, 2004 (1794).

Shane, Scott. 'The Moral Case for Drones'. The *New York Times*, 14 July 2012.

Singer, Peter W. *Wired for War: The Robotics Revolution and Conflict in the 21st Century*. New York: Penguin, 2009.

Smith, Andreas Whittam. 'Death by Drone Is Swift and Efficient – It's Also Murder'. *The Independent*, 6 October 2011.

Swift, Christopher. 'The Drone Blowback Fallacy'. *Foreign Affairs*, 1 July 2012. Online. Available at www.foreignaffairs.com/articles/137760/christopher-swift/the-drone-blowback-fallacy (accessed 6 July 2012).

Tesón, Fernando R. 'Targeted Killing in War and Peace: A Philosophical Analysis'. In *Targeted Killings. Law and Morality in an Asymmetrical World*, edited by Claire Finkelstein, Jens David Ohlin and Andrew Altman. New York: Oxford University Press, 2012: 403–433.

Thakur, Ramesh. 'United Nations'. In *The Oxford Companion to American Politics*, edited by David Coates. New York: Oxford University Press, 2012: 388–396.

Thakur, Ramesh. 'A Balance of Interests'. In *The Oxford Handbook of Modern Diplomacy*, edited by Andrew F. Cooper, Jorge Heine and Ramesh Thakur. Oxford: Oxford University Press, 2013a: 70–87.

Thakur, Ramesh. 'Follow the Yellowcake Road: Balancing Australia's National Interests against International Anti-Nuclear Interests'. *International Affairs* 89, No. 4 (2013b): 943–961.

The New America Foundation. 'Drone War Pakistan: Analysis 2004–2012'. Online. Available at http://counterterrorism.newamerica.net/drones (accessed 9 September 2013).

U.S. Department of Justice. 'Lawfulness of a Lethal Operation Directed against a U.S. Citizen Who Is a Senior Operational Leader of Al-Qa'ida or an Associated Force'. edited by DOJ: White Paper, 2013. Online. Available at http://msnbcmedia.msn.com/i/msnbc/sections/news/020413_DOJ_White_Paper.pdf (accessed 2 March 2013).

U.S. National Intelligence Council. *Global Trends 2030: Alternative Worlds*. Washington DC: NIC Document 2012–001, December 2012. Online. Available at www.dni.gov/nic/globaltrends (accessed 5 January 2013).

Weiss, Thomas G. and Thakur, Ramesh. *Global Governance and the UN: An Unfinished Journey*. Bloomington, Ind.: Indiana University Press, 2010.

'Yemeni Man Brings the Horror of Drone Strikes Home to US Senate'. *The Independent*, 26 April 2013.

6 Access to international justice

Law and practice of the European Court of Human Rights

Vesselin Popovski

Introduction

All states – to different extents – may violate human rights. What makes a difference is whether or not the state is willing to investigate and compensate victims of human rights violations. If not, the victims should have access to justice and approach various domestic mechanisms – citizens advice bureaux, ombudsman offices, members of parliament's offices, ministerial complaints offices, or other dispute resolution organs. If these non-judicial mechanisms cannot help, victims should have access and file a legal case in a domestic court and seek remedies. Often courageous independent judges rule in favour of an individual victim and against a state – a state that has violated human rights. But when the domestic law fails to deliver remedies, citizens should have access to international justice. They should be able to challenge the government's actions or inactions that violate their human rights. The European Convention on Human Rights (ECHR) adopted in 1950 created the first international mechanism – the European Court of Human Rights (ECtHR) – where individual applications can be filed by any person whose rights are violated,[1] against any state which is a party of the Convention.

This chapter reflects on some achievements and shortages in the practice of the ECtHR and contributes to the theme of the book by arguing that access to international justice is a crucial element to achieve several tasks:

- to satisfy victims when domestic mechanisms fail to deliver a sufficient and just remedy;
- to develop the domestic legislation and improve practices, as well as to influence policymakers and judges to take seriously into consideration the international standards; and
- to help reduce similar human rights abuses in the future.

Human rights originate in various texts and forms from different traditions and regions of the world, accepting that all people are born free and equal and that their rights and freedoms need protection. The Code of Hammurabi, set down in 1772 BC, already prescribed that accusations of crimes cannot be arbitrary and need to be substantiated – a very early text that signals the important notion of access to justice. Therefore, human rights are not exclusively 'Western'; they can be found in the history and territory of Iraq, Iran (Persia), Afghanistan and elsewhere. Human rights in their modern form were developed during the period of Enlightenment (eighteenth century) and written into some early constitutions. It took two more centuries until human rights became universally accepted: the 1948 Universal Declaration of Human Rights[2] and the subsequent 1966 International Covenants for Civil and Political Rights and for Economic Social and Cultural Rights;[3] regional conventions and charters of human rights such as the 1950 ECHR, the 1969 American Convention on Human Rights,[4] the 1981 African Charter on Human and People's Rights,[5] and most recently the ASEAN Intergovernmental Commission on Human Rights (AICHR)[6] established in 2009. Human rights are universal and natural in origin, belonging to and applicable to all people; however, they exist in different cultural environments and different economic and social contexts, and these affect their implementation. In Europe the ECtHR has developed a solid case law over the past 60 years, which demonstrates how crucial the access to international justice is for victims of human rights violations. This chapter demonstrates the importance of access to justice presenting the following cases from the practice of the ECtHR:

1 *Kalashnikov v. Russia*[7] – a long pre-trial detention of a suspect in an overcrowded and unhygienic condition was ruled as a violation of Art. 3 (torture, inhuman or degrading treatment). The *Kalashnikov* judgment had a significant influence and has consequently been referred to in many later cases. It had an effect on the Russian government, which took measures to decrease the number of people in pre-trial detention and reform its old penitentiary system.
2 *Budayeva and others v. Russia*[8] – a precedent-setting case wherein state negligence before natural disasters (mudslides) resulting in failure to evacuate was ruled as a violation of human rights (including the right of life) in an international court for the first time in history. It led to other successful applications of victims of natural disasters in later cases (*Kolyadenko and others v. Russia*).[9]
3 *Bankovic v. NATO*[10] demonstrates how the ECtHR can provide additional access to international justice when an existing international criminal tribunal – the International Criminal Tribunal for Former Yugoslavia (ICTY), in this case – fails to establish jurisdiction and satisfy the victims.

Kalashnikov v. Russia

On 5 May 1998, the Russian Federation (henceforth 'Russia') ratified the ECHR and its citizens became eligible to file individual applications to the ECtHR for violations of human rights committed by Russia. Three years earlier, in June 1995, Valery Kalashnikov, at the time president of the Northeast Commercial Bank in Magadan, Siberia, was charged with embezzlement, and he spent the next four and half years in pre-trial detention and a few months in prison, before being released on 26 June 2000. After his release he filed an application to the ECtHR, complaining about the conditions of the detention centre where he was held.

Kalashnikov was not an easy case, and this demonstrates how important access to justice is in principle, even if every claim of the plaintiff cannot be found justiciable. Those who feel that injustice has been done to them have the right to apply to courts, even if the final ruling of the judges might be that in fact there was no injustice done. The first challenge in *Kalashnikov* was eligibility, according to the generally recognized principles of international law. Conventions are binding on contracting parties only in respect of facts occurring after their entry into force. The ECHR applies to Russia only after 5 May 1998, and seen from that dateline – less than two years – Kalashnikov's detention could not be regarded as a very long one. The Russian government further argued that its decision to grant Kalashnikov amnesty in 2000 showed that it had no intention whatsoever of ill treatment towards him. However, assessing the effect of the conditions of detention on the applicant, which were generally the same throughout his period of detention, both on remand and following his conviction, the ECtHR extraordinarily took the overall period of detention, including the period prior to 5 May 1998, as relevant to the case.

Kalashnikov's major complaint was that the detention cell was overcrowded – in 17 square metres[11] there were between 18 and 24 inmates,[12] most of them heavy smokers. It was difficult to sleep as the light and the TV were never turned off. More seriously, the cell was not only 'continuously, severely overcrowded' but also unsanitary, and Kalashnikov contracted skin infections and was not given proper medical treatment. Many detention centres in Russia at the time would have been in similarly poor, if not worse, conditions. Ironically, one of the defences of the Russian government was actually to admit the similar situation in other detention centres, as evidence that there was nothing prejudicial and nothing individually intentional against Kalashnikov. The response of the judges in the ECtHR was that finding of purpose, or intention to humiliate Kalashnikov, is applicable only to 'torture' but not to 'inhuman or degrading treatment', therefore they did not see the lack of intention as a barrier to proceed with the case and establish a violation of Art. 3 of the ECHR.[13]

Kalashnikov then faced another challenge – the judges had to interpret the threshold of 'minimal assessment of severity', an inevitable task in all cases of torture or inhuman or degrading treatment where one has to distinguish 'degrading treatment' from some feelings of humiliation connected with any form of legitimate detention or punishment. Kalashnikov was denied liberty, and correctly so, if he may have committed a crime; and the detention itself may involve a certain feeling of 'degradation', so the actual and difficult test was whether Kalashnikov suffered additional humiliation, in excess of what anyone would feel when denied liberty. The legal team representing Kalashnikov[14] (further 'the team') searched the ECtHR's previous case law to find, disappointingly, only a few cases where naked strip-searches of prisoners

(*Iwanczuk v. Poland*; *Valasinas v. Lithuania*)[15] were qualified as 'degrading' by the ECtHR. Kalashnikov was not stripped naked, nor handcuffed, so his case was not an easy one to argue. There was also the burden of *Raninen v. Finland*[16] where the ECtHR denied that the 'minimal assessment of severity' was met, despite their agreement that the handcuffing of Raninen was unnecessary. The deliberations in *Kalashnikov* also brought some light on the old definitional debate about the difference between 'torture', 'inhuman treatment' and 'degrading treatment'. Many international lawyers[17] attempted, but mostly failed, to establish such definitional clarity between the three qualifications. Nigel Rodley wrote:

> [H]ow severe or aggravated inhuman treatment has to be for it to amount to torture is virtually impossible. Only the organs of the ECHR have attempted to conceptualize the difference between the various limbs of the formula of the prohibition (torture, inhuman treatment, degrading treatment).[18]

The ECtHR in its decision in *Kalashnikov* found only a violation of the third category – 'degrading treatment', not of the first (torture) and the second (inhuman treatment). Kalashnikov, they ruled, was not tortured and his treatment was not 'inhuman', but it was still 'degrading treatment', establishing an Art. 3 violation. Curiously, had the ECHR Art. 3 equated 'inhuman' and 'degrading' in the same category of ill treatment (simply by using 'and' instead of 'or' between them), Kalashnikov would have lost the case on the Art. 3 violation. By definition, a treatment would be 'inhuman' if there is intense physical or mental suffering. No evidence of physical suffering above the 'minimal assessment of severity' was found. The team attempted to establish 'mental suffering' but could not find enough material to impress the European judges. However, for treatment of detained persons to be defined as 'degrading', the bar is lower. All that needed to be proven was that the treatment had aroused feelings of fear, anguish and inferiority in Kalashnikov, and that such feelings were humiliating and debasing. In its practice the ECtHR usually regarded whether the treatment was humiliating and debasing to the prisoner and whether it adversely affected his personality in a manner incompatible with the Art. 3 prohibition. The *Raninen* precedent was against Kalashnikov. But the team found another precedent that could help Kalashnikov – *Peers v. Greece*[19] – and it is worth revisiting the details of *Peers*, as it is instructive how the access to justice of one person can help another person in similar conditions.

In August 1994 Donald Peers, a UK citizen, was arrested in the airport of Athens for drug offences and transferred to Korydallos Prison where he was medically tested, issued a certificate of drug user and placed in a segregation unit. In July 1995 Peers was found guilty of drug offences by the Athens Court of Appeal and sentenced to 13 years' imprisonment. In September 1996 he was transferred from Korydallos to Tyrintha Prison 'to ensure better conditions of detention'. In November 1997, a court of appeal upheld the applicant's conviction, but reduced the sentence to nine years and ordered his expulsion from

Greece. In June 1998 Peers applied for release on probation; it was granted, and he left Greece, spending fewer than four years in total in detention. Peers submitted an Art. 3 application to ECtHR, arguing that he never wanted to be placed in the segregation unit in Korydallos, but forcefully was put there, and he alleged that the conditions in segregation were degrading – in particular, he had to spend a considerable time confined to his bed with no ventilation and no window in the cell. Peers complained that the prison administration did not provide him with sheets, pillows, toilet paper and toiletries and he slept with no sheets or pillow during the hottest period of the year. He also had to use the toilet in the presence of another inmate and be present while the toilet was being used by the other inmate. The applicant claimed that he felt humiliated and distressed and that the conditions of his detention had adverse physical and mental effects on him. The Greek government responded at ECtHR that the applicant himself asked to be left in the segregation unit, but because there were no cells available, he had to share a cell with another inmate, hence the problem with the toilet. Greece argued that Peers could have moved to another part of the prison at any time, if he so wished, but he never asked for this because he developed a friendly relationship with his fellow inmate, and the two continued sharing a cell when they were both moved to Alpha wing two months later. Greece disputed the 'minimum level of severity' and stressed that the conditions of detention in no way contemplated lack of respect for Peers, even less any physical or mental suffering. On the contrary, the prison authorities allowed him extra phone calls and frequent contact with a psychiatrist. The ECtHR accepted that there was no evidence proving a positive intention of humiliating or debasing Peers. However, it noted that, although the question whether the purpose of the treatment was to humiliate or debase the victim is to be taken into account, the absence of such purpose cannot conclusively rule out a finding of violation of Art. 3. The fact remains that the authorities took no steps to improve the unacceptable conditions of detention and this omission denotes lack of respect for the applicant. The Court took into account that for at least two months the applicant had to spend a considerable time confined to his bed in a cell with no ventilation and no window, which would at times become unbearably hot. He also had to use the toilet in the presence of another inmate and be present while the toilet was being used. The Court therefore was of the opinion that the prison conditions diminished the applicant's human dignity and aroused in him feelings of anguish and inferiority capable of humiliating and debasing him and possibly breaking his physical or moral resistance. In sum, the Court considered that the conditions of the detention in the segregation unit amounted to degrading treatment within the meaning of Art. 3 of ECHR.

The *Peers* judgment was exactly what the team in *Kalashnikov* needed – overcrowded cell, use of the toilet in visibility of other inmates, and so forth, could be 'degrading', no matter whether there was a direct intention to humiliate or debase Kalashnikov or not. The fact that inmates had to sleep in turns on eight beds gave the judges a good ground to find that the 'deprivation of sleep must have constituted a heavy physical and psychological burden'[20] on Kalashnikov.

The judges further observed the 'absence of adequate ventilation in the cell, which held an excessive number of inmates, who were permitted to smoke'.[21] Although Kalashnikov was 'allowed outdoor activity for one or two hours a day, the rest of the time he was confined to his cell, with a very limited space for himself and a stuffy atmosphere'.[22] The ECtHR noted that the cell was 'infested with pests' and 'no anti-infestation treatment was effected'.[23] Throughout his detention Kalashnikov contracted various skin illnesses, and though he received some treatment, the illnesses' recurrence signalled that the very poor conditions remained unchanged.

The ECtHR, based on these findings, ruled at the end that 'the applicant's conditions of detention, in particular the severely overcrowded and insanitary environment and its detrimental effect on the applicant's health and well-being, combined with the length of the period in such conditions, amounted to degrading treatment'. The Court also found a violation of Art. 5§3 (illegal detention) and Art. 6§1 (unfair trial) and ordered compensations – 5,000 euros in respect of non-pecuniary damage and 3,000 in respect of costs and expenses. These compensations were not the main victory; Kalashnikov, rather, wanted a moral satisfaction. The important outcome was the impact of *Kalashnikov* on Russian domestic legislation and practice, giving hope for millions of victims suffering in similar conditions. In 2002, Russia adopted a new Criminal Procedure Code, aligning its standards with the European laws. After *Kalashnikov* Russia took some measures to reduce the number of detainees,[24] improve the conditions in pre-trial detention, and carry out other legal reforms. Lawyers, inspired and guided by *Kalashnikov*, subsequently filed numerous similar cases in ECtHR.[25]

Budayeva v. Russia

States historically have never accepted liability for natural disasters. They would blame God, the sky, the ocean, or Mother Nature for human suffering but would never admit their own negligence. *Budayeva v. Russia* broke this taboo and found that state negligence – both before and after natural disasters – can be the primary cause of human suffering from natural disasters and this can amount to a violation of human rights, including Art. 2 (right of life). If states delay or do not deliver remedies and compensations after natural disasters, these could also amount to violations of human rights, which can be litigated – in domestic courts first, or when victims are not satisfied with domestic remedies, they can utilize international human rights machinery. *Budayeva* – similarly to *Kalashnikov* – opened the door for many victims in similar circumstances to approach courts and seek remedies and compensations.

Before analysing *Budayeva*, I would like to briefly present how the ECtHR had expanded the state's responsibility for negligence regarding industrial environmental disasters. A first breakthrough judgment came in *Guerra v. Italy*.[26] The applicants lived near a fertilizer factory, which often released inflammable gases and accidents occurred, the most serious being when the factory tower exploded and arsenic trioxide escaped into the air, poisoning 150 people in 1976. The applicants alleged violation of ECHR Art. 10 right to information, resulting from authorities' failure to inform of the risks and the evacuation plans in case of accidents. The ECtHR ruled that in this case the right to information could not be construed as imposing positive obligations on Italy to disseminate information of its own volition; however, the ECtHR found that the direct effect of toxic emissions on Guerra and others was a violation of another human right – ECHR Art. 8 respect for private and family life, the main logic of which is essentially the protection of an individual against arbitrary interference by public authorities. *Guerra* illustrates how the access to justice is crucial, even if the victims of human rights violations might not be fully legally capable of dealing with the exact legal technicalities – the Court itself can work these out. In *Guerra*, the applicants failed in their Art. 10 claim, but the Court found an Art. 8 violation, asking whether the authorities had taken all necessary steps to ensure effective respect for private and family life and ruling that this failure and potential air pollution might affect Guerra and others' well-being and prevent them from enjoying their homes. The applicants had waited, right up until the production of fertilizers had ceased in 1994, for essential information that would have enabled them to assess the risks that they and their families might run if they continued to live near the factory; therefore, Italy violated its Art. 8 obligation to secure applicants' right to respect for their private and family life.

A more serious case involving loss of life was *Oneryildiz v. Turkey.*[27] A methane explosion killed nine members of Oneryildiz family, who lived in a slum in Istanbul surrounding a rubbish tip. The applicants listed violations of Art. 2 (right to life), 8 (right to respect for private and family life), and 13 (right to an effective remedy) in their claim that the authorities did not prevent the deaths, caused by the explosion of the rubbish tip, which operated under the authorities' control. The applicants stressed that Art. 2 does not solely concern deaths resulting from actions of state agents but also inaction because of negligence, laying down a positive obligation to take appropriate steps to safeguard the lives of those within state jurisdiction. The Court unanimously found a violation of Art. 2 – negligence to prevent death – and that Turkey had known or ought to have known that there was a real risk to persons living near the tip but failed to take operational measures to protect them. Taken together, the *Guerra* and *Oneryldiz* decisions frame responsibility of states to protect citizens from hazards, causing a risk to their life and well-being.

In another case, *Murillo Saldías v. Spain,*[28] heavy rains caused flooding of a campsite and resulted in a loss of life. The surviving victims approached the ECtHR and, although in their decision (28 November 2006) the judges found the application inadmissible on procedural grounds (non-exhausted domestic remedies), they at least signalled the state's responsibility to protect right of life from floods caused by rain, a purely natural, not industrial, disaster.

Budayeva v. Russia[29] became the first precedent in international court of establishing state negligence – and violations of human rights – for natural disasters, applicable both before the disaster and the failure to evacuate, and also to post-disaster rescue, recovery, investigation and compensating victims. The sad story of Budayeva goes back to 1937, when a town in Caucasus was reported as having repeatedly been exposed to mudslides, mostly in the summer. Various mud-retention dams had protected the town, but these had been damaged by earlier mudslides and never repaired, despite repeated warnings. Two weeks before the murderous mudslide in July 2000, meteorologists warned the local Ministry for Disaster. Seeing no action from the authorities, they requested to establish emergency 24-hour observation points, so as to issue warnings for people to evacuate. Even such a desperate, last-minute measure was ignored and not undertaken. At about 11 p.m. on 18 July, a flow of mud and debris hit and flooded the town. The next morning (19 July), the mud level fell and some people went back home, seeing no barrier or police warning them not to do so. Budayeva and her family, not being aware of any order to evacuate, also went back home, and at 1 p.m. a second powerful mudslide hit the town. Budayeva and her eldest son managed to escape while the younger son was rescued with serious injuries. But her husband, Vladimir Budayev, who stayed behind to help his parents-in-law, was killed when the house collapsed. The town was subsequently hit by a succession of mudslides over a period lasting until 25 July 2000. Eight people were officially reported dead in total, and many homes and possessions were destroyed.

In the ECtHR the Russian government's representatives replied – unsurprisingly – that the natural disaster could not have been predicted nor could the damages be prevented. They pointed to a decision from 12 August 2000 to grant those who lost properties with free replacement housing and an emergency allowance of 530 euros.[30] The applicants, however, were not satisfied and subsequently brought civil proceedings for proper compensation. The claims were rejected in domestic courts on the grounds that the authorities had taken all reasonable measures to mitigate the damage from the mudslides and that the local population was informed of the risk of possible mudslides by the media.

The applicants pointed to three major shortcomings of the authorities: the failure to maintain mud-protection facilities, in particular to repair the mud-retention dam, damaged in 1999, and the failure to clear a mud-retention collector, blocked by debris; the lack of official warning and evacuation order, which would have avoided casualties, injuries and panic; and the absence of an enquiry to assess the authorities' conduct before and after the mudslides. The application was supported by witness statements, financial documents showing that funds were allocated but not for the repair of the dam required after the 1999 mudslides, and letters from the Mountain Institute (a state agency responsible for monitoring weather hazards in high-altitude areas) issued between August 1999 and July 2000 warning about high mudslide risks and recommending that the damaged dam be repaired and observation posts be set up to facilitate the evacuation in the event of a mudslide. One of the last warnings referred to possible record losses and casualties if those measures were not carried out as a matter of urgency. Referring to Art. 2 (right to life), 8 (right to respect for private and family life), 13 (right to an effective remedy), and Article 1 of Protocol No. 1

(protection of property), the applicants alleged that the Russian authorities failed to mitigate the consequences of the mudslides, put the applicants' lives at risk, were responsible for the death of Budayev and others, and for the destruction of their homes. They also mentioned the authorities' failure to carry out a judicial enquiry after the disaster, which is also part of Russia's Art. 2 obligations.

The ECtHR decision on *Budayeva v. Russia*[31] is the first in history when state negligence before and after natural disasters was explicitly found as constituting violations of human rights in international court. The judges pronounced Russia's 'failure to discharge its positive obligation to protect the right to life',[32] its omission to implement land-planning and emergency relief policies, and its ignorance of the fact that the area was particularly vulnerable to mudslides, thus exposing the residents to mortal risk. The ECtHR in its *Budayeva* decision crystallized the state's responsibility for mitigating natural disasters both in terms of substance – not maintaining protective defensive infrastructure and not issuing warnings to citizens to evacuate – and in procedure – lack of investigation of the authorities' conduct. It affirmed that states should bear such responsibility and protect human rights both before and after natural disasters.

Following the precedent-setting *Budayeva v. Russia*, other victims of natural disasters also filed successful applications and claimed compensations. In a recent case, *Kolyadenko and others v. Russia*,[33] the applicants lived in the city of Vladivostok near a river, close to a water reservoir, an area subject to periodic flooding during heavy rains. On 6 August 2001 a regional meteorological service forwarded a storm warning to Vladivostok city authorities, stating that heavy rainfall was expected with a risk of over-flooding. The local water company calculated that the water inflow to the reservoir would be dangerous and started releasing water from the reservoir. The intensity of the rain proved to be much higher than forecast, and accordingly the water company increased the rate of release to the maximum. The applicants claimed that no emergency warning had been given, and each of them was caught by surprise. One of them, Kolyadenko, a disabled woman, found out about the flood from her children, who came running to help her out when the water started rising rapidly, reached waist level in the flat, and was much deeper in the courtyard. Another applicant was at home with her 21-month-old son when the flat was instantly flooded, but she managed to dress the boy and escape, wading breast-deep to a nearby motorway. Another applicant and her 19-year-old son opened the door, and when their home was instantly flooded, they rushed out into the street, where within 15 minutes the water had risen to breast height. She could not swim, but her son swam away and brought a ladder, which enabled them to climb onto the roof of a garage. Defending the case the Russian government, as in *Budayeva*, argued that the infringements of the applicants' rights resulted from a natural disaster, exceptionally heavy rain, which could not have been foreseen and could therefore not be imputed to the state. The ECtHR did not accept this argument and reiterated that the flooding occurred after the urgent release of water from the reservoir, the likelihood and potential consequences of which the authorities should have foreseen. The ECtHR stressed that the main reason for the flooding was the poor state of repair of the river channel because of the authorities' manifest failure to keep it clean and to make sure its capacity was adequate. The ECtHR concluded that this failure, as well as the failure to apply town planning restrictions corresponding to the technical requirements of the exploitation of the reservoir, put the lives of applicants at risk. Although nobody died from the flooding, the ECtHR nevertheless found a violation of Art. 2 (right of life) because no evacuation had been organized, the applicants' lives had been put at risk, and they had had to find their own way to safety and cope with all the consequences of the flooding on their own.

The examples above manifest how the evolving practice of the ECtHR has firmed in ruling state negligence in case of natural disasters as a violation of human rights. Still, the limit of the applicability of the Convention to European states renders similar litigation for disasters in other parts of the world possible only in domestic courts. But even if not directly applicable, the judgments in *Budayeva* and *Kolyadenko* can serve at least as a guide for lawyers, defending the rights of victims of natural disasters and demanding proper compensations.

Access to justice, and to international justice when the domestic courts fail, is important no matter whether all cases will be successfully litigated or not. The third case presented here did not succeed for the applicants, but nevertheless it showed an alternative access to international justice for the victims after their previous attempt to have their case heard at the International Criminal Tribunal for former Yugoslavia (ICTY) failed.

Bankovic v. NATO

From March to May 1999, NATO bombed targets in Serbia over 72 days without authorization from the UN Security Council, urging Serbian authorities to stop the policy of ethnic cleansing in Kosovo. One of the controversial targets of these bombings was the TV station in Belgrade (Radio Televizije Srbije), and the building of the TV station was partially destroyed, 16 people were killed, and another 16 were seriously injured. The relatives of the victims approached the ICTY, a body established by the UN Security Council in 1992 to investigate and prosecute war crimes.[34] In June 2000, the ICTY Prosecutor appointed a Panel of Experts to verify whether the air strikes were conducted in accordance with the international humanitarian law (IHL), and the Panel concluded that no violation of IHL was ascribed to NATO forces. They considered the TV station to be a legitimate target, as it was part of the Serbian integrated system of command and control, and the attack aimed to disrupt this whole system. Furthermore, NATO authorities announced the raid in advance; therefore, Bankovic and the other civilians were in the building at their own risk.[35]

Failing at the ICTY, the relatives of Bankovic and others decided to approach the ECtHR. If the IHL, with its strict threshold of military necessity in time of armed conflict, restricted their chances for remedy and compensation, they hoped that the human rights law – applicable at all times, including in time of peace[36] – would be a better choice of court to file the case as a violation of Art. 2 (right of life).

On 19 December 2001, the ECtHR announced its decision on *Bankovic*, declaring the application inadmissible as the impugned act fell outside the jurisdiction of the respondent states. The ECtHR came to the conclusion that there was no jurisdictional link between the persons who were victims of the act and the respondent states. The judges ruled that the applicants and their deceased relatives did not fall within the jurisdiction of the respondent states on account of the extraterritorial act in question. One interesting legal issue was whether the exclusion of Bankovic and others from the respondent states' jurisdiction would defeat the public order mission of the European Convention and leave a regrettable vacuum in its system of human rights protection; one of the Court's obligations is to regard the special character of the Convention as a constitutional instrument of European public order for the protection of individual human beings, and its role was to ensure the observance of the engagements undertaken by the contracting states within their legal space. Kosovo, the judges decided, did not fall within this legal space, and they wrote that the Convention is not considered to be designed for application throughout the world, even in respect of the conduct of the contracting states. The Court concluded that the impugned action of the respondent states does not engage such responsibility and declared *Bankovic* inadmissible.

Bankovic is a disappointing judgment as it excludes the victims from the jurisdiction of the NATO countries by virtue of questioning NATO's absolute control of the airspace above former Yugoslavia, declaring that acts of war, performed under NATO command and control within the territory of Serbia, could not be ascribed to the respondent NATO states. Serbia could not have control of its airspace either during the NATO invasion of that same airspace. The judges in fact opined that if Bankovic died on a NATO country territory the case would be admissible, but she was unlucky to die from NATO bombs on Serbian territory. The ECtHR could have determined whether the victims were within the jurisdiction of the respondent NATO states by virtue of an extraterritorial act, but it decided to define such extraterritoriality depending on the effective control of the relevant territory and its inhabitants, as a consequence of military occupation or through the consent, invitation or acquiescence of the government of the territory concerned. In sum, as NATO bombed Yugoslavia without, ironically, the consent of Yugoslavia, *Bankovic* had no jurisdiction and the case was inadmissible.

Conclusion

This chapter presented how important it is for individuals to gain access to international justice where they can effectively challenge states – even major ones such as Russia and NATO members – for violations of human rights. The successfully litigated examples *Kalashnikov* and *Budayeva* are remarkable achievements – individuals being denied justice domestically could achieve justice in an international court. These important precedent-setting cases in ECtHR opened chances for others, suffering from similar violations, to file applications and successfully receive remedies, as it happened with *Kolyadenko and others*. Access to justice does not mean that every claim will necessarily always be successfully litigated. As with *Murillo Saldías v. Spain* and *Bankovic v. NATO*, even when individuals may fail to win their cases, the mere opportunity to present and deliberate human rights violations in international court can be useful in building up case law and caution states to face their responsibilities and respect human rights in the future.

Cases

Bankovic and others v. Belgium and others (NATO members) (52207/99) ECHR 970 (19 December 2001).
Budayeva v. Russia (15339/02) ECHR (29 September 2008).
Iwanczuk v. Poland (25196/94) ECHR 15 (15 November 2001).
Kalashnikov v. Russia (47095/99) ECHR 591 (15 July 2002).
Kolyadenko and others v. Russia (Applications 17423/05, 20534/05, 20678/05, 23263/05, 24283/05, 35673/05) ECHR (judgment from 9 July 2012).
Murillo Saldías v. Spain (dec.) (No. 76973/01) *ECHR* (28 November 2006).
Oneryildiz v. Turkey 41 ECHR 20 (2005).
Peers v. Greece (28524/95) ECHR (14 September 1997).
Raninen v. Finland (152/1996/771/972) ECHR (6 December 1997).
Sukhovoy v. Russia (Application 63955/00) ECHR (27 March 2008).
Trepashkin v. Russia (Application No. 14248/05) ECHR (23 November 2005).
Valasinas v. Lithuania (44558/98) ECHR 2001-VIII (29 July 2001).

Notes

1 The applicant does not necessarily need to be a European citizen.
2 UN General Assembly 1948: 217 A (III).
3 UN General Assembly 1966, vol. 999: 171.
4 Organization of American States (OAS) 1969.
5 Organization of African Unity (OAU) 1981: CAB/LEG/67/3 rev. 5, 21 I.L.M. 58 (1982).
6 See Association of Southeast Asian Nations (ASEAN) 2009.
7 *Kalashnikov v. Russia* (47095/99) ECHR 591 (15 July 2002).
8 *Budayeva v. Russia* (15339/02) ECHR (29 September 2008).
9 *Kolyadenko and others v. Russia* (Applications 17423/05, 20534/05, 20678/05, 23263/05, 24283/05, 35673/05, judgment from 9 July 2012).
10 *Bankovic and others v. Belgium and others* (NATO members) (52207/99) ECHR 970 (19 December 2001).
11 The Russian government claimed it was 20 square metres, but the Court was not interested in investigating – 20 square metres was still far less than the minimum standard.
12 The government put the figure between 11 and 14, and again the court showed no appetite to find the exact numbers because at any given time it makes 0.9–1.9 square metres of cell space per inmate.
13 Art. 3 of ECHR prohibits torture, or inhuman or degrading treatment.
14 The author worked with this legal team in Moscow in 2002.
15 *Iwanczuk v. Poland*, No. 25196/94, 15, ECHR; *Valasinas v. Lithuania*, No. 44558/98, ECHR 2001–VIII.

16 *Raninen v. Finland* (152/1996/771/972, 16 December 1997).
17 O'Boyle 1977: 674–706; Klayman 1978.
18 Rodley 1999: 77–106.
19 *Peers v. Greece* (28524/95), ECHR 14 (September 1997).
20 *Kalashnikov v. Russia* (47095/99) ECHR 591 (15 July 2002) at 15.
21 *Kalashnikov v. Russia* (47095/99) ECHR 591 (15 July 2002) at 16.
22 *Kalashnikov v. Russia* (47095/99) ECHR 591 (15 July 2002) at 17.
23 *Kalashnikov v. Russia* (47095/99) ECHR 591 (15 July 2002) at 20.
24 From 199,000 in October 2001 to 137,000 in October 2002.
25 For example, *Sukhovoy v. Russia* (Application 63955/00); *Trepashkin v. Russia* (Application No. 14248/05) ECHR. For a full list see: http://hudoc.echr.coe.int/sites/eng/pages/search.aspx# (accessed 30 February 2014).
26 *Guerra v. Italy* 26 EHRR 357 (1998).
27 *Oneryildiz v. Turkey* 41 EHRR 20 at 56 (2005).
28 *Murillo Saldías v. Spain (dec.)* (No. 76973/01) ECHR (28 November 2006).
29 *Budayeva v. Russia* (Appl. No. 15339/02, 21166/02, 20058/02, 11673/02).
30 People evacuated from Fukushima got 5 million yen (50,000 euros).
31 *Budayeva v. Russia* (Judgment of 20 March 2008).
32 *Budayeva v. Russia* (Judgment of 20 March 2008) at 207 [2].
33 *Kolyadenko and others v. Russia* (Applications 17423/05, 20534/05, 20678/05, 23263/05, 24283/05, 35673/05, judgment from 9 July 2012).
34 UN Security Council, 'Resolution 808 (1993) Adopted by the Security Council at its 3175th meeting', 22 February 1993(a), S/RES/808; UN Security Council, 'Resolution 827 (1993) Adopted by the Security Council at its 3217th meeting', 25 May 1993, S/RES/827 (1993b).
35 ICTY 2008.
36 I discussed the difference in Popovski 2008.

References

Association of Southeast Asian Nations (ASEAN). 'Terms of Reference of ASEAN Intergovernmental Commission on Human Rights'. July 2009. Online. Available at www.refworld.org/docid/3ae6b3630.html (accessed 31 March 2014).

ICTY. 'Final Report to the Prosecutor by the Committee Established to Review the Nato Bombing Campaign against the Federal Republic of Yugoslavia'. (2008). Online. Available at www.icty.org/sid/10052 (accessed 22 February 2014).

Klayman, Barry M. 'The Definition of Torture in International Law'. *Temple Law Quarterly* 51 No. 3 (1978): 449–517.

O'Boyle, Michael. 'Torture and Emergency Powers under the European Convention on Human Rights: Ireland V. United Kingdom'. *American Journal of International Law* 71, No. 4 (1977): 674–706.

Organization of African Unity (OAU). 'African Charter on Human and Peoples' Rights ("Banjul Charter")'. 27 June 1981, CAB/LEG/67/3 rev. 5, 21 I.L.M. 58 (1982).

Organization of American States (OAS). 'American Convention on Human Rights, "Pact of San Jose", Costa Rica'. 22 November 1969.

Popovski, Vesselin. 'Protection of Children in International Humanitarian Law and Human Rights Law'. In *International Humanitarian Law and Human Rights Law: Towards a New Merger in International Law*, edited by Roberta Arnold and Noelle Quenivet. New York: Brill, 2008: 391–410.

Rodley, Nigel. *The Treatment of Prisoners under International Law*. 2nd edn. Oxford: Oxford University Press, 1999.

UN General Assembly. 'Universal Declaration of Human Rights'. 10 December 1948, 217 A (III).

UN General Assembly. 'International Covenant on Civil and Political Rights'. In *United Nations Treaty Series*, edited by United Nations, 16 December 1966, vol. 999.

UN Security Council. 'Resolution 808 (1993) Adopted by the Security Council at its 3175th meeting'. S/RES/808 (1993a).

UN Security Council. 'Resolution 827 (1993) Adopted by the Security Council at its 3217th meeting'. S/RES/827 (1993b).

7 Access to justice for victims of the use of force in international affairs

Individual civil responsibility for aggression

Edwin Bikundo

Introduction

Peace and justice are literally emblematic of the ICC. That Court's emblem consists of the scales of justice framed and supported by the olive laurels of peace. That is hardly an accidental occurrence. On the contrary, it is a careful choice that was consciously and deliberately made as the visual presentation of the Court. And yet, holding individuals civilly responsible for the crime of aggression is a proposition yet to be legally tested. Accessing justice for violations of the law on the use of force is replete with dualisms concerning forums, bodies of law, legal regimes and personal status. Both the international Criminal Court (ICC) and the International Court of Justice (ICJ) have jurisdiction over violations of the law of the use of force in different yet overlapping ways. The use of force also has two different bodies of law regarding resort to force – *jus ad bellum* – and regulating force *jus in bello*. Breaches of the *jus ad bellum* or acts of aggression can attract compensation as international delicts (being contrary to 'the renunciation of war as an instrument of national policy', contained within the title of the Kellogg-Briand Pact, or Pact of Paris, officially General Treaty for Renunciation of War as an Instrument of National Policy) as well as entail punishments as crimes (planning, preparation, initiation or execution of an act of aggression contrary to the UN Charter). More dualism is in that the persons with status or legal standing can be either states or individuals, and so on. This chapter inquires into the forms access to justice for victims of the use of force in international affairs take. For these purposes, it looks at the different regimes to which recourse may be had. It then analyses various doctrinal, theoretical and practical aspects to interrogate the efficacy of access to justice involving the use of force.

Testing access to justice

Access to justice denotes ideas revolving around improving access to formal legal procedures or providing supplemental mechanisms outside of those procedures to promote justice. Both of those approaches are after the fact. How about preventing injustice to potential victims of the use of force? This paper focuses on the symbolic role of the international criminal trial in providing justice by preventing injustice. That is to say access to preventive justice as distinct from either rehabilitative or retributive justice.

This dichotomy still persists even though only 'persons in a position effectively to exercise control over or to direct the political or military action of a State'[1] can be individually liable for the crime of aggression. The *jus in bello* includes 'Hague Law' (generally derived from the 1907 Hague Conventions), governing the conduct of hostilities and 'Geneva Law' (principally derived from the 1949 Geneva Conventions) providing for the protection of the victims of war. Hague Law renders military personnel and military targets open to the application of deadly force, while Geneva Law stipulates when military personnel may no longer be targeted, even as it protects civilians from the brunt of the deliberate use of force. Although both the Hague and Geneva regimes are of course not applicable prior to force being used, the two are considered discrete areas of the law with no bearing on the legality of the resort to force as opposed to its use.

Aggression at the ICJ: armed activities on the territory of the Congo (*Democratic Republic of the Congo v. Uganda*)

On 19 December 2005, the ICJ found that Uganda had violated the principle of the non-use of force in international relations by, among others, engaging in military activities against the Democratic Republic of the Congo (DRC). Furthermore, the Court found that Uganda violated its obligations under international human rights law and international humanitarian law, by the conduct of its armed forces, which committed acts of killing, torture and other forms of inhumane treatment of the Congolese civilian population, and failed to distinguish between civilian and military targets and to protect the civilian population in fighting with other combatants, and so forth. Uganda, too, failed to take measures to respect and ensure respect for human rights and international humanitarian law in its area of occupation in DRC territory. These findings cover both the *jus ad bellum* as well as *jus in bello* aspects of the use of force. Jurisdictionally, however, individual victims do not have standing except through their state taking up their grievances within the ICJ. This is where the ICC can potentially provide a difference in terms of widening access for victims.

A 'right to peace'[2]

The first attempt to legalize war in the Western tradition was through the doctrine of 'just war'. The just war doctrine aimed to reconcile might with right though recognizing only just wars as legal and unjust wars as aggression and therefore illegal.[3] War, therefore, could only be a just response to aggression and in this way was the ultimate means for both restoring a 'right' of some sort that had been violated and simultaneously punishing the offender.[4] It therefore seems that, in discussing the legality or illegality of the use of force and its normative manifestation, there is a universal yet inarticulate soft law background presumption that at its simplest says 'there is a right to peace'[5] that could be violated, but such violation would attract penal consequences. This so-called right to peace and concomitant duty to keep the peace[6] inheres in the nation state but arguably also in individuals[7] through the operation of customary international law.[8] It may not be part of the positive law as such but it does provide interpretative capacity by conceiving of peace as the norm and war/armed conflict the undesirable exception.

At the foreground of this right to peace is the reality of war or armed conflict as acknowledged in the hard law. The laws that govern entry into and conduct of war and armed conflict have traditionally been divided into two: *jus ad bellum* and *jus in bello*.[9] The contemporary arguments extending *jus in bello* principles into internal armed conflict just as cogently apply to *jus ad bellum*.[10] Peace at its most basic is the absence of armed conflict. Armed conflict is resort to force by state or non-state actors which may be legal or illegal. *Jus ad bellum* law governs resort to war or force in general (the *why* questions), while *jus in bello* governs the conduct of war or armed conflict (the *how* questions).

Aggression falls on the *jus ad bellum* side of the ledger. The dearth of trials for the crime of aggression, despite the wealth of perpetrators, gives cause for comment.[11] If indeed it is irrefutable that present-day positive international law reflects the Nuremberg Judgment[12] and United Nations declarations,[13] is the lacuna observed in normative application merely a result of realpolitik or are there largely suppressed, legally reasoned and underlying reasons subsisting?

Under contemporary international law, the prosecution of international crimes is generally the responsibility of the state as the oldest, most traditional and indeed appropriate subject of international law.[14] Although the Nuremberg Charter itself was established without prejudice to the jurisdiction of national courts,[15] it in turn was set up 'as an act of the will of the conqueror'.[16] Even with the advent of the International Criminal Court, this responsibility to prosecute is still mainly with the state as expressly provided under the Rome Statute on issues of admissibility.[17] This statute provides that due regard must be given to paragraph 10 of the Preamble[18] and the first article of the statute,[19] both of which unequivocally lay stress on the principle of complementarity. It is laid down that the court shall determine that a case is inadmissible where, *inter alia*, the case is being or has been investigated or prosecuted by a state which has jurisdiction over it, except where the state is either unwilling or unable in good faith to carry out such investigation or prosecution.[20] Under the Statute of the International Criminal Court, the accent and emphasis is thus clearly on the primary duty of the state to prosecute violators of international criminal law.

Further, with a few relatively minor exceptions, the statute does not create, codify or legislate new types of crime but only provides a novel collective mechanism for dealing with the most serious crimes of international concern. Even then, this is only when the state primarily responsible for investigation and/or prosecution has abdicated its responsibility and another state has not taken it upon itself to investigate and/or prosecute such a crime.[21] Moreover, the ICC has jurisdiction only over the most serious crimes of international concern.[22] The rest remain within the purview of states.

With particular reference to the crime of aggression, the ICC will exercise the jurisdiction already vested over the crime of aggression once a provision is adopted containing a definition and procedure of how aggression should be dealt with. However, this should be consistent with the relevant provisions of the Charter of the United Nations.[23]

The public international law prohibition on the use of force

Historical developments up to the Second World War

The Hague peace conferences of 1899 and 1907 contained the first, albeit modest, restrictions on the use of force but did not go so far as to comprehensively outlaw its use outright.[24] Prior to this century, no prohibition of the use of force had existed and states were free to resort to war as yet another tool in the diplomatic kitbag.[25] Public international law at the time permitted the use of force in the relations between states.[26] During the era of the League of Nations, its covenant went some way towards progressively regulating and restricting the use of force amounting to war between states.[27] A further welcome development was the Geneva Protocol for the Pacific Settlement of International Disputes of 1924 outlawing aggressive war and labelling it an international crime.[28] In the Kellogg-Briand Pact (that is, the General Treaty for the Renunciation of War 1928), the state parties to it not only condemned recourse to war for the solution of international controversies, but renounced it as an instrument of national policy and agreed that only peaceful means were to decide all disputes or conflicts among them.[29] The provisions of this treaty may be taken accordingly as evidence of international customary law rules. However, the position as it stands now is markedly different.

Criminalization of the use of force

After the First World War, through the Treaty of Versailles 1919, Wilhelm II of Hohenzollern, former German emperor, was indicted for 'a supreme offence against international morality and the sanctity of treaties and essential rules of justice'.[30] However, the Netherlands, where he was exiled, declined to give him up for trial after receiving assurances that the Allied Powers would not vigorously pursue the point.

Aggression under contemporary international law

But the real watershed in terms of individual criminal responsibility came in Article 6 of the Constitution of the International Military Tribunal appended to the London Agreement for the Prosecution and Punishment of the Major War Criminals of the European Axis.[31]

The tribunal set-up had the power to try to punish persons who, as individuals, had committed crimes against peace: namely, planning, preparation, initiation or waging of a war of aggression, or a war in violation of international treaties, agreements or assurances. The judgment of the court said that crimes against international law were committed by persons, not abstract entities, and only by punishing individuals who committed such crimes could the provisions of international law be enforced.[32] As for the critical matter of individual criminal responsibility, the High Command case ruled that the criminality of aggressive war was attached only to individuals at the policymaking level.[33]

The aforementioned General Assembly Resolution[34] affirmed the rules of law developed by the Nuremberg Charter and Judgment and directed the International Law Commission to draft them into a code. Still on this point, the International Law Commission said 'the law of the Charter concerning the prohibition of the use of force in itself constitutes a conspicuous example of a rule in international law having the character of *jus cogens*'.[35]

The first time criminal aggression was defined in a legal text was for the Nuremberg trials. The Charter of the International Military Tribunal (IMT) defined the jurisdiction and set out the general principles for the criminalization and prosecution of 'the major war criminals of the European Axis countries' for *inter alia* aggression, as set out in the following terms:

> (a) CRIMES AGAINST PEACE: namely, planning, preparation, initiation or waging of a war of aggression, or a war in violation of international treaties, agreements or assurances, or participation in a common plan or conspiracy for the accomplishment of any of the foregoing.[36]

During the negotiations leading to the adoption of the text, the United States' position, as put forward by its representative Justice Jackson, was that 'sterile legalisms developed in the age of imperialism to make war respectable' justified acts which otherwise would be crimes, indistinguishable from piracy and brigandage. Jackson, however, distinguished between international law of the nineteenth century and that of the early twentieth century, which declared that war-making was not illegal as both parties to war were regarded as being in an identical legal position. This was a departure from the doctrine taught by Hugo Grotius (favoured by Jackson), distinguishing between just (defence) and unjust (aggression) war.[37] According to Jackson, international law went beyond 'abstract and immutable principles' but originated in state action.[38] There was, therefore, no need for precedent to justify the trial because when the Nazis came to power aggressive war was already illegal and criminal.

According to Jackson this followed on from the texts already cited above, together with some notable inclusions:[39]

1 The Briand-Kellogg Pact of 1928 with which Germany, Italy and Japan renounced war as an instrument of national policy, which mentioned the Geneva Protocol of 1924 for the Pacific Settlement of International Disputes, which declared aggressive war criminal.
2 The unanimous resolution of the Eighth Assembly of the League of Nations in 1927, including Germany, to declare wars of aggression criminal; and (most interestingly from the perspective of this inquiry).
3 The unanimous resolution of the Sixth Pan-American Conference of 1928 stating that 'war of aggression constitutes an international crime against the human species'.[40]

These justifications for prosecuting aggression readily divide into the more traditional horizontal/geopolitical plane (including Germany with its consent) and the radically inclusive vertical/biopolitical plane (including Germany regardless of its consent).

The point consistently emphasized during drafting of the IMT Charter was that only actual attack or invasion constituted aggression, and any possible arguments that such attack or invasion was in defence against political or economic measures were headed off in the drafting. This was despite the drafters' awareness that from Germany's perspective such an attack was considered a defensive action. Defining the 'aggressor' beforehand would exclude any argument in the courtroom over characterization in which the Germans would participate.[41] Aggression was therefore defined to exclude 'resort to war to redress economic or political disadvantages or threats of encirclement, et cetera, as a defence'.[42] Neither political or military nor other considerations could excuse resorting to war. That is, for the purposes of prosecution in 1945 peaceful settlement of grievances between states was considered compulsory *ex ante* due to a prohibition of aggression deemed by that point to be customary.[43]

Sir David Maxwell Fyfe, representing the United Kingdom and speaking in support of Jackson, presented the available options as stark choices: first, exclude aggression which was the essential complaint against the Germans; second, allow political argument as to the meaning of aggression at trial; and third, define aggression for the purposes of the tribunal. Jackson expressed his fears that, if argument was allowed over the political and economic causes of the war, controversy would arise regarding whether Germany invaded Norway just before a British invasion of Norway or whether France, in declaring war, was the real aggressor. These considerations would also apply to Russia.[44] In this way, therefore, aggression was defined as a crime by reference to states but with or without their consent through the strategic use of the term 'humanity'. The usual concerns of international law – criminal law and legality – were left by the wayside in creating the new jurisdiction.

Developments post-Nuremberg

Article 2(4) of the United Nations Charter instructs states to 'refrain in their international relations from the threat or use of force against the territorial integrity or political independence of any state'. This provision is an improvement of the language of the Kellogg-Briand Pact in replacing the term 'war' with 'force'. This is in anticipation of aggressors qualifying the force they use as not amounting to war.

In the Nicaragua (Merits) Case,[45] the International Court of Justice considered the principle of non-use of force a rule of customary international law. The court went on to say that the United Nations Charter by no means covered the whole area of the regulation of the use of force in foreign relations, and stated that relevant customary rules still applied, some of which, being in the nature of *jus cogens*, could not be varied by treaty.

According to Bruno Simma, neither Article 2(4) nor any Charter provision provides a basis for the criminal prosecution of individuals violating the prohibition of the use of force.[46] Therefore, the international community has not yet succeeded in completely transforming the respective principles emanating from the Nuremberg and Tokyo trials regarding aggression into valid international law.[47] Another commentator has expressed the opinion that the Charter does not per se declare war illegal or criminal, but merely a breach of treaty subject to the sanctions embodied in that treaty.[48] However, another view is that as pre-existing international crimes already entailed individual liability, it is therefore reasonable to extend the same principle by analogy to the international crime of aggression.[49] Further, under customary international law, war crimes and crimes against peace are subject to universal jurisdiction, so that all states are entitled to bring offenders to trial.[50]

Another matter to be taken into consideration is that the principles laid down in the Charter and Judgment of the Nuremberg Tribunal concerning individual criminal responsibility for aggression or crimes against peace had been approved by the United Nations General Assembly.[51] Moreover, the initial title for the then proposed International Criminal Court statute was 'Draft Code of Crimes against the Peace and Security of Mankind' (1954)[52] and later (1996).[53] However, both the General Assembly and the International Law Commission remained silent on punishment as this was envisaged to be provided for in the future by the then proposed but not putative International Criminal Court (ICC).[54] The advent of the ICC was the occasion for slightly more than glacial progress in further codifying aggression. A question of some merit is whether the judicial enforcement of peace is compatible with the role of the Security Council. However, this is addressed by the statute itself, which gives a perpetually renewable 'veto' to the Security Council concerning deferral of investigations or prosecutions.[55]

The 1998 International Criminal Court Rome Conference

The ICC negotiations led to the following compromise formula regarding aggression in Article 5 of the Rome Statute, which confers aggression and withholds its exercise pending a definition:

1. The jurisdiction of the Court shall be limited to the most serious crimes of concern to the international community as a whole. The Court has

> jurisdiction in accordance with this Statute with respect to the following crimes:
>
> [...]
>
> (d) The crime of aggression.
>
> 2. The Court shall exercise jurisdiction over the crime of aggression once a provision is adopted in accordance with articles 121 and 123 defining the crime and setting out the conditions under which the Court shall exercise jurisdiction with respect to this crime. Such a provision shall be consistent with the relevant provisions of the Charter of the United Nations.

However, the majority of participants at the conference to establish the ICC were in favour of including the crime of aggression. For instance, Mr Westdickenberg, who was the German representative, expressed strong support for inclusion of the crime of aggression.[56] He believed that a non-political, workable and precise definition of the crime of aggression could be found that conformed to the Charter of the United Nations.[57] Mr Baibourtian, the Armenian delegate, was of the view that the ICC should have jurisdiction over aggression. However, a clear definition of aggression was needed in order to avoid misinterpretation over the right to self-defence (a traditional right expressed externally by a state against other states) and self-determination (a non-traditional right expressed internally within the state between factions that otherwise owe allegiance to the state).[58] The latter was problematic because it undermined the legitimacy of the state by raising a right to self-determination that seemed to trump the presumed 'right to peace'.

Mr Bill Richardson presented a somewhat revised position for the United States from the view expressed at Nuremberg by saying that acts not clearly criminalized under international law should be excluded from the definition of aggression and that it was therefore premature to attempt to define aggression in terms of individual criminal responsibility.[59]

Leading up to Article 5 reproduced above, Mr van der Wind for the Netherlands said that it was unclear whether the crime of aggression should be included.[60] He suggested that although the number of states accepting inclusion had risen over the years, much would depend on the definition and the role of the Security Council. He identified two precedents for the definition of aggression: the statutes of the Nuremberg and Tokyo Tribunals and General Assembly resolution 3314 (XXLX) of 14 December 1974.[61] Regarding the Security Council, the issue was whether the ICC might consider the crime of aggression only after the Council had determined that a state had committed such an act (and the ICC would then have the duty to look into the criminal responsibility of the person who had ordered that act) or whether the ICC might also consider a crime of aggression without such a prior determination by the Council.[62] Further, the crime of aggression had been discussed in the Preparatory Committee on the Establishment of an International Criminal Court, initially on the basis of the definition included in the Nuremberg Charter and of the definition included in General Assembly resolution 3314 (XXIX) of 14 December 1974. During those discussions, it had become clear that neither of the precedents was considered acceptable or appropriate for full inclusion.[63]

Mr Lloyd, representing the United Kingdom and speaking on behalf of the European Union, the central and Eastern European countries associated with the European Union, the associated country of Cyprus and the European Free Trade Association countries of Iceland and Norway, said that the ICC should have jurisdiction over the crime of aggression, properly defined, but without detracting from the role of the Security Council in maintaining international peace and security.[64]

Mr Omar, representing South Africa and speaking on behalf of the Southern African Development Community (SADC), said that the ICC was a necessary element for peace and security in the world and must therefore have inherent jurisdiction over aggression.[65]

Mr Hassouna, who was the observer for the League of Arab States, expressed support for the principle of including the crime of aggression in the list of crimes within the jurisdiction of the ICC, taking into account the definition of aggression contained in General Assembly resolution 3314 (XXDQ) of 14 December 1974 and the distinction between aggression and the right of peoples to armed struggle.[66] There being no agreed definition of the crime of terrorism, Mr Hassouna stated that he would prefer not to see that crime included in the statute, but if it was included, he suggested that it might be guided by the definition of the crime of aggression and the crime of terrorism laid down in the Arab Convention for the Suppression of Terrorism adopted in Cairo in April 1998.[67]

Mr Mirzaee Yengejeh, the delegate for the Islamic Republic of Iran and speaking on behalf of the member states of the Movement of Non-Aligned Countries, expressed disappointment over not including the crime of aggression. Mr Yengejeh's view was that the difficulties that allegedly would result from aggression's inclusion were pretexts for excluding the 'mother of crimes' as recognized by the Nuremberg Tribunal and as called for in the declaration by the Ministerial Meeting of the Coordinating Bureau of the Movement of Non-Aligned Countries, held at Cartagena de Indias, Colombia, on 19 and 20 May 1998.[68] In saying this, the delegate was probably referring to the Nuremberg International Military Tribunal, which famously characterized 'a war of aggression as the supreme international crime in that it contained within itself the accumulated evil of the whole'.[69]

In opposing the inclusion of aggression, Israel and Pakistan found themselves in close agreement. Mr Nathan, representing Israel, was not convinced that the crime of aggression should be included in the ICC's jurisdiction.[70] This was because he believed penal sanctions should be based on precise and universally accepted definitions and not politically motivated ones.[71] Although there were the precedents of the Nuremberg crimes against peace and the General Assembly resolution 3314 (XXIX), no exhaustive enumeration of acts of aggression was possible.[72] Further, according to Nathan, acts of aggression were committed by states against states. In addition, even if the crime was included, it would be subject to Security Council determination which would prejudice both the defence and the ICC's independence.[73] His suggestion, therefore, was that aggression be postponed for a future review conference, pending the development of an acceptable definition.[74]

Mr Mahmood, speaking for Pakistan, opposed the inclusion of aggression for its controversial nature.[75] The definition of aggression that had been adopted by the General Assembly in 1974 was considered by Pakistan as not only non-binding but more political than legal.[76] Any role for the Security Council would introduce a political element which would undermine the state sovereignty.[77] Furthermore, aggression was traditionally considered a crime committed by states, whereas Pakistan favoured the principle that the ICC's jurisdiction should be limited only to crimes committed by individuals.[78] Mr Sadi, the Jordanian delegate, stated that he would prefer to maintain the reference to aggression as a crime subject to the jurisdiction of the ICC, but was open to deferring its definition to a later stage if an acceptable formula could not be found.[79] This was what transpired eventually.

What the diplomats sounding a discordant note at the negotiations neglected to mention was that a clear distinction must be maintained between a finding of factual aggression under the United Nations Charter[80] and a charge of criminal aggression, such as that under the contemplations of the Rome Statute for the International Criminal Court[81] and domestic penal legislation in Germany, Japan, Switzerland, Austria, Russia and Sweden.[82] The former entails state responsibility, the latter individual criminal responsibility. One is political and the other is judicial. Presumably, the latest effort under the ICC process will allay such concerns should the states have maintained their position.

The ICC Special Working Group on the Crime of Aggression

The ICC Special Working Group on the Crime of Aggression is mandated by the State parties to prepare a draft definition and conditions for the exercise of jurisdiction for discussion at the next review conference. They are at the forefront of the development of the law and have developed a possible definition of the crime of aggression as per draft Article 8*bis*:[83]

> 'crime of aggression' means the planning, preparation, initiation or execution, by a person in a position effectively to exercise control over or to direct the political or military action of a State, of an act of aggression which, by its character, gravity and scale, constitutes a manifest violation of the Charter of the United Nations.

This provision is plainly a marriage between the Nuremberg definition and the United Nations General Assembly definition of aggression. This is clearly so when 'act of aggression' for the purpose of the provision means the use of armed force by a state against the sovereignty, territorial integrity or political independence of another state, or in a way otherwise inconsistent with the Charter of the United Nations.[84] This definition is explicitly derived from United Nations General Assembly resolution 3314 (XXIX) of 14 December 1974.

The exercise of jurisdiction over the crime of aggression is addressed in draft Article 15*bis*, which lays down alternative options for acting after ascertaining whether the Security Council has made a determination of an act of aggression committed by the state concerned.

Access to justice in the ICC: victims' participation

The ICC's Trial Chamber II had occasion to review the relevant law concerning victims' participation on 3 November 2011 (ICC 2010). The Chamber noted specifically Articles 68(3), 21(2) and (3) of the Rome Statute, rules 85 to 93 of the Rules of Procedure and Evidence and regulations 86 and 87 of the Regulations of the Court.

Article 68(3) of the Statute states that where the personal interests of the victims are affected, their views and concerns should be presented and considered at appropriate stages of the proceedings. The question as to whether the victims' personal interests are affected by those judicial proceedings is to be assessed on a case-by-case basis.

Other relevant international human rights instruments the Chamber looked at included the 'Declaration of Basic Principles of Justice for Victims of Crime and Abuse of Power', the 'Basic Principles and Guidelines on the Right to a Remedy and Reparation for Victims of Gross Violations of International Human Rights Law and Serious Violations of International Humanitarian Law', and the 'Convention on the Rights of the Child'. Moreover, the 'right to an effective remedy' and the 'right to have access to justice', which lie at the heart of victims' rights are also found in Articles 2(3)(a) and 14(1) of the International Covenant on Civil and Political Rights, Articles 6(1) and 13 of the (European) Convention for the Protection of Human Rights and Fundamental Freedoms, Article 7(1)(a) of the African Charter on Human and Peoples' Rights, and Articles 8(1) and 25(1) of the American Convention on Human Rights.

Individuals, therefore, have standing at the ICC but at the moment only for breaches of the *jus in bello* given the slow progress in invoking ICC jurisdiction over the crime of aggression. Strictly speaking, breaching *jus ad bellum* is not a violation of individuals' rights. However, because of the factual as opposed to theoretical interplay between the *jus ad bellum* and the *jus in bello* even where there is no access to justice for the former there is still recourse to justice mechanisms for the latter. Moreover, domestic aspects of the law regulating force have a powerful role to play in this regard.

Individual civil responsibility for aggression

Individual civil responsibility for aggression or violations of the *jus ad bellum* is uncharted territory. This situation of limbo will not last indefinitely however.

The ICC Statute in Article 75 provides for reparations to victims including restitution, compensation and rehabilitation against a convicted person or through the Trust Fund established under Article 79.

Who is the victim of aggression is the crucial question here. The ICC has jurisdiction with respect to the crime of aggression under Article 8. There 'crime of aggression' means the planning, preparation, initiation or execution, by a person in a position effectively to exercise control over or to direct the political or military action of a state, of an act of aggression that, by its character, gravity and scale, constitutes a manifest violation of the Charter of the United Nations. On the other hand 'act of aggression' means the use of armed force by a state against the sovereignty, territorial integrity or political independence of another state, or in any other manner inconsistent with the Charter of the United Nations.

Certain acts (drawn from United Nations General Assembly resolution 3314 (XXIX) of 14 December 1974) qualify as acts of aggression. These are blockading, invading, attacking, military occupation or the use of any weapons against the territory of another state, and an attack on the armed forces of another state. Those examples suffice to demonstrate that the 'victim' of aggression in most instances is the state. The only exception is attacks on the armed forces of a state. At this stage, therefore, the only hypothetical possibility would be an attack on the armed forces of another state where members of the armed forces would be the victims in question.

It must be noted that the ICC under Article 258 exercise jurisdiction through individual criminal responsibility over natural persons. In respect of the crime of aggression, that applies only to persons in a position effectively to exercise control over or to direct the political or military action of a state. This does not affect the state responsibility under international law.

Friedrich Rosenfeld finds it 'tempting to apply the concepts and principles that have emerged in the field of state responsibility by analogy to individual civil responsibility'.[85] In the end he finds that:[86]

> Acknowledging an individual right for violations of the *ius ad bellum* is not irreconcilable with the proposition that the *ius ad bellum* protects the sovereignty of states. As has been shown above, the notion of sovereignty has changed. Due to the advent of international human rights, states are – to put it in Hobbesian terms – no longer comparable to a Leviathan, *legibus solutus*. Instead, they are bound to secure the autonomy claims of individuals. Individual rights are thus an integral aspect of sovereignty. Hence, there are good reasons to argue that individuals can fall within the protective ambit of the *ius ad bellum*.

The law as it stands does not support Rosenfeld's position. The better view is that any putative victims of the crime of aggression would be better served under the current regime of state responsibility. This is because the individuals responsible for acts of aggression would generally not be in the same financial position of a state to compensate the victims.

Cases

Prosecutor v. Dusko Tadic A/K/A 'Dule' (Case No. IT-94–1-T) decision of 2 October 1995, 'On the Defence Motion for Interlocutory Appeal on Jurisdiction', Before: Cassese, J (Presiding), Li, Deschênes, Abi-Saab, Sidhwa JJ.

Notes

1 UN General Assembly 1998: 18, Annex 1, Article 8*bis*, 'Crime of Aggression'.
2 This section is substantially based on work I have already done in Bikundo 2014.
3 Grotius 2005: 39.
4 Grotius 2005.
5 'All peoples have the right to national and international peace and security.' Organization of African Unity (OAU) 27 June 1981, entered into force 21 October 1986 Art. 23.
6 See, for example, UN General Assembly 1970.
7 '1. Every nation and every human being, regardless of race, conscience, language or sex, has the inherent right to life in peace.' 'Declaration on the Preparation of Societies for Life in Peace', (UNGA/Res/33/7315 December 1978), see Clause 1.
8 See, for example, 'Declaration of the Right of Peoples to Peace', (UNGA Res 39/1112 November 1984). It expressed 'the will and the aspirations of all peoples to eradicate war from the life of mankind' and in Art. 1: 'Solemnly proclaims that the peoples of our planet have a sacred right to peace'.
9 Kolb 1997: 553.
10 See *Prosecutor v. Dusko Tadic* A/K/A 'Dule' (Case No. IT-94–1-T) decision of 2 October 1995, 'On the Defence Motion for Interlocutory Appeal on Jurisdiction', before: Cassese, J (Presiding), Li, Deschênes, Abi-Saab, Sidhwa JJ paras 83 and 134.
11 Paulus 2004: 21.
12 Dinstein 2002: 109.
13 UN General Assembly, 'Definition of Aggression', (UNGA Resolution 3314 (XXIX)14 December 1974), Art 1. 'Aggression is the use of armed force by a State against the sovereignty, territorial integrity or political independence of another State, or in any other manner inconsistent with the Charter of the United Nations'; 'Definition of Aggression', (UNGA Resolution 3314 (XXIX)14 December 1974), Art. 2. 'The first use of armed force by a State in contravention of the Charter shall constitute prima facie evidence of an act of aggression although the Security Council may, in conformity with the Charter, conclude that a determination that an act of aggression has been committed would not be justified in the light of other relevant circumstances, including the fact that the acts concerned or their consequences are not of sufficient gravity.'
14 See, generally, Charney 2001: 120.
15 Article 6 of the United Nations, 'Agreement for the Prosecution and Punishment of the Major War Criminals of the European Axis ("London Agreement")', (82 U.N.T.C. 2808 August 1945a).
16 Glueck 1946: 25.
17 Article 17 of UN General Assembly, 'Rome Statute of the International Criminal Court', (2187 UNTS 3, Art. 83(2) (entered into force 1 July 2002), 17 July 1998).
18 Emphasizing that the International Criminal Court established under this Statute shall be complementary to national criminal jurisdictions.
19 Article 1 provides that the International Criminal Court shall be complementary to national criminal jurisdictions. Article 1 of UN General Assembly, 'Rome Statute of the International Criminal Court'.
20 Article 17 para 1 clause (a) ibid.

21 Ibid.
22 Article 17 para 1 clause (d) ibid.
23 Article 5 para 2 ibid.
24 Article 1: 'The Contracting Powers recognize that hostilities between themselves must not commence without previous and explicit warning, in the form either of a reasoned declaration of war or of an ultimatum with conditional declaration of war.' International Peace Conference, 'Opening of Hostilities', (The Hague III: ICRC, 18 October 1907). Article 7: 'The acceptance of mediation cannot, unless there be an agreement to the contrary, have the effect of interrupting, delaying, or hindering mobilization or other measures of preparation for war. If mediation, occurs after the commencement of hostilities it causes no interruption to the military operations in progress, unless there be an agreement to the contrary.' 'Convention (I) for the Pacific Settlement of International Disputes', (The Hague I: ICRC, 29 July 1899).
25 Maogoto 2005: 22. See also Simma and Mosler (eds.) 2002: 127.
26 Maogoto 2005.
27 Article 10: 'The Members of the League undertake to respect and preserve as against external aggression the territorial integrity and existing political independence of all Members of the League. In case of any such aggression or in case of any threat or danger of such aggression the Council shall advise upon the means by which this obligation shall be fulfilled.' League of Nations, *Covenant of the League of Nations*, (28 April 1919).
28 Alexandrov 1996: 43.
29 Kellogg and Briand 1928, vol. 46, part 2, 2343, Articles 1–3.
30 Israel 1967: 1265.
31 United Nations. 'Charter of the International Military Tribunal (London Agreement): Nuremberg Trial Proceedings'. London: United Nations, 8 August 1945b.
32 The International Military Tribunal of Nuremberg 1947.
33 *USA v. Von Leeb et al. Case No. 72 (The German High Command Trial)* 1949.
34 UN General Assembly, 'Definition of Aggression', 29(1).
35 United Nations International Law Commission 1966: 247.
36 United Nations 1945b, vol. 1.
37 International Conference on Military Trials 1949.
38 Ibid.
39 Ibid.
40 Ibid.
41 Ibid.
42 Ibid.
43 Ibid.
44 Ibid.
45 International Court of Justice 1986.
46 Simma and Mosler 2002: 127.
47 See, 'Formulation of Nurnberg Principles' (1950) in United Nations 1951: 191.
48 Green 2000.
49 Malanczuk 1997: 354.
50 Akehurst 1970: 18. Cited in Dinstein 1966: 16.
51 UN General Assembly 1946.
52 United Nations 1954.
53 United Nations 1996.
54 Dinstein 1966.
55 UN General Assembly 1998, (entered into force 1 July 2002).
56 International Criminal Court, summary records of the plenary meetings and of the meetings of the Committee of the Whole Official Records, 1998: 171, para 19.
57 International Criminal Court, summary records of the plenary meetings and of the meetings of the Committee of the Whole Official Records, 1998.

58 International Criminal Court 1998: 78, paras 83–84.
59 International Criminal Court 1998: 95, para 61.
60 International Criminal Court 1998: 146, paras 1–6.
61 International Criminal Court 1998.
62 Ibid.
63 International Criminal Court 1998: 171, paras 15–19.
64 International Criminal Court 1998: 66, paras 31–33.
65 International Criminal Court 1998: 65, para 15.
66 International Criminal Court 1998: 88, para 67.
67 International Criminal Court 1998.
68 International Criminal Court 1998: 321, para 17.
69 International Military Tribunal (Nuremburg) 1946: 13, reprinted in 1947: 41.
70 International Criminal Court 1998: 172 paras 45–51, see above note 55.
71 Ibid.
72 Ibid.
73 Ibid.
74 Ibid.
75 Ibid. 173, paras 41–3.
76 Ibid.
77 Ibid.
78 Ibid.
79 Ibid. 52, para 72.
80 United Nations 24 October 1945, Art. 39: 'The Security Council shall determine the existence of any … act of aggression'.
81 Ibid. Art. 5(1): 'The Court has jurisdiction … with respect to … the crime of aggression'.
82 Gewehr 2003, www.publiclaw.uct.ac.za/usr/public_law/LLMPapers/gewehr.pdf (accessed 2 August 2014).
83 Annex II Report of the Special Working Group on the Crime of Aggression ICC-ASP/6/20/Add.1.
84 See Annex II International Criminal Court 2009: 12–14.
85 Rosenfeld 2012: 251.
86 Rosenfeld 2012: 265.

References

Akehurst, M. 'Reprisals by Third States'. *British Yearbook of International Law* 44, No. 1 (1970): 1–18.

Alexandrov, Stanimir A. *Self-Defense against the Use of Force in International Law*. The Hague: Kluwer Law International, 1996.

Bikundo, E. *International Criminal Law: Using or Abusing Legality?*. International and Comparative Criminal Justice Series. Aldershot: Ashgate, 2014.

Charney, J.I. 'International Criminal Law and the Role of Domestic Courts'. *The American Journal of International Law* 95 (2001): 120–124.

Dinstein, Yoram. 'The Distinctions between War Crimes and Crimes against Peace'. In *War Crimes in International Law*, edited by Yoram Dinstein and Mala Tabory. The Hague: Kluwer Law International, 1966: 1–18.

Dinstein, Yoram. *Yoram Dinstein, War, Aggression and Self-Defence*. Third edn. Cambridge: Cambridge University Press, 2002.

Gewehr, J. 'Defining Aggression for the International Criminal Court: A Proposal'. (2003). Online. Available at www.publiclaw.uct.ac.za/usr/public_law/LLMPapers/gewehr.pdf (accessed 4 August 2014).

Glueck, Sheldon. *The Nuremberg Trial and Aggressive War*. New York: Knopf, 1946.
Green, Leslie C. *The Contemporary Law of Armed Conflict*. Manchester: Manchester University Press, 2000.
Grotius, Hugo. *The Rights of War and Peace*. Natural Law and Enlightenment Classics, edited by Richard Kolb III vols. Vol. II, Indianapolis: Liberty Fund, 2005.
International Conference on Military Trials. 'Report of Robert H. Jackson – United States Representative to the International Conference on Military Trials London 1945'. Washington DC: US Department of State, 1949.
International Court of Justice. 'Case Concerning Military and Paramilitary Activities in and against Nicaragua (Nicaragua V. United States of America): Merits'. ICJ REP 14, 27 June 1986.
International Criminal Court. 'United Nations Diplomatic Conference of Plenipotentiaries on the Establishment of an International Criminal Court Rome, 15 June–17 July 1998'. Summary records of the plenary meetings and of the meetings of the Committee of the Whole Official Records, 1998.
International Criminal Court. 'Assembly of States Parties to the Rome Statute of the International Criminal Court Resumed Sixth Session New York, Official Records'. Annex II: Report of the Special Working Group on the Crime of Aggression ICC-ASP/6/20/Add.1, 20 August 2009.
International Military Tribunal (Nuremberg). 'Judgment and Sentences'. 1 October 1946, reprinted in Vol. 41(1) *American Journal of International Law* (1947): 186.
International Peace Conference. 'Convention (I) for the Pacific Settlement of International Disputes'. The Hague I: ICRC, 29 July 1899.
International Peace Conference. 'Opening of Hostilities'. The Hague III: ICRC, 18 October 1907.
Israel, Fred L. *Major Peace Treaties of Modern History, 1648–1967*. Vol. 3, New York: Chelsea House Publishers, 1967.
Kellogg, Frank and Briand, Aristide. 'The Kellogg-Briand Pact and Associated Documents'. In *United States Statues at Large*, 27 August 1928.
Kolb, Robert. 'Origin of the Twin Terms Jus Ad Bellum and Jus in Bello'. *International Review of the Red Cross* 320 (1997): 555–562.
League of Nations. *Covenant of the League of Nations*. League of Nations, 28 April 1919.
Malanczuk, Peter. *Akehurst's Modern Introduction to International Law*. New York: Routledge, 1997.
Maogoto, Jackson Nyamuya. *Battling Terrorism: Legal Perspectives on the Use of Force and the War on Terror*. Aldershot: Ashgate, 2005.
Organization of African Unity (OAU). 'African Charter on Human and Peoples' Rights ("Banjul Charter")'. CAB/LEG/67/3 rev. 5, 21 I.L.M. 58 (1982), 1520 UNTS 217, 27 June 1981, entered into force 21 October 1986 Art. 23.
Paulus, Andreas L. 'Peace through Justice? The Future of the Crime of Aggression in a Time of Crisis'. *Wayne Law Review* 50 (2004): 1–35.
Rosenfeld, Friedrich. 'Individual Civil Responsibility for the Crime of Aggression'. *Journal of International Criminal Justice* 10, No. 1 (2012): 249–265.
Simma, Bruno and Mosler, Hermann, eds. *The Charter of the United Nations: A Commentary*. Oxford: Oxford University Press, 2002.
The International Military Tribunal of Nuremberg. 'Trial of the Major War Criminals before the International Military Tribunal: 14 November 1945–1 October 1947'. Nuremberg: The International Military Tribunal of Nuremberg, 1947.

UN General Assembly. 'Affirmation of The Principles of International Law Recognized by the Charter of The Nuremberg Tribunal'. New York: UNGA Resolution 95(1), 11 December 1946.

UN General Assembly. 'Declaration on Principles of International Law Concerning Friendly Relations and Cooperation among States in Accordance with the Charter of the United Nations'. A/RES/2625(XXV) 24 October 1970.

UN General Assembly. 'Definition of Aggression'. UNGA Resolution 3314 (XXIX), 14 December 1974.

UN General Assembly. 'Declaration on the Preparation of Societies for Life in Peace'. UNGA/Res/33/73, 15 December 1978.

UN General Assembly. 'Declaration of the Right of Peoples to Peace'." UNGA Resolution 39/11, 12 November 1984.

UN General Assembly. 'Rome Statute of the International Criminal Court'. 2187 UNTS 3, Art. 83(2) (entered into force 1 July 2002), 17 July 1998.

United Nations. 'Agreement for the Prosecution and Punishment of the Major War Criminals of the European Axis ("London Agreement")'. 82 U.N.T.C. 280, 8 August 1945a.

United Nations. 'Charter of the International Military Tribunal (London Agreement): Nuremberg Trial Proceedings'. London: United Nations, 8 August 1945b.

United Nations, *Charter of the United Nations*, 24 October 1945, 1 UNTS XVI, Art. 39.

United Nations. 'Yearbook of the International Law Commission: Documents of the Third Session Including the Report of the Commission to the General Assembly'. New York: UN Doc A/CN.4/22, 1951.

United Nations. 'Draft Code of Offences against the Peace and Security of Mankind'. United Nations, 1954.

United Nations. 'Draft Code of Crimes against the Peace and Security of Mankind'. United Nations, 1996.

United Nations International Law Commission. *Yearbook of the International Law Commission*. Vol. II, New York: United Nations, 1966.

USA V. Von Leeb et al. Case No. 72 (The German High Command Trial), XII Nuremberg (1948) Law-Reports of Trials of War Criminals. London: HMSO (1949).

8 Access to justice before international criminal tribunals

An evaluation of the scheme of victim participation adopted by the Extraordinary Chambers in the Courts of Cambodia (ECCC)

Susan Lamb

Introduction

The Extraordinary Chambers in the Courts of Cambodia (ECCC), an internationalized criminal tribunal established with United Nations assistance and located within the domestic legal system of Cambodia, adopted from its inception an ambitious form of victim participation in its trials of the senior leadership of the Khmer Rouge regime and others most responsible for atrocities committed during the Democratic Kampuchea period. Those urging the adoption of victim participation before the ECCC responded to perceptions that the ad hoc International Criminal Tribunals for Rwanda and the former Yugoslavia had failed to sufficiently empower victims.[1] They also drew inspiration from a much broader movement in recent decades towards the achievement of restorative justice by allowing victims to participate in proceedings and by providing compensation to victims for their harm suffered.[2] In addition to involving victims as witnesses and complainants, the ECCC is the first and only internationalized criminal tribunal to follow the civil law practice of including victims as parties to the proceedings.[3] The model of victim participation initially adopted before the ECCC permitted extensive rights of participation by victims within the ECCC's first trial (Case 001)[4] and fuelled early hopes that it may represent an innovative model of access to justice for victims in relation to trials of atrocity crimes before international courts and tribunals.[5]

Experience during the ECCC's first trial, however, forced a radical retrenchment of this scheme in advance of its second case (against the four surviving members of the Khmer Rouge leadership) in the interests of safeguarding the Trial Chamber's ability to render any timely verdict in Case 002, the tribunal's core case. While these reforms successfully neutralized the trial management impact of victim participation and preserved the possibility of obtaining a verdict in Case 002, critical questions remain regarding the overall impact of these measures on a tribunal already overburdened with insuperable trial management and financial challenges, and their efficacy in meeting the core objectives of the victims of Khmer Rouge-era crimes themselves.

Initial form of victim participation before the ECCC

Although a comprehensive system of victim participation was not a feature of the ECCC's framework agreement or other founding instruments, the ECCC's Internal Rules were drafted to provide victims the opportunity both to submit complaints to the Co-Prosecutors and to participate in the proceedings as full parties. The victim participation scheme adopted by the ECCC plenary permitted appeals of decisions by victims (as to be required by Article 36 new of the ECCC Law).[6] The initial form of victim participation enshrined in the ECCC Internal Rules, which drew heavily on the French model of civil party participation, was also a feature of the domestic legal system of Cambodia, within which the ECCC is embedded.[7] The original version of the ECCC's Internal Rules were adopted by the Court's plenary session on 12 June 2007, following which the ECCC became operational.[8]

Features of the original form of civil party participation adopted before the ECCC

Although championed enthusiastically by victim advocates, elements of civil society and some actors within the ECCC itself, the actual nature of the system of civil party participation adopted before the ECCC was poorly understood.[9] In its essence, civil party participation, a feature of many civil law legal systems, permits victims of crime to seek compensation from its perpetrators within the course of an ongoing criminal trial.[10] It follows that civil parties (victims admitted to participate in criminal proceedings) must substantiate their alleged linkage between the harm suffered and the alleged acts of the accused. All victims seeking to participate in ECCC proceedings were thus required by the ECCC Internal Rules to be clearly identified and to show direct harm stemming from the crimes for which an accused is charged.[11] Available forms of compensation were from the outset limited to measures which were 'collective and moral', and the costs borne by the perpetrator of the harm in question, i.e. the convicted person.[12] As victims participate in an ongoing trial, prior to any determination of the accused's guilt or innocence, victims were admitted to participate in ECCC proceedings following a determination that the facts alleged in support of the civil party application are more likely than not to be true.[13]

Once joined as a civil party and admitted to participate in criminal proceedings, victims enjoyed a broad cluster of rights. Amongst others, civil parties under the original scheme of victim participation before the ECCC were entitled to:

- receive all filings and access all information relevant to the case;
- request that investigations be carried out;

- request that witnesses be heard, or that they themselves be heard at trial;
- file motions on most issues at trial; and
- seek reparation for injury suffered at the hands of the accused.[14]

The ECCC Internal Rules also provided a separate complaints procedure, enabling victims of crimes to inform the ECCC Co-Prosecutors of their harm suffered or crimes they personally witnessed during the Khmer Rouge era.[15] Although complainants do not testify or otherwise participate in ECCC trials as of right, there is no barrier to their inclusion on the witness lists of any party where their testimony is considered relevant and probative.[16]

Impact of civil party participation upon the ECCC's first trial

In its original context, civil party participation enhances access to justice by removing the need for victims to initiate separate and later civil proceedings in order to recover financial compensation for their harm suffered. While civil party participation promotes judicial economy and cost-saving within domestic criminal proceedings, it was less clearly suited to the demands of complex, large-scale trials of atrocity crimes, which often have many thousands of victims and which frequently operate under significant time and financial pressure. Where the locus of these trials is a country and legal system still struggling to overcome the effects of armed conflict, and suffering from severe infrastructural and resource constraints, these difficulties are magnified.

A number of challenges to the operation of the civil party system manifested more or less from the outset of the ECCC's first trial, of Kaing Guek Eav (alias Duch) – the director and head of the notorious S-21 extermination facility. This trial, which commenced in March 2009, was by the standards of international criminal proceedings relatively straightforward, involving a single accused, essentially one crime site, and a relatively finite victim class. The accused in large measure also accepted responsibility for the allegations against him and generally showed little interest in contradicting the evidence of those victims who testified at trial.

Experience over the course of Case 001 nevertheless highlighted a number of trial management and other challenges stemming from the implementation of this initial form of civil party participation before the ECCC. First, relatively low levels of literacy and Internet penetration in Cambodia meant that notification of the right to participate at trial on the ECCC website would have been unlikely on its own to have located the majority of victims of S-21 or to have adequately informed them of their right to participate at trial. In order to ensure that as many potential victims as possible could be informed in a timely manner of their right to take part in the trial rights, a significant outreach campaign throughout Cambodia was necessary and could only be accomplished with the support of intermediary organizations. Many NGOs responded to this need and deployed their often scarce resources in disseminating victim information forms (the document which victims were required to complete in order to become civil parties, detailing the basis on which they sought to be joined to proceedings) throughout Cambodia. As many civil parties were illiterate, victim information forms were sometimes completed by the intermediaries themselves, on the basis of information conveyed orally by the victims and translated by an interpreter. To ensure that all parties to the proceedings could be identified and the trial commence without undue delay, a deadline was set for the submission of civil party applications, ensuring that some victim information forms were either completed in haste or submitted late.[17]

A total of 94 victims sought to be joined to the proceedings as civil parties on the basis of a claim to be either a survivor of the S-21 extermination facility or a descendant of a victim of the atrocities that occurred there. Ninety were provisionally admitted to participate at trial, on the basis of the information provided in their victim information forms.[18] From the outset, the ECCC was unable to fulfil its obligation to distribute to civil parties all documentation relevant to the trial, due to the voluminous quantity of documents at issue in Case 001, and the absence of a reliable postal service across vast segments of the country. This right to receive all material on the case file also extended to confidential documents. Although there was no suggestion that civil parties deliberately disregarded their obligations of non-disclosure in relation to confidential material in their possession, this obligation was difficult in practice for illiterate civil parties to fulfil, and documentary management was usually undertaken by the civil parties' lawyers. Indeed, meaningful exercise of most of the rights accorded to civil parties under this scheme in practice required victims to be legally represented; a role played by numerous civil party lawyers, frequently working on a *pro bono* basis. The civil party lawyers representing Case 001 victims spontaneously organized into four groups, all of which sought to routinely intervene on most questions at trial, often repetitiously and occasionally in contradiction to the stance of the Co-Prosecutors on some issues.[19]

Once the trial commenced, proceedings were slowed by difficulties faced by civil parties in establishing even basic features of their civil party claim, such as their identity. Even the establishment of one's identity is frequently difficult to substantiate in the Cambodian context, due principally to the widespread destruction of official documentation under the Khmer Rouge regime and its haphazard replacement over the years that followed. In many instances, inconsistencies in the spelling of names and dates of birth in civil parties' identifying information required considerable courtroom time to resolve. Some civil parties during their testimony also disavowed the contents of their victim information forms, citing interpretative or communication errors at the time they were recorded. Other civil parties, whilst undoubtedly having suffered profound trauma during the Khmer Rouge era, could not substantiate their claim to have been victimized at S-21 in particular or to be related to someone who was: an indispensable prerequisite for participation in Case 001. Questions regarding the accuracy or otherwise of information contained in victim information forms raised the issue of the proper weight to be accorded to them, especially where the authors of these statements could not be summoned to testify at trial.[20] As a result, victim information forms not subject to in-court challenge were ultimately declared by the Trial Chamber to be entitled to relatively little probative weight, on grounds that it would be contrary to fair trial principles to rely unduly on them in determining the guilt or innocence of an accused.[21]

Over the course of ECCC proceedings, the defence frequently questioned whether the presentation of statements of harm suffered in consequence of alleged crimes was unfairly prejudicial to the accused. It was also alleged that the accused, when confronted by civil party lawyers in court, thereby confronted a 'second Prosecution', in contravention of the principle of the equality of arms.[22] Although these concerns are mitigated by the fact that ECCC trials are not conducted before professional judges rather than a jury, the issue of how to most appropriately balance victims' rights of participation against the accused's fair trial rights was frequently contested and divisive.[23]

The clearest illustration of the inherent limitations of this system in relation to victims came with the issuance of the Case 001 verdict.[24] Delivered on 26 July 2010, the Case 001 trial judgement convicted the accused of crimes against humanity and grave breaches of the Geneva Conventions in relation to the more than 12,272 deaths that occurred at S-21 and related crime sites.[25] In consequence of a failure to substantiate their alleged link to S-21 or any of the crimes for which the accused was convicted, the claims of 26 of the 90 civil parties provisionally admitted to participate at trial were declared inadmissible in the verdict.[26] Although a handful of civil parties were reinstated following a successful appeal of the Trial Chamber decision to the ECCC's Supreme Court Chamber, this feature of the original scheme of victim participation was roundly criticized by victim advocates for having granted the appearance of full participation throughout the trial, only for this to be invalidated in the judgement.[27] Many victims are reported to have experienced the rejection of their civil party claims in the Case 001 verdict as re-traumatization.[28]

Nor did the reparations, which could be awarded in Case 001 appear to provide any significant succour to victims. Given the unfeasibility of individual financial compensation in light of the mass victimization of the Khmer Rouge era, reparation before the ECCC had been limited from the outset to measures which are 'collective and moral'.[29] The only avenue of financing reparations available under the civil party scheme was an award against the accused – a former schoolteacher who had, prior to his conviction, been incarcerated for 12 years – and who was declared to be indigent.[30] There were accordingly no funds available to support any of the reparations requests made by the civil parties in Case 001. Many of these requests – e.g. requests for the construction of memorials, preservation of the S-21 archives and sites, and for the provision of access to free medical care and educational measures to civil parties – also fell outside the jurisdiction of the ECCC as they were not measures which could be satisfied through orders made against the accused. Indeed many of the measures sought as reparation, such as improved access to health care and educational facilities, appeared inherently incapable of being satisfied by a convicted person and instead appeared to require state-wide implementation or governmental endorsement. Other measures, such as the institution of a national commemoration day for victims or the issuance of official statements of apology, also fell exclusively within national governmental prerogatives, which the ECCC had no competence to compel.[31]

Although victim needs in these areas were undisputed and deserving, many of these requests could not provide the basis of enforceable orders against Kaing Guek Eav. While the Chamber sought to grant all it could within the constraints of the prevailing legal framework the outcome appeared to be profoundly disappointing to the civil parties in Case 001.[32]

Reform of the system of civil party participation before the ECCC

In addition to disillusionment on the part of victims, the operation of the original system of civil party participation was also a source of concern to the Trial Chamber as it contemplated the inevitably far more complex trial management demands that lay ahead in Case 002. While victim participation had proved cumbersome in Case 001 and undoubtedly contributed to a prolongation of these proceedings, its impact was not fatal in the context of a trial of an accused who was only 67 years of age, in good health, and which took place before the ECCC Trial Chamber was seised of its second, core case. Case 001 also possessed a relatively finite victim class, and an accused who generally showed little inclination to challenge the basis of the victims' participation at trial or the substance of their reparations claims.

By contrast, the Trial Chamber in Case 002 confronted four elderly and frail accused who, at the time of the Case 001 verdict, ranged in age between late seventies and mid-eighties. All sought to challenge a broad range of the allegations against them. Further, approximately 4,000 individuals (represented by over 30 civil party lawyers) had sought to be joined as civil parties in this case. It was apparent that if the Case 002 accused sought to challenge the admissibility or substance of even a small fraction of this total number of applicants, the Trial Chamber would have been mired in the resolution of these challenges for months, if not years, in advance of either a trial or verdict in this case. A scheme granting rights of individualized participation in proceedings to this number of victims could not be meaningfully exercised by anything other than a small percentage of them without seriously retarding progress in Case 002, if not its viability. It was, however, considered imperative to conclude Case 002 expeditiously in the light of the advanced age and physical frailty of many of the four accused and the undoubted significance of ensuring that the ECCC's core case, against the surviving Khmer Rouge leadership, reached a verdict.[33] Whilst the individualized participation of approximately 4,000 individuals threatened to overwhelm the ECCC with insuperable administrative and trial management demands, the estimated total number of survivors from the Khmer Rouge era numbered approximately 1 million. The application by merely 4,000 victims simultaneously represented a significant outreach failure on the part of the ECCC in relation to the totality of the potential victims of Case 002, whose reach encompassed the entirety of the Democratic Kampuchea period and multiple crime sites across the entire country. Finally, and given the unlikelihood of the accused cooperating with any reparations awarded in the event of conviction or of significant assets being identified or seized within the likely lifespan of the ECCC, nor was Case 002 considered any more likely than Case 001 to deliver meaningful reparation for the victims.[34]

The potentially vast number of victims entitled to participate at trial in Case 002 thus threatened to overwhelm the ECCC's core trial and frustrate its main objective, including from the perspective of the victims – i.e. the achievement of a timely verdict. Substantial reforms were therefore necessary to the original victim participation scheme not merely to enhance the experience of victims but in order to safeguard the Trial Chamber's ability to reach any timely verdict in Case 002. [35]

The ECCC legislative bodies undertook systematic reform of the ECCC's Internal Rules over the course of 2010 and 2011. Given the widespread disappointment of victims with the outcomes in Case 001, this exercise was also seen by the ECCC as an opportunity to craft mechanisms better able to meet the legitimate aspirations of victims to achieve timely justice and meaningful – even if inevitably symbolic – reparation for the overwhelming harm suffered by so many over the course of the Democratic Kampuchea period.

Nature of the reforms to the civil party system in advance of Case 002

Although all members of the ECCC plenary acknowledged the need for substantial reform of the Court's civil party system ahead of the significantly greater trial management challenges in Case 002, the reform process itself was protracted and difficult.[36] This ambivalence was also reflected in the views expressed by civil society organizations engaged with the Court, whose input had been sought by the ECCC for consideration within the reform process.[37] As the Trial Chamber expected to be seised of Case 002 around January 2011, there was simultaneously little time available to conceptualize, build consensus around and implement all required amendments to the Internal Rules.[38]

The Sixth ECCC Plenary Session, which concluded on 11 September 2009, considered numerous proposals to amend the Internal Rules and adopted or formalized several measures to promote more expeditious trial proceedings. The Sixth Plenary voted to support proposals to adapt civil party participation before the ECCC in order to meet the requirements of trials of mass crimes and the specific Cambodian context, to promote greater efficiency in trial management and to safeguard the ability of the ECCC to reach a verdict in any future trials. These proposals were also intended to ensure that ECCC proceedings could respond more fully to the needs of victims.

The Plenary Session delegated to a subcommittee the task of drafting proposed new Internal Rules to give effect to the agreed concept.[39] The Plenary agreed that the key features of this concept, to apply at the trial and appeal stage in Case 002, would include:

- a single claim for collective and moral reparation, to be formulated on behalf of all civil parties. Civil parties would henceforth not participate individually at trial but would instead comprise a single, consolidated group; and
- streamlining of the representation of this consolidated group to enable it to be represented by two lead co-lawyers, supported by civil party lawyers.[40]

Having undertaken consultations with civil society in order to identify alternative participatory mechanisms better designed to meet the needs of victims, the Plenary also agreed to adopt other supplementary forms of victim participation, which would instead occur outside of formalized court proceedings.[41]

As the Plenary was aware that the judicial investigation in Case 002 was expected to conclude shortly, a number of measures concerning civil party participation were adopted immediately to safeguard the smooth conduct of the trial. These included:

- amendments to ensure that civil party applications can no longer be received during the trial. The deadline for the filing of all civil party applications in Case 002 was amended to ensure that all victims admitted to participate at trial were instead conclusively determined during the pre-trial stage;[42] and
- parties and victims may appeal orders by the co-investigating judges concerning the admissibility of civil party applications. Once this avenue of appeal is exhausted, no further admissibility challenges to civil parties are possible.[43]

The Rules and Procedure Committee reconvened to finalize the proposed rule amendments later that year and a Plenary Session was held to consider these proposed amendments in February 2010.

At the core of the reforms ultimately adopted by the ECCC Plenary was the removal of the right of individualized victim participation at the trial stage and beyond. In consequence of these amendments, victims admitted to participate at trial formed a single, consolidated group of civil parties. The purpose of these amendments was not to remove rights previously conferred upon civil parties but instead to ensure that these rights would henceforth be exercised collectively.[44]

Representation and articulation of the interests of this consolidated group of civil parties was vested in two newly created civil party lead co-lawyer positions;

one Cambodian and one international.[45] The creation of this office was intended to provide greater coherence, stability and continuity of the representation of victims at trial. The lead co-lawyers were entrusted with the 'effective organization of civil party representation during the trial stage and beyond', but could be supported in this role by civil party lawyers representing particular groups of civil parties or individual victims.[46] Although vested with the ultimate responsibility to the Court for the 'overall advocacy, strategy and in-court presentation of the interests of the consolidated group of civil parties at trial and beyond', the lead co-lawyers were enjoined to consult with individual civil party lawyers, and to endeavour to reach consensus to the extent possible when coordinating the representation of civil parties at trial.[47]

The February 2010 Plenary Session further empowered a subcommittee to explore possibilities for expanding the scope of the previous reparations scheme before the ECCC beyond reparations awarded exclusively against convicted persons. As experience under the previous rules had shown that where convicted persons are indigent, reparations awards under the classic civil party model were unlikely to yield significant tangible results for civil parties, the ECCC Plenary sought to identify and adopt a reparations model capable of achieving at least some tangible outcomes for civil parties participating in ECCC trials and for Khmer Rouge-era victims more generally.

The subcommittee addressed these limitations by proposing alternative reparations avenues that could instead utilize external resources or third-party funding in support of reparations. The amendments forwarded by the Rules and Procedure Committee to the Plenary proposed the creation of two reparations avenues additional to the traditional civil party claim against the convicted person.

The first allowed the civil party lead co-lawyers to request the Trial Chamber to recognize that specific reparations measures, designed or identified in coordination with the Victims Support Section, are appropriate for implementation with external funding. These amendments, which were ultimately adopted by the Plenary, clarify that such measures may be funded by donor contributions and developed in collaboration with governmental and non-governmental organizations external to the ECCC.[48]

As many reparations sought by civil parties in Case 001 were measures requiring the exercise of governmental authority, the subcommittee also proposed to empower the Trial Chamber to make non-binding recommendations to the Royal Government of Cambodia. These proposed amendments were not ultimately adopted by the Plenary, as they were considered to be beyond the scope of the ECCC's powers.[49]

Finally, and in recognition of the fact that many measures for the overall benefit of all Khmer Rouge era victims in Cambodia are best pursued outside of formalized court proceedings, the ECCC Plenary also empowered the ECCC Victim Support Section to develop and implement 'non-judicial programs and measures addressing the broader interests of victims'.[50]

Impact of these reforms on the ongoing trial in Case 002

Although the Trial Chamber could not eliminate all vestiges of duplication and unwieldiness from the courtroom over the course of Case 002/01, the lead co-lawyer's ability to coordinate and consolidate civil party participation and in-court representation significantly improved the manageability of trial proceedings. While vigorous debate as to the appropriate balance to be struck between the rights of victims participating at trial and the fair trial rights of the accused was a continuous feature of Case 002, these concerns did not predominate at trial. Conclusive determination of the right of victims to participate at trial during the pre-trial phase and removal of the right to challenge during the trial phase and beyond not only safeguarded the Trial Chamber's ability to conclude proceedings expeditiously, but also succeeded in ensuring a measure of certainty for those civil parties admitted to participate in proceedings.[51] Overall, the revised scheme of victim participation thus contributed to enhanced trial manageability and ameliorated a number of the undesirable features of the previous regime from both the victims' and Trial Chamber's perspectives.

Despite the criticisms that followed the rejection of some civil parties in Case 001, the ECCC was instead criticized for an overly permissive approach to admissibility in Case 002.[52] Undoubtedly, the broad inclusion of large numbers of victims within Case 002 complicated a number of the Trial Chamber's strategic decisions, such as the severance of proceedings in that case: a step which it considered to be vitally necessary in view of the size and complexity of the proceedings in Case 002 and the increasingly fragile health of its elderly defendants.[53] In determining the scope of Case 002/01 – the first trial in Case 002 – to be limited principally to forced evacuations and related offences, the Trial Chamber ultimately determined that these crimes have impacted virtually all survivors of the Khmer Rouge era, and that the continued participation of all individuals previously admitted to Case 002 therefore has no adverse impact upon the fair trial rights of the remaining Case 002/01 accused.[54] Experience before the ECCC therefore shows that joining of large numbers of victims to large-scale international proceedings may thus on occation hamper a Trial Chamber's ability to effectively manage already complex trials, or at the very least limit its operational flexibility.

Expanding the basis upon which reparations can be awarded before the ECCC has not been universally welcomed, and the overall direction of the revised scheme has been criticized by some as incoherent.[55] While valid, these criticisms assume, erroneously, that reforms made to the ECCC civil party system reflect efforts to devise a coherent model of reparation. In reality, they were measures designed solely to create *any* possibility of meaningful recovery by the victims in the light of the reparations outcome in Case 001. Despite the laudable aims of these reforms, the financing and implementation of this new and alternative reparations avenue have nonetheless proved challenging.[56] In support of reparations financed through project management, the lead co-lawyers have sought donor funding for reparations projects in a context of budgetary scarcity, and at a time when the ECCC itself has struggled significantly to marshal adequate financial resources to remain operational. To ensure that proceedings in Case 002/01 may result in meaningful reparation for victims, and in view of limited donor funds and finite human resources in both the lead co-lawyers' and Victims' Support Sections, the Chamber had suggested that the lead co-lawyers prioritize for development a small number of reparations awards out of the totality currently contemplated, and to commence preparation for their implementation as soon as possible.[57] In response, the lead co-lawyers indicated seven prioritized reparations projects for implementation and detailed fundraising efforts undertaken to date. While earlier indicating that no financial guarantees or funds have yet been secured in support of these initiatives, recent indications show that most priority projects have garnered the funds necessary to ensure their implementation.[58] Although it is perhaps too early to draw definitive conclusions, the extent to which significant progress has in practice been made by the Victims' Support Section in developing and promoting non-judicial measures is also presently unclear.[59]

Victim participation in international trials of atrocity crimes has undoubtedly led to a number of positive outcomes, principally in terms of the enhanced visibility it provides to victims, and the empowerment and succour it may provide for the relatively few individual victims who are granted the opportunity to take part in proceedings. However, many of the benefits claimed for victims from civil party participation could arguably be better or more simply obtained through other, less burdensome, methods – whether via testimony as witnesses, through the presentation of victim impact statements or through the official recognition provided to victims by the complaints procedure. In relation to the latter, the ECCC co-prosecutors developed a practice of acknowledging receipt of each complaint. This standard-form letter thanked complainants for their efforts to inform the Court of their experiences under the Khmer Rouge regime, explaining that information of this type was of vital assistance to the co-prosecutors in building a coherent prosecutorial strategy and understanding of events in Democratic Kampuchea. Anecdotal reports indicate that these letters are much valued by victims. Other stated benefits of victim participation, such as enabling the presence of victims as observers of the trial – could also be achieved outside of formal courtroom processes. To the contrary, the ECCC's somewhat bureaucratic, legalistic system of victim participation appeared often to be alienating to victims and ill-suited to fulfilling their genuine needs whilst risking the accomplishment of the ECCC's core objective – namely, delivery of a timely verdict.

Finally, difficulties of implementing the civil party system were often misdiagnosed as examples of individual failures of planning, prioritization or resource allocation, or of institutional lassitude.[60] Those tasked with the implementation and later reform of this scheme to the contrary came to realize that the problem was instead a systemic one: the objectives sought were inherently incapable of being achieved, at least within the real-world constraints in which the Trial Chamber operated, including the age and physical frailty of the Case 002 accused, size and scope of these proceedings, and myriad trial management challenges, and available resource levels, both human and financial.

Conclusion

The Trial Chamber concluded the hearing of evidence in Case 002/01 – its first trial in Case 002 – in July 2013 and announced that judgment would be delivered in this case on 7 August 2014.[61] While the ECCC confronted many challenges in obtaining a timely verdict in Case 002 – principally due to the advanced age and physical frailty of the accused – civil party participation on its own thus can no longer be described as an existential threat to the viability of ECCC trial proceedings. To this extent, the reforms to the civil party system were a qualified success. Questions nonetheless remain as to the overall impact and legacy of this system of victim participation on trials of this type, and its efficacy in satisfying the core objectives of the victims of large-scale atrocities. It also demonstrates some of the perils of transplanting domestic measure into immeasurably more complex international criminal proceedings.

The ECCC's original scheme of victim participation, in granting individual party status to all victims admitted to participate in proceedings, rapidly proved unworkable in the light of the overwhelming number of surviving Khmer Rogue era survivors, the size and complexity of Case 002, and unique features of the specific Cambodian context. Substantial remodelling of this system, while necessary to safeguard the ability of the ECCC to reach any timely verdict in its core case, nonetheless attracted fierce internal and external opposition, and was challenging to accomplish in a timely fashion. The need to undertake sustained, systemic reform of the victim participation regime also coincided with many other complex trial management and financial challenges. It is at least possible that many of the benefits for victims of civil party participation could instead be accomplished through measures outside the formal trial process, and which do not carry the same attendant risks to the expeditiousness of proceedings.

Although the ECCC's model of victim participation differs in important respects from the system enshrined in the Rome Statute, the ICC appears to confront similar challenges of manageability and coherence. The ECCC's experiences in victim participation have much to contribute to an overall understanding of the balance to be struck between trial manageability, and satisfying the legitimate aspirations of growing numbers of victims of atrocity crimes in relation to trials of alleged perpetrators. These experiences show that there is a high cost in disregarding systemic and practical constraints when embarking on ambitious restorative justice schemes within international criminal proceedings. Rather than burdening these trials with an ever-increasing list of ambitious extraneous goals, there may instead be benefits of greater clarity and modesty in one's objectives from the outset. In attempting to graft an inclusive system of restorative justice onto an already dangerously overburdened international criminal trial process, the ECC example shows that it is easy to risk the latter while falling far short of the former.

Cases

Extraordinary Chambers in the Courts of Cambodia, Case against Kaing Guek Eav, Case No. 001/18–07–2007-ECCC-TC.
Extraordinary Chambers in the Courts of Cambodia, Case against Nuon Chea and Khieu Samphan, File No. 002119–09–2007/ECCC/TC.

Notes

1 See, for example, Thomas and Chy 2009: 286, describing most national and international legal systems as failing to accord survivors an active role within proceedings, reducing them to mere witnesses for the prosecution, and claiming that 'this exclusionary understanding of survivors' role may cause survivors to feel marginalized and disempowered'; see also, 'The Victims before the International Criminal Tribunal for the Former Yugoslavia and Rwanda', op-ed by Swiss NGO Trial (alleging that victims are excluded from the conduct of proceedings before the ICTY and ICTR and that the victim 'can only be heard in his capacity as a witness' before theses tribunals, attributing this to the adversarial nature of these proceedings).
2 See SaCouto and Cleary 2008: 79–77, 'Advocates of victims' participation in criminal justice mechanisms believe that participation has a number of potential restorative benefits, including the promotion of victims' healing and rehabilitation [and] a sense of empowerment and closure'.
3 Ciorciari and Heindel 2014: 59.
4 Extraordinary Chambers in the Courts of Cambodia, Case against Kaing Guek Eav, Case No. 001/18–07–2007-ECCC-TC.
5 See, for example, Mohan *et al.* 2011, describing the ECCC's reparations scheme as having 'the potential to be the Court's most remarkable contribution to Cambodian victims and society, and the development of international law'; see also Thomas and Chy 2009: 155, 'With a groundbreaking scheme for survivor participation – stretching far beyond that of the International Criminal Court – the Extraordinary Chambers in the Courts of Cambodia (ECCC) have the potential to succeed where other tribunals have failed'.
6 'The Extraordinary Chamber of the Supreme Court shall decide appeals made by the accused, *the victims*, or the Co-Prosecutors against the decision of the Extraordinary Chamber of the trial court' [*sic*] (Law on the Establishment of Extraordinary Chambers in the Courts of Cambodia for the Prosecution of Crimes Committed During the Period of Democratic Kampuchea, 10 August 2001 with inclusion of amendments as promulgated on 27 October 2004 ('ECCC Law'), Article 36 new (emphasis added).
7 Cambodia's legal system, which is primarily based on the French civil law tradition, suffered significant setbacks as a result of policies adopted during the 1975–1979 period. While existing Cambodian criminal procedure applies before the Court, if that procedure does not deal with a particular matter, or if there is a question regarding its consistency with international standards, guidance is sought in rules established at the international level; see generally Agreement between the United Nations and Royal Government of Cambodia Concerning the Prosecution under Cambodian law of Crimes Committed During the Period of Democratic Kampuchea, 6 June 2011. See also Kaing Guek Eav alias Duch, Trial Judgment, E188, 26 July 2010 ('Case 001 verdict'), para 661: 'Although the Internal Rules depart from Cambodian national law in significant respects, the notion of Civil Party participation before the ECCC is derived from analogous forms of participation recognized before some national jurisdictions, including in the Kingdom of Cambodia'.

8 Internal Rules of the ECCC, adopted 12 June 2007 ('original Internal Rules'); see generally Internal Rules 18–20 (detailing the composition of the ECCC plenary body and other rule-making mechanisms of the ECCC). Unless otherwise stated, the Internal Rules cited below refer to the rules as amended following their eighth and most recent revision, which came into effect on 3 August 2011.

9 See, for example, Ciorciari and Heindel 2014: 62, 'Although admissibility standards applied by the [ECCC] Chamber[s] were in conformity with the Internal Rules and Cambodian procedures, they were apparently not clear to all parties in advance'.

10 Rule 23(1), Internal Rules: 'The purpose of Civil Party action before the ECCC is to: (a) Participate in criminal proceedings against those responsible for crimes within the jurisdiction of the ECCC by supporting the prosecution; and (b) Seek collective and moral reparations'.

11 Rule 23*bis*(1), Internal Rules:

> In order for civil party action to be admissible, the civil party applicant shall a) be clearly identified; and b) demonstrate as a direct consequence of at least one of the crimes alleged against the charged person, that he or she has … suffered physical, material or psychological injury upon which a claim of collective and moral reparation might be based.

12 Rule 23(11), original Internal Rules: '[T]he Chambers may award only collective and moral reparations to Civil Parties. These shall be awarded against, and be borne by convicted persons'.

13 Rule 23*bis(*1), Internal Rules.

14 See, for example, Rules 23(3), 23(6), 23(7), 55(10), 58(5), 58(5), 67(5), 74(4), 76(2), 79(5), 86, 89(1), 90(2), 91(3), 92, 94 and 105(1)(c) of the original Internal Rules.

15 See Rule 49(2), Internal Rules:

> The Co-Prosecutors shall receive and consider all written complaints or information alleging commission of crimes within the jurisdiction of the ECCC. Such complaints or information may be lodged with the Co-Prosecutors by any person … or other source who witnessed or was a victim of such alleged crimes, or who has knowledge of such alleged crimes.

16 Ultimate determinations of which individuals are to be heard at trial are made by the Trial Chamber (Internal Rule 80*bis*(2)). As more than 1,000 individuals were cumulatively sought to be heard by the parties during the first phase of the trial in Case 002, the Chamber was obliged repeatedly to stress over only a fraction of the individuals sought could ultimately be heard, in the interests of ensuring a fair and expeditious trial (see, for example, Agenda for Initial Hearing from 27 to 30 June 2011, E86/1, 14 June 2011; see also Confidential Annex A: partial list of witnesses, experts and Civil Parties to be heard during the first trial in Case 002, E131/1.1, 25 October 2011). Although civil parties may, and did, testify before the Trial Chamber in Case 002, the Chamber, in the interests of an expeditious trial, had to limit their number to a representative sample of those able to speak to facts relevant to the scope of the case (in support of the prosecution) and others who instead provided evidence in relation to suffering (in support of reparations claims) (see Direction to the Parties, E108, 8 July 2011, para 5).

17 See, for example, Decision on Request to Extend Deadline for the Filing of Civil Party Applications, E2/92/2, 10 March 2009 (rejecting, for lack of substantiation, a request of Civil Party Group 1 to belatedly admit the civil party application of Norng Chanphal (E2/92). One of the few known survivors of S-21, Norng Chanphal was, in view of his relevance, called to testify at trial as a witness.

18 Three victims withdrew their applications, whereas a fourth was rejected following late submission of his victim information form: see Case 001 verdict, p. 250, para 11.

19 See Ciorciari and Heindel 2014: 60–61. The four civil party legal teams in Case 001 for the most part 'worked independently, resulting in questioning repetitive not only with the Prosecution, but with each other'; cf. Internal Rule 23(1)(a) (providing that a purpose of civil party action before the ECCC is to '[p]articipate in criminal proceedings against those responsible for crimes within the jurisdiction of the ECCC by supporting the prosecution'.

20 As only a relatively small proportion of those civil parties provisionally admitted at trial were called to give evidence before the Chamber, the majority of victim information forms at issue in Case 001 could not be subject to adversarial scrutiny by the defence (see Case 001 verdict, p. 251, para 12 (of the 90 civil parties provisionally admitted to testify at trial, only 7 were called to testify before the Chamber. A further 15, however, testified regarding their suffering, in support of reparations claims)).

21 Decision on co-prosecutors' Rule 92 Submission Regarding the Admission of Witness Statements and other Documents before the Trial Chamber, E96/7, 20 June 2012, para 29 (finding that victim information forms, which were often completed by various intermediary organizations on behalf of civil party applicants, may ultimately be entitled to little, if any, probative weight in the absence of information regarding the circumstances in which they were recorded). Case 002 included statements of 3866 civil parties who were not called to testify at trial.

22 The principle of equality of arms between the prosecution and the accused is a core principle of fairness in a criminal trial and implies that each party must be afforded a reasonable opportunity to present his case – including his evidence – under conditions that do not place him at a substantial disadvantage vis-à-vis his opponent (*Prosecutor v. Tadic* Appeal Judgment, ICTY Appeals Chamber, 15 July 1999, paras 44, 48).

23 See, for example, Decision on Civil Party Co-Lawyers' Joint Request for a Ruling on the Standing of Civil Party Lawyers to Make Submissions on Sentencing and Directions Concerning the Questioning of the accused, Experts and Witnesses Testifying on Character, E72/3, 12 October 2009 (where, following a joint civil party request, the Trial Chamber delivered two decisions by a majority (Judge Lavergne dissenting in part) declaring that the civil party lawyers lacked standing to make submissions on sentencing, including submissions on a sentence to be imposed. The Trial Chamber also denied the civil parties' request to put questions relevant to the accused's character to the accused, two experts and nine witnesses).

24 Kaing Guek Eav alias Duch, Judgment, ECCC Trial Chamber, E188, 26 July 2010 ('Case 001 verdict').

25 Case 001 verdict, disposition.

26 Case 001 verdict, paras 639–649 (finding that despite the undoubted physical and psychological harm suffered by a number of the civil parties claiming to be survivors of S-21, the Trial Chamber could not satisfy itself to the required standard that these civil parties were in fact victims of crimes committed by Kaing Guek Eav. Other civil parties had been unable to establish either the identity of victims to whom they claimed to be related and/or their kinship to them).

27 See, however, Rule 100(1), original Internal Rules: 'The Chamber shall make a decision on any Civil Party claims in the judgment. It shall rule on the admissibility and the substance of such claims against the Accused'.

28 See, for example, Ciorciari and Heindel 2014: 62, noting research conducted by the Transcultural Psychosocial Organization (TPO), a Cambodian NGO, in the immediate aftermath of the verdict, which suggested that those civil parties who were rejected 'reacted with intense emotional distress' and viewed it as shameful and a personal failure 'as they could not fulfil the felt obligation to seek justice for the spirits of their relatives' (citing Report on TPO's After-Verdict Intervention with Case 001 Civil Parties, 27 July 2010: 2).

29 See Rule 23(11), original Internal Rules: '[T]the Chambers may award only collective and moral reparations to Civil Parties. These shall be awarded against, and be borne by convicted persons'; see also Case 001 verdict, footnote 1144:

> unlike ordinary Cambodian courts, the ECCC lacks the competence to award individual monetary compensation to Civil Parties. Reparations awards in the ECCC context are instead "collective and moral" (Internal Rule 23(1)(b)). Such departures from national law were considered necessary in view of the large number of civil parties expected before the ECCC and the inevitable difficulties of quantifying the full extent of losses suffered by an indeterminate class of victims. Reparations before the ECCC were therefore intended to be essentially symbolic (aimed at conferring official recognition upon victims, and assisting to restore dignity and preserve the collective memory) rather than compensatory.

30 Case 001 verdict, para 666: 'In the present context, constraints also stem from the overwhelming losses suffered by the Civil Parties and the unlikelihood of recovery from KAING Guek Eav, who appears to be indigent'; see also para 664: 'Where an Accused [is] indigent, there is currently no mechanism allowing the ECCC to substitute or supplement awards made against them with funds provided by national authorities or other third parties'.

31 Case 001 verdict, paras 670–675 (also rejecting all requests which, whether directly or indirectly, sought individual monetary awards for Civil Parties, or the establishment of a trust fund for victims, as these were beyond the scope of available reparations before the ECCC).

32 See, for example, Case 001 verdict, paras 667 and 668 (granting civil parties' requests that their names and those of the immediate victims be included in the final judgment, noting that although reparations before the ECCC are, strictly speaking, limited to measures ordered against the accused, the Chamber alone was capable of honouring the request to include the names of civil parties and their relatives who died at S-21 in the judgment. It noted that comparable, official acknowledgments of suffering before other international bodies have been characterized as reparation of considerable symbolic significance for victims. The Chamber also granted the civil parties' request that the statements of apology and expressions of remorse made by Kaing Guek Eav during the trial be compiled, on grounds that these may provide some satisfaction to victims and as they are in substance the only tangible means by which Kaing Guek Eav may acknowledge his responsibility and the collective suffering of the victims of his criminal conduct); see further original Rule 23(12), which provided that these awards may take the following forms:

1 an order to publish the judgment in any appropriate news or other media at the convicted person's expense;
2 an order to fund any non-profit activity or service that is intended for the benefit of victims; or
3 other appropriate and comparable forms of reparation.

33 Over the course of the trial, proceedings against two of the original four Case 002 accused were discontinued, following the death of one (Ieng Sary) on 7 March 2013 and the determination of unfitness to stand trial of another (Ieng Thirith) due to the impact of a progressive, dementing illness, most likely Alzheimer's disease. On 17 November 2011, the Trial Chamber declared Ieng Thirith to be unfit to stand trial and declared proceedings against her to be stayed (see, for example, Decision on IENG Thirith's Fitness to Stand Trial, E138, 17 November 2011 (and Decision on Reassessment of the Accused IENG Thirith's Fitness to Stand Trial Following Supreme Court Chamber Decision of 13 December 2011, E138/1/10, 19 September 2012); see also

Death Certificate of Accused IENG Sary, E270, 14 March 2013 and [Order Terminating] Proceedings Against the Accused IENG Sary, E270/1, 14 March 2013.

34 The ECCC, which is a criminal tribunal, lacks the capacity to enforce civil claims; see Case 001 verdict, para 661: 'The ECCC lacks the competence to enforce reparations awards. Reparations awarded by the ECCC against an accused can therefore only be enforced, where necessary, within the ordinary Cambodian court system'.

35 As the Trial Chamber noted, '[l]imitations of this nature cannot be circumvented through jurisprudence but instead require Rule amendments' (Case 001 verdict, para 662 (also acknowledging the principles expressing the right of victims of gross violations of international human rights to redress, as reflected in a number of international treaties and other instruments, but noting that the Chamber was nonetheless constrained in its task by the requests before it and type of reparations permitted under its Internal Rules)).

36 To give effect to these reforms, approximately 60 Internal Rules required either adoption or amendment. This workload comprised most of the agenda of three biannual ECCC Plenary Sessions held over the course of 2009 and 2010: see ECCC Internal Rules (revision 8), 3 August 2011.

37 See, for example, Diamond, 2009, acknowledging the ongoing reform process and the factors which gave rise to it, while describing the Chambers as 'seeking to further restrict the role of civil parties and their lawyers'. This paper, one of many submitted by interested civil society organizations upon the invitation of the ECCC, urged that the revised Rules 'not be used as a Trojan horse where, in the name of judicial management, the rights of civil parties are undercut to the extent that they could no longer in good faith be properly considered parties to the proceedings'. It considered that such an outcome would 'seriously undermine the very credibility of the Chamber itself' and described failure to retain certain minimum rights of individual civil parties as 'unconscionable'.

38 The need for the governing legal framework to be prospective added increased urgency to the amendment process, as it was considered necessary to enact any required amendments at the latest before the commencement of trial proceedings in Case 002, which were expected to commence around January 2011. The undesirability of retroactive amendments to rules in the midst of ongoing proceedings also ensured that no measures adopted in relation to civil party participation were applicable to Case 001 (Rule 114, Internal Rules).

39 ECCC Plenary Press Release 11 September 2009).

40 Ibid.

41 Ibid.

42 See Internal Rule 23*bis*(2)–(3) (determinations on the admissibility of all applicants are to be made by the Co-Investigating Judges within 15 days of notification of the conclusion of the judicial investigation).

43 See Rule 77*bis*, Internal Rules (challenges may be brought to any decision to admit or reject a civil party via an expedited appeal process). Although admissibility decisions by the co-investigating judges were still made on an individualized basis, those civil parties admitted to participate at trial form a single, consolidated group during the trial stage and beyond. If, after the Trial Chamber is seised of the case, the application of an individual civil party is declared inadmissible on appeal, that individual can no longer form part of the single, consolidated group (Internal Rule 23*bis*(3)).

44 See Internal Rule 23*ter*(3):

> At the pre-trial stage, Civil Parties participate individually. Civil Parties at the trial stage and beyond shall comprise a single, consolidated group, whose interests are represented by the Civil Party Lead Co-Lawyers.... The Civil Party Lead Co-Lawyers are supported by the Civil Party Lawyers.... The ... Lead Co-Lawyers shall file a single claim for collective and moral reparations.

45 See generally Rule 12*ter*, Internal Rules. The civil party lead co-lawyers derived their powers from the Internal Rules rather than from any power of attorney conferred upon them by pre-existing groups of civil parties or individual victims (Rule 12*ter*(2), Internal Rules).

46 Rule 12*ter*(5)(a), Internal Rules. Civil party lawyers were enjoined to 'endeavour to support the Civil Party Lead Co-Lawyers in the representation of the interests of the consolidated group', as mutually agreed between the civil party lawyers and the lead co-lawyers (Internal Rule 12*ter*(6)). This support could take the form of oral and written submissions, in-court examination of their clients and witnesses and other procedural actions. Such support is coordinated by the lead co-lawyers, who were further enjoined to 'balanc[e] the rights of all parties and the need for an expeditious trial within the unique ECCC context' (Internal Rule 12*ter*(3) and (6)).

47 Rule 12*ter*(3) and (5)(b), Internal Rules.

48 Internal Rule 23*quinquies*(3)(b) provides that:

> [i]n deciding the modes of implementation of the awards, the Chamber may, in respect of each award, either:
>
> a order that the costs of the award shall be borne by the convicted person; or
> b recognize that a specific project appropriately gives effect to the award sought by the Lead Co-Lawyers and may be implemented. Such project shall have been designed or identified in cooperation with the Victims Support Section and have secured sufficient external funding.

See also Internal R*ule* 23*quinquies*(1), concerning the general conditions for the grant of reparations before the ECCC. It was also amended by the September 2010 Plenary, but does not differ substantially from the previous Rule 23(11). It provides:

> If an Accused is convicted, the Chambers may award only collective and moral reparations to Civil Parties. Collective and moral reparations for the purpose of these Rules are measures that:
>
> a acknowledge the harm suffered by Civil Parties as a result of the commission of the crimes for which an Accused is convicted; and
> b provide benefits to the Civil Parties which address this harm.
>
> These benefits shall not take the form of monetary payments to Civil Parties.

49 ECCC Press Release, 17 September 2010.

50 In addition to requiring the Victims Support Section (VSS) to assist the lead co-lawyers in identifying, designing and implementing reparations measures (Internal Rule 12(2)), Rule 12*bis*(3) empowered the VSS to develop and implement 'non-judicial programs and measures addressing the broader interests of victims'. Non-judicial measures may, where appropriate, be developed and implemented in collaboration with governmental and non-governmental organizations external to the ECCC (Rule 12(3)).

51 This of course did not eliminate the workload stemming from admissibility determinations, but merely shifted these risks and burdens to an earlier phase of proceedings: see, for example, Internal Rules 23*bis*(2)–(3) (requiring all admissibility determinations to be made by the co-investigating judges within 15 days of the conclusion of the judicial investigation) and 63(6)–(7) (indicating 3 years to be the maximum allowable period of pre-trial detention of an accused before the ECCC).

52 See, for example, Ciorciari and Heindel 2014: 63, 'The Pre-Trial Chamber has arguably applied the admissibility standard too inclusively, admitting most of the nearly 4000 applicants'.

53 Decision on Severance of Case 002 Following Supreme Court Chamber Decision of 8 February 2013, E284, 26 April 2013 ('Severance Decision'), para 114:

> A further relevant feature of the ECCC legal framework is that approximately 4000 Civil Parties were joined to these proceedings during the pre-trial phase, following individual determinations by the Co-Investigating Judges that their harm suffered is linked to one or more allegations in the entirety of the Case 002 Closing Order. There is no possibility (legally or practically) of revisiting the basis of these admissibility decisions at trial or following the severance of proceedings in Case 002.

See also para 157 (finding that the Severance Order had no impact on the nature of civil party participation at trial. The Trial Chamber did not seek to reopen admissibility decisions taken during the pre-trial phase and the membership of the consolidated group remained unchanged following the severance of Case 002).

54 Cf. Ciorciari and Heindel 2014: 63, noting that out of the 3,872 victims joined to the case, only about 750 were formally admitted due to harm related to crimes at issue in Case 002/01.

55 See, for example, Ciorciari and Heindel 2014: 65, citing the perceptions of a civil party lawyer that the funding of reparations through donor contributions sets

> a horrible legal precedent, as reparations should be paid for either by the convicted person or by the state, not by NGOs through third party funding. Most concerning, the Court is putting the burden on victims to design and fund reparations themselves.

56 See, for example, Severance Decision, para 158:

> The Chamber has ... previously provided guidance to the Lead Co-Lawyers to assist their efforts in formulating requests that may result in meaningful measures in reparation and encompass the entire consolidated group of Civil Parties. [S] everance has no impact whatsoever in relation to the new and separate reparations avenue created by Internal Rule 23*quinquies*(3)(b), pursuant to which the initiatives proposed as possible measures do not result in enforceable claims against an accused, and may be developed in parallel with the trial.

57 See, for example, Indication of Priority Projects for Implementation as Reparation, E218/7, 4 December 2012 (clarifying that implementation of the civil parties' prioritized list of reparation projects began prior to the verdict in Case 002/01 and requesting, in consultation with the VSS, information regarding the current status of the financing of these projects in order to ensure that measures sought pursuant to Rule 23*quinquies*(3)(b) are able to be realized, with the support of donor assistance and external collaborators, within a meaningful time frame).

58 ECC Press Release of 21 April 2014.

59 See, for example, Ciorciari and Heindel 2014: 59, noting that the VSS, two years after the enactment of these reforms, had neither identified what non-judicial projects it would pursue nor clearly differentiated these projects from court-ordered reparations, concluding that '[i]nitial hopes that with its expanded mandate the VSS would undertake broader outreach to the general victim population during the Case 002 trial proceedings thus far remain unrealized'.

60 It was often alleged by civil society and critics of the court that if only sufficient goodwill, intelligence, effort, planning or resources had been allocated to victims, all difficulties associated with victim participation may have been overcome; see for example, Ciorciari and Heindel 2014 (alleging that the ECCC's challenges in the area of victim participation reflected in part 'UN neglect', unpreparedness, willingness to address problems 'only as they arose rather than [through] forethought', and 'inadequate planning and preparation on the Court's behalf').

61 Scheduling Order for the Pronouncement of the Judgment in Case 002/01, E310, 29 May 2014.

References

Ciorciari, John D. and Anne Heindel, Anne. 'Experiments in International Criminal Justice: Lessons from the Khmer Rouge Tribunal'. *Michigan Journal of International Law* (2014(forthcoming)): 1–77.

Diamond, Andrew F. 'Public Comment on Proposed Changes on Civil Party Participation before the ECCC'. Online. Available at www.cambodiatribunal.org/assets/pdf/reports/public_comment_on_proposed_changes_to_civil_party_participation_12_2_09.pdf (accessed 4 August 2014). Documentation Center of Cambodia (DC-Cam) 2009.

Extraordinary Chambers in the Courts of Cambodia (ECCC Agreement). 'Press Release: Sixth ECCC Plenary Session Concludes'. ECCC, 11 September 2009.

Extraordinary Chambers in the Courts of Cambodia (ECCC Agreement). 'Press Release: Eighth ECCC Plenary Session Concludes'. ECCC, 17 September 2010.

Extraordinary Chambers in the Courts of Cambodia (ECCC Agreement). 'Agreement between the United Nations and the Royal Government of Cambodia Concerning the Prosecution under Cambodian Law of Crimes Committed During the Period of Democratic Kampuchea ("Agreement")'. UN, 6 June 2011.

Extraordinary Chambers in the Courts of Cambodia (ECCC Agreement). 'Internal Rules (Revision 8)'. ECCC, 3 August 2011.

Extraordinary Chambers in the Courts of Cambodia (ECCC Agreement). 'Press Release: Wide Ranging Support Secured for The Reparations for Victims of The Khmer Rouge Regime'. ECCC, 21 April 2014.

Mohan, Mahdev *et al.* 'Victims' Right to Remedy: Awarding Meaningful Reparations at the ECCC'. *Asian Business and Rule of Law Initiative* (2011): 1–16. Online. Available at http://ink.library.smu.edu.sg/cgi/viewcontent.cgi?article=1020&context=sol_aprl (accessed 5 June 2014).

SaCouto, Susana and Cleary, Katherine. 'Victims' Participation in the Investigations of the International Criminal Court'. *Journal of Transnational Law and Contemporary Problems* 73 (2008): 74–99.

Thomas, Sarah and Chy, Terith. 'Including the Survivors in the Tribunal Process'. In *On Trial: The Khmer Rouge Accountability Process*, edited by John D. Ciorciari and Anne Heindel. Phnom Penh: Documentation Centre of Cambodia, 2009: 269–294.

'The Victims before the International Criminal Tribunal for the Former Yugoslavia and for Rwanda'. TRIAL. Online. Available at www.trial-ch.org/en/resources/international-law/ (accessed 5 June 2014).

9 'Visions of a distant millennium'?[1]

The effectiveness of the UN Human Rights Petition System

Darren O'Donovan and Patrick Keyzer

Introduction

A later injunction of the then UN Secretary-General: 'We must move from an era of legislation to an era of implementation',[2] represents a fundamental challenge to the norm-laden, fragmented UN human rights treaty system. The past decade has seen much academic work questioning its effectiveness.[3] The question whether international monitoring bodies can cross conceptual, political and cultural barricades to ensure outcomes for individuals is at the core of a new focus upon implementation. Despite the ever-expanding corpus of human rights instruments, an allegation can be made that 'without (an) understanding of the connection of law and behaviour, an explanation for the very function of the international legal system is missing'.[4]

The ability of the UN human rights petition processes to deliver outcomes for individuals is a particularly challenging subset of the implementation problem. In this chapter, we discuss the relationship between Australia and the Human Rights Committee (HRC), the monitoring body under the International Covenant on Civil and Political Rights.[5] This relationship provides a stark example of what may be termed normative dissension between an international body and a nation state, illustrating the dynamics of 'decoupling', where a state effectively separates its international legal commitments from practical implementation. Focusing in particular on the reaction of the Australian government to the *Fardon v. Australia* and *Tillman v. Australia* communications,[6] we examine the discourses which Australia has adopted to insulate itself from the decisions of international institutions. Much of the scholarship about implementation has focused upon developing countries and developed arguments about incapacity as a ground for non-implementation.[7] The material traversed in this chapter demonstrates that even rich, developed, liberal democracies can pursue a policy of deliberate and persistent non-compliance. Ultimately, access to international justice in this context is meaningless if the parties to international human rights instruments fail to comply. In examining the patterns which mark the denial of justice, we hope to identify where the pressure points for greater compliance may lie.

Rights without remedies? *Fardon v. Australia* and *Tillman v. Australia*

The Optional Protocol to the International Covenant on Civil and Political Rights is the most prominent international forum for the vindication of the human rights of individual Australian residents. As Australia lacks a domestic national bill of rights, petitions under the ICCPR have emerged as a primary space for visibility and contestation. While complaints often result in increased advocacy platforms, the substantive implementation of the HRC's findings has regularly been refused by the Australian government.

Fardon v. Australia and *Tillman v. Australia* provide concrete illustrations of the dynamics of the system. These communications centred upon legislation in the Australian states of Queensland and New South Wales, respectively, which authorize the Supreme Court of each state to order the continuing imprisonment of a serious sex offender after the conclusion of the offender's prison term if they are judged to be an unacceptable risk to the community if released.[8] The Queensland law was different from the well-known regimes for the detention of sexually violent predators in the United States, which require a finding of mental abnormality and only authorize detention in a secure treatment facility (not a prison).[9] The Queensland law requires no finding of mental abnormality and authorizes civil commitment to prison.[10] The Queensland legislation survived a constitutional challenge in Australia's High Court.[11] It had been argued that the law infringed the separation of judicial power effected by the Australian constitution by authorizing a court capable of exercising federal judicial power (the Supreme Court of Queensland) to order the imprisonment of a person without a predicate finding of criminal guilt. Previously, three members of the seven-member High Court had expressed the opinion that, subject to a number of exceptions that did not include the re-imprisonment of sex offenders on the basis of a risk assessment, 'the involuntary detention of a citizen in custody is penal or punitive in character and, under our system of government, exists only as an incident of the exclusively judicial function of adjudging and punishing criminal guilt'.[12] This principle was applied by two members of the High Court in a subsequent decision,[13] but only by the dissentient, Kirby J, in the High Court.[14] A majority of the High Court held that the legislation's purpose was preventive and not punitive and that it did not violate the institutional integrity of the Supreme Court.[15]

The findings of the High Court majority diverge from pre-existing judicial pronouncements regarding the punitive character of imprisonment.[16] The Queensland government's assertion of a rehabilitative purpose was not and cannot be supported by the substantive content of the legislation, as Justice Kirby underlined in his dissent:

> If the real objective of the Act were to facilitate rehabilitation of certain prisoners retained in prison under a 'continuing detention order', significant, genuine and detailed provisions would have appeared in the Act for care,

> treatment and rehabilitation. There are none. Instead, the detainee remains effectively a prisoner. He or she is retained in a penal custodial institution, even as here the very prison in which the sentences of judicial punishment have been served. After the judicial sentence has concluded, the normal incidents of punishment continue. They are precisely the same.[17]

The grounded nature of Kirby J's critique underscores the forced quality of the reasoning of the majority – that such extraordinary forms of civil commitment sat comfortably within the traditional modes of criminal process and sentencing that had hitherto operated in Australia.[18] As noted above, the Queensland law was completely unprecedented – the systems in the states of the United States only authorize detention in a special treatment facility, not a prison.[19]

With domestic remedies now exhausted, counsel on behalf of Robert Fardon and Ken Tillman[20] took communications to the HRC, which were filed in 2007. These alleged that the preventive detention regimes that were applied to them inflict arbitrary detention contrary to Article 9(1),[21] violate the right to a fair trial under Article 14(1),[22] violate the rule against double punishment in Article 14(7)[23] and constitute a retroactive infliction of further punishment contrary to Article 15(1) of the ICCPR.[24] In its existing jurisprudence, the HRC had stressed that the concept of 'arbitrariness' proscribed detention 'that is inappropriate, unjust and unpredictable'.[25] This does not prohibit state parties to the Covenant from authorizing their courts to order indefinite sentences that contain a preventive component.[26] However, if a state party is able to achieve its legitimate ends by means less invasive than that of detention, then detention will be considered to be arbitrary. In *Fardon* and in *Tillman* it was accepted by the HRC that the rehabilitation and treatment of sex offenders was a legitimate objective, but the unmodulated use of re-imprisonment was not proportionate to this goal. A more balanced approach would require the use of purpose-designed, non-punitive facilities directed towards the objectives of offender treatments, together with long-term strategies contemplating monitored release into community settings.[27] The Australian government opposed this, stating:

> The complainant argues that the mere fact that the detention takes place in a prison gives it a predominantly punitive character and that detention would need to take place in a special mental facility or hospital to avoid this.... The Australian Government submits that this is not the case. As stated above, the complainant has access to the best available rehabilitative resources and facilities within the prison system. This enables the government to achieve the dual goals of ensuring the safety of the community through detention in a secure facility and rehabilitation by providing the individual with the most appropriate therapy.[28]

On 18 March 2010 the HRC, in an 11–2 ruling, upheld Fardon and Tillman's complaints under Article 9. The Committee also concluded that the Queensland legislation breached the Article 14 guarantee of a fair trial and the Article 15 guarantee against the retroactive infliction of punishment. It underlined that imprisonment is penal in character and cannot be ordered following a civil trial. As Australia had conceded that the system of continuing detention orders 'was designed to be civil in character', it did not meet the due process guarantees required under Article 14, which require a fair trial in which a penal sentence is imposed.

The government's response to the Committee's views in the separate decisions was a bare document of five pages, half of which was devoted to a description of events that had occurred since the HRC communication. It took a confusingly passive view of the prevailing situation, rather than accepting responsibility for it:

> In relation to less restrictive means of rehabilitation, the New South Wales Government has advised that, in imposing a continuing detention order on Mr Tillman, the New South Wales Supreme Court was satisfied that at the relevant time, there was no treatment available in the community suitable to address his long standing offending behaviour. The Queensland Government has advised that the intensive counselling and rehabilitation programs Mr Fardon was required to undergo during his preventive detention were not available in psychiatric facilities outside of the prison environment.[29]

The non-existence of sufficient facilities and alternatives *is the* issue, yet the government response is to actually rely on these very shortcomings as somehow overruling the HRC's recommendations. Legally unacceptable practices are projected as realities that cannot be overcome. This is an extraordinarily constricted vision of how international legal obligations are to be translated to concrete circumstances, perhaps indicating that the stultifying effects of Australian legalism do leak into the international sphere. The passive circularity of the content of the response may also reflect a distancing by the Commonwealth based on the (illusory obstacle of) federal-state relationships, which are, of course, not cognizable or relevant under international law.[30]

Further reliance was placed by the Australian government upon the involvement of the State Supreme Court and Australian High Court decisions to defeat the Committee's findings. Yet the provisions of the ICCPR were not directly examined by these bodies, with traditional judicial views of the separation of powers and prevailing ideologies regarding the involvement of courts in distributive justice also mandating only bounded judicial oversight. The Australian government response thus tacitly relied upon the provisions of its own domestic criminal law to defeat international obligations. On 25 March 2013, the Australian Permanent Mission filed a letter responding to a follow-up *note verbale* from the Human Rights Committee with the Registry of the Office of the High Commissioner for Human Rights. This stated that having considered submissions from the parties, the government did not consider further action is necessary and that it now regards both communications as 'finalized'.

The response to *Fardon* and *Tillman* is only one recent iteration in Australian government resistance to the findings of the HRC. In this instance the HRC were open to objectives of the legislative scheme – and sought to focus the government on striking a more sensitive balance between the needs of the community and the human rights of the complainants under the Covenant. There were many ways for the government to engage with the Committee, even if it wished to reject its findings. The response provides no reassurance that the relevant government departments engaged in fact-finding or in ongoing communication with prison staff and state-level politicians. It does not seek to assure that Australia will endeavour to improve the existing prison environments. The absence of any constructive elements underlines the extreme nature of the government's conduct. The denial of justice and the disregard of international legal obligations, which previously triggered public confrontations and strong rhetoric, now occur with a whimper of administrative obfuscation.

The follow-up to *Fardon* and *Tillman* allows us to map the factors that aid or obstruct the effectiveness of human rights treaty bodies as access to justice institutions. Clearly, prisoners' rights, especially those of serious offenders, have consistently lain at the bottom of the 'hierarchies of sympathy' of the Australian public.[31] Yet, it is also clear that there were many pressure points that could operate to strengthen the case for reform, such as the cogency of Kirby J's dissent in the High Court, the critical perspective of psychiatric professionals and the fact that the Committee's views could not be characterized as absolutist or as a rejection of the interests of the community. In the remainder of this chapter, we use the *Fardon* and *Tillman* cases as a backdrop for a critical assessment of the 'compliance pull' of HRC findings within Australia. What factors operate to prevent or support national compliance with the Committee's recommendations? Can advocates counter the allegation that the findings of international human rights institutions are ultimately shibboleths valued only by a discrete human rights community but unpronounceable by other social actors?

Australia and the ICCPR

The prevailing view upon the ratification by Australia of the Optional Protocol to the ICCPR was that, 'should there be legitimate concerns remaining, after an individual's domestic remedies have been exhausted, in relation to an alleged violation of human rights, then it is entirely appropriate that the problem should be brought to our attention'.[32] Australia's compliance with the HRC views ironically reached its high point with the first communication heard before it – *Toonen v. Australia*.[33] There the HRC found a breach of Article 17 (the right to privacy) as a result of the criminalization of homosexual acts in Tasmania. The HRC-nominated remedy was the repeal of sections 122(a) and (c) and 123 of the Tasmanian Criminal Code. This was an early signal that the federal government would be called upon to implement the Covenant, even where state legislation governed the conduct in question. The Keating government responded by enacting the *Human Rights (Sexual Conduct) Act 1994*. The legislation was plainly inconsistent with the Tasmanian Criminal Code provisions and rendered the Tasmanian provisions invalid to the extent of their inconsistency, pursuant to

Section 109 of the Australian constitution.[34] Tasmania grimly declined to repeal the provisions however,[35] and so Rodney Croome, Mr Toonen's partner, citing his fear that he might yet be prosecuted under the Tasmanian law as a justification for standing, sought a declaration in the High Court that the Tasmanian law should be struck down under s109.[36] Tasmania conceded that if Croome had standing, the Tasmanian Code provisions would be held incompatible with this federal legislation and thus constitutionally invalid.

With the arrival of the Howard government in 1996, *Toonen* was destined to be an outlier. The pattern that emerged was one of non-compliance, which even went so far as to contest the competence of the HRC to make findings. In the years following *Toonen*, the federal government, across a variety of subject matters, from the mistreatment of children (*Bakhtiyari v. Australia*),[37] the right to family life (*Winata v. Australia*)[38] and arbitrary detention (*A v. Australia*),[39] rejected the substantive views of the Committee. The direct conflict with treaty bodies arguably reached its highpoint when the then Minister for Immigration Phillip Ruddock appeared before the Committee on the Elimination of Racial Discrimination upon its consideration of Australia's third and fourth reports. The minister directly challenged the competence of the Committee to assess the actions of the Australian government:

> I said to the distinguished delegate from India yesterday, that I remembered many years ago meeting Mrs Gandhi, and she asked me how long I was going to be in India.... I said to her, nine days, and she said, well that's good. Most come for two and then think they can write a book. And I think there is a sense of that in what we are discussing here.[40]

The confrontation led to an Australian government announcement that it would be bringing forward proposals for the reform of treaty bodies, a step widely construed as an attack upon their legitimacy. These directly confrontational approaches did not persist however, as the government ultimately decided to starve the treaty system of the oxygen of publicity, with the result that upon later instances of criticism by UN bodies 'silence effectively killed the story'.[41] The central plank of prevailing government responses has thus shifted to an emphasis upon resisting the authoritative legal status of the Committee's findings.

While it is legitimate to argue that decisions of the HRC are not formally binding, there is a growing recognition amongst academics and states that the decisions represent authoritative interpretations of the Covenant.[42] As a result, strong weight should be accorded to the decisions of UN treaty bodies by all organs of the state, and if a government seeks to reject a decision, it must do so with substantial, *objectively assessed* reasons. This latter requirement is best expressed by Scheinin:

> It would be wrong to categorise the Committee's views as mere 'recommendations'. They are the end result of a quasi-judicial adversarial international body established and elected by the States Parties for the purpose

> of interpreting the provisions of the Covenant and monitoring compliance with them. It would be incompatible with these preconditions of the procedure if a state that voluntarily has subjected itself to such a procedure would, after first being one of the two parties in a case, then after receiving the Committee's views, simply replace the Committee's position with its own interpretation as to whether there has been a violation of the Covenant or not. If a state wishes to question the correctness of a legal interpretation of the Committee, it should at least resort to some other procedure before an international court or independent expert body. As this is not likely to happen in practice, the presumption should be that the Committee's views in Optional Protocol cases are treated as the authoritative interpretation of the Covenant under international law.[43]

The Australian government has not put in place any objective mechanism to ensure it has itself properly construed its obligations under the Covenant. This could include an alternative international forum (as Scheinin suggests) but also a domestic mechanism such as an independent evaluator who would, in accordance with the rule of law, evaluate the legal position of the executive. This fulfils the requirement, forwarded by Tomuschat, that there is a weighty presumption in favour of the Committee's correctness, and any counterarguments must be detailed, tested and specific.[44]

Prominent academic studies of the Covenant support the position that Committee Views are 'in effect' binding.[45] Joseph *et al.* argue that 'rejection of [HRC] decisions is good evidence of a State's bad faith attitude towards its ICCPR obligations'.[46] The Human Rights Committee itself addressed the issue in *General Comment 33: The Obligations of States of Parties under the Optional Protocol to the ICCPR*, adopted on 5 November 2008.[47] It accepted that while its function is not 'as such, that of a judicial body', its 'Views' exhibit 'some important characteristics of judicial decisions'.[48] This included *inter alia*, 'the impartiality and independence of Committee members, the considered interpretation of the language of the Covenant, and the determinative character of the decisions'.[49] Thus, the *General Comment* established that views represented 'an authoritative determination' and state parties 'must use whatever means lie within their power in order to give effect to the views of the Committee'.[50] The adoption of the *General Comment* was not merely a self-referential process as the opinions of states supporting the draft *General Comment* represent state practice supporting the binding nature of its content.

The legal quality of the Human Rights Committee views has been further strengthened in recent years. Internationally, the International Court of Justice recognized the normative value of the findings in its *Diallo* judgment:

> Although the Court is in no way obliged, in the exercise of its judicial functions to model its own interpretation of the Covenant on that of the Committee, it believes that it should ascribe great weight to the interpretation adopted by this independent body that was established specifically to supervise the

> application of that treaty. The point here is to achieve the necessary clarity and the essential consistency of international law, as well as legal security, to which both the individuals with guaranteed rights and the States obliged to comply with treaty obligations are entitled.[51]

At first blush, the initial sentence seems conservative, but the Court's recognition endorses the prevailing approach of the HRC and links it to the fulfilment of the purpose of the Covenant. Australia's use of executive responses, which lack independence or adherence to the rule of law, to reject HRC findings is entirely inappropriate. Such responses fundamentally defeat the functional roots of the body identified by the International Court of Justice – 'clarity and consistency of obligations' and 'legal security'. They therefore represent not merely instances of non-compliance but also a threat to the fundamental purpose of the entire framework. It is important, therefore, that cases such as *Fardon* and *Tillman* be seen not simply as controversial cases but also as an attack by the Australian executive on the fundamental premises of access to international justice. Australia not only fails the test of compliance, but it also fails the far lower test of properly engaging with the deliberative equilibrium implicit in the entire treaty body system.

This argument is further supported by Australia's rejection of another core component of treaty body mechanisms: interim measures. A request for interim measures allows the Committee to ensure that irreparable harm is not caused while a complaint awaits examination. Such a step can frustrate the entire existence of the Optional Protocol process, as any subsequent finding by the HRC would have no possibility of influencing the conduct of the state which could not accord it any weight. *General Comment 33* recognizes the disruptive force of such conduct with an unambiguous statement that a failure to implement interim measures is incompatible with the Covenant. The illegitimate and expansive nature of Australia's resistance to treaty bodies is underlined by its rejection of the legally binding nature of interim measures and by instances where it refused to obey direct requests. This occurred, *inter alia*, in the *Bakhtiyari v. Australia* communication,[52] where the Committee's request that the Bakhtiyari family be released from detention while there were outstanding court cases was rejected. Since the passage of *General Comment 33*, the Labor government rejected an interim measures request relating to Sheikh Leghaei in April 2010. The HRC's request for interim measures was ultimately dropped without written reasons.[53] In 2012, the federal government returned a Tamil asylum seeker to Sri Lanka, with a spokesman stating that the HRC's urgent request not to deport 'carried with it no obligation'.[54]

Criticism of government non-compliance with Human Rights Committee findings has featured prominently in human rights scholarship in Australia. The debate about the 'legal quality' of HRC decisions can be frustrating for the individual clients given the manner in which it ultimately collapses into normatively sound, but practically disempowering, legalism. To return to practical action, we would propose an independent evaluation mechanism for any rejection of the

HRC's findings. If the government believes it possesses the correct legal interpretation, then this claim should be tested. The executive is disempowering the role of the legislature, particularly given parliament's new role in judging the human rights compatibility, as discussed later in this chapter. Existing government responses do not meet rule of law principles in the sense of objectivity or scrutiny. Such a mechanism would also undermine the polemical props that have marked Australia's rejections, particularly the rhetoric of nationalistic exceptionalism regarding the competence and legitimacy of a body, to which Australia has, ultimately, committed itself.

An ineffective forum? Enforcement typologies and the 'compliance pull' of HRC findings

In assessing HRC actions as an access to justice option, we must supplement the legal analysis above with an assessment of the enforcement matrix underlying the instrument. This reflects the reality that even if the decisions were binding according to legalistic criteria, their practical enforcement would remain dependent upon distinct enforcement processes. This was seen in the evolution in the enforcement of the European Convention on Human Rights, which is often conditioned by extra-legal processes such as European Union accession, democratic acceptability, attitudes amongst the domestic judiciary and the pressure of the Committee of Ministers of the Council of Europe.

The Open Society Foundation has estimated that only 12 per cent of the Human Rights Committee views are actually complied with.[55] On the basis of General Assembly reports from 2006–2011, Ulfstein estimates only 54 out of 474 findings were implemented. While such stark figures are bracing, it is also the case that the individual complaints mechanism serves other, more indirect rights-promotion purposes, such as raising the profile of issues and laying the groundwork for advocacy. Martin Scheinin underlines such diversity by highlighting that treaty bodies' most significant function may be 'to contribute towards the concretization and evolution of international human rights law'.[56] This evolution of a body of jurisprudence reflects a broader process than remedying individual cases. The HRC's view in *Young v. Australia*, where it identified violation of the Covenant due to the non-recognition of Mr Young, who was in a same-sex relationship, as a dependent for the purposes of the *Veterans Entitlement Act*,[57] provides a good illustration of this broader impact. Although it did not lead to remedies for the individual, it arguably advanced public debate on welfare and pension entitlements for same-sex partners towards its recent legislative recognition.[58] There remains merit in the HRC argument that 'all attempts to categorise follow-up replies by States parties are inherently imprecise and subjective: it accordingly is not possible to provide a neat statistical breakdown of follow-up replies'.[59]

Unlike other more general treatments of compliance, however, our analysis can be tailored towards a single national context. The figures above may reflect many trends at a state level, particularly incapacity of developing states.

Australia must be distinguished as it is an instance not of incapacity but of direct insolence. Specificity must also be attended to in analysing petitions taken under the ICCPR. The fact that 114 states have accepted the Optional Protocol may not be positive, as it may indicate an assumption that the costs of doing so may not be high.[60] Only 70 states, for instance, have accepted the compulsory jurisdiction of the International Court of Justice.[61] While the sample sizes are dramatically lower, other United Nations committees would seem to have higher compliance rates than those of the ICCPR complaints mechanism.[62] Finally, while the term 'compliance' has been used throughout this chapter, it is important that in the following section we are dealing with the effectiveness of the HRC actions. Compliance may not correlate with international law's impact on behaviour, as high levels of compliance could merely indicate easily met, low standards. Thus, the ICCPR may be more effective in countries which are more non-compliant than Australia. Furthermore, Australia's compliance levels may be built upon pre-existing correlation of existing laws with the standards at the time of ratification.

Cluster one: coercion and incentives

This cluster of enforcement resources relies upon activating rationalist responses within government elites, emphasizing in particular coercion based upon cost–benefit calculations and material incentives. While the Human Rights Committee does not possess direct coercive power, there are some possible material inducements and reputational constraints to be unpacked and assessed.

Reputational constraints

The past number of years have seen an emphasis upon reputational constraints as influencing state compliance.[63] There are several dangers in applying this approach to human rights. First, reputation must be disaggregated; the calculation that a country's reputation may be damaged by human rights breaches can easily be balanced by a government that wishes to project a reputation for toughness throughout its region. Furthermore, unlike other public international law, where obligations are interstate, human rights law addresses the relationship between the state and the individual.[64] Adverse perceptions of a country as an unreliable future contracting party are less likely to arise in such a context. Downs and Jones have found that 'reputation promotes compliance with international law most in trade and security and least in environmental regulation and human rights'.[65] This reflects the fact that fear of reciprocal violation does not arise where the legal norms are regulating interactions.

The introduction of the peer-to-peer review Universal Periodic Review (UPR) system seeks to reignite interstate engagement. Australia's first review under this system was completed in 2011. It occurred at a time when reputational concerns were at their highest: Australia was pursuing a candidacy for a seat on the UN Security Council. Its election manifesto included the claim that Australia would be a 'principled advocate of human rights for all'.[66] Clearly such statements yielded a heightened sensitivity to the operation of the UPR process, whereby the United Nations Human Rights Council would be examining Australia's domestic human rights record. The process secured a headline commitment by the Australian government to implementing, in full or in part, 90 per cent of the 145 recommendations made by 53 member states of the Council.[67] Yet the ambiguities and abstractness of these commitments were underlined by recommendation 17, which called upon Australia to bring 'domestic law and practice into line with international obligations'.[68] Australia accepted this recommendation, but a passive posture was immediately registered by the supporting statement that 'Australian practice is to satisfy itself that legislation and policies necessary to implement a treaty are in place before Australia becomes bound by it'.[69]

Perceptions that the treaty bodies are linked to the Human Rights Council must be avoided to ensure the legal nature of Australia's obligations are not obscured. The nature of the UPR process allows it to be easily politicized; Iran, for instance, was one of the few states highlighting prisoners' rights, something which could be easily exploited by Australian politicians. The selective visibility and generality of the process leads to selective oversight of rights and less than specific recommendations and responses. The sole mention of prisoners' rights, outside of the specific issue of unacceptable incarceration rates and treatment of Australia's indigenous peoples, came in recommendation 71.[70] This called for Australia to 'enact legislation to ensure the humane treatment of prisoners'. Australia's response was a putative acceptance, but one bearing a tone of normative and functional distancing more than of legal responsibility:

> States and Territories are responsible for managing and operating prisons and consider that existing legislation and policies ensure humane treatment of prisoners. States and Territories will continue to deliver corrective services in accordance with standard guidelines which comply with the UN Standard Minimum Rules for the Treatment of Prisoners.[71]

This is not to undermine some laudable commitments generated by the UPR.[72] The implementation of these will now be monitored regularly by the Australian Human Rights Commission, until Australia's second UPR assessment in 2016. It must be recognized, however, that with the successful election of Australia to the Security Council in 2012 there is an argument that the sensitivity of Australian officials to adverse human rights findings may lessen. The overarching pattern for Australian foreign policy is that any allegations of non-implementation of human rights obligations can be compartmentalized, a calculation underlying current refugee resettlement policies in particular. Australia rarely appears to suffer any ripple effects upon its broader credibility as an international partner.

Norm internalization

Estimating the role of coercion or material inducements to compliance also depends upon the ability to connect, if not incorporate, international legal obligations with the domestic legal system. Australia, however, remains largely resistant to the internalization of international law rules whether within the courts or through executive and legislative actions.

The Australian judiciary, with the exception of Kirby J,[73] have largely eschewed any prominent role for international law in applying Australian law. The high point in judicial recognition was the finding in the *Teoh* case that an unincorporated international treaty can raise legitimate expectations that its provisions be taken into account in citizens' dealings with government.[74] That decision drew a sharp reaction from successive Labor and Coalition (Conservative) governments, who both issued executive pronouncements opposing the principle though not seeking to limit its impact. The *Teoh* precedent continues to live a half-life, teetering on the brink of being distinguished. The personal and often visceral reaction of Australian judges to human rights reasoning has also been evident, most controversially in the statement of former Chief Justice Gibbs that 'nowadays bills of rights are to be found in most democratic countries in the world—like AIDS'.[75] Attempts by Kirby J to employ international law to interpret the Australian constitution were described by McHugh J as 'heretical'.[76]

The judiciary and political actors have also engaged in a potent form of identity politics around rights, which projects their rejection as a core part of Australia's legal culture. The comments of Prime Minister Malcolm Fraser upon the ratification of the ICCPR and the creation of the Human Rights Commission illustrate how this fundamental perception of the role of law influences Australia's attitude to international oversight:

> When people resort to the law to protect their rights, they typically do so only because their rights have already been infringed. It is a trap to depend too much upon law for the enjoyment of rights, or to imagine that more laws, different kinds of laws, or a greater resort to law, can be a substitute for attitudes and relationships between people, and it is worth remembering Cicero's words, 'the more law, the less justice'.[77]

This belief was central to the failure to pass implementing legislation upon Australia's ratification of the ICCPR. Mr Fraser has since recanted this belief and supports a bill of rights for Australia, a viewpoint based particularly upon the historical exclusion of indigenous peoples.[78] Yet the historical claim that rights have done little as a practical bulwark against abuse has lain at the core of the philosophies of successive chief justices.[79]

The answer to the fundamental conundrum of which is the central step in constituting a nation, 'good people' or 'good law', has haunted political science and legal theory for centuries.[80] Construing the relationship of human rights with democracy in such an unmodulated manner is an act of dubious historicity and intellectual closure for Australia. Yet even proposals for legislative protection of human rights are alleged to be anti-democratic and uniquely polycentric. Rights language is claimed to be uniquely 'turbid' or 'cloudy'.[81] The degree to which the United Nations system, with its marked abstractness and politicization, aggravates this perception needs to be reflected upon. Certainly, modes of interpretation such as proportionality balancing and dialogic constitutionalism, which would illuminate the grossly simplified image of rights amongst prominent Australian commentators, are less than developed within the reasoning of UN treaty bodies than other regional or comparative jurisdictions. It is at least arguable that rights opponents have used the programmatic emphasis and high level of generality within the UN system to undermine the 'legal' nature of rights at home. The impact of the United Nations system upon domestic rights advocacy cannot be analysed as travelling in one direction, particularly when existing state-level rights legislation appears to substantially echo ICCPR provisions. There is a danger of domestic innovation being crowded by excessively linking international and domestic frameworks.

Both the benefits and pitfalls of relying upon the UN treaties as engines for domestic rights discussion can be seen in the *Human Rights (Parliamentary Scrutiny) Act 2011*. This requires Commonwealth ministers, when passing legislation, to provide a statement of compatibility or to declare non-compatibility with Australia's international human rights obligations. Such a mechanism empowers parliament to be primary overseers of Australia's obligations, internalizing and systemizing consideration of them across the legislative process. The concern is that imposing a requirement that parliament check the compatibility of legislation against the substantive content of each of the seven central human rights treaties may lower the quality of oversight. If the practical machinery of the system can function, however, it could provide a greater mandate for courts to take into account the compatibility statements when constructing the parliamentary intention in statutory interpretation. Queensland and New South Wales legislation, however, remain occluded from such processes, and indeed parliamentary scrutiny procedures requiring analysis of bills for compatibility with 'the rule of law' (interpreted by counsel to the now defunct Scrutiny of Legislation Committee of the Queensland Parliament as including compliance with human rights principles) have recently been replaced by review by the Office of Parliamentary Counsel, a greater distance from public scrutiny.[82]

Ultimately, international legal obligations are not yet sufficiently linked with the Australian domestic legal system to ensure the HRC views are implemented through, or even properly valued by, domestic legal institutions. Thus, in dedicating their energy to the pursuit of justice internationally, Australian actors must attend to the specificity of the political dynamics behind their case. As we shall see, practical realities support the claim of Risse and Ropp that international norms are more effective when they 'resonate or fit with existing collective understandings embedded in domestic institutions and political cultures'.[83]

Cluster two: persuasion

International legitimacy

The concept of legitimacy owes its origin to Professor Thomas Franck, who defined it as:

> [a] property of a rule or rule-making institution which itself exerts a pull toward compliance on those addressed normatively because those addressed believe that the rule or institution has come into being and operates in accordance with generally accepted principles of right process.[84]

A core part of 'compliance pull' should be generated through the substantive content of HRC views, its procedure and the high standing of member experts.

The cogency of the views of the HRC can highlight the nature of a state's violation. It is clear after *Fardon* and *Tillman* that Australia's human rights violations are conscious, in that the prevailing policy is not rooted in a lag between the treaty's adoption and implementation or ambiguous directives on the part of the HRC or national inability to comply. The Committee must continually reflect upon its ability to deliver not just a bare finding but also a consolidated account of violation causes and mapping its vision of future actions. There are hurdles to achieving this in practice, however, particularly the reality that the communication process is conducted entirely 'on the papers' with no oral hearing or cross examination. This damages the expressive value of the process, when compared to (more structured and public) court action. Given the backlogs within the system, the Committee is unlikely to engage deeply with the facts to draw out the political and organizational dynamics that led to the violation or to challenge the putative evidence base for such actions.[85]

Despite the characterization of the HRC as a political body, it has historically been dominated by high-level legal experts. Its current membership consists of eight professors and four judges, including two retired chief justices, with only one or two members not being lawyers. The system is chronically under-resourced, and as a result, while the members are independent, they are able to work for government or international organizations, with the HRC currently having three members in governmental service.[86] Rule 90 of the HRC's rules of procedure does contain conflict of interest procedures, however.[87] Ironically, given the comments of some Australian politicians, the treaty bodies have historically over-represented the 'Western Europe and Other Group' of which Australia is a member.

Some commentators have argued for a more active division of labour within treaty bodies, which would look to retain and concentrate legal expertise in a number of individuals, while appointing experts from other fields. The latter group would focus on producing precise and actionable authoritative advice to states and other stakeholders on implementing the legal determinations. This would, according to John Morijn, allow the committees to combine human rights discourse with 'politics, policy and programming'.[88] In our view, such a diversity of views could have aided the implementation of the *Fardon* and *Tillman* findings. For instance, the availability of a leading forensic psychiatrist would have provided an evidence base for the Committee's recommendations, or a prison official could have identified comparative perspectives and best practice innovations. A greater cross-referencing of the work of other human rights bodies such as the Special Committee on Torture would be a partial measure to secure such elements.

The legitimacy of the treaty bodies is also affected by the priority accorded to them within the United Nations system. Recent debates about the reform of the treaty bodies have focused upon centring the process on distinctive ground. The rise of regional systems does, in some geographical areas, decrease the distinctive position of the individual petition mechanism. This general trend does not apply to Australia, where the actions under the Optional Protocol remain central, given the absence of a regional human rights instrument and the limited litigation opportunities offered by the Australian Capital Territory and Victorian statutory rights provisions. The introduction of the Universal Periodic Review system, which focuses upon peer-to-peer state interaction, is also seen as potentially redefining the role of the treaty bodies. The desire of many international reformers to systemically centre the treaty bodies upon distinctive ground such as norm clarification must not lead to a drift away from processes which are uniquely valuable to Australia.

The Australian government has at times made prominent use of cultural relativism to undermine the legitimacy of the findings. First, the Australian government has argued that UN committees fail to appreciate Australia's status as a 'model member' of the UN. This is also supplemented by attacks upon the make-up and competence of the Committee, for instance, through the argument that government representatives would not 'dance attendance on the views of committees that are a long way from Australia'.[89]

The political and judicial reactions to the *Fardon* and *Tillman* findings have reflected these trends but are distinctive in that most prominent reflections upon the legitimacy of the Human Rights Committee have come from members of judges. The legitimacy of the Committee was attacked by Justice Kaye of the Victorian Supreme Court in *WBM v. Chief Commissioner for Police*, a case concerning the registration of an individual as a sex offender:

> That Committee does not perform the same judicial role, which is performed by the courts of this state. In particular, it is not the independent judicial arm of a parliamentary democracy, the other arms of which are the legislature and the executive. Further, it is fair to observe that the majority of the members of that Committee do not come from countries which have the same system of democracy as ours, or indeed any system of representative democracy at all. The opinions of that Committee, to which I was referred, involve the expressions by the Committee of value judgments in a manner and to an extent which is at odds with the traditional judicial function of the courts of this State and this nation.[90]

On this basis, Kaye J refused to use Human Rights Committee decisions to interpret the concept of 'arbitrary interference' with the right to privacy despite a direct statutory provision, s32(2)[91] of the Victorian Charter of Human Rights, encouraging overseas decisions to be taken into account. As outlined by the Victorian Human Rights and Equality Commission, Kaye J's comments err in portraying members of the Human Rights Committee as 'representatives' of their governments; they are independent experts of high standing.[92] It also does not reflect the authoritative character of the HRC's views, which we have already justified above. We would not expect Australian judges to take a similar approach to other streams of international law, such as trade law or investment arbitration decisions. Justice Kaye's comments were countered by more progressive findings on appeal, with members of the Victorian Supreme Court of Appeal, in particular Bell J, stressing the continuing utility of international human rights law in construing the domestic principle of legality.[93] Positive recognition in Queensland of the Human Rights Committee's findings in *Fardon* and *Tillman* has been led by Atkinson J. In a footnote to her judgment in *Attorney-General for the State of Queensland v. Fardon* Her Honour stressed the findings in the *Fardon* communication 'serves to emphasise the respect for human rights that ought to be applied by this court' when interpreting state legislation.[94] In *Attorney-General for the State of Queensland v. Beattie*, Atkinson J invoked the HRC findings in stressing the need for regular reviews of post-sentence preventive detention orders.[95] Such recognition of the legitimacy of the HRC is a prerequisite for norm internalization through statutory interpretation.

Domestic legitimacy and mobilization

The vagaries of media coverage that arise around HRC communications are best illustrated by the preparation of a complaint centring upon the mandatory sentencing of youths in the Northern Territory in 2000. Due to the involvement of Cherie Booth, wife of the then United Kingdom prime minister, the issue attracted an unprecedented level of coverage. The communication ultimately never proceeded as the mandatory sentencing statutes were repealed.[96] Both major political parties in Australia have displayed a strong propensity to instrumentalize and override international legal obligations in the name of perceived political imperatives. Charlesworth *et al.* provide an illustration of this in their work, *No Country Is an Island – Australia and International Law*. They contrast the political discourse surrounding the Howard government's decision to join the Iraq War with the introduction of a supervised drug injection room in Sydney by the New South Wales government.[97] The parties reversed roles in these cases, with the Howard government calling for compliance with the Single Convention on Narcotic Drugs of 1961 after it had dismissed the applicability of international law as a restraint in Iraq.[98] This led to the statement by Prime Minister Howard that:

> [i]n the end Australia makes its own decisions on what is good for Australia. But part of what is good for Australia is paying some regard to treaties that we've signed, and part of the cooperation between a federal government and state government is for a state government to recognise that we have our responsibilities.[99]

The controversy for Charlesworth *et al.* underlined the 'fluidity in arguments about international law' in Australia. It embodies the limited impact upon

Australian politicians of what Jon Elster terms the 'civilising force of hypocrisy'.[100] This idea argues that even shallow commitments to human rights norms can evolve into deeper commitments due to a 'consistency constraint', whereby international legal commitments allow political opportunism to be clearly identified. Similar fluidity is evident in invocations of the concept of national sovereignty. Anne Kent argues that historically it has proved 'endlessly malleable' and not centred upon any consistent values such as democratic legitimation.[101] As a result, sovereignty is never consolidated in a manner that represents a principled interrogation of international access to justice mechanisms but is used as a political trope.

Politicians have continually relied upon what they perceive as negative attitudes towards human rights in the community. Alexander Downer, Minister for Foreign Affairs under the Howard government, confidently predicted that 'if a UN Committee wants to play domestic politics here in Australia, it will end up with a bloody nose'.[102] Across the aisle, former Commonwealth Attorney General, Gareth Evans, a proponent of a domestic bill of rights, nevertheless concluded in 1999 that 'most Australians seem to regard fundamental matters of political and civil liberty as of no concern to themselves but only to noisy and unattractive minorities'.[103] Evans concludes that as a nation 'we are monumentally indifferent, if not positively hostile, to most matters of civil liberty and law reform'.[104]

Turning to the *Fardon* and *Tillman* action, prisoners' rights, and in particular the rights of serious offenders, are far less likely to attract domestic mobilization. The operation of preventive detention represents just one iteration of a broader devaluing of the rule of law and of the failure of government interventions to incorporate objective scientific evidence, but such a framing struggles to shift the underlying political culture of crime control. Evidence that 'state of exception' leaks out into other government actions and policy structures is not yet subjectively valued by the Australian public.[105] The bounded impact of appeals to the principle of legality and the need for a culture of justification within government in *Fardon* and *Tillman* underlines that test case selection will remain a politically pragmatic and inequitable process. Thus the effectiveness of persuasive approaches remains heavily conditioned by underlying domestic political opportunity structures.

Cluster three: socialization and acculturation

This category within 'compliance pull' literature is perhaps the most recently championed, with Goodman and Jinks, in particular, arguing for its distinctive role in 'designing effective global regimes'.[106] They recognize the applicability of the foregoing two clusters: materially inducing states (whether by direct sanction, reputational impact) or persuading them (by convincing them of the international regime's legitimacy). What is intriguing about the acculturation school of empirical international relations, and its potential descriptive validity to Australia, is its embrace of the realities of 'decoupling'. This latter idea refers to a phase (often persistent) where formal international commitments fail to change concrete practices on the ground. Yet within this space, where persuasion or material inducement fail, there is still room for actors to be socialized in human rights culture. Goodman and Jinks define such a process:

> By acculturation, we mean the general process by which actors adopt the beliefs and behavioural patterns of the surrounding culture. More specifically, this mechanism induces behavioural changes through pressures to assimilate—some imposed by other actors and some imposed by the self. Acculturation encompasses a number of micro-processes including mimicry, identification, and status maximization.[107]

As the reference to micro-processes suggests, the vision of acculturation is in many respects wildly different in its emphasis than a legalistic focus upon directly binding obligations. Its development is linked to insights from behavioural sciences and behavioural economics. Acculturation is propelled by both 'internal pressures' and 'social pressures', which include:

1 social-psychological costs of non-conformity (such as dissonance associated with conduct that is inconsistent with an actor's identity and social roles) [internal];
2 social-psychological benefits of conforming to group norms and expectations (such as the 'cognitive comfort' associated with both high social status and membership in a perceived 'in-group' [internal];
3 imposition of social-psychological costs of shaming or shunning [social]; and
4 the conferral of social-psychological benefits through back-patting and other displays of public approval [social].[108]

These mental and social processes can operate both for and against human rights. Certainly where identifying violations would trigger a ground level 'naming and shaming' in core surrounding relationships, human rights compliance may be increased. But in a negative prison culture, the acculturative pressures may align to influence a particular guard or administrator to act in a non-compliant manner. Ironically, therefore, Goodman and Jinks note that an excessive focus upon cataloguing violations may lead to a 'boomerang effect'. Such an approach may 'reinforce the sense that human rights abuses ... are commonplace and other priorities of good governance such as economic growth, public order and national security, routinely trump the protection of individual rights'.[109] If an impression is gained that deviance from human rights standard is prevalent and socially accepted by others, the mental models and pressures listed above function to ensure non-compliant acts persist. So one core practical conclusion of acculturative models of enforcement is that it is essential to focus energy upon the circulation of positive best practice models. Further emanations may include the integration of human rights within professional training and reward structures, the facilitation of transnational experts in human rights consultancy and the strengthening of local 'receptor sites' for transmitting global norms.

The Optional Protocol on the Convention against Torture (OPCAT), which Australia signed in 2009, may represent a mechanism which is ideally suited for harnessing acculturative methods of enforcing Australia's international human rights obligations. On 21 June 2012, the Australian Parliament Joint Standing Committee on Treaties tabled its review of OPCAT recommending that Australia take 'binding treaty action' and that federal and state governments cooperate to implement a national preventive mechanism upon ratification.[110] The National Human Rights Action Plan committed to ratification in 2013, with the government delaying commencement of domestic monitoring obligations 'for up to three years'.[111] OPCAT is an action-based protection mechanism, which links international obligation with a national preventative mechanism, allowing for the ongoing monitoring of all places of detention. While the United Nations Subcommittee on the Prevention of Torture also has the right to conduct inspections, the independent National Preventive Mechanism is to be placed upon a statutory footing and free access to closed environments.[112]

Bronwyn Naylor has recently discussed the distinctive benefits of such an ongoing process by reference to the experiences of the Council of Europe's Committee for the Prevention of Torture.[113] Its former president, Silvia Casale, appears implicitly to foreground the place of acculturation and socialization practices in describing its work.[114] She notes that the Committee attempts to mobilize 'the pressure of example'[115] and, somewhat counter-intuitively for observers, prefers to announce its visits to allow facilities to make its own improvements. The Committee thus 'tend to smell a lot of fresh paint', and the naming and shaming process is counterbalanced.[116] At a minimum the OPCAT mechanism may result in an institutional attentiveness to the lived experience of those within preventive detention, particularly the extremely substandard nature of their current accommodation and lack of effective rehabilitation options.

At a minimum the acculturative model can offer a counter-discourse to the politicization of clinical judgments and administration of the preventive detention regimes, though it cannot be wholly insulated from the adverse political context. Such interventions within Australia's prison context are also profoundly shaped by the realities of privatization. The ability to exploit social pressures within a shifting body of temporary employees regulated by contract may be much more difficult than engaging a body of career public servants with a long established collective culture. The empirical basis for acculturation is not yet wholly secure, and attentiveness to its insights should not be confused with unsubstantiated claims of pre-eminence. Equally, acculturation approaches should also involve interventions in the political and legal spheres that wield the most significant regulatory power.

Conclusion

> [International law is] those premises and obligations that make it materially more likely that a state behave in a manner consistent with those promises and obligations than would otherwise be the case.[117]

This functional definition of international law by Guzman nominates access to justice as a fundamental characteristic of international legal orders. An analysis that seeks to measure effectiveness often raises deep discomfort amongst human rights lawyers, particularly when it culminates in the claim that human rights law may be reduced to a form of critical morality about law and not fully legal. This is not our belief, and we argue that a fuller appreciation of how human rights instruments are enforced will yield evidence of their effectiveness. Yet, the non-implementation of *Fardon* and other HRC views underlines that outcomes for the individual litigant are not the primary orientation of the system.

Within the Australian context, distinct, well-entrenched barriers exist to securing improved outcomes through invocation of the ICCPR. The *Fardon* case, as an iteration of Australia's resistance to the Human Rights Committee, underlines that accessing justice in the international plane through human rights treaties requires complex strategic judgments informed by political, legal and cultural insights. In concluding this chapter, we wish to avoid a collapse into outright pessimism, or to simply announce an impasse. In charting a road towards greater access to justice, we would urge the following advocacy steps:

- Build pressure upon existing government intransigence by lobbying for an independent national evaluation mechanism of executive rejections of Human Rights Committee findings.
- NGOs and academics supporting individual petitions must attempt to improve the substantive content of HRC findings – in particular remedies must be disaggregated and concretized. Furthermore, any core factual economic, scientific or political assumptions upon which government policy is constructed should be addressed and critiqued.
- Discourage the compartmentalization of human rights violations from the broader United Nations system.
- Conduct an honest appraisal of the factors increasing and decreasing 'compliance pull' and resulting patterns of effectiveness. The goal should be to mediate in any dormant but appropriate enforcement possibilities such as acculturative approaches.

None of this alters the significant headwinds presented to international human rights lawyers in Australia, an advanced liberal democracy which nevertheless continues to cultivate an intransigent normative dissension with an international law oversight body.

Cases

A-G (Qld) v. Beattie (2010) QSC 217 [2].
A-G (Qld) v. Fardon (2003) QCA 416 (McMurdo P, dissenting).
A-G (Qld) v. Waghorn (2010) QSC 183, fn 1.
A-G v. Fardon (2003) QSC 200.
Al-Kateb v. Godwin (2004) 219 CLR 562 [175].

Chu Kheng Lim v. Minister of Immigration (1992) 176 CLR 1, 27.
Croome v. Tasmania (1997) 191 CLR 119.
Fardon v. A-G (Qld) (2004) 223 CLR 575.
Fardon v. Australia UN Doc CCPR/C/98/D/1629/20.
Kable v. DPP (NSW) (1996) 189 CLR 51.
Minister for Immigration and Ethnic Affairs v. Teoh (1995) 183 CLR 273.
Momcilovic v. The Queen (2011) HCA 34 [429].
Power v. The Queen (1974) 131 CLR 623, 627.
Tillman v. Australia UN Doc CCPR/C/98/D/1635/2007.
Victoria v. Commonwealth (1996) 187 CLR 416.
WBM v. Chief Commissioner of Police (2010) VSC 219 [49].
WBM v. Chief Commissioner of Police (2012) VSCA 159.

Notes

1 The phrase used in the title of this chapter comes from the 1941 State of the Union address of Franklin D. Roosevelt, which outlined a global vision of governance centred upon fundamental human rights. He stressed:

> That is no vision of a distant millennium. It is a definite basis for a kind of world attainable in our own time and generation.... The world order which we seek is the cooperation of free countries working together in a friendly, civilized society.... Our support goes to those who struggle to gain those rights or keep them.

See Roosevelt 1941. Kind permission granted by Gerhard Peters and John T. Woolley, American Presidency Project.

2 United Nations 26 May 2005, para 132.

3 See, for example, Goodman and Jinks 2013; Morijn 2011: 299–333; Hathaway 2002.

4 Burgstaller 2007: 39–71.

5 'International Covenant on Civil and Political Rights ("ICCPR")', (999 UNTS 171, opened for signature 16 December 1966 (entered into force 23 March 1976)). The communication process was established by the Optional Protocol to ICCPR.

6 *Tillman v. Australia*, UN Doc CCPR/C/98/D/1635/2007 and *Fardon v. Australia*, UN Doc CCPR/C/98/D/1629/20.

7 This reflects work that engages in system-wide analyses of the impacts of treaty ratification in democratic and non-democratic countries. See, for example: Hafner-Burton *et al.* 2008: 115–141; Hathaway 2007.

8 *Fardon v. A-G (Qld)* (2004) 223 CLR 575. This type of legislation exists in four of the six Australian states and one of its self-governing territories: *Dangerous Prisoners (Sexual Offenders) Act 2003* (Qld); *Dangerous Sexual Offenders Act 2006* (WA); *Crimes (Serious Sex Offenders) Act 2006* (NSW); *Serious Sex Offenders (Detention and Supervision) Act 2009* (VIC); *Serious Sex Offenders Act 2013* (NT).

9 Slobogin 2013: 38–43.

10 Keyzer *et al.* 2004: 248–249.

11 *Fardon v. A-G (Qld)* (2004) 223 CLR 575. It had previously survived constitutional challenges in the Supreme Court of Queensland and the Queensland Court of Appeal: see *A-G v. Fardon* (2003) QSC 200 and *A-G (Qld) v. Fardon* (2003) QCA 416 (McMurdo P, dissenting).

12 *Chu Kheng Lim v. Minister of Immigration* (1992) 176 CLR 1, 27. For further analysis of this case, the decisions that followed it and the High Court's treatment of

this principle in the High Court's decision in *Fardon v. A-G (Qld)*, see Keyzer 2008: 101–113.

13 *Kable v. DPP (NSW)* (1996) 189 CLR 51, 97–98 (Toohey J) and 131–132 (Gummow J).

14 *Fardon v. A-G (Qld)* (2004) 223 CLR 575 at 633–636 (Kirby J).

15 Ibid. 575, 592 (Gleeson CJ), 597 (McHugh J, 'the Act is not designed to punish the prisoner'), 613, 647 (Gummow J, with whom Hayne J agreed), 653 (Callinan and Heydon JJ).

16 In *Power v. The Queen* (1974) 131 CLR 623, 627, a unanimous High Court had said that we 'cannot understand how … imprisonment, either with or without hard labour, can, however enlightened the prison system is, be regarded as otherwise than a severe punishment'.

17 Dissenting judgment of Kirby J in *Fardon v. A-G (Qld)* (2004) 223 CLR 575, 631–632.

18 The claim that the scheme reflected the traditional values and aims of criminal sentencing shaped the judgments of Callinan and Heydon JJ in particular.

19 LaFond 2011: 51–62.

20 Fardon was serving a 14-year sentence for rape, sodomy and unlawful assault on a female committed in October 1988 when he was subjected to an order under the Queensland regime. Tillman was serving a 10-year sentence for sexually assaulting a minor when he was subjected to an order under the equivalent New South Wales legislation.

21 Article 9(1) of the Covenant provides:

> Everyone has the right to liberty and security of person. No one shall be subjected to arbitrary arrest or detention. No one shall be deprived of his liberty except on such grounds and in accordance with such procedure as are established by law.

22 Article 14(1) of the Covenant provides:

> All persons shall be equal before the courts and tribunals. In the determination of any criminal charge against him, or of his rights and obligations in a suit at law, everyone shall be entitled to a fair and public hearing by a competent, independent and impartial tribunal established by law.

23 Article 14(7) provides: 'No one shall be liable to be tried or punished again for an offence for which he has already been finally convicted or acquitted in accordance with the law and penal procedure of each country'.

24 Article 15(1) provides:

> No one shall be held guilty of any criminal offence on account of any act or omission which did not constitute a criminal offence, under national or international law, at the time when it was committed. Nor shall a heavier penalty be imposed than the one that was applicable at the time when the criminal offence was committed.

For details of the arguments advanced see Keyzer and Blay 2006: 407–424 (referred to by the HRC in the *Fardon* decision) and Keyzer 2010b.

25 In, Human Rights Committee 23 July 1990, para 5.8 (*Van Alphen v. The Netherlands*).

26 See Human Rights Committee 2003, paras 7.2, 7.3 (*Rameka v. New Zealand*).

27 See Carroll *et al.* 2004: 407–425 (which was referred to the HRC in the *Tillman* decision).

28 *Tillman v. Australia*, UN Doc CCPR/C/98/D/1635/2007 and *Fardon v. Australia*, UN Doc CCPR/C/98/D/1629/20 at [4.4].

29 Australian Government, 'Response of the Australian Government to the Views

of the Committee in Communication No 1635/2007 Tillman V Australia and Communication No 1629/2007 Fardon V Australia'. Online. www.ag.gov.au/RightsAndProtections/HumanRights/DisabilityStandards/Documents/TillmanvAustralia-AustralianGovernmentResponse.pdf, para 15 p. 3 (accessed 2 August 2014).

30 We would argue that these obstacles are illusory, since it is trite law in Australia that the Australian parliament could enact legislation implementing the ICCPR into domestic law, and that such a law, if it was reasonably capable of being considered appropriate and adapted to the Covenant, would be valid and override the inconsistent Queensland and New South Wales laws at issue here to the extent of their inconsistency: see *Victoria v. Commonwealth* (1996) 187 CLR 416, 486–488 and Keyzer 2013: 208 and Ch. 21.
31 See Dunn 2012: 515.
32 Thomson 1991: 83.
33 Human Rights Committee 25 December 1991, para 8.3 (*Nicholas Toonen v. Australia*).
34 'When a law of a State is inconsistent with a law of the Commonwealth, the latter shall prevail, and the former shall, to the extent of the inconsistency, be invalid.'
35 See Keyzer 2010a: 55–64.
36 *Croome v. Tasmania* (1997) 191 CLR 119.
37 Human Rights Committee 2003 (*Bakhtiyari v. Australia*).
38 Human Rights Committee 2001 (*Winata v. Australia*).
39 Human Rights Committee 30 April 1997 (*A v. Australia*).
40 'Transcript of Australia's Hearing before the CERD Committee', cited by Charlesworth *et al*. 2006.
41 Marr 2005.
42 Blay and Piotrowicz 2000: 1–21.
43 Hanski and Scheinin 2007.
44 Tomuschat 2008: 220.
45 Steiner *et al*. 2008: 915.
46 Joseph *et al*. 2004: 24.
47 Human Rights Committee 5 November 2008.
48 Human Rights Committee 5 November 2008, para 11.
49 Human Rights Committee 5 November 2008.
50 Human Rights Committee 5 November 2008, para 13.
51 *Ahmadou Sadio Diallo (Republic of Guinea* v. *Democratic Republic of the Congo)* (2011) ICJ (Nov 30) para 66.
52 Human Rights Committee 2003 (*Bakhtiyari v. Australia*).
53 This sequence of events is described fully in Saul 2010: 629.
54 See Lynch 2012. As Lynch discusses, the asylum seeker was detained and interrogated for 16 hours straight following his arrival in Sri Lanka, after which, at a government organized press conference, he 'recanted' allegations of torture.
55 Baluarte and De Vos 2010.
56 Hanski and Scheinin 2007.
57 Violation of Article 26 (right to equality).
58 *Same Sex Relationships (Equal Treatment in Commonwealth Laws – General Law Reform) Act 2008* (Cth) and Same Sex Relationships (Equal Treatment in Commonwealth Law Superannuation) Act 2008 (Cth).
59 United Nations 2004, para 227.
60 The First Optional Protocol to the ICCPR also has 35 signatures.
61 International Court of Justice, 'Declarations Recognizing the Jurisdiction of the Court as Compulsory'. Online.
62 Geir Ulfstein's analysis conducted in 2012 found compliance in 4 out of 20 findings of the CERD Committee, 22 out of 45 findings of the Convention Against Torture and 3 responses of 4 findings of CEDAW Committee. Ulfstein 2012: 105.

63 For a helpful overview of this and other trends in compliance literature see Pulkowski 2006: 511–554.
64 Moravcsik 2000: 217.

> Unlike international institutions governing trade, monetary, environmental or security policy, international human rights institutions are not designed primarily to regulate policy externalities arising from social interactions across borders, but to hold governments accountable for purely internal activities.

65 Downs and Jones 2002: 95, 112.
66 Department of Foreign Affairs and Trade 2011: 1.
67 An excellent summary of Australia's initial review under the UPR process is available at the Australian Human Rights Commission website: www.humanrights.gov.au/australias-universal-periodic-review-human-rights.
68 United Nations Human Rights Council 2011, para 86.17. 69 Australian Government, 'Formal Response of the Australian Government to the Universal Periodic Review Recommendations of the Human Rights Council'. Online.
70 United Nations Human Rights Council 2011 para, 86.71.
71 Australian Government, 'Formal Response of the Australian Government to the Universal Periodic Review Recommendations of the Human Rights Council', p. 4.
72 These included the establishment of a full-time Race Discrimination Commissioner in the Australian Human Rights Commission, the tabling in parliament of concluding observations of human rights treaty bodies and UPR recommendations, and establishing a systematic review process of Australia's reservations to international human rights treaties.
73 The high point of this valuing of international law was Kirby J's statement in *Al-Kateb v. Godwin* (2004) 219 CLR 562 [175]:

> Whatever may have been possible in the world of 1945, the complete isolation of constitutional law from the dynamic impact of international law is neither possible nor desirable today. That is why national courts, and especially national constitutional courts such as this, have a duty, so far as possible to interpret their constitutional texts in a way that is generally harmonious with the basic principles of international law, including as that law state human rights and fundamental freedoms.

74 *Minister for Immigration and Ethnic Affairs v. Teoh* (1995) 183 CLR 273.
75 The inappropriateness of this statement in 1995 was explained by His Honour as an attempt to 'be frivolous and to adapt Malcolm Williamson's remark about the music of Andrew Lloyd Webber'. Gibbs 1995.
76 McHugh J in *Al-Kateb v. Godwin* (2004) 219 CLR 562 [62].
77 Fraser 1981, cited in Charlesworth *et al.* 2006: 69.
78 Fraser 2000.
79 French 2012. In support of this belief, French CJ cited United States Justice Learned Hand:

> Liberty lies in the hearts of men and women; when it dies there, no constitution, no law, no court can save it; no constitution, no law, no court, can even do much to help it. While it lies there it needs no constitution, no law, no court to save it.

80 See Honig 2007: 1.
81 *Momcilovic v. The Queen* (2011) HCA 34 [429]. The authors remain puzzled as to why a judiciary that invests so heavily in both heavily relative concepts such as jurisdictional error and such penumbral concepts as market impact or efficiency should single out human rights as uniquely open-textured. Nor do commentators who allege that human rights concepts are unenforceable explain why legislatures cannot cure such putative drawbacks with carefully executed drafting.

82 *Legislative Standards Act 1992* (Qld) §4.
83 Risse and Ropp 1999: 271.
84 Franck 1990: 24.
85 See generally Viljoen 2004: 646–651. The rules of procedure (rules 86(1) and 97(4)) do allow for the UN Secretariat to request further information, or the Committee can establish a working group or designate the Rapporteur to do so.
86 Human Rights Committee, 'Membership Office of the United Nations High Commissioner for Human Rights'. Online.
87 United Nations Human Rights Committee 1994, Rule 90.
88 Morijn 2011: 320.
89 Wright 2000.
90 *WBM v. Chief Commissioner of Police* (2010) VSC 219 [49].
91 This provided: 'International law and the judgments of domestic, foreign and international courts and tribunals relevant to a human right may be considered in interpreting a statutory provision'.
92 Victorian Commission on Human Rights, 'Reply Submission of the Victorian Equal Opportunity and Human Rights Commission (Intervening) in the Case of *R V Kelun Wang*', paras 5–13.
93 *WBM v. Chief Commissioner of Police* (2012) VSCA 159.
94 *A-G (Qld) v. Waghorn* (2010) QSC 183, fn 1.
95 *A-G (Qld) v. Beattie* (2010) QSC 217 [2].
96 Australian Broadcasting Corporation 14 July 2000.
97 Charlesworth *et al.* 2006: Ch. 3, 64–105. See also Hovell 2003: 297.
98 In this regard it was upholding the view of the International Narcotics Control Board, the relevant treaty agency, which expressed concern that the injecting facility would violate Australia's international legal obligations.
99 See Charlesworth *et al.* 2006: 18. ABC Radio National 1999.
100 Elster 1998: 111.
101 Kent 2005.
102 Australian Broadcasting Corporation 29 August 2000.
103 Evans 1999: 151.
104 He accepts that 'reform in this area will always be hard to sell, but decency and humanity demand that it be made': 'Democratic Socialism and Human Rights'" in Evans 1999.
105 Agamben 2005. For the sketching of the challenges for the traditional rule of law when confronted by such discourses, see Poole 2009: 247. In support of the point we make here, we would note that similar selective invocations of 'risk' prevention appear to be shaping the Queensland government's Youth Justice Action policy and, in particular, its advocacy of 'boot camps' for juvenile offenders.
106 Goodman and Jinks 2008: 725.
107 Goodman and Jinks 2004: 621.
108 The tacit nature of these mental and social pressures are what distinguishes acculturation from persuasion: Goodman and Jinks 2004: 640.
109 Goodman *et al.*, 'Coda to Chapter Two', in Goodman *et al.* 2012: 45.
110 Joint Standing Committee on Treaties Parliament of Australia 2012: Chapter 6, Recommendation 6.
111 Department of the Commonwealth Attorney General 2012. Draft state legislation in furtherance of this has begun to circulate, see for example, the Australian Capital Territory 2013.
112 In Australia there are already existing independent mechanisms for the monitoring at state and federal levels, including the Australian Human Rights Commission and Ombudsmen. Clearly OPCAT will require increased funding and a firmer statutory basis for such practices.
113 Naylor 2012: 233. See also Fletcher 2012: 233.

114 Casale 2006: 217.
115 Casale 2006: 223.
116 Ibid.
117 Guzman 2002: 1823, 1878.

References

ABC Radio National. 'PM Urges States to Stop Heroin Trials'. 15 December 1999.

Agamben, Giorgio. *State of Exception*. Trans. Kevin Attel. Chicago: University of Chicago Press, 2005.

Australian Broadcasting Corporation. 'Governments Unfazed at Challenge to Mandatory Sentencing'. *7.30 Report*, 14 July 2000.

Australian Broadcasting Corporation. 'Government Calls for UN Overhaul'. *7.30 Report*, 29 August 2000.

Australian Capital Territory. *Monitoring of Places of Detention (Optional Protocol to the Convention against Torture) Bill 2013*. Canberra: ACT Government, 2013. Online. Available at www.legislation.act.gov.au/b/db_47444/default.asp (accessed 20 December 2013.

Australian Government. 'Formal Response of the Australian Government to the Universal Periodic Review Recommendations of the Human Rights Council'. Online. Available at www.ag.gov.au/RightsAndProtections/HumanRights/UniversalPeriodicReview/Documents/AustraliasformalresponsetotheUPRrecommendations.pdf (accessed 14 April 2014).

Australian Government. 'Response of the Australian Government to the Views of the Committee in Communication No 1635/2007 Tillman V Australia and Communication No 1629/2007 Fardon V Australia'. Online. Available at www.ag.gov.au/RightsAndProtections/HumanRights/DisabilityStandards/Documents/FardonvAustralia-Australian GovernmentResponse.doc (accessed 14 April 2014).

Baluarte, David C. and De Vos, Christian. *From Judgment to Justice: Implementing International and Regional Human Rights Decisions*. New York and London: Open Society Foundation, 2010.

Blay, Sam and Piotrowicz, Ryszard. 'The Awfulness of Lawfulness: Some Reflections on the Tension between International and Domestic Law'. *Australian Yearbook of International Law* 21 (2000): 1–19.

Burgstaller, Markus. 'Amenities and Pitfalls of a Reputational Theory of Compliance with International Law'. *Nordic Journal of International Law* 76, No. 1 (2007): 39–71.

Carroll, Andrew, Lyall, Mark and Forrester, Andrew. 'Clinical Hopes and Public Fears in Forensic Mental Health'. *The Journal of Forensic Psychiatry & Psychology* 15, No. 3 (2004/09/01 2004): 407–425.

Casale, Silvia. 'Mechanisms for Custodial Oversight: The United States and Europe'. *Washington University Journal of Law and Policy* 22 (2006): 217–229.

Charlesworth, Hilary, Chiam, Madelaine, Hovell, Devika and Williams, George. *No Country Is an Island – Australia and International Law*. Sydney: University of New South Wales Press, 2006.

Department of Foreign Affairs and Trade. *Australia: Candidate for the United Nations Security Council 2013–14*. Canberra: Commonwealth of Australia, 2011.

Department of the Commonwealth Attorney General. *National Human Rights Action Plan 2012*. Canberra: Commonwealth of Australia, 2012.

Downs, George W. and Jones, Michael A. 'Reputation, Compliance and International Law'. *Journal of Legal Studies* XXXI No. 1 part 2 (2002): S95–114.

Dunn, Kevin. 'Do Australians Care About Racism? Awareness, Hierarchies of Sympathy and Universality of Human Rights'. In *Contemporary Perspectives on Human Rights Law in Australia*, edited by Melissa Castan and Paula Gerber. Rozelle, NSW: Thomson Reuters, 2012, Ch. 21

Elster, Jon. 'A Plea for Mechanisms'. In *Social Mechanisms: An Analytical Approach to Social Theory*, edited by Peter Hedstrøm and Richard Swedberg. Cambridge: Cambridge University Press, 1998: 45–73.

Evans, Gareth. 'Democratic Socialism and Human Rights'. In *Gareth Evans*, edited by Keith Scott. Sydney: Allen & Unwin, 1999.

Fletcher, Adam. 'Australia and the Opcat'. *Alternative Law Journal* 37, No. 4 (2012): 233–237.

Franck, Thomas M. *The Power of Legitimacy Amongst Nations*. Oxford: Oxford University Press, 1990.

Fraser, Malcolm. 'Inauguration of the Human Rights Commission'. In *Inauguration of the Human Rights Commission*. Canberra, 10 December 1981.

Fraser, Malcolm. 'The Past We Need to Understand'. *Fifth Vincent Lingiari Memorial Lecture Northern Territory University*, 24 August 2000. Online. Available at www.abc.net.au/specials/lingiari/print.htm (accessed 20 March 2013).

French, Robert. 'Human Right Protection in Australia and the United Kingdom: Contrasts and Comparisons'. In *Anglo-Australasian Lawyers Society and Constitutional and Administrative Law Bar Association*. London, 5 July 2012.

Gibbs, Harry. 'Does Australia Need a Bill of Rights?', *Proceedings of the Sixth Conference of The Samuel Griffith Society* 6, (17–19 November 1995). Online. Available at www.samuelgriffith.org.au/papers/html/volume6/v6chap7.htm (accessed 14 April 2014).

Goodman, Ryan and Jinks, Derek. 'How to Influence States: Socialization and International Human Rights Law'. *Duke Law Journal* 54 No. 3 (2004): 621–703.

Goodman, Ryan and Jinks, Derek. 'Incomplete Internalization and Compliance with Human Rights Law'. *European Journal of International Law* 19, No. 4 (2008): 725–748.

Goodman, Ryan and Jinks, Derek. *Socializing States: Promoting Human Rights through International Law*. New York: Oxford University Press, 2013.

Goodman, Ryan, Jinks, Derek and Woods, Andrew K. 'Coda to Chapter Two'. In *Understanding Social Action, Promoting Human Rights*, edited by Ryan Goodman, Derek Jinks and Andrew K. Woods. New York: Oxford University Press, 2012: 44–46.

Guzman, Andrew J. 'A Compliance Based Theory of International Law'. *California Law Review* 90, No. 6 (2002): 1823–1887.

Hafner-Burton, Emilie, Tsutsui, Kiyoteru and Meyer, John W. 'International Human Rights Law and the Politics of Legitimation: Repressive States and Human Rights Treaties'. *International Sociology* 23, No. 1 (2008): 115–141.

Hanski, Raija and Scheinin, Martin. *Leading Cases of the Human Rights Committee*. Second edn. Turku, Finland: Institute for Human Rights, Åbo Akademi University, 2007.

Hathaway, Oona A. 'Do Human Rights Treaties Make a Difference?'. *Yale Law Journal* 111, No. 8 (2002): 1935–2042.

Hathaway, Oona A. 'Why Do Countries Commit to Human Rights Treaties?'. *Journal of Conflict Resolution* 51, No. 4 (2007): 588–621.

Honig, Bonnie. 'Between Decision and Deliberation: The Political Paradox in Democratic Theory'. *American Political Science Review* 101, No. 1 (2007): 1–17.

Hovell, Devika. 'The Sovereignty Stratagem: Australia's Response to UN Human Rights Treaty Bodies'. *Alternative Law Journal* 28, No. 6 (2003): 297–301.

Human Rights Committee. 'Communication No 305/88'. UN Doc CCPR/C/39/D/305/1988, 23 July 1990.

Human Rights Committee. 'Communication No 488/1992'. UN Doc CCPR/C/50/D/488/1992, 25 December 1991.

Human Rights Committee. 'Communication No 560/1993'. UN Doc CCPR/C/59/D/560/1993, 30 April 1997.

Human Rights Committee. 'Communication No 30/2000'. UN Doc CCPR/C/72/D/930/2000, 2001.

Human Rights Committee. 'Communication No 1069/2002'. UN Doc CCPR/C/79/D/1069/2002, 2003.

Human Rights Committee. 'General Comment No 33: The Obligations of States Parties under the Optional Protocol to the International Covenant on Civil and Political Rights'. 97th sess: UN Doc CCPR/C/GC/33, 5 November 2008.

Human Rights Committee. 'Membership'. Office of the United Nations High Commissioner for Human Rights. Online. Available at www.ohchr.org/EN/HRBodies/CCPR/Pages/Membership.asp (accessed 6 August 2014).

International Court of Justice. 'Declarations Recognizing the Jurisdiction of the Court as Compulsory'. Online. Available at www.icj-cij.org/jurisdiction/?p1=5&p2=1&p3=3 (accessed 14 April 2014).

Joint Standing Committee on Treaties Parliament of Australia. 'Review into Treaties: Tabled on 7 and 28 February 2012'. Canberra: Report No. 125, 2012, Ch. 6, Recommendation 6.

Joseph, Sarah, Schultz, Jenny and Castan, Melissa. *The International Covenant on Civil and Political Rights: Cases, Materials and Commentary*. Second edn. Oxford: Oxford University Press, 2004.

Kent, Anne. 'Influences on National Participation on International Institutions: Liberal V Non-Liberal States'. In *The Fluid State: International Law and National Legal Systems*, edited by Hilary Charlesworth. Sydney: Federation Press, 2005: 251–276.

Keyzer, Patrick. 'Preserving Due Process or Warehousing the Undesirables: To What End the Separation of Judicial Power of the Commonwealth?'. *Sydney Law Review* 30, No. 1 (2008): 100–113.

Keyzer, Patrick. *Open Constitutional Courts*. Annandale, NSW: Federation Press, (2010a).

Keyzer, Patrick. 'The United Nations Human Rights Committee's Views About the Legitimate Parameters of the Preventive Detention of Serious Sex Offenders'. *Criminal Law Journal* 34, No. 5 (2010b): 283–291.

Keyzer, Patrick. *Principles of Constitutional Law*. Fourth edn. Chatswood, NSW: LexisNexis, 2013.

Keyzer, Patrick and Blay, Sam. 'Double Punishment? Preventive Detention Schemes under Australian Legislation and Their Consistency with International Law: The Fardon Communication'. *Melbourne Journal of International Law* 7, No. 2 (2006): 407–424.

Keyzer, Patrick, Pereira, C. and Southwood. S. 'Pre-Emptive Imprisonment for Dangerousness in Queensland under the Dangerous Prisoners (Sexual Offenders) Act 2003: The Constitutional Issues'. *Psychiatry, Psychology and Law* 11, No. 2 (2004): 244–253.

LaFond, John Q. 'Sexual Offender Commitment Laws in the USA: The Inevitable Failure of Misusing Civil Commitment to Prevent Future Sex Crimes'. In *Dangerous People*, edited by Bernadette McSherry and Patrick Keyzer. New York: Routledge, 2011: 51–62.

Lynch, Phillip. 'Australia's Duplicitous Approach to the UN'. (13 August 2012). Online. Available at www.abc.net.au/unleashed/4190968.html (accessed 14 April 2014).

Marr, David. 'Geneva V Canberra'. *Sydney Morning Herald*, 28 March 2005.

Moravcsik, Andrew. 'The Origins of Human Rights Regimes: Democratic Delegation in Postwar Europe'. *International Organization* 54, No. 2 (2000): 217–252.

Morijn, John. 'Reforming United Nations Human Rights Treaty Monitoring Reform'. *Netherlands International Law Review* 58, No. 3 (2011): 295–333.

Naylor, Bronwyn. 'Protecting the Human Rights of Prisoners in Australia'. In *Contemporary Perspectives on Human Rights Law in Australia*, edited by Melissa Castan and Paula Gerber. Rozelle, NSW: Thomson Reuters, 2012, Ch. 16

Parliament of Australia, Joint Standing Committee on Treaties. 'Review into Treaties: Tabled on 7 and 28 February 2012'. Canberra: Report No. 125, 2012, Ch. 6.

Poole, Thomas. 'Constitutional Exceptionalism and the Common Law'. *International Journal of Constitutional Law* 7, No. 2 (2009): 247–274.

Pulkowski, Dirk. 'Testing Compliance Theories: Towards US Obedience of International Law in the Avena Case'. *Leiden Journal of International Law* 19, No. 2 (2006): 511–554.

Risse, Thomas and Ropp, Stephen C. 'International Human Rights Norms and Domestic Change: Conclusions'. In *The Power of Human Rights International Norms and Domestic Change*, edited by Thomas Risse, Stephen C. Ropp and Kathryn Sikkink. Cambridge and New York: Cambridge University Press, 1999: 234–278.

Roosevelt, Franklin D. 'Annual Message to Congress on the State of the Union'. Edited by Gerhard Peters and John T. Woolley, The American Presidency Project, 6 January 1941. Online. Available at www.presidency.ucsb.edu/ws/?pid=16092 (accessed 10 April 2014).

Saul, Ben. 'The Kafka-Esque Case of Sheikh Mansour Leghaei: The Denial of the International Human Right to a Fair Hearing in National Security Assessments and Migration Proceedings in Australia'. *University of New South Wales Law Journal* 33, No. 3 (2010): 629–661.

Slobogin, Christopher. 'Preventive Detention in Europe, the United States, and Australia'. In *Preventive Detention: Asking the Fundamental Questions*, edited by Patrick Keyzer. Cambridge: Intersentia, 2013: 31–54.

Steiner, Henry, Goodman, Richard and Alston, Philip. *International Human Rights in Context: Law, Politics, Morals*. Third edn. New York: Oxford University Press, 2008.

Thomson, Peter. 'Implications of Australian Ratification and Potential Ratification of International Human Rights Treaties'. In *International Law Weekend*. Canberra: Centre for International Law and Public Law, 10–12 May 1991.

Tomuschat, Christian. *Human Rights: Between Idealism and Realism*. Second edn. New York: Oxford University Press, 2008.

'Transcript of Australia's Hearing before the CERD Committee'. 1394th Meeting, 56th Session of the Committee on the Elimination of Racial Discrimination, 22 March 2000.

Ulfstein, Geir. 'Individual Complaints'. In *UN Human Rights Treaty Bodies: Law and Legitimacy*, edited by Helen Keller and Geir Ulfstein. Cambridge: Cambridge University Press, 2012: 73–115.

United Nations. 'International Covenant on Civil and Political Rights ("ICCPR")'. 999 UNTS 171, opened for signature 16 December 1966 (entered into force 23 March 1976).

United Nations. 'Report of the Human Rights Committee: Covering the Seventy-Ninth Session (20 October–7 November 2003) Eightieth Session (15 March–2 April 2004) Eighty-First Session (5–30 July 2004). General Assembly Fifty-Ninth Session, Supp No 40'. UN Doc A/59/40, 2004.
United Nations. 'In Larger Freedom: Towards Development, Security and Human Rights for All: Report of the Secretary-General of the United Nations'. UN Doc A/59/2005, 26 May 2005.
United Nations Human Rights Committee. 'Rules of Procedure'. UN Doc CCPR/C/3/Rev3, 1994.
United Nations Human Rights Council. 'Working Group on the Universal Periodic Review of Australia'. Tenth Session Geneva: UN Doc A/HRC/17/10, 24 January–4 February 2011.
Victorian Commission on Human Rights. 'Reply Submission of the Victorian Equal Opportunity and Human Rights Commission (Intervening) in the Case of *R V Kelun Wang*'. Online. Available at www.humanrightscommission.vic.gov.au/index.php/component/k2/item/560-wk-charter-intervention-jul-2010 (accessed 7 August 2014).
Viljoen, Frans. 'Fact-Finding by UN Human Rights Complaints Bodies – Analysis and Suggested Reforms'. *Max Planck Yearbook of United Nations Law* 8 (2004): 49–100.
Wright, Lincoln. 'Howard Softens Stand on UN'. *The Canberra Times*, 3 April 2000.

10 The International Committee of the Red Cross and access to international justice

A carefully considered paradox

David P. Forsythe

Introduction

In this chapter, I first reflect on the concept of justice, noting its two prominent meanings of legal justice and social justice. I then present the concept of International Committee of the Red Cross (ICRC) social justice in the form of applied humanitarian protection and assistance. I next discuss legal justice and ICRC policy positions. My central point is to show that the ICRC prioritizes social justice in the sense of service to victims of violent politics. The organization is active on questions of international legal justice, including criminal justice, but only in ways that do not impede its policies and programmes of social justice. Those in legal circles who think of access to international justice solely in terms of individual access to courts and criminal prosecutions might want to rethink their assumptions, taking into account that some humanitarian organizations as well as many of those they represent or support prioritize a more pressing need for social justice.

Theoretical reflections

The *Random House Dictionary of the English Language* (1967) lists ten definitions for the term 'justice'. So the word 'justice' is similar to other words in the English language that have multiple and unclear meanings – words such as 'politics', 'power', 'sovereignty', and so on. The disciplines of law, philosophy, political science and many more do not manifest agreement on when or how to use these terms. They remain contested concepts.

According to the *Random House Dictionary*, one meaning of 'justice' relates to legal rules, and use of the term 'legal justice' is widespread. Accordingly, what is just is what is in accord with legal norms. Access to international justice is frequently assumed to refer to legal processes, especially judicial proceedings. Another meaning of 'justice' relates to equity or fairness. Accordingly, what is just is what is moral, understood here as equitable or fair. Access to this conception of international justice may turn out to be distinct from legal standards, at least in part. These two mainstream meanings do not automatically conflate. What is legal may not be moral, whereas what is moral may not be legal. Law schools are called law schools, not schools of justice, for a reason.

The 1999 NATO bombing of Serbia, ostensibly in response to human rights violations in Kosovo, was said by many to have been morally just, but likewise to many people its commencement was not in accord with the norms of international law. The killing of Osama bin Laden was seen by many as morally just, but if he were unarmed and unresisting at the time of his death, shooting him may have been legally unjustified. Thus, those who discuss access to justice in international relations should be aware of the differing conceptions of justice. An assumption favouring legal institutions and processes may be, and often is, incomplete. Such an assumption may, in global perspective, reflect a Western bias.

The discussion above is indeed relevant to the International Committee of the Red Cross, initial appearances to the contrary notwithstanding. The ICRC, a non-governmental organization recognized in public international law, defines its mandate as working for humanity in situations of violence. It is, therefore, a humanitarian organization active in international and internal armed conflict and situations of major domestic violence perceived as political but said to fall short of some type of war. Those attuned to law associate it with international humanitarian law (IHL) in general and the 1949 Geneva Conventions[1] and Additional Protocols in particular. It is said to be the guardian of IHL, and there is no lack of lawyers at its Geneva headquarters. It is certainly attentive to law and legal justice, including international criminal justice.[2]

But as I have previously argued, much of what it does is based on what it believes is ethical or moral or equitable in context.[3] It often operates in a context where legal categories are contested. At what precise point in Syria did the violence during 2012 constitute an internal armed conflict, as the ICRC asserted? Or did it remain, as the Assad government maintained, caused by a violent movement of terrorists? Moreover, the ICRC often operates in a context in which precise legal standards are not, and never have been, clear. If Syria did manifest an internal armed conflict at some point, how much assistance to the civilian population was legally required, and what conditions could properly be cited as blocking the delivery of that assistance? Given such ambiguities, either because of the imprecision of the law or the contested labels applied to the situations of concern, the ICRC often is compelled to fall back on its judgments about the contextual social justice it can safely provide for victims of war and other situations of violence.

The central point of this essay is to show that the ICRC prioritizes social justice to victims of war and of other forms of violent politics. Its priority is to provide humanitarian services on the ground (*sur place*). It is certainly interested in, and active for, legal justice as applied to its métier, including criminal justice. But it pursues the latter in a way that does not jeopardize the former. This strategy to implement its mandate, actually well considered, can be paradoxical. It identifies with the pursuit of legal justice for potential or actual victims of large-scale political violence, but it only pursues this conception of justice in ways that do not interfere with social justice – namely, bringing services of protection and assistance to needy victims *sur place*. Its unique role in international relations is, in fact, tied primarily to social justice. Its association with legal justice is often misunderstood.

The primacy of social justice

Even within the womb, so to speak, what became the ICRC prioritized non-legal social justice in the form of medical assistance to wounded soldiers. Henry Dunant, the Swiss businessman who originated the idea of the ICRC and the International Red Cross and Red Crescent Movement, took action in the aftermath of the Battle of Solferino in 1859 in what is now northern Italy, as the clashing French and Austrian armies left the wounded unattended. Driven by a sense of Christian compassion, his concern was to organize medical aid then and there. Legal considerations came later, when the ICRC was created in Geneva in 1863 and developed under the leadership of its second president, the lawyer Gustav Moynier.

From 1863 until today, the ICRC has carved out a unique role for itself in world affairs primarily through the provision of humanitarian protection and assistance – in general, focusing on the basic human needs of sick, wounded or detained combatants and of the similar needs of civilians. It has always considered states and other fighting parties as having the primary obligation or duty to respond to these needs: and if it can help create laws and institutions to get others to meet these needs it will do so. But in the last analysis, if contesting authorities and their associated aid agencies (such as National Red Cross or Red Crescent Societies) cannot or will not respond adequately to human suffering in violent situations, the ICRC will try to fill the void with practical action. Thus, individuals victimized by violence have access to social justice in the form of goods and services provided by the ICRC (and its partners) – to the extent that the organization is allowed to operate in zones of conflict and is provided with the resources to meet the basic human needs of those victims.

The relevant historical pattern is that social justice has preceded legal justice. Just as Dunant acted without legal authority in 1859, so the ICRC began visiting detained fighters during the First World War before it was authorized to do so by international law. The 1929 Geneva Convention covering detention matters obviously came later. Likewise, the ICRC projected itself into the (internationalized) Spanish Civil War from 1935. Common Article 3 of the 1949 Geneva Conventions, providing fundamental humanitarian norms for internal armed conflict, obviously came later.

The ICRC began trying to protect and assist what some call political prisoners in the aftermath of the First World War and continued its ad hoc efforts into the 1930s and beyond. There still is no treaty specifically for that category of victims of politics, in general owing to governmental sensitivity about state sovereignty and domestic jurisdiction. Yet, trying to bring a modicum of social justice to such persons remains today a major aspect of ICRC activity. Trying to avoid legal controversies, it refers to such persons as those 'detained by reason of events'. Its primary objective is curtailment of various forms of prisoner abuse and deprivation, not securing a legal definition of political prisoner or the prosecution of those authorities responsible for detention on arbitrary or political grounds.

In fact, there are many organizations, agencies and individuals who comment on IHL, and human rights law for that matter, in order to secure compliance with existing norms and/or to develop new norms. But there is no other entity in the world that does so many systematic and structured prison visits on a global basis except for the ICRC. Now from time to time Amnesty International or a UN agency or some unit of the Salvation Army may do some prison visits on a very limited and ad hoc basis. But what distinguishes the ICRC and sets it apart on prisoner affairs is its long experience (from 1920), its global reach, its well-established procedures, and the scope of its work (namely, number of visits made and detainees seen).

The priority in its prisoner policy across different legal categories of prisoners is a focus on what is equitable in context, not legal justice. It does not prioritize the release of prisoners 'unjustly' held, although it may ask for release on occasion on humanitarian grounds – for example, age, sickness, family hardship, etc. It does not prioritize legal proceedings, although it may ask for due process in judicial matters and it does engage in some judicial observation. What it does prioritize as a form of social justice is prohibition of torture or cruel treatment of prisoners and provision of adequate food, clothing, shelter and medical care (including mental health aspects). Its prison visits are directed to securing these minimal forms of social justice. Persons have access to this form of international justice to the extent that the ICRC is allowed to carry out its visits and to the extent that the detaining authority carries out the recommendations of the organization.

The same general analysis can be made about its work for the civilian population as a whole in conflict areas (detained civilians being covered in the points already made above). While the early focus of the ICRC was on sick and wounded combatants, and then detained combatants, from the First World War it was also concerned with civilians in need. This focus was finally codified in 1949 Geneva Convention IV pertaining to civilians under occupation or in international armed conflict. Its work for the civilian populations in situations of internal armed conflict proceeded apace, finally receiving some further legal support via Additional Protocol II of 1977. If we use concrete examples, we can say that Palestinian civilians living under Israeli occupation, or Syrian civilians in need because of the violence in Syria after 2011, have access to social justice to the extent that the ICRC (and its partners) is able to meet their basic human needs when the relevant authorities, including armed non-state actors, are unable or unwilling to do so.

Now in the case of the civilian population in general, many actors may be active in trying to provide food, clothing, shelter, medical care and psychiatric services to this type of victim. There is also the matter of tracing missing persons. The ICRC has no monopoly on delivery of such goods and services. Often the size of the need mandates a role for multiple actors. The UN World

Food Programme, the UN Office of the High Commissioner of Refugees, and United Nations Children's Emergency Fund (UNICEF) join the ICRC as being almost always present in violent situations working for the civilian population. Moreover, dozens if not hundreds of NGOs are usually also active, from Doctors Without Borders (MSF) to World Vision to Caritas to Oxfam, and so forth. Still, the ICRC can be considered one of the big four relief agencies present in political conflict.[4] The Red Cross Code of Conduct (initiated by the Federation of Red Cross and Red Crescent Societies) has had broad impact on all relief agencies. Particularly the Red Cross values of independence, neutrality and impartiality inform much international assistance activity today – both in conflicts and natural or technological disasters.[5]

Despite much treaty law in the domain of IHL, a considerable amount of ICRC activity is not precisely shaped by that law but is dependent on the organization's decisions about what is equitable or morally appropriate in context. The nature of its prison visits has never been specified in law but is the product of practice over time. One might make the argument that these procedures are now part of customary international law, but this author knows of no court case indicating so. When the organization asked for reading material for Nelson Mandela and the other black detainees held on Robben Island in South Africa in the 1980s, or long pants, or eating utensils, no legal norm specified the correctness or legitimacy of those ICRC requests. When the organization decided that the US regime at the Guantanamo Bay detention facility was injurious to the mental health of the detainees held there after 2001, no legal norm specified how to judge the situation or indeed that public disclosure of the situation was merited. In these and other situations featuring ICRC protection and assistance activities on the ground, much depends on Geneva's notions of social justice in context. Geneva decides what is fair, equitable or moral in context, relying on its global experience, and then pursues the matter – mostly discreetly – with detaining authorities.

To be sure, international legal justice through the codification of IHL, and some parts of human rights law, does manifest certain general norms or principles: hospitals are not to be made the object of attack; medical personnel are to be recognized as neutral and likewise not to be attacked; goods and facilities essential to the survival of civilians are likewise legally protected; those operating under the Red Cross, Red Crescent, and Red Diamond emblems are to be considered neutral and immune from attack, and so on. Individuals are never to be tortured, regardless of any other consideration. Yet, the many details of such matters remain subject to practice on the ground. To secure the safety of its personnel, resources and facilities, the ICRC usually engages in ad hoc negotiations with fighting parties. Only if those with the guns *sur place* know who the ICRC is and where it will be and what it will be doing can independent, neutral and impartial action occur. So a form of legal justice is not entirely absent in humanitarian activity in conflict situations, but most practical arrangements require a decision about what Geneva finds morally acceptable and consistent with its mandate and principles – and feasible when bullets are flying. The simple invoking of legal standards is rarely sufficient for the advancement of humanitarian protection and assistance.

From one point of view, victims in need because of violent politics have access to international justice to the extent that the ICRC and its partners are able to carry out their humanitarian protection and assistance activities at appropriate levels. This is basically a matter of social justice, of implementing equitable programmes that meet at least minimal standards of human dignity. To those without safe water, adequate food and nutrition, minimal health care, knowledge of loved ones, or who suffer torture or cruelty while detained, notions of traditional legal justice may seem distant, theoretical or academic. What good is legal justice, especially in the form of *ex post facto* criminal justice, if one in the meantime has died from hypothermia or malnutrition or dysentery or torture?

The question of legal justice

From its beginnings the ICRC tried to turn Dunant's charitable zeal into legal obligation via public international law. It drafted what became the 1864 Geneva Convention[6] for victims of war, which legally neutralized the international war wounded and those who tended to their needs. Since then the ICRC has continued to draw on its field experience in order to translate its pragmatic endeavours for social justice into legal justice. It has tried to get states to consent to legal restrictions on violence in the name of protecting human dignity. Its early slogan of '*inter arma caritas*' was fully indicative of its objectives until the notion of (Christian) charity became widely seen as politically incorrect, smacking as it did of (Western) cultural superiority and imperialism.[7] The organization, especially when Dunant faded into temporary oblivion and the general Henri Dufour was replaced as president by the lawyer Gustav Moynier, manifested a pronounced legal orientation.

In fact, the ICRC saw its early role as facilitating legal developments and field action by others, not itself. Its early intention was to help National RC Societies act and to get states to do the right thing as codified in IHL.[8] It was during the Franco-Prussian War of 1870 that the central defect in Dunant's vision became clearly evident: the French and Prussian RC Societies were not going to be neutral. As nationalistic supporters of their military establishments, they could only operate in limited ways. Moreover, the French RC left something to be desired in terms of effectiveness. So the ICRC, claiming to be neutral and tied in many ways to the permanently neutral Swiss state, expanded its own field activities. (It had sent two Swiss delegates to observe the previous war in Schleswig-Holstein, thus engaging in very limited 'field work'.) This ICRC new focus on action in the field by itself was made permanent by the experience of the First World War (despite the considerable size, efficiency and resources of the American Red Cross (ARC), which nevertheless was far from being neutral – with the US commander-in-chief, Woodrow Wilson, being also titular head of the ARC.

The ICRC has never deviated from part of its original objectives, namely to translate applied social justice through its pragmatic fieldwork into legal justice.

The first step was to construct a legal framework in which states consented to limit violence in the name of sparing as many victims as possible in the light of 'military necessity'.[9] From 1864 to 1949 and beyond, the ICRC succeeded at least in terms of legal theory, serving as drafting secretariat and sometimes low-key lobbyist for 'Geneva Law', which restricted the scope of military necessity and expanded the scope of humanitarian protection and assistance for victims. From 1977, the two Additional Protocols introduced further restrictions on military action based not only on revised Geneva Law but also on: (1) means and methods of warfare, thus updating parts of The Hague tradition of the laws of war; and, (2) human rights conceptions. (The third Protocol in late 2005 dealt with neutral emblems.) In this first sense, legal justice has to do with states (and other fighting parties) endorsing Geneva Law so as to inject a minimal humanity into an otherwise violent and brutalizing process – whether taking the form of international or internal armed conflict. (Major domestic political violence remains unregulated by IHL.)

Here, it should be noted that while actively developing and supporting IHL, the ICRC has progressively sought to avoid some (but not all) specific and public commentary about who has violated the norms and who should be labelled a war criminal – at least for ongoing controversies (compared to fully historical events). The subject is complex.

Because of prioritizing its quest for effective access to war victims, it mostly prefers to leave to others specific charges about specific violations of IHL. Recognizing through bitter experience that as a matter of subjective perception it is not likely to be regarded as independent, neutral and impartial if making such public charges, it has mostly left most specific and public accusations of wrongdoing to others. It will certainly make general and public comments about how in a given situation, say, the Yugoslav Wars of the 1990s, there needs to be more effective attention to IHL. Or it may indicate that in another situation, say, Israeli occupation of foreign territory after 1967, various terms of the Fourth Geneva Convention (1949)[10] are not yet fully implemented. But it tries to avoid specific commentary in most contemporary cases about particular war crimes and particular war criminals.

Thus in 2001, President Jacob Kellenberge recalled to Geneva the head of the ICRC delegation to Israel and the Occupied Territories, Rene Kosirnik, because of his public statement that a certain Israeli action constituted a war crime. Having a multitude of projects in process in Israel and the territories, and manifesting a complicated history of interactions with Israel and European Jewry, the ICRC wanted to leave to others such public accusations if possible. The ICRC internal rule is that any such public statement has to receive advance clearance by the Geneva headquarters. Now one could reasonably infer from ICRC publications on the subject that the ICRC was unhappy about certain Israeli policies in the territories. And eventually when ICRC archives are open on the subject, a researcher will be able to find out what the ICRC was saying to Israeli authorities in discreet statements. Still, in 2001 the ICRC sought to avoid finding itself in the role of public prosecutor regarding a high-profile issue like the introduction of more Jewish settlements into the West Bank area. This policy position the ICRC adopted not out of lack of conviction in the light of IHL but in order to prioritize and optimize its chances for social justice through its fieldwork.[11]

Relevant also are events in 1962. During the Cuban Missile Crisis, as the United States and the Soviet Union belatedly sought to defuse the clash that might lead to nuclear war, there was discussion of some sort of fact-finding mission that might resolve the question of whether the Soviets had installed attack missiles with Castro's permission and whether Soviet military vessels then in transit contained missile equipment. ICRC officials and UN Secretary-General U Thant discussed options. The ICRC took the position that as an exceptional matter it would play a role in the selection of such a panel but that it would not serve itself as factfinder. This position reflected not only its willingness to act beyond its traditional métier but also to avoid finding itself in possible public conflict with a superpower. Presumably the Soviets were just buying time for further diplomacy through discussion of a fact-finding commission, and the commission never was constructed. But the ICRC was consistent in seeking to avoid the role of public protagonist on specific and controversial matters.[12]

The ICRC, whether because of Swiss culture or an accurate understanding of events, or some combination of the two, mostly believes in the efficacy of discreet humanitarianism. (The leadership of the organization remains all Swiss, although the staff was internationalized in the early 1990s.)[13] When one of its non-public detention reports was leaked to the press concerning CIA torture and cruelty in secret prisons after 2001, the organization was unhappy. It believes that such unauthorized publicity on controversial subjects imperils its access to detainees and undermines its status as a reliable partner of governing authorities. The fact that the ICRC was never granted access to the CIA black sites (it did interviews with prisoners after they were moved to Guantanamo Bay where it did have access), and the fact that brutal abuse was directed to most if not all of the 'high-value' detainees held by the CIA, did not alter the ICRC's view that publicity about specifics was unhelpful. The ICRC did publicly 'deplore' its lack of access to CIA prisons, and it did publicly criticize some aspects of the Guantanamo Bay operation (that commentary meeting with vociferous attacks from the American right-wing).[14]

But in general the ICRC does not believe in the efficacy of public 'naming and shaming', and it does believe that it can advance more social justice through its fieldwork via discreet engagement – most of the time. (Large-scale assistance operations do not raise the issue of discretion so much. Still, from time to time the question does arise as to what actor is blocking progress and why, as in Syria at the time of writing.)

Against this background one can understand the ICRC position on international criminal justice. It is in favour of prosecution of individuals for grave breaches of IHL. It agrees that states have a duty to prevent and repress such breaches. It supported the creation of the first two UN ad hoc criminal tribunals (the International Criminal Tribunal for the Former Yugoslavia, or ICTY, and the International Criminal Tribunal for Rwanda, or ICTR), other contemporary criminal courts, and the permanent International Criminal Court. In its early history it favourably discussed the creation of precisely such a court.

Nevertheless, in order to facilitate its access to victims of violent politics, it decides itself whether or not to exercise a right of testimonial immunity. This right of the ICRC has been accepted in public international law. In general it refuses to allow its delegates to testify in national and international investigative or judicial proceedings about what they have seen. As an exceptional matter it might allow testimony, but it reserves that decision to itself. It objects to a court holding the final say on such matters, perhaps using a balancing test of the importance of testimony versus the importance of ICRC fieldwork. Thus the organization demands the authority to judge the wisdom of testifying, and that demand has been accepted by states who fashion international criminal law and institutions. The rules of the International Criminal Court exempt the ICRC from testimony in criminal cases. States either appreciate ICRC fieldwork or do not want ICRC statements about the dirty laundry in their messy backyards, or both.[15]

In other words, to do justice the ICRC distances itself from justice. To effectuate social justice, the ICRC distances itself in certain ways from legal justice, specifically criminal justice. This is not really a contradiction but rather a paradox. It appears to be a contradiction but it is not. It is a well-considered paradox.

Conclusion

The ICRC through word and deed manifests an appropriately broad notion of justice in the world. Its view of justice not only includes but actually prioritizes social justice, through direct services of protection and assistance to victims of violent politics. It does not eschew legal justice, but the organization pursues that dimension in ways that do not undercut its version of social justice.

The ICRC view of international justice is a conception that resonates well in many circles of opinion. Nelson Mandela, who was visited in prison by the ICRC over many years, praised the ICRC for its sense of 'justice, fairness, [and] humane compassion'.[16] A survey indicates that in Nepal, wracked by violence, what those in need want is:

1 knowledge about the fate of loved ones;
2 economic assistance; and (in last place)
3 legal remedies.[17]

For the ICRC, all victims need to know the fate of loved ones, and therefore the ICRC pushes for exhumation of remains for all as part of the search for missing persons, not just when there is a legal case pending.[18]

For the ICRC, physical rehabilitation for those wounded from political violence is a matter of 'basic justice'.[19]

In the ICRC annual report of 2010, it is clear that the ICRC strategy for action is first and foremost to meet the needs of the victims of violent politics by direct access to such persons through its fieldwork. A distinctly secondary focus is 'shaping the legal debate' that sets the framework for humanitarian action. As for international criminal justice, the organization insists on testimonial immunity. The ICRC prioritizes social justice over legal justice.[20]

Notes

1 International Committee of the Red Cross (ICRC) 12 August 1949, 75 UNTS 287).
2 The ICRC is often treated as if it were an international organization, although it is a Swiss civic society organization. See further Forsythe 2005. And see www.ICRC.org.
3 Forsythe 1993: 131–51.
4 See Natsios 1997.
5 International Federation of Red Cross and Red Crescent Societies and the ICRC n.d.
6 International Committee of the Red Cross (ICRC) 1864.
7 On early humanitarian efforts as reflecting the mindset of Western imperialism, see Barnett 2011.
8 The abbreviation 'RC' has utility because it obviates the need to write out the phrase 'Red Cross or Red Crescent' each time.
9 To be sure, states consented to the 1864 Geneva Convention in part for self-interested political reasons and not entirely for humanitarian ones. With improved communications, journalists and others were reporting on the distressing fate of many soldiers at the front, which gave rise to popular unrest. In order to preserve wars and conscripted armies as viable options, state leaders were motivated to improve humanitarian arrangements. See especially Hutchinson 1996.
10 International Committee of the Red Cross (ICRC), 'Geneva Convention Relative to the Protection of Civilian Persons in Time of War (Fourth Geneva Convention)'. Online.
11 The ICRC manifests a 'doctrine' on discretion in which it reserves the right to 'go public' when certain conditions are met, including that any public statement must be in the interest of victims. This last caveat constitutes a loophole even when humanitarian progress is not evident to most observers. In the practice of ICRC detention visits and other activities, it is rare to find ICRC public statements of criticism of particular actors because of particular problems. Discretion is the rule and pointed public commentary about the specific defects of authorities is the rare exception.
12 Bugnion 2012. It seems an ICRC official on his own approached U Thant and not the other way around.
13 The ICRC Assembly, or governing board, must be all Swiss according to the statutes of the organization. In theory the top of the management side, namely the director-general and director of operations, etc., can be of any nationality. To date, they have always been Swiss (males).
14 See further Forsythe 2011.
15 Rona 2002, updated February 2004.
16 International Committee of the Red Cross (ICRC) n.d.
17 International Committee of the Red Cross (ICRC) 2009.
18 Kirasiolumb and Kalebi Yakub 2002.
19 International Committee of the Red Cross (ICRC) 2012.
20 International Committee of the Red Cross (ICRC) 2011: www.icrc.org/eng/resources/documents/annual-report/icrc-annual-report-2010.htm.

References

Barnett, Michael J. *Empire of Humanity: A History of Humanitarianism*. Ithaca, NY: Cornell University Press, 2011.

Bugnion, Francois. 'The ICRC and the Cuban Missile Crisis, October–November 1962'. *Intercross Magazine*, 26 October 2012. Online. Available at http://intercrossblog.icrc.org/blog/icrc-and-cuban-missile-crisis-october-november-1962 (accessed 30 October 2012).

Forsythe, David P. 'Choices More Ethical Than Legal: The International Committee of the Red Cross and Human Rights'. *Ethics & International Affairs* 7, No. 1 (1993): 131–151.

Forsythe, David P. *The Humanitarians: The International Committee of the Red Cross*. Cambridge: Cambridge University Press, 2005.

Forsythe, David P. *The Politics of Prisoner Abuse: The United States and Enemy Prisoners after 9/11*. Cambridge: Cambridge University Press, 2011.

Hutchinson, John F. *Champions of Charity: War and the Rise of the Red Cross*. Boulder, CO: Westview Press, 1996.

ICRC. 'Geneva Convention for the Amelioration of the Condition of the Wounded in Armies in the Field (First Geneva Convention)'. 1864.

ICRC. 'Geneva Convention Relative to the Protection of Civilian Persons in Time of War (Fourth Geneva Convention)'. 12 August 1949, 75 UNTS 287.

ICRC. *Families of Missing Persons in Nepal: A Study of Their Needs*. Geneva: ICRC, 2009. Online. Available at www.icrc.org/eng/assets/files/2011/families-of-missing-persons-nepal-report.pdf (accessed 26 March 2014).

ICRC. 'Annual Report 2010'. 21 June 2011. Online. Available at www.icrc.org/eng/resources/documents/annual-report/icrc-annual-report-2010.htm (accessed 26 March 2014).

ICRC. *Towards Social Inclusion: Physical Rehabilitation Programme*. Geneva: ICRC, 2012. Online. Available at www.icrc.org/eng/resources/documents/publication/p4090.htm (accessed 4 August 2014).

ICRC. 'Nelson Mandela: Red Cross a "Beacon of Humanity" for Political Prisoners'. N.d. Available at www.icrc.org/eng/resources/documents/misc/5pkj9a.htm (accessed 26 March 2014).

International Federation of Red Cross and Red Crescent Societies and the ICRC. 'Code of Conduct for the International Red Cross and Red Crescent Movement and Non-Governmental Organizations (NGOs) in Disaster Relief'. ICRC, n.d. Online. Available at www.icrc.org/eng/resources/documents/publication/p1067.htm (accessed 26 March 2014).

Kirasiolumb, Alex and Yakub, Ahmed Kalebi. 'Management, Exhumation and Identification of Human Remains: A Viewpoint of the Developing World'. *IRRC* 84 (2002): 893–902. Online. Available at www.icrc.org/eng/resources/documents/misc/5hvjfz.htm (accessed 26 March 2014).

Natsios, Andrew. *U.S. Foreign Policy and the Four Horsemen of the Apocalypse: Humanitarian Relief in Complex Emergencies*. Westport, CT: Praeger, 1997.

Rona, Gabor. 'The ICRC Privilege Not to Testify: Confidentiality in Action'. *International Review of the Red Cross* 845 (March 2002). Online. Available at www.icrc.org/eng/resources/documents/misc/59kcr4.htm (accessed 6 July 2004).

11 Convergence, fragmentation and sustainability in access to international justice*

Simon Chesterman

Introduction

A problem when contemplating a term like 'access to justice' is that justice means many things to many people. This is all the more true at the international level, where justice may not always be matched with an avenue to pursue it. Such a mismatch partly explains the tension within some international lawyers, balancing the idealism of the human rights activist against the cynicism of the lawyer. Susan Lamb's account of victim participation in Cambodia's Khmer Rouge Tribunal may suggest what happens when such idealism is not balanced by legal cynicism. Even so, there may routinely be no access to justice in response to a clearly and widely perceived wrong. The drone attacks that Ramesh Thakur describes are an obvious example of this. Less obvious may be how one should respond to larger, more inchoate wrongs such as poverty and the looming impact of climate change.

For this chapter, I prefer to write not of access to justice per se but 'accountability'. This term is also invoked routinely without much rigour, but it is a little clearer in that it implies a relationship, traditionally with an obligation to give an account. That merely begs the question, of course, of *who* is accountable *to whom* and *for what*. Such questions highlight an underlying concern in this volume that looms large but often silent: the problem of governance.

The chapter first considers how we conceive of the problem of access to international justice, examined through the lens of accountability and governance deficits. It then turns to a possible answer in the form of an emerging global administrative law regime, the impact that this might have in practice and some possible critiques. A key question is how convergence in the international order is also leading to fragmentation of the institutions intended to enforce these norms. The modest contribution of this chapter is that if such an order is to be sustainable then processes moderating governance and providing measures of accountability must be cultivated.

The accountability deficit: politics or institutions, networks or norms?

The question of how the globe should be governed depends, crucially, on one's diagnosis of its challenges. My response to this question will build on two insights that have now become commonplaces. The first is that the liberal order constructed in large part by the United States after the Second World War is losing its claim to legitimacy. The second is that globalization has revealed governance gaps suggesting that the present order is in any case no longer effective.

The first may be understood as a political challenge to the top-down hierarchy that dominates this order, the second as a bottom-up practical challenge to the relevance of existing institutions. Though these crises of legitimacy and effectiveness are of course related, different prescriptions emphasize one or the other.

To the crisis of legitimacy, political solutions are sometimes proposed: a reallocation of seats on the various institutions of global governance such as the UN Security Council, the World Bank, the International Monetary Fund, the G8 and so on.[1] For the crisis of effectiveness, new institutions are frequently mooted and sometimes created: recent modest examples include the Group of Twenty (G-20) Finance Ministers and Central Bank Governors that first met in 1999,[2] the Leaders-20 (L20) established in 2003[3] and the UN Peacebuilding Commission created in 2005.[4]

Yet the viability of any system-wide prescriptive approach depends on political will that, historically, has been available only in times of crisis. It took the First World War to bring about the establishment of the League of Nations, and a Second World War to see the creation of the United Nations and the Bretton Woods Institutions. The only amendments to the UN Charter took place during the organization's expansion in the wake of decolonization. It is possible that current crises – of climate change, public health, financial markets – will be sufficient to bring about similar tectonic shifts, but overcoming the underlying collective action problems requires a level of enlightened self-interest that is rare in international affairs, even if one assumes that political or institutional solutions to these crises exist.[5]

Other accounts therefore eschew major political or institutional change and focus on processes; often they are more descriptive than prescriptive, advocating a change in perspective rather than a wholesale change in political reality – evolution rather than revolution. Anne-Marie Slaughter, for example, has argued compellingly that government networks are an underutilized tool of global governance that operate in parallel to traditional institutions.[6] Advocacy of greater reliance on such networks can loosely be termed the *deformalization* of global processes and could lay the foundation for greater legitimacy in decision-making in so far as the various participating officials can be linked back to traditional domestic accountability structures.[7] The limitations of such an approach are that it remains subject to the power disparities of the political order and cannot easily overcome the collective action problems identified earlier.[8]

An alternative (though not mutually exclusive) approach thus emphasizes instead the *formalization* of global processes. It is this account, largely descriptive of developments already occurring, that is the subject of the present chapter.

Global administrative law

The intentionally unexciting name given to this formalization of certain global processes is 'global administrative law'.[9] Blandness can be a virtue if it is equated with harmlessness, and indeed there is little to fear from global administrative law. The emerging set of rules to which it refers encompasses procedures and normative standards for regulatory decision-making that fall outside domestic legal structures and yet are not properly covered by public international law. The standards that are being imported into this new sphere of regulatory activity draw upon administrative law principles common in many jurisdictions, such as transparency, participation and review.[10]

As a response to the demand for accountability in globalization, then, this is distinct from demands that globalization be made more *democratic*; instead, these developments aim to make it more *reasoned*.[11] Nevertheless, though most of the discussion here is descriptive of existing phenomena, consolidation of this emerging body of norms would improve both the quality of decision-making and the ability of those affected by decisions to protect their legitimate rights and interests.

The fragmented nature of activity in this area to date is easily seen. The forums in which regulatory decisions are being made range from treaty-based organizations such as the United Nations and the World Trade Organization (WTO) to networks of government officials such as the Basel Committee of national bank regulators. In addition to government representatives, the actors include experts such as the technical committees of the International Organization for Standardization (ISO) and the non-profit Internet Corporation for Assigned Names and Numbers (ICANN). And, increasingly, less formal networks of interested parties play a role in developing standards in areas as diverse as 'fair trade' coffee and 'dolphin-friendly' tuna.

Participation in these disparate decision-making processes varies widely, but there is rarely a general right for affected parties to challenge a decision; frequently it is not possible even to seek reasons as to why a particular decision was made. The disparate regimes may overlap – sometimes quite intentionally, as the market comes to be regulated by a market of regulation. In some areas, competing standards may be adopted on a 'voluntary' basis, though the global marketplace quickly leads to standards becoming mandatory as a commercial reality if not a legal requirement.

Mechanisms that have sought to regulate these activities tend to come from traditional governance institutions operating at the limits of or beyond their traditional boundaries. At the national level, courts and legislatures have increasingly asserted a capacity to review domestic implementation of global standards and national officials' participation in global administrative decisions. At the international level, accountability may depend on specific mechanisms established for a particular regime, such as the WTO's inspections panels and Appellate Body,[12] or reactive ad hoc bodies such as the Independent Inquiry Committee into the United Nations Oil-for-Food Programme. For many regimes, there is no formal review procedure at all and no means of calling for one.[13]

Though such activities are far from uniform, they mark a paradigm shift in the governance activities of bodies that do not fit neatly into historic categories of national or international law. The former typically controls activities within the jurisdiction of one state; the latter the relations between states. This schema was never particularly neat – a separate body of law deals just with conflicts of jurisdiction – but the activities considered here frequently operate in the interstices *between* jurisdictions, while encompassing activities that would normally be undertaken by domestic governance authorities.[14]

Seeing such activity as 'global administration' reflects those qualities and pointedly raises the legitimacy issues that would follow from a government asserting such powers. A government that runs a trading regime for pollution credits, determines capital adequacy requirements for banks or freezes the assets of suspected terrorist financiers, for example, would typically be subject to some form of administrative law process, perhaps requiring varying degrees of transparency, rights of participation and review of decisions. These procedural remedies are not available against the Kyoto Protocol's Clean Development Mechanism, the Basel Committee or the UN Security Council's 1267 Al-Qaida Sanctions Committee, respectively.[15]

Whether it makes sense for these activities to be thought of as a coherent whole is an open question. Similarly, analogies between national legal regimes, such as administrative law, and international or transnational law must be drawn carefully. Nevertheless, the increasing demands for accountability are suggestive of the manner in which administrative activity by governments came to be subject to review.[16]

A more basic difficulty in applying administrative law principles to global administration is the structure of authority.[17] National institutions of governance tend to be organized hierarchically with power distributed in accordance with a constitution or basic law. Global institutions of governance, such as they are, frequently operate in a less structured environment driven by negotiation; formally, much authority comes from the states whose consent gives them legitimacy. This is reflective of larger problems with any conception of an international 'rule of law': in a domestic legal order, the sovereign stands in a vertical hierarchy with other subjects of law; at the international level, sovereignty tends to be conceived of as remaining with states, at least nominally operating in a horizontal plane of sovereign equality.[18]

In practice

Is it *possible*, then, to have meaningful accountability in this area? (This is separate from the question of whether accountability is always *desirable* – a point that is considered below.)

There are many ways of holding power to account. Mechanisms are available at the global level, but they tend to be responsive in nature and ad hoc in structure. Accountability should not simply be a reaction to scandal, however. To be effective it should normally exist as of right, which requires the creation of institutions, the elaboration of standards and the potential for sanctions.[19]

This is not, of course, the only way to constrain power. Other means include negotiation constraints, checks and balances, the threat of unilateral action and so on. Such constraints fall outside 'accountability' as it is used here but point to an important distinction between legal and political accountability. *Legal* accountability typically requires that a decision-maker has a convincing reason for a decision or act. Compliance with a rule will normally be a sufficient reason, though some administrative agencies may be established with a requirement to provide substantive reasons on the merits of a particular decision. *Political* accountability, by contrast, can be entirely arbitrary. In an election, for example, voters are not required to have reasons for their decision – indeed, the secrecy of the ballot implies the exact opposite: it is generally unlawful even to ask a voter why he or she voted one way or another.[20]

These forms of accountability may be seen as lying on a spectrum, with other variations possible. In a legislature individual legislators may have specific reasons for voting in favour of or against a piece of legislation, sometimes demonstrated through speeches made before or after it was adopted. But if such reasons are inconsistent, it may be unclear what significance is to be attributed to them.[21]

In the absence of political or what we might loosely term 'democratic' accountability, is it desirable to provide for legal accountability mechanisms? Two concerns immediately present themselves. First, it is unclear that the objective implementation of standards implied by legal accountability can adequately substitute for a democratic deficit: such an approach presumes that holding power to specified standards is a sufficient form of accountability, while ignoring that the standards themselves are contestable – it loses the essentially arbitrary character of democratic accountability.[22]

Second, the relationship between those making decisions and those affected by them is different in the global administrative sphere than it is in national institutions. In a democracy, power is delegated through elections by the same population that is typically affected by decisions; in global administration, there is no corresponding link between those affected and those delegating power. As a result, those with the most leverage to demand and enforce accountability may be those with least interest in doing so.[23]

It is necessary, therefore, to look more closely at different structures of accountability across the spectrum of legal and political remedies. Ruth W. Grant and Robert O. Keohane have identified seven such structures, reflecting different relationships between those who delegate power, those who make decisions, and those who bear the consequences:

1 *hierarchical* accountability within a bureaucracy, such as the UN Secretariat;
2 *supervisory* accountability, such as the government representatives on the executive boards of the World Bank and the International Monetary Fund (IMF);
3 *fiscal* accountability, such as through the Advisory Committee on Administrative and Budgetary Questions (ACABQ) of the UN General Assembly or the unilateral withholding of UN dues;
4 *legal* accountability, where a disinterested independent third party, such as a

court, is vested with decision-making powers, for example, arbitral tribunals set up under the International Centre for Settlement of Investment Disputes (ICSID) or the International Criminal Court;

5 *market* accountability, where decisions are left to the operation of the market, such as pressure on developing economies to adopt standards attractive to global capital markets or consumer pressure against inadequate labour standards on running shoes;
6 *peer* accountability, such as the desire of diplomats to maintain credibility and influence among their colleagues; and
7 *public reputational* accountability, which applies to all the preceding categories but also embraces 'soft power' connected with the prestige and esteem of a given state.[24]

Such broader conceptions of accountability may provide tools for shaping and improving global administrative decisions, even if they are unlikely to offer the revolution that may be called for in response to specific problems.

Critiques

Global administrative law is appropriately described as an 'emerging' phenomenon.[25] It is not suggested here that it offers a comprehensive response to the problems identified earlier. The global decision-making processes that are subject to administrative law type remedies are limited, and it is unlikely that such remedies will be extended to cover every such decision.

Nor should they. As indicated earlier, the formalization of certain decision-making processes is supplementary to other efforts to address global governance deficits. The argument here is that such procedures will improve the *quality* of decision-making and responsiveness to those affected by decisions. The intention is not to make such decision-making structures more democratic but to make the decisions themselves more reasoned.

Not all of these problems are technical questions to be resolved by lawyers, of course. Objective implementation of standards is not neutral unless the standards themselves are legitimate. For this reason, purely legal forms of accountability will never be sufficient to address underlying political and institutional deficits. The advantage offered is that such an approach at least clarifies political choices and avoids the illusion of change that is merely rhetorical.

A second criticism of global administrative law is that the formalization of existing processes may entrench the interests of the powerful.

It probably will. Nevertheless, law's capacity to restrain power and prevent the co-optation of norms to serve the ends of the powerful has always been questionable. Writing on the development of the rule of law in eighteenth-century England, the historian E.P. Thompson endorsed the Marxist view that law systematized and reified inequality between the classes. Even so, he argued, law also mediated those class relations through legal forms, constraining the actions of the ruling class. For this reason, unusually for a Marxist, he termed the rule of law an 'unqualified human good'.[26] Global administrative law will not bring about a New International Economic Order, but it might enable those most affected by globalization to hold those with influence to their rhetoric.

The goals of a global administrative law go beyond constraining decision-makers, however. In addition to providing 'input legitimacy' to decision-making processes, broadening participation, shining light on deliberations and providing the possibility of revisiting bad or unfair choices should improve the decisions themselves. This may be thought of as 'output legitimacy'.[27]

What, then, might this mean in some key areas of convergence and sustainability in international affairs? In the area of environment and energy (discussed by Yasunabe Sato),[28] global administrative law is unlikely to answer the high political questions of who pollutes and who pays. But it could improve, among other things, environmental impact assessments or the workings of a cap-and-trade system and other mechanisms, enhancing both substantive decisions and the legitimacy accorded to those decisions.[29] In relation to aggression (discussed by Edwin Bikundo[30] as well as Mirinda O'Gorman and Charles Sampford),[31] global administrative law is unlikely to force states to do the right thing.[32] But it may make it harder to do the wrong thing. Or to do nothing at all.

In other areas such as public health, this approach will not resolve the problems of resources or how intellectual property rights held by the rich should be balanced against the medical needs of the poor. Yet it can offer concrete improvements to the work of the World Health Organization (WHO) as well as insights into effective reporting systems for epidemics and the rational allocation of scarce resources.[33]

And in the area of finance, global administrative law will not address the basic structure of global capitalism or conjure regulatory tools to prevent speculative bubbles. Nevertheless it may improve the accountability of institutions such as the WTO, the IMF and the World Bank, as well as the procedures of credit-rating agencies and other actors that can affect national economies.[34]

These are all, evidently, partial answers to the governance and accountability deficits identified earlier. Even if present crises make possible more ambitious political and institutional transformations, however, and even if networked governments supplement those transformations with informal relationships, those seem inadequate safeguards for the exercise of powers that, in a domestic environment, would naturally be regarded as 'public' and thus subjected to public law limitations.

These are, of course, incomplete answers to a call for access to justice. But as global regimes are granted greater powers to address global problems, the starting point is ensuring that such powers are subject to, as well as enforced by, law.

Notes

* This chapter draws on some material first published as Simon Chesterman, "Globalization Rules: Accountability, Power, and the Prospects for Global Administrative Law", *Global Governance* 14 (2008), 39–52.

1 See, for example, Mahbubani 2008: 103–104; Emmott 2008: 262–264.

2 Germain 2001.

3 See, for example, Linn and Bradford 2006; Xue 2007.
4 See, for example, Chesterman 2005.
5 Cf. Talbott 2008: 393–401; Zakaria 2008: 231–232.
6 Slaughter 2004.
7 Ibid.: 230–244. Cf. Barnett and Finnemore 2004; Khagram 2006.
8 Kingsbury *et al.* 2005: 50.
9 See the materials available at the Global Administrative Law website. Online. Available at: www.iilj.org/GAL (accessed 2 April 2014).
10 Kingsbury *et al.* 2005: 15–18.
11 Esty 2006.
12 See, for example, Clark *et al.* (eds.) 2003; Hunter 2003.
13 Kingsbury *et al.* 2005: 33–34.
14 Cohen and Sabel 2005.
15 On the Basel Committee in particular, see Barr and Miller 2005.
16 See Stewart 1975, 2005.
17 See Cassese 2005; Dyzenhaus 2008.
18 See further, Chesterman 2008.
19 Kingsbury 2005. See also, United Nations 2008.
20 See Ferejohn 1999: 131–153.
21 Kingsbury 2005.
22 Cf. Ferejohn 2002.
23 Grant and Keohane 2005. Cf. Krisch 2006.
24 Grant and Keohane 2005.
25 Kingsbury *et al.* 2005: 50.
26 Thompson 1977: 264.
27 Böhmer 2005.
28 In this volume.
29 See, for example, Jagers and Stripple 2003; Craik 2007; David B. Hunter 2008; MacDonald 2008; Wara 2008.
30 In this volume.
31 In this volume.
32 Cf. Tzanakopoulos 2011.
33 See, for example, Krisch 2004: 38; Esty 2006: 1550–1554; Stiglitz 2006: 21; Choi 2008.
34 See, for example, Anghie 2000; Porter 2001; Sinclair 2001: 441–451; Saoul 2002: 127–137; Bridgeman and David B. Hunter 2008; Gadinis 2008; Howse 2008; Sokol 2008.

References

Anghie, Antony. 'Time Present and Time Past: Globalization, International Financial Institutions and the Third World'. *New York University Journal of International Law and Politics* 32 (2000): 243.

Barnett, Michael and Finnemore, Martha. *Rules for the World: International Organizations in Global Politics*. Ithaca, NY: Cornell University Press, 2004.

Barr, Michael S. and Miller, Geoffrey P. 'Global Administrative Law: The View from Basel'. New York: New York University, 2005.

Böhmer, Martín. 'Who Benefits from Administrative Remedies? Mobilization and Access to Justice in Impoverished Areas'. Paper presented at the Global Administrative Law Conference, New York University School of Law, 22–23 April 2005.

Bridgeman, Natalie L. and Hunter, David B. 'Narrowing the Accountability Gap: Toward a New Foreign Investor Accountability Mechanism'. *Georgetown International Environmental Law Review* 20 (2008): 187–236.

Cassese, Sabino. 'Administrative Law without the State? The Challenge of Global Regulation'. *New York University Journal of International Law and Politics* 37 (2005): 663–694.

Chesterman, Simon. 'From State Failure to State Building: Problems and Prospects of a United Nations Peacebuilding Commission'. *Journal of International Law and International Relations* 2, No. 1 (2005): 155–176.

Chesterman, Simon. 'An International Rule of Law?'. *American Journal of Comparative Law* 56 (2008): 331–361.

Choi, Kathleen J. 'A Journey of a Thousand Leagues: From Quarantine to International Health Regulations and Beyond'. *University of Pennsylvania Journal of International Law* 29 (2008): 989–1022.

Clark, Dana L., Fox, Jonathan and Treakle, Kay, (eds). *Demanding Accountability: Civil Society Claims and the World Bank Inspection Panel*. Lanham, MD: Rowman and Littlefield, 2003.

Cohen, Joshua and Sabel, Charles F. 'Global Democracy?'. *New York University Journal of International Law and Politics* 37 (2005): 763–797.

Craik, Neil. 'Deliberation and Legitimacy in Transnational Environmental Governance: The Case of Environmental Impact Assessment'. *Victoria University Wellington Law Review* 38 (2007): 381–405.

Dyzenhaus, David. 'Accountability and the Concept of (Global) Administrative Law'. New York: New York University School of Law, 2008.

Emmott, Bill. *Rivals: How the Power Struggle between China, India and Japan Will Shape Our Next Decade*. London: Allen Lane, 2008.

Esty, Daniel C. 'Good Governance at the Supranational Scale: Globalizing Administrative Law'. *Yale Law Journal* 115 (2006): 1490–1652.

Ferejohn, John. 'Accountability and Authority: Toward a Theory of Political Accountability'. In *Democracy, Accountability, and Representation*, edited by Adam Przeworski, S.C. Stokes and B. Manin. Cambridge: Cambridge University Press, 1999: 131–153.

Ferejohn, John. 'The Law of Politics: Judicializing Politics, Politicizing Law'. *Law and Contemporary Problems* 65, No. 3 (2002): 45–68.

Gadinis, Stavros. 'The Politics of Competition in International Financial Regulation'. *Harvard International Law Journal* 49 (2008): 447–507.

Germain, Randall D. 'Global Financial Governance and the Problem of Inclusion'. *Global Governance* 7 (2001): 411–426.

Grant, Ruth W. and Keohane, Robert O. 'Accountability and Abuses of Power in World Politics'. *American Political Science Review* 99, No. 1 (2005): 29–44.

Howse, Robert. 'The End of the Globalization Debate: A Review Essay'. *Harvard Law Review* 121 (2008): 1528–1554.

Hunter, David. 'Using the World Bank Inspection Panel to Defend the Interests of Project-Affected People'. *Chicago Journal of International Law* 4 (2003): 201–211.

Hunter, David B. 'Civil Society Networks and the Development of Environmental Standards at International Financial Institutions'. *Chicago Journal of International Law* 8 (2008): 437–477.

Jagers, Sverker and Stripple, Johannes. 'Climate Governance Beyond the State'. *Global Governance* 9 (2003): 385–399.

Khagram, Sanjeev. 'Possible Future Architectures of Global Governance: A Transnational Perspective/Prospective'. *Global Governance* 12 (2006): 97–117.

Kingsbury, Benedict. 'The Rules and Institutions of Accountability'. Paper presented at the A Rules-Based International Order, seminar convened by the Institute for International Law and Justice and the Permanent Mission of Austria to the United Nations, UN Headquarters, New York, 5 May 2005.

Kingsbury, Benedict, Krisch, Nico and Stewart, Richard B. 'The Emergence of Global Administrative Law'. *Law and Contemporary Problems* 68 (2005): 15–62.

Krisch, Nico. 'Imperial International Law'. New York: New York University School of Law, 2004.

Krisch, Nico. 'The Pluralism of Global Administrative Law'. *European Journal of International Law* 17 (2006): 247–278.

Linn, Johannes F. and Bradford, Colin I. Jr. 'Pragmatic Reform of Global Governance: Creating an L20 Summit Forum'. Washington DC: Brookings Institution, 2006.

MacDonald, Euan. 'Gal and the Intergovernmental Panel on Climate Change'. New York: Institute for International Law and Justice, 2008.

Mahbubani, Kishore. *The New Asian Hemisphere: The Irresistible Shift of Global Power to the East*. New York: Public Affairs, 2008.

Porter, Tony. 'The Democratic Deficit in the Institutional Arrangements for Regulating Global Finance'. *Global Governance* 7 (2001): 427–439.

Saoul, Graham. 'Transparency and Accountability in International Financial Institutions'. In *The Right to Know, the Right to Live: Access to Information & Socio-Economic Justice*, edited by Richard Calland and Alison Tilley. Cape Town: Open Democracy and Advice Centre, 2002: 127–137.

Sinclair, Timothy. 'The Infrastructure of Global Governance: Quasi-Regulatory Mechanisms and the New Global Finance'. *Global Governance* 7 (2001): 441–451.

Slaughter, Anne-Marie. *A New World Order*. Princeton: Princeton University Press, 2004.

Sokol, D. Daniel. 'Order without (Enforceable) Law: Why Countries Enter into Non-Enforceable Competition Policy Chapters in Free Trade Agreements'. *Chicago-Kent Law Review* 83 (2008): 231–291.

Stewart, Richard B. 'The Reformation of American Administrative Law'. *Harvard Law Review* 88 (1975): 1667–1813.

Stewart, Richard B. 'US Administrative Law: A Model for Global Administrative Law?'. *Law and Contemporary Problems* 68 (2005): 127–167.

Stiglitz, Joseph E. *Making Globalization Work*. New York: W.W. Norton, 2006.

Talbott, Strobe. *The Great Experiment: The Story of Ancient Empires, Modern States, and the Quest for a Global Nation*. New York: Simon & Schuster, 2008.

Thompson, E.P. *Whigs and Hunters: The Origin of the Black Act*. Harmondsworth: Penguin, 1977.

Tzanakopoulos, Antonios. *Disobeying the Security Council: Countermeasures against Wrongful Sanctions*. Oxford: Oxford University Press, 2011.

United Nations. 'The UN Security Council and the Rule of Law'. A/63/69-S/2008/270, 2008.

Wara, Michael. 'Measuring the Clean Development Mechanism's Performance and Potential'. *UCLA Law Review* 55 (2008): 1759.

Xue, Lan. 'Breaking Deadlocks in Global Governance: How to Make the L–20 Work'. *Global Governance* 13 (2007): 320–323.

Zakaria, Fareed. *The Post-American World*. London: Allen Lane, 2008.

12 Accessing ecological justice in the Anthropocene epoch!

Afshin Akhtarkhavari[1]

Introduction

In the past few years a range of scientists have argued that in geological terms planet earth has reached the end of what is known as the Holocene epoch.[2] This epoch is a stage in the Cenozoic era that, generally speaking, stands for the flourishing of mammalian life. The name given to this new geological epoch is the Anthropocene epoch. It is defined in terms of the significance of the anthropogenic impact that human beings have had on earth's subsystems. A perspective that the Anthropocene epoch forces on us is the idea that, as a species, the significance of our footprint raises questions about fairness and justness of who we are as a species because what we do is no longer local but truly global in terms of its impact on planet earth. The idea of entering the Anthropocene epoch raises concerns about our capacity as a collective force at the international level to achieve long-term environmental or ecological justice. 'Ecological justice' as compared to environmental justice is a term used to describe the justness of the kind of relationship that humans have with the natural world.[3] The term 'environmental justice' is more commonly used as a way of describing the distribution of interests that humans have in relation to each other when it comes to their use of the natural environment.[4] As such, ecological justice and access to it, as opposed to just environmental justice, raises important intellectual concerns going forward in the Anthropocene epoch.

Commentators and scholars often turn to existing constructs in analysing the idea of ecological justice. One such instance is around granting access in courts and other public institutions for adjudicating and addressing the rights and interests of nature. Drawing on the work of Michel Serres in *The Natural Contract*, this chapter suggests that what is more important is for us to avoid excluding the natural world from the social and cultural agreements or contracts that define us and what we value outside of our self-interest. It argues that we narrow our social and cultural constructions of the world and objects in a way necessary for achieving ecological justice in the Anthropocene epoch. Establishing a symbiotic or reciprocal partnership that is more holistic than the one that draws simply on the rights of nature discourse is more likely to enable cultural changes that will assist us to appreciate the gravity of the collective way in which we are responsible for ensuring ecological justice in the Anthropocene Epoch.

The chapter has two parts: the first will trace developments in adjudicating environmental issues and shows how varieties of courts and adjudicative bodies exist creating fragmented ways for judging human interests in matters that also raise environmental issues. These institutions are suited to arbitrating 'environmental' as compared to 'ecological' justice claims because in most cases they are functionally important bodies for reducing conflicts amongst states. Their fragmentation adds to the challenge of accessing ecological justice in a systematic manner. The second part departs dramatically from the descriptive view of fragmentation and offers a view on the cosmopolitan, public and collective expression of judgment about our relationship with nature through the well-known cultural icon and text, namely a painting by Edvard Munch which in English is titled the *The Scream of Nature*.

The analysis suggests that relying on individual expressions of what is ecological justice is currently more about us as a human species than a global partnership or a natural contract. This is followed by a description and brief assessment of the work of Michel Serres in *The Natural Contract* and places emphasis on a few parts that have meaning for this chapter. This chapter analyses and engages with the work of Serres as an alternative to the rights of nature discourse and as a means to rethink the collective way in which we need to respond to accessing ecological justice issues in the Anthropocene epoch.

Accessing ecological justice through international dispute settlement institutions

Since 1893 and the *Bering Sea Arbitration*,[5] parties have brought disputes before international dispute resolution bodies involving environmental issues. The global concern with environmental matters and a raft of international instruments promulgated in the environmental field means that there is a 'growing number of international fora within which environmentally related disputes can now be addressed'.[6] Commentators have noted that less than 30 years ago '[t]he courts were usually not the kinds of places in which decent professionals would always feel comfortable raising full-scale environmental claims'.[7] Nowadays, there is a 'willingness of international actors – States, corporations and individuals – to engage in international litigation'.[8] Increasingly, environmental considerations also emerge in disputes relating to trade (for example, in the World Trade Organization's (WTO) dispute resolution bodes) and through international investment arbitration.

With the international law movement gaining importance in the 1990s, the creation of a specialized environmental chamber of the International Court of Justice (ICJ) heralded a new category of forum catering specifically for environmental disputes. Despite this start, the ICJ has disbanded the specialized chamber for lack of case law presented to it. However, the jurisprudence of the International Court of Justice has long been a fertile ground for discussions of principles of environmental law, and since the 1970s there have been dozens of cases before the court that have involved environmental issues.[9] There have also been calls for an international environmental court although initiatives in this regard have not significantly progressed.[10] This is partly because the various treaties and conventions that have been negotiated on aspects of environmental protection and conservation have also spawned their own non-compliance mechanisms. Suggestions have been made that this situation reflects the wariness of states to subject environmental matters to an independent 'contentious and conflictual procedure'.[11]

Although litigation to do with environmental concerns has expanded some scholars have observed that '[e]nvironmental claims are invariably made through the lens of the human person'.[12] The growing number of cases before international forums that harness the body of international human rights law is a testament to that fact: groups seek to protect and preserve their environments through the use of human rights norms and agreements. Despite being able to access justice through a variety of dispute settlement procedures, some have noted that the proliferation of available international dispute resolution forums has increased the 'risk of inconsistent judicial decisions on identical or similar matters'.[13] For instance, in the recent *Pulp Mills Case*,[14] the case was not only litigated before the ICJ but was also brought before an arbitration panel (unsuccessfully) and a petition lodged with the Inter-American Commission on Human Rights,[15] illustrating the lack of exclusive jurisdiction over such matters. Much has been written on the problem of fragmentation in international law generally and dispute settlement in particular. Stephens, for instance, has analysed the fragmentation, noting that the *Southern Bluefin Tuna* dispute came before the International Tribunal for the Law of the Sea (ITLOS) and an arbitral tribunal, who reached completely different conclusions on the matter.[16] In broadly describing the nature and features of following dispute resolution mechanisms, it is important to come back to the point that whilst the cases studied often raise important points of international environmental law, often these environmental considerations are subsumed by other legal issues considered more central to the dispute. Importantly, because the cases are embedded in more complex circumstances involving a range of issues, it is human beings that are ultimately the subjects of the justice delivered by the dispute settlement bodies.

The International Court of Justice and environmental matters

The International Court of Justice is the most prominent and preeminent dispute settlement body capable of dealing with wide-ranging disputes involving environmental issues. Noting the growing concern for environmental protection and 'the parallel development of environmental law',[17] in 1993 the ICJ formed a Chamber for Environmental Matters (CEM). However in its 13 years of existence, no case was brought before the specialist chamber and as such it was disbanded in 2006.[18] As the members of the CEM were drawn from the general members of the bench of the ICJ, there existed no specialized knowledge unique to the judges on the CEM. 'There appears to be little benefit for States to bring a dispute before the CEM, rather than the full court of the ICJ or an ad hoc chamber.'[19]

While the jurisprudence of the court has given much discussion to concepts of international environmental law, access to the court is limited to states, and only then with the consent of both state parties. This situation has created challenges for non-state entities who are often the most ardent advocates of environmental concerns and issues including individuals and corporations who can be severely affected by state actions within or outside their own territories.[20] However, a number of ICJ cases have contributed to developments in international environmental law with subsequent effects on a range of activities and actors internationally. These included the *Nuclear Weapons Advisory Opinion*,[21] the *Case Concerning the Gabcikovo-Nagymaros Project*,[22] and most recently, the *Pulp Mills* decision.[23]

In the *Nuclear Weapons Advisory Opinion*, the Court considered the potential threat to the environment stemming from the use of nuclear weapons. While the Court did not find that environmental law specifically prohibited the use of nuclear weapons, it did note 'important environmental factors that have to be properly considered in the context of the implementation of the principles and rules of law applicable in armed conflict'.[24] A more explicit consideration of the developing principles of international environmental law took place in the *Danube Dam Case*, concerning a dispute between Hungary and Czechoslovakia over the construction of barrages on the river Danube.[25] Some have argued that the ICJ missed an opportunity to develop international environmental law but the Court made comments that have generated commentary in terms of the principle of sustainable development and also fair and equitable use of rivers.[26] Recently the Court had occasion to consider a case that raised clear environmental law arguments.[27] The *Pulp Mills Case* concerned a dispute between Uruguay and Argentina over their shared riparian resource, the river Uruguay, and Uruguay's construction of a pulp mill on the banks of the river. Although the Court effectively sidestepped addressing the substantive arguments concerning the environment, they did consider the requirement to undertake an environmental impact assessment (EIA) – an established principle of customary international law in cases involving the potential for transboundary impact. The Court in this case also emphasized 'the link between the principle of equitable and reasonable utilization and the goal of sustainable development'.[28]

The World Trade Organization dispute settlement procedures[29]

The potential for trade disputes to involve environmental matters is now clearly established, and, as such, the dispute settlement body (DSB) of the WTO (and prior to 1995, the GATT tribunals) provide an important forum for environmental issues to present during international litigation. Owing to the subject matter of the disputes, environmental matters are often incidental to the main issue being litigated but may come to the fore during the decision-making process.

The *Tuna-Dolphin* cases[30] that came before the General Agreement on Trade and Tariffs (GATT) tribunals in the early 1990s are emblematic of how such commercial bodies dealt with environmental issues which impinge on trade issues raised during litigation. The disputes, which 'raised squarely the question of whether environmental considerations could justify import prohibitions under GATT law',[31] concerned the US restrictions on importation of tuna caught in a manner which contravened certain US regulations on 'dolphin-friendly' fishing methods. Despite the environmental arguments put forward by the US, the decisions proved that, at the time, there was no room within the provisions of the GATT for a nation to apply its environmental protection laws 'extra jurisdictionally' and, as such, the provisions of the GATT prevailed over environmental concerns.[32]

Since the *Tuna-Dolphin* cases and the creation of the WTO dispute settlement procedures, a number of cases concerning environment-related trade disputes have come before the WTO DSB. A seminal case in the shifting of the WTO's environmental stance came about in the *Shrimp Turtle Case*[33] which contained similar facts to the *Tuna-Dolphin Case*. In this instance, the US sought to restrict imports of shrimp to those harvested in accordance with sea turtle preservation strategies. Although the panel found in favour of the complainants (India, Malaysia, Pakistan and Thailand), they did recognize the legitimate environmental objective of the domestic policy. Importantly, the case was a first in recognizing that 'amicus curiae submissions from environmental groups could be considered in the WTO DSB process',[34] allowing such groups space to voice their concerns within the trade dispute framework.[35] The case drew attention for the clear consideration of international environmental law, including numerous environmental treaties, as well as the focus on sustainable resource management. Although commentators have noted that no state has explicitly relied on environmental law to derogate from their obligations under the WTO,[36] the jurisprudence of the WTO DSB shows a willingness to consider the interface between trade and environmental protection.

UN Convention on the Law of the Sea (UNCLOS) dispute resolution mechanisms

The UN Convention on the Law of the Sea (UNCLOS) makes strong contributions to establishing environmental norms and a number of important cases have come before the various dispute resolution bodies of UNCLOS supporting an emerging jurisprudence. The dispute resolution procedures provided for under UNCLOS include 'the International Tribunal for the Law of the Sea (ITLOS), the International Court of Justice (ICJ), an arbitral tribunal constituted in accordance with Annex VII of UNCLOS, and a special arbitral tribunal constituted in accordance with Annex VIII'.[37]

The dispute, which has drawn the most commentary thus far, is the *Southern Bluefin Tuna* litigation between Australia and New Zealand (claimants) and Japan.[38] Parties to this dispute were involved in a dispute over the numbers of southern bluefin tuna to be fished each year; in particular, Australia and New Zealand sought a resolution on Japan's unilateral experimental fishing programme.[39] While waiting for an arbitral panel to be constituted under Annex VII of the UNCLOS, Australia and New Zealand sought provisional measures before ITLOS, who determined that the panel would ultimately have jurisdiction and therefore ordered provisional measures. However, when the arbitral panel came to consider the issue, the panel found that they lacked jurisdiction and therefore were unable to consider the merits of the case. Despite no actual consideration of the merits, the litigation 'did facilitate the eventual conclusion of the EFP (exempted fishing permit) dispute and assisted the Commission to move towards an agreed scientific basis for its work', which notes the role that litigation can take in encouraging parties to engage in dialogue.[40] Since the *Southern Bluefin Tuna Case*, several other litigations of importance to environmental law have arisen under UNCLOS. They include the *MOX Plant Case*[41] (another example of a case litigated before several forums) and the *Straits of Johor Case*,[42] concerning the environmental impact of Singapore's land reclamation policies.

Investor state arbitration and environmental considerations

International environmental law rules and principles are potentially applicable to investor-state dispute though no tribunal has yet actively engaged with them in deciding a dispute. It is possible that they have not yet become strategically significant to the success of any particular litigation. Pavoni and Samuele have noted that '[i]n recent arbitration squarely involving environmental and human rights issues … investor-state tribunals have had the occasion to address the relevance of the concept of SD [sustainable development], but have failed to do so'.[43] They point, for instance, to the case of *Biwater Gauff*[44] where the International Centre for Settlement of Investment Disputes (ICSID) tribunal failed to apply the principle of sustainable development when the government of the United Republic of Tanzania appropriated the licence granted to Biwater Gauff, a German and English company, for the provision of water and sanitation in the city of Dar es Salaam in Tanzania.

Balancing the interests of the private sector along with those of the state in cases involving environmental issues presents challenges for investor-state arbitration bodies. This problem was played out in the case of *Southern Pacific Properties*[45] where the tribunal 'unhesitatingly declared the [World Heritage Convention] relevant as applicable law'[46] despite finding against Egypt. Pavoni and Samuele, who have studied this decision, have suggested that the overall nature of the decision that in that case protecting a world heritage site was clearly the preferred outcome which had to override overall investor protections.[47] The idea that investor-state tribunals will at times favour environmental interests over investor-state protection was reversed in the *Santa Elena* decision[48] where the tribunal held that the fact that Costa Rica was acting in furtherance of several international environmental agreements did not preclude available compensation owed to the investor. As such, Pavoni and Samuele have suggested that the decision in *Santa Elena* implies 'the investor-state process may turn out to operate as a powerful disincentive for genuine efforts by host states to act for the protection of the environment in line with international and national law'.[49]

The challenge with the work of investor-state arbitral bodies is generally the ad hoc nature of the tribunals and courts that often function in different political and cultural contexts and regions of the world. Also, the only exposures we have to their work are judgments that parties have agreed to release to the public. As such, it is difficult to know the extent to which investor-state arbitration contributes to shifting perception around justice issues beyond isolated cases.

Permanent Court of Arbitration

There have been a number of important cases referring to environmental principles that have come before the Permanent Court of Arbitration (PCA) in recent years. In 2001, the PCA adopted special rules to handle environmental and natural resource claims on the basis that these kinds of cases required specialized knowledge and skills.[50] The PCA can adjudicate disputes between a range of actors including corporations and states. Recognizing the need for specialized knowledge when arbitrating such disputes, the PCA has established a list of arbitrators with specialized knowledge in this field as well as a list of scientific and technical experts.[51] In 1991, the arbitral tribunal considered the case on the *Protection of the Rhine Against Pollution by Chlorides* (*France v. Netherlands*).[52] The dispute between France and the Netherlands concerned the amount of chlorides that France was discharging into the Rhine River, which is arguably one of the most regulated river systems in the world. In another arbitration before the PCS involving the Rhine River, the arbitral body commented that current transboundary projects:

> must today include necessary environmental protection measures as an integral component of such a project.... [R]ules of international law on protection of the environment are applicable law between the Parties in the interpretation of the conventional regime for the Iron Rhine railway.[53]

Little has happened as a result of these cases, and given their isolated and ad hoc nature of the judgments it is not surprising either. Further, the open nature of these statements in the context of very specific issues has meant that they have contributed little to development in achieving environmental justice. However, there is no doubt that arbitration, whether driven entirely by corporations or states, is likely to continue making incremental gains on contributing to developments in environmental law.

International courts and tribunals reason through international law in all the dispute settlement bodies mentioned above and aim to avoid conflicts from escalating further than they have. In most cases, these bodies deliver some kind of environmental justice by ensuring that parties are better aware of how their interests are distributed relative to the other parties in the dispute. The paradox inherent in the work done by these dispute settlement bodies is that they are bound to apply international law and not to reason through the inherent justice of the relationship that the parties have with respect to the natural environment that is a feature of their dispute with each other as litigants. As such, the most that these bodies can deliver is a version of environmental justice that articulates the interests that the parties have in their relationship with each other in the particular context of the case. The deeply anthropocentric foundations of environmental justice as such becomes central to the work of the dispute settlement bodies which seek to balance and distribute interests to avoid further interstate or intrastate conflict.

This is not to say that dispute settlement bodies do not adjudicate important ecological concerns and issues. In fact, the dispute between Australia and Japan currently before the ICJ on the issue of protecting and preserving whales in Antarctica is an important process in terms of achieving ecological justice.[54] The claims by Australia are that Japan, by whaling in the Antarctic region, is in breach of its obligations under the International Convention for the Regulation of Whaling as well as other international agreements.[55] This case shares similarities with the *Tuna Dolphin Case* referred to earlier. Despite these cases suggesting that the international community in the Anthropocene epoch has an avenue for being ecologically just, the fragmentation in the system prevents these opportunities from having much effect outside of the immediate context within which they are addressed. Further, the nature of the adjudicative reasoning processes narrows the potential of cases that are meaningful for ecologically just outcomes. Finally and most importantly, dispute settlement processes have no capacity to address the problem that the Anthropocene epoch throws at us, namely that we as humans are deeply and collectively involved in the current global ecological challenges. Despite international law's concerns for the global commons, it does not have capacity, nor has it entertained the possibility, for finding humanity at fault. As such, from the brief survey above, there is little evidence suggesting that the international community allows access to courts and tribunals for addressing ecological justice but that even when it happens the fragmentation inherent in the system means that, potentially, it has little effect on ongoing concerns. The idea of collective fault and ecological justice in the Anthropocene epoch is even a further removed possibility.

Nature as the excluded subject for accessing ecological justice

The Anthropocene epoch describes the variety of stratigraphical signals that we leave by building cities, dams, roads and so on. During the Holocene epoch, the precursor to the proposed Anthropocene epoch, major changes to planet earth and its various subsystems were through subsystem activities such as shifts in plate tectonics, the weight of glaciers or melting ice. Human species in the Anthropocene epoch are significant in geological and morphological ways not just because of the size of our population but in terms of the anthropogenic impact we have on earth's subsystems. These impacts have come from increased carbon and nitrogen oxide levels in the atmosphere, biodiversity loss or a range of other conditions that place pressure on one of the earth's subsystems. In terms of changes to the biosphere, for instance, humans are as powerful, through the release of carbon and nitrogen, if not more so than the forces of climate itself.

The Anthropocene epoch is said to have possibly started from the industrial age or maybe even as far back as when humans cleared trees, cultivated land for the purposes of agriculture, or domesticated animals. Some scientists have argued that from the 1850s onwards the levels of carbon dioxide in the atmosphere, as a result of increased fossil fuel usage in urbanized areas, made significant differences in terms of the human impact on earth systems and which explain the onset of the Anthropocene epoch. In previous geological epochs, particularly the Holocene epoch, human species flourished because of stable and clement conditions that allowed us to build communities and societies to flourish. In 2016, the International Commission of Stratigraphy, which has set up a Working Group on the Anthropocene, will decide whether planet earth has officially entered into the Anthropocene epoch.[56]

The commitment of science to objectivity has been increasingly criticized for its political, cultural and moral agendas.[57] For instance, environmental sciences can point to the mathematics of planetary boundaries establishing thresholds whose breach could cause irreversible harm,[58] but fail to contextualize it within particular modes of ecological thought. The geological sciences use stratigraphical signals and data to make objective assessments about the content of sedimentary layers. As such, the geological sciences establish the basis for discourses around how we got there and what the data means. The cultural and social stories that the information tells are as significant as the scientific ones in terms of how the law can better deal with changing conditions. Berry and Swimme in *The Universe Story* have referred to the cultural stories developing out of the geological sciences as helping us see through to the 'larger patterns of functioning of the biosystems of the planet'.[59] The geological sciences have an advantage in relative terms to ecology, for instance, because the significance of events are defined and evaluated in terms relative to time measured in epochs or eras. This method of evaluation increases the geological sciences' ability to point to long-term and generational impacts of human beings on objects such as planet earth.

The idea of the Anthropocene epoch echoes in scientific terms the cries of scholars who have described our relationship to nature in very dramatic, catastrophic and dire terms.[60] Arguably, our ability to live symbiotically with and in nature is affected by the deep institutional and cultural commitments to anthropocentrism. The tendency to imbue a discourse with anthropocentrism is common and deeply entrenched in a range of approaches to thinking about our relationship to our natural surroundings. The last section described and analysed this argument in the context of accessing ecological justice through dispute settlement. However, this problem is also evident in globally important cultural motifs. For instance, the work of Edvard Munch's now very famous and still relevant painting, titled *The Scream*, created between 1893 and 1910, represents in art form a very profound description of our relationship to our natural surroundings. This painting represents to some people[61] the deafening scream of the landscape and the severe impact on the figure represented in the image. The original German title given by Munch to this work is *Der Schrei der Natur* which can be translated into English as *The Scream of Nature.*

This painting, as a narrative, describes or represents a particular but, as will be argued below, not necessarily an unproblematic way of articulating our relationship to nature. It suggests a universal and inherently personal relationship to nature. The normative aspect of the work is a suggestive one, in that the orange and red in it can be interpreted as a metaphor for blood that we have been responsible for shedding. The work captures the disturbance, violence and chaotic presence of nature in our lives and is something we react to, and represents the reason we find ourselves worrying about its protection, preservation or conservation. Munch himself is central to the representation of nature in this work. At the same time, the capacity of his surroundings to scream at him also represents the potential of our environment to press itself upon us whether we like it or not.

This painting or text,[62] which is more than 100 years old, is still very representative of the dialogue that is had amongst a range of academic disciplines concerned with our relationship to nature. However, it is also representative of a distinctly bifurcated view of nature which divides our philosophical landscape into anthropocentric or ecocentric terms. Munch's work portrays our anthropocentric tendencies that describe nature only in terms that have effects on us. At the same time, it represents nature through the metaphor of the unnatural state it is in, which indicates the hurt and harm it is experiencing. The brilliance of this piece is perhaps in the metaphor that however we conceptualize nature and our relationship to it, humanity is incapable of responding to its cry and scream.

Two critical and missing features in this narrative are important to point out as they help explain our limited views of the relationship we have to nature in the context of the Anthropocene epoch. Importantly, they reflect the missing components in the work of international dispute settlement bodies described above. The first is that we need to better understand what aspects of our social relations enable our violence in nature and against planet earth as an object of our attention. Munch portrays a solitary and independent existence from nature and other human beings by the distance he has from other human characters in the painting. This gives the impression that he is alone in feeling the pain of nature's suffering and which ignores the contractual foundations that imbues his and not nature's embodiment as a subject of the painting. This ensures that we all see the natural surroundings described in this work as a particular kind of an experience or as an 'object' of a particular kind – one that is hurting rather that morphing into something different or better – that we must all access. The subject of this painting is therefore the character in it rather than nature itself.

Second, the painting gives us a localized view of the violence that nature experiences. This means that we are excluded from seeing the broader context within which we can experience the harm or damage and which is absent from what one might extract from the painting. In other words, Munch only describes a localized experience of nature that is then turned into a universal and subjective experience by viewers. These two perspectives and critiques of both the work of Munch and also, perhaps indirectly, international dispute settlement bodies, are central to what Michel Serres sees in *The Natural Contract*. This work is described and examined next to set up the philosophical underpinnings of an alternative and broader ecological position to rethink access to justice.

Michel Serres and The Natural Contract

The work of Michel Serres explores some of the themes raised so far in this chapter. In particular his work called *The Natural Contract* (1990) is both the title for the work discussed below but, as noted by a known commentator on his work, it is 'a full-blown philosophical concept' or an 'ecological concept'.[63] This makes summarizing the work in this book particularly difficult because his arguments develop, and are sometimes contextualized by his other writings, such as those of *The Parasite*,[64] *Biogea*,[65] *Les Cinq Sens*[66] and also *Malfeasance*.[67] The breadth of *The Natural Contract* is significant and important, in that Serres talks about it as a contribution to the history and philosophy of science and culture or their juxtapositions as nature and law. As such, the work is not directly about the idea of nature, ecology, environment but rather jurisprudence, justice broadly conceived and the nature and culture dichotomy.

Although analytical thought and reasoning processes form the basis of processes for developments in science/nature and culture/law, the former pair 'demonstrate' it whereas the latter is a form of judgment through it. In recent times, however, as Serres argues, science and its commitment to objectivity has prevailed to the detriment of cultural and legal understandings about how we understand and relate to nature. What emerges from Serres' reading of the historical tensions between science and culture is how we have included or excluded certain objects from our social and cultural constructions and relations and also the way in which we have continued to localize what we see as real, rather than also focus on globally significant 'objects' such as planet earth.

In *The Natural Contract*, Serres discusses the idea of building a 'partnership' with the natural world where there is a genuine symbiotic and reciprocal relationship between human beings and global objects such as planet earth itself. Our exclusionary social contractual relationships with each other have given science its dominance over how we reason and continue to support a culture where we are parasites on our surroundings. The pendulum, according to Serres, needs to be rebalanced so that science and culture work in harmony to support our partnership with the natural world. This symbiosis also requires a new vision of who we are as human beings not as individual local actors but as a collective mass with impacts that have global implications for the natural world and planet earth. Serres avoids words and concepts such as 'anthropocentrism' and 'deep ecology' by reorganizing his engagement and relationship with nature around objects such as planet earth. It is in this sense that Serres' work contributes to rethinking ecological justice, not in terms of how interests over the natural world are distributed amongst human beings but, instead, how as partners with the natural world we have to be just to ensure that the partnership can continue. The rest of this section describes these ideas.

Contracts, exclusions and parasites

The idea of a reciprocal or symbiotic partnership with nature or global objects such as planet earth seems vague and abstruse. In this work, Serres evokes Rousseau's conception of the social contract as a metaphor to critique our obsession with ourselves and build an alternative paradigm from that.[68] Rather than use the concept of the social contract directly, he draws on its metaphorical power and imagery rather than how it analytically constructs our social relations. He argues that at the foundations of culture are a series of contractual relationships but, importantly, every time we contract with each other we exclude something from the relationship that we express through our agreements with each other. Our cultural and social engagements with each other have excluded the idea of nature and planet earth by virtue of the 'exclusionary gesture' that contracts generally facilitate.[69] This exclusionary relationship has consequences for how humanity has managed to place itself at the centre of how we see and value life on planet earth. For instance, the word 'environment' itself assumes that humans are at the 'centre of a system of nature'.[70] Serres argues that this 'idea'

> recalls a bygone era, when the Earth (how can one imagine that it used to represent us?), placed in the centre of the world, reflected our narcissism, the humanism that makes of us the exact midpoint or excellent culmination of all things. No. The Earth existed without our unimaginable ancestors, could well exist today without us, will exist tomorrow or later still, without any of our possible descendants, whereas we cannot exist without it. Thus we must indeed place things in the center and us at the periphery, or better still, things all around and us within them like parasites.[71]

This narcissism is supported by examples such as the *Declaration of the Rights of Man and of the Citizen* as well as the *Universal Declaration of Human Rights*, which pretend to be universal in their reach but exclude nature.[72] The *Universal Declaration of Human Rights*, according to Serres, will 'achieve full universality when it resolves that living creatures and inert objects – in short, everything we see as encompassed by nature – are invested with rights'.[73] The centrality of this idea for *The Natural Contract* is because the book and the idea are about the philosophical treatment of 'who has the right to be a legal person'.[74] This idea that both Planet Earth and humanity need to be at the centre of our systems of thought is critical to repositioning the former as a subject in legal philosophy.

Despite the nature of this work, Serres never uses the word 'nature' in its normal sense but rather focuses on planet earth as a unit or object independent of our subjective or localized perceptions of it.[75] He has several reasons for using the words 'planet earth' or 'world' instead of nature or the environment. In part, it is a direct criticism of the schism between the humanities and science or technology as disciplines. Serres has argued that science no longer talks about nature in its totality and uses it only allegorically,[76] which is why Serres himself uses the word 'nature' as an 'ensemble or referent' rather than anything in particular.[77] For him, science only now gives us experiences of particular aspects of nature. As such, 'our technology has analysed nature so pervasively that only the volatile froth remains'.[78]

Despite, how we through science particularize our relationship with 'matter', we have also used it to develop global conceptions of planet earth, which, for instance, the human eye can see from outer space.[79] This is significant in that: '[t]he new counterpart of these new plates of humanity is global nature, Planet Earth in its totality, the seat of reciprocal and crossed interrelations among its local elements and its giant components – oceans, deserts, atmospheres, or stocks of ice'.[80] It is not just that we can see planet earth as an object or as a whole but that our actions and activities have global effects. It is our capacity for turning planet earth as a whole into an actor through climate change, ozone depletion and so on that makes it an actant.[81]

Most significantly, however, and a point which Assad makes most poignantly, Serres sees the 'contractual conscious' as 'always local' or always acting 'locally'.[82] As such, no matter what our achievements, they are always particular or limited to localized matters even if their significance is widespread. This observation is common to all cultural and symbolic activities according to Assad's reading of the work of Serres.[83] This analysis requires that we rethink the conceptual basis of our contractual relationships: that is, the foundations of our cultural engagements with each other, to bring together the way that human beings think and relate symbiotically with planet earth.

The idea that planet earth can be a 'subject' rather than object in legal philosophy is important for Serres. As long as it remains an object in terms of our engagement with it, it is incapable of being a genuine actant in a partnership. For Serres, a 'subject takes everything and gives nothing while the object gives everything and receives nothing'.[84] This idea is significant in that so far, human beings have been the only subjects of legal philosophy but this has turned us, as a result, into 'parasites'. In this following paragraph, Serres combines a number of concepts which highlight the logic behind being parasites rather than partners with the natural world:

> Back to nature, then! That means we must add to the exclusively social contract a natural contract of symbiosis and reciprocity in which our relationship to things would set aside mastery and possession in favour of admiring attention, reciprocity, contemplation, and respect; Where knowledge would no longer imply property, nor action mastery, nor would property and mastery imply their excremental results and origins. An armistice contract in the objective war, a contract of symbiosis, for a symbiont recognizes the

> host's rights, whereas a parasite – which is what we are now – condemns to death the one he pillages and inhabits, not realizing that in the long run he's condemning himself to death too.[85]

'Parasite' is not a simple term in French in that it has three different meanings. Serres actually develops the logic behind the term 'parasite' in a later book that he called *The Parasite*.[86] Brown has neatly summarized the different meanings that Serres has ascribed to this term in *The Parasite*:

> In informational terms, the parasite provokes a new form of complexity, it engineers a kind of difference by intercepting relations. All three meanings then coincide to form a 'parasite logic' – analyse (take but do not give), paralyse (interrupt usual functioning), catalyse (force the host to act differently). This parasite, through its interruption, is a catalyst for complexity.[87]

In *The Natural Contract*, the idea of the parasite is deployed not in terms of how human relations are structured with respect to one another but rather against the object, being planet earth. In this respect, Serres argues that the natural contract will seek to reposition humanity – not as simply taking from nature – as an equal partner benefitting from a symbiotic relationship and partnership with planet earth. He argues that it will break us away from the parasitic nature of our social contracts which exclude important subjects from its purview, namely nature or planet earth.

Humanity, the individual and education

A critical feature of the natural contract is the idea that humans as 'individuals' or 'subjects' have evolved and become 'dense tectonic plates of humanity'.[88] Serres repeats this idea in many different forms throughout *The Natural Contract* to emphasize the scale of the change and also to emphasize the various ways that this idea has implications for his philosophy on our partnership with planet earth. Two ideas are discernable from this metaphor. The first is the connections between being human that define us in terms of what he refers to as the 'new Grand Narrative of our paleoanthropolitical origins'.[89] Our ability to communicate not just through the Web but also through the language and contracts of science and technology is critical in defining us as an entity or as a subject in his philosophy.[90] This, it should be mentioned, is not the same as creating a universal culture of any kind but rather acknowledging the idea that we, as humans, are a particular kind of prokaryote[91] with potential to have collective impacts on our surroundings.

He also talks about how humanity exists 'on a natural scale' and how the '[m] ind has grown into a beast and the beast is growing into a plate'.[92] It is not just the scale, in terms of moving from 'I' to 'we' or local to global, that we are being asked to consider, but also the sheer power of our footprint on planet earth itself. He talks about how 'our collectivities are becoming as powerful as seas and share the same destiny. We have invaded not only the space of the world, but, if I dare say so, ontology'.[93] In his work he compares humanity to significant elements of change within nature itself in order, perhaps, or precisely because he wants to, to ensure that we recognize why we are different to other living things. He writes that 'from now on there will be lakes of humanity, physical actors in the physical system of the Earth. Man is a stockpile, the strongest and most connected of nature. He is a being-everywhere. And bound'.[94] Again, he points out that 'Europe weighs at least a quarter-billion souls ... it behaves like a sea'.[95] The capacity and the scale of it, to have an impact on planet earth appears to Serres to have established the necessary philosophical conditions for why the time has come for us to sign the implicit natural contract.

In much of Serres' works, he is concerned with the way that war and conflict has dominated our history as humans. However, in *The Natural Contract* he takes this further and suggests that in '[i]n its burning heat, history remains blind to nature'.[96] At the start of his book, he uses a painting by Francisco Goya to introduce the significance of the idea of the natural contract that is represented by this painting. In this painting, the dualists do not realize that the harder they fight and battle with each other the faster they are sinking in the quicksand that they are standing on. Their rivalry and battle with each other is directly proportionate to the speed with which they actually lose a different battle for survival. This painting is to Serres a metaphor not just for actual real wars but also for those involved in a crusade through politics and dialogue about our relationship to nature.[97] In *The Natural Contract*, Serres suggests that what we have so far ignored in our history is that planet earth has become the common enemy of humanity. He writes that '[w]e must decide on peace among ourselves to protect the world, and peace with the world to protect ourselves'.[98]

What remains is to point to the significance of the various ideas described above in terms of change and what must happen to ensure the natural contract. Serres does not advocate adopting a particular kind of moral conduct or ethical standard. Unlike much recent work on ecological thought, instead of focusing on the significance of the object[99] Serres talks about our own capacity to rethink ourselves in this partnership. However, he does not specify anything in particular like the kind of structured 'democratic ecology' suggested, for instance, by Luc Ferry.[100] The natural contract in his view requires that as individuals we become 'sages' who can combine:

> a mixture of the Legislator of Heroic times and the modern titleholder of rigorous knowledge; he knows how to weave together the truth of the sciences with the peace of judgment; he blends together our Egyptian and Roman heritages, the source of our laws, with our Semitic and Greek legacies, givers of knowledge; he integrates quick and effective sciences into our slow and prudent laws.[101]

This sage is not the hero that nature requires to be saved or the defender of the rights of nature in a world driven by production and consumption. Instead, he needs to possess qualities that will help to balance the ways that science reasons through what he observes and culture is more prudent about its capacity to judge what is good or bad in terms of the natural contract. The sage, it appears, is needed to transcend the cartesianism and localized perspectives of science that have continued to prevail in terms of how to relate to and judge our relationship to the environment or planet earth. Further, the sage must develop the capacity for 'prudent judgment' over our culture/legal relationships.[102] Serres assumes that 'education' and 'instruction' are necessary to see this 'sage' emerge and be 'cast off' into the world that can construct a more harmonious relationship between science and culture which ultimately appears to be the crucial foundations of the critique that forms the basis for the natural contract.[103]

Analysis

The foundations of Serres' comments about how we have become as parasites towards planet earth and the natural world is founded on a range of philosophical traditions. Others, such as Luc Ferry, have similarly argued but with differing conclusions. In *The New Ecological* Order,[104] for instance, he describes how science, particularly through physics, emphasizes the randomness or meaninglessness of matter whether in living or inert objects. In this way, he argues that science continues to challenge cultural norms of all kinds, particularly those established in Christian theology. One consequence of seeing nature as meaningless or lacking in purpose is that we have come to construct cultures that do not value it. There are many theories ascribing particular teleological orientations for how the natural world is organized and functions.[105] Instead of working with these alternate and contradictory approaches to nature, Ferry has suggested that a kind of 'democratic ecology' is necessary to build a culture of stewardship and care towards the natural world. This approach, argues Ferry, is necessary because human beings are distinctly different to other living creatures who are simply driven by 'instinct'.[106] Ferry founds his ideas of 'democratic ecology' on the potential of humanist philosophy, and our capacity to transform ourselves and build a culture of stewardship towards the natural world. Serres and Ferry are not ideologically very far apart, in that neither advocates the use of deep ecology or the other extreme opposite to it, which is the sense that human beings control and are masters over nature. Unlike Ferry, Serres does not develop a particular theory about the role for the human collective other than to require that we 'cast off' from foundations that can sustain a more harmonious relationship between science and culture.

Ferry has criticized Serres for using and adopting the language of rights, and particularly the discourse around the rights of nature, which is popular in ecological movements, particularly in the English-speaking world. The idea that nature must have access to justice or rights has been the subject of commentary and one can trace this back to Christopher Stone whose seminal work in this area is a call for trees to have standing.[107] The effect of Stone's work has been to identify the 'rights' of nature and to have them represented in institutional structures that can in turn allow them to have access to rights and remedies.[108] In a different way, the wild law movement has also been driven by jurisprudential concerns around nature's access to survival through the medium of human legal institutions.[109] What this body of law and jurisprudential literature has done is to use rights discourse and dispute settlement institutions to embody concerns around who the 'legal subject' is and what it can do to access what is claimed to be an inherent feature of its existence and survival.

Ferry's criticism of Serres is that he adopts the rights discourse as a solution without thinking about the political consequence of what this means. The rights discourse is generally problematic in that it is neutral in terms of which species or who in particular is prioritized and whose interests and to what extent they are recognized.[110] Also, the discourse has no particular way of prioritizing between the different rights. As such, what and how something is protected depends on the context that issues are raised in. Ferry does not acknowledge the complexity of Serres' critique of how culture and nature have dominated each other in different stages of human history and assumes that he adopts the language of rights as a way to establish the natural contract. The partnership that Serres calls for does not elevate rules and legal rights per se to ethical and moral standards that we have to aspire to. Rather, it operates to construct a new legal subject who can ideologically play an important role in shaping politics, culture and all that gives meaning to law and jurisprudential thought.

The idea of a symbiotic or reciprocal partnership goes beyond notions such as showing respect or having an obligation towards the natural world. Since its formulation, *The Earth Charter*, for instance, has been the prime vehicle for articulating the notions of respect towards the natural world.[111] It has sought to bridge the gap that exists between the interests that human beings have to exploit and consume, and the integrity that exists in the natural world. The partnership, however, that Serres calls for in his view does not presume that the natural world is good or bad and has to be respected or guarded.[112] Instead, he is neutral about its role in the partnership to the extent that we cannot be predisposed in particular ways towards a subject that has to be seen as an active agent in the process of creating meaning for others who exist in its world. It is, in this sense, that Serres argues that what is needed is not just the capacity for us to judge whether we have met our obligations towards the natural world but that we have to balance this judgment with the kind of reason that can adequately search for and understand the natural world in its various emanations, rather than just in the form that impacts on our interests. It is arguable that, in this sense, Serres ask us to go beyond just ascribing value to nature but that he presumes it. In this way, he encourages us to move away from ideas and concepts of stewardship, respect and a sense that we have to comply with ethical obligations that we have towards the natural world. Instead, he suggests, although not as directly, that we have to better understand our own capacities to engage with nature as reciprocal partners in a world where our as well as the natural world's existence depends on it.

Conclusion

This chapter argues that the narratives driving our views of what interests are valuable, are as important (if not more so), as simply allowing access to ecological justice. Our international institutions granting access to justice are embroiled in a political environment that denies the fact that in most cases it exists for the interests of human beings that are central to the disputes before them. Additionally, the kind of cosmopolitanisms that can force a less anthropocentric view on the international community are still a long way off. This notwithstanding, discourses that press upon us to become deeper ecologists can prove to be as problematic when examined in the context of international law and its institutions as is the case with the discourse around the rights of nature. Further, theories that take a deep ecological view and ascribe particular institutional form to their potential meaning have also come under attack. For instance, the Gaia theory has been in one instance described as 'a theory of high technology, a theory of imperialism and a theory that is hostile to socially-aware environmental policy-making'.[113]

The Anthropocene epoch, on the other hand, forces upon us the notion that the size and scope of the harm that humanity can do to planet earth is enormous and has to be taken seriously. Two key aspects of the work of Serres fuel criticisms for simply relying on what is currently available for accessing ecological justice through courts and tribunals. The first is the metaphor drawn on by Serres through the painting by Goya, which suggests that dialogues and conflicts, whether hard or soft, are, in themselves, contributing to the acceleration of planet earth becoming even more fragile. Although this notion is confirmed by the idea of the Anthropocene epoch, we are no better off in terms of our responses to harm through international courts and tribunals.

Second, the Anthropocene epoch is a description of the fact that despite our actions in one area of the globe, it is likely to influence biospheres' patterns in other parts of the planet. While this contention is a generalization, the main point is that through disciplinary studies such as earth system science, we are starting to move away from local to possible global causes and consequences of our actions and desires. Serres also makes this point but in a different way when he says that a 'local causal chain becomes more effective when thought is limited to plans for raising a stone wall or taming a plow ox. But nothing in such plans concerns global nature, which alone is decisive today'.[114] As such, we are likely to rely more and more on international tribunals and courts to resolves conflicts over interests without recognizing that the equity of those cases is potentially harmful to our wider survival as a species.

These arguments raise the significance of the idea that we need to rethink the jurisprudential foundations of what we do to allow access to ecological justice. It was argued in this chapter that the work of Serres is important for rethinking the ecological foundations of jurisprudential thought away from stewardship, respect and care towards one that recognizes the natural world as a potential subject of a reciprocal partnership with human beings. The significance of this idea is not necessarily vested in creating categories of rights and institutional structures that will accommodate and create anthropomorphic visions of the natural world. The significance lies in recognizing that our social and cultural relationships with each other, as human beings and as a species with considerable impacts on the world around us, have come to exclude the natural world from what we see as real. This foresight requires that we rely less on expressions of the law in and through courts and tribunals but rather work on cultural and political environments that will build on our reciprocal and symbiotic 'partnership' with the natural world.

Cases

Biwater Gauff (Tanzania) Ltd. v. United Republic of Tanzania, ICSID Case No. ARB/05/22, Award (24 July 2008).

Case Concerning Land Reclamation by Singapore In and Around the Straits of Johor (Malaysia v. Singapore) (Provisional Measures) (8 October 2003) (available at www.itlos.org).

Case Concerning Pulp Mills on the River Uruguay (*Argentina v. Uruguay*) (2010) ICJ Reports 14.

Case Concerning the Gabikovo-Nagymaros Project (Hungary/Slovakia) (Merits) (1997) ICJ Rep 7.

Compañía del Desarrollo de Santa Elena, S.A. v. Costa Rica, ICSID Case No. ARB/96/1.

Legality of the Threat or Use of Nuclear Weapons, Advisory Opinion (1996) ICJ Rep 226.

MOX Plant (Ireland v. United Kingdom) (Provisional Measures) (2002) 41 ILM 405.

MOX Plant case (Ireland v. United Kingdom) (Suspension of Proceedings on Jurisdiction and Merits and Request for Further Provisional Measures) (2003) 42 ILM 1187.

Southern Bluefin Tuna Cases (New Zealand v. Japan; Australia v. Japan) (Provisional Measures) (1999) 38 ILM. *Southern Bluefin Tuna Case (Australia & New Zealand v. Japan) (Jurisdiction and Admissibility)* (2000) 39 ILM 1359.

Southern Pacific Properties (Middle East) Ltd v. Egypt, ICSID Case No. ARB/84/3.

Notes

1 My thanks go to attendees at the 'Access to International Justice' international workshop and Charles Sampford in particular for inviting me to be a part of it. The following people participated in a reading group that I organized around Michel Serres' *The Natural Contract* and helped encourage me to think more critically about his work: Chris Butler, Edward Mussawir and William MacNeil. I also want to thank Louis Kotze and Peter Burdon for their comments on parts of this chapter. Significantly, my thanks go to Fiona Lubett who helped greatly with some of the research in the early sections of this chapter.

2 For instance, Crutzen 2002: 526; Steffen *et al.* 2007; Zalasiewicz *et al.* 2010. For social science and humanities examinations of the impacts of humans on nature in the Anthropocene epoch see Dipesh 2009.
3 On this topic, see Bosselmann 2008, Chapter 3 in particular; Schlosberg 2009.
4 See generally the work of Gonzalez 2012: 77–98.
5 *Bering Sea Fur Seals (Great Britain v. United States)* (1893) 1 Moore 755.
6 Sands 2008: 27–28.
7 Sands 2012: 3.
8 Sands 2012: 5.
9 On this, see Akhtarkhavari 2009: 91–129.
10 See Murphy 2000: 333–334.
11 Sands 2008.
12 Sands 2012.
13 Pavoni and Samuele 2009: 526.
14 *Case Concerning Pulp Mills on the River Uruguay* (*Argentina v. Uruguay*) (2010) ICJ Reports 14.
15 Pavoni and Samuele 2009: 526.
16 Stephens 2006: 232.
17 4 March 2002, 'Press Release – Composition of the Chamber for Environmental Matters', www.icj-cij.org/presscom/index.php?pr=106&pt=&p1=6&p2=1 (accessed 4 August 2014).
18 The ICJ published the following comments on its website following the disbandment of the CEM:

> With respect to the formation of a Chamber pursuant to Article 26, paragraph 1, of the Statute, it should be noted that, in 1993, the Court created a Chamber for Environmental Matters, which was periodically reconstituted until 2006. In the Chamber's 13 years of existence, however, no State ever requested that a case be dealt with by it. The Court consequently decided in 2006 not to hold elections for a Bench for the said Chamber'

(ICJ website, 'Chambers and Committees'. Online. Available at www.icj-cij.org/court/index.php? (accessed 6 September 2013).
19 Kalas 2001: 209.
20 On the involvement of non-state entities in litigation before the international courts see, for instance, Kalas 2001: 208.
21 *Legality of the Threat or Use of Nuclear Weapons, Advisory Opinion* (1996) ICJ Rep 226.
22 *Case Concerning the Gabikovo-Nagymaros Project (Hungary/Slovakia) (Merits)* (1997) ICJ Rep 7. Hereinafter *Danube Dam Case*.
23 *Case Concerning Pulp Mills on the River Uruguay* (*Argentina v. Uruguay*) (2010) ICJ Reports 14.
24 Fitzmaurice 2012: 40.
25 See A-Khavari and Rothwell 1998.
26 Ibid.; Akhtarkhavari 2009.
27 See Anton 2010.
28 McIntyre 2010: 475.
29 World Trade Organization 2014, available at www.wto.org/english/tratop_e/envir_e/edis00_e.htm.
30 United States 1991, 1994.
31 Sands 1999: 1624.
32 Hurlock 1992: 2098.
33 United States 1998.
34 Stephens 2009: 327.
35 See also Ahn 1998–1999.

36 Stephens 2009: 344.
37 Churchill 2010: 145.
38 *Southern Bluefin Tuna Cases (New Zealand v. Japan; Australia v. Japan) (Provisional Measures)* (1999) 38 ILM 1624; *Southern Bluefin Tuna Case (Australia & New Zealand v. Japan) (Jurisdiction and Admissibility)* (2000) 39 ILM 1359.
39 See Stephens 2004: 177, note 1.
40 See Stephens 2004: 183.
41 *MOX Plant (Ireland v. United Kingdom) (Provisional Measures)* (2002) 41 ILM 405; see also *MOX Plant case (Ireland v. United Kingdom) (Suspension of Proceedings on Jurisdiction and Merits and Request for Further Provisional Measures)* (2003) 42 ILM 1187.
42 *Case Concerning Land Reclamation by Singapore In and Around the Straits of Johor (Malaysia v. Singapore) (Provisional Measures)* (8 October 2003) (available at www.itlos.org).
43 Pavoni and Samuele 2009: 529.
44 *Biwater Gauff (Tanzania) Ltd. v. United Republic of Tanzania*, ICSID Case No. ARB/05/22, Award (24 July 24 2008).
45 *Southern Pacific Properties (Middle East) Ltd v. Egypt*, ICSID Case No. ARB/84/3.
46 Pavoni and Samuele 2009: 535.
47 Pavoni and Samuele 2009: 536.
48 *Compañía del Desarrollo de Santa Elena, S.A. v. Costa Rica*, ICSID Case No. ARB/96/1.
49 Pavoni and Samuele 2009: 539.
50 For the rules see the Permanent Court of Arbitration 2001.
51 See website of the Permanent Court of the Environment, 'Environmental Dispute Resolution', (Permanent Court of the Environment 2006).
52 Permanent Court of Arbitration 2008: 107.
53 Permanent Court of Arbitration 2007: 37, para 222. For commentary on this case see Salman 2006.
54 The proceedings are at a very early stage of their development at the time of writing. For more, see the press releases on the following page on the site for the ICJ International Court of Justice, 'Press Releases: Whaling in the Antarctic (Australia V. Japan: New Zealand Intervening)', www.icj-cij.org/presscom/index.php?p1=6&p2=1 (accessed 4 August 2014).
55 161 *UNTS* 72.
56 Zalasiewicz *et al.* 2010.
57 On this subject see, for instance, Latour 1991; Serres and Latour 1995. There are many examples of works exploring these issues practically. See Bruno Latour's work in Latour 1999); Latour and Woolgar 2013.
58 On the subject of planetary boundaries, see Rockström *et al.* 2009b; Rockström *et al.* 2009a, www.ecologyandsociety.org/vol14/iss2/art32/ (accessed 4 August 2014).
59 Rockström *et al.* 2009a: 243.
60 See, for instance, McKibben 1989.
61 My thanks go to Patrick Keyzer and Peter Burdon (amongst others) who have kindly read and commented on this work and who pointed out that my description of *The Scream* is only one of many interpretations of this important piece of art.
62 Munch's hand-painted poem appears on the frame of a version of *The Scream*, it ends with the words: 'Shivering with Anxiety/I felt the great Scream in Nature'. See Aspden 2012.
63 The idea of the natural contract is as complex, creative and nuanced as is the work of Serres himself. Serres has written over 30 books but the complexity of his style has meant that scholars working within their very niche areas of scholarship cannot readily access him. His eclecticism and the connections he makes between disciplines is precisely what makes his philosophical work very inventive. William

Paulson has translated Serres into English on a number of occasions and has talked about how his work does 'not correspond to the expectations of the humanities community. They do not provide justification or material for the task of cultural critique'. Paulson 2000: 216. Huyghe, 'The UNESCO Courier', available at www.huyghe.fr/. There is a lot in *The Natural Contract* and this section that will not fully describe the range of metaphysical innovations behind his work. For instance, an interesting and perhaps critical aspect of his work is the potential of objects to have the capacity for intentionality or to be perceived outside of the subjective reality or perceptions of humans. This has been the subject of extensive work and debate in philosophy. For traditions that reflect what Serres does with respect to object-oriented philosophy see, for instance, the work of Bruno Latour or Quentin Meillassoux. For a good description of both the work of Latour and also the object-oriented philosophy that he is well known for see Harman 2009. Assad 1999: 149.

64 Serres 2007a.

65 Serres 2012.

66 Serres 1985.

67 Serres 2008.

68 Serres 1995: 20.

69 Assad 1999: 151.

70 Serres 1995: 33. For more on this idea see, for instance, Margulis and Sagan 2007.

71 Serres 1995: 33.

72 Serres 2007b: 131–132.

73 Serres 2007b: 132. Despite the use of the language of rights Serres does not, as will be argued later, assume that nature can exist independent of its partnership with humanity. As such, it is doubtful that he uses the language of rights in the same way that modern jurists have come to interpret it in relation to nature. See Grear (ed.) 2012; Stone 2010; Burdon 2010: 69.

74 Serres 2007b: 131. Importantly, and as discussed later, this is not the equivalent of granting a right to nature which it can then assert in juridical circles.

75 Huyghe, 'The UNESCO Courier'.

76 Serres 2007b: 134.

77 Serres 2007b: 133.

78 Serres 2007b: 135.

79 Huyghe, 'The UNESCO Courier'. On this idea, the emerging disciplinary field of earth systems science has developed extensive approaches to better understanding the functioning of the earth itself as a totality. On the aspect of governance in earth systems science see Biermann *et al.* 2012; Allen *et al.* 2010; Biermann 2007.

80 Serres 1995: 20.

81 Serres 2006.

82 Assad 1999: 155.

83 Ibid.

84 Serres 2006.

85 Serres 1995: 38.

86 Serres 2007a.

87 Brown 2002: 16.

88 Serres 1995: 16.

89 Serres 2006.

90 Ibid.

91 Huyghe, 'The Unesco Courier'.

92 Serres 1995: 19.

93 Serres 1995: 20.

94 Serres 1995: 18.

95 Serres 1995: 16.

96 Serres 1995: 7.

97 See, for instance, Serres 1995: 7–10.
98 Serres 1995: 25.
99 See, for instance, Morton 2010); Bennett 2010.
100 Ferry 1995).
101 Serres 1995: 95.
102 Ibid.
103 Serres 1995: 95, 97.
104 Ferry 1995.
105 For example, see the work of theorists around the Gaia hypothesis: Lovelock 2009; Margulis and Sagan 2007. For a critical view of the Gaia hypothesis see Marshall 2002, Chapter 3 in particular.
106 See in particular part one of Ferry 1995. See also Ferry 2010.
107 Stone 2010. See also Grear 2012.
108 Burdon 2010: 69–89.
109 For instance, Cullinan 2012.
110 For a general critique of the rights discourse see Douzinas 2000 and 2007.
111 The Earth Charter Initiative, 'Values and Principles to Foster a Sustainable Future', Earth Charter Associates, available at http://earthcharterinaction.org/content/pages/Read-the-Charter.html.
112 In an important and interesting way he eschews identifying himself with the kind of teleological view of the natural world associated with Aristotelian versions of naturalism. On this see, for instance, Pinkard 2013.
113 Marshall 2002: 53.
114 Serres 1995: 19.

References

Ahn, Dukgeun. 'Environmental Disputes in the GATT/WTO: Before and after US – Shrimp Case'. *Michigan Journal of International Law* 20, No. 4 (1998–1999): 819–870.

Akhtarkhavari, Afshin and Rothwell, Donald. 'The ICJ and the Danube Dam Case; a Missed Opportunity for International Environmental Law?'. *Melbourne University Law Review* 22 (1998): 507–537.

Akhtarkhavari, Afshin. 'Power, Environmental Principles and the International Court of Justice'. *Australian Yearbook of International Law* 28 (2009): 91–129.

Allen, S.K., Biermann, Frank, Betsill, Michele M., Camargo Vieira, Susana, Gupta, Joyeeta, Kanie, Norichika and Lebel, Louis. 'Strategy Paper: Navigating the Anthropocene: The Earth System Governance Project Strategy Paper'. *Environmental Sustainability* 2 (2010): 202–208.

Anton, Donald. 'Case Concerning Pulp "Mills on the River Uruguay (Argentina V Uruguay)" (Judgment) (2010) ICJ Rep (20 April 2010)'. *Australian International Law Journal* 17 (2010): 213–223.

Aspden, Peter. 'So, What Does "The Scream" Mean?'. *The Financial Times*, 21 April 2012.

Assad, Maria L. *Reading with Michel Serres: An Encounter with Time*. New York: State University of New York Press, 1999.

Bennett, Jane. *Vibrant Matter: A Political Ecology of Things*. Durham, NC and London: Duke University Press, 2010.

Biermann, Frank. '"Earth System Governance" as a Crosscutting Theme of Global Change Research'. *Global Environmental Change* 17 (2007): 326–337.

Biermann, Frank, Abbott, Kenneth and Andresen, Steiner. 'Navigating the Anthropocene: Improving Earth System Governance'. *Science*, 2012, 1306–1307.

Bosselmann, Klaus. *Principle of Sustainability: Transforming Law and Governance*. Aldershot: Ashgate, 2008.

Brown, Steven. 'Michel Serres: Science, Translation and the Logic of the Parasite'. *Theory, Culture & Society* 19, No. 3 (2002): 1–27.

Burdon, P. 'The Rights of Nature: Reconsidered'. *Australian Humanities Review* 49 (2010): 69–89.

Churchill, Robin. 'Trends in Dispute Settlement in the Law of the Sea: Towards the Increasing Availability of Compulsory Means'. In *International Law and Dispute Settlement: New Problems and Techniques*, edited by Duncan French, Matthew Saul and Nigel D. White. Portland, OR: Hart Publishing, 2010: 139–160.

Crutzen, P.J. 'Geology of Mankind'. *Nature* 415 (2002): 23.

Cullinan, Cormac. *Wild Law: A Manifesto for Earth Justice*. Second edn. London: Green Books, 2012.

Dipesh, Chakrabarty. 'The Climate of History: Four Theses'. *Critical Inquiry* 35, No. 2 (2009): 197–222.

Douzinas, C. *The End of Human Rights: Critical Legal Thought at the Turn of the Century*. Oxford: Hart Publishing, 2000.

Douzinas, C. *Human Rights and Empire: The Political Philosophy of Cosmopolitanism*. Oxford: Routledge-Cavendish, 2007.

Ferry, Luc. *The New Ecological Order*. Trans. Carol Volk. Chicago: University of Chicago Press, 1995.

Ferry, Luc. *A Brief History of Thought*. Trans. Theo Cuffe. New York: Harper Perennial, 2010.

Fitzmaurice, Malgosia. 'The International Court of Justice and Environmental Disputes'. In *International Law and Dispute Settlement: New Problems and Techniques*, edited by D. French, M. Saul and N. White. Oxford: Hart Publishing, 2012: 17–56.

Gonzalez, Carmen G. 'Environmental Justice and International Environmental Law'. In *Routledge Handbook of International Environmental Law*, edited by Shawkat Alam, Jahid Hossain, Bhuiyan Tareq, M.R. Chowdhury and Erika Techera. London: Routledge, 2012: 77–98.

Grear, A., (ed.) *Should Trees Have Standing?: 40 Years On*. Cheltenham: Edward Elgar, 2012.

Harman, Graham. *Prince of Networks: Bruno Latour and Metaphysics*. Melbourne: re. press, 2009.

Hurlock, Matthew Hunter. 'The Gatt, U.S. Law and the Environment: A Proposal to Amend the Gatt in Light of the Tuna/Dolphin Decision'. *Columbia Law Review* 92, No. 8 (1992): 2098–2161.

Huyghe, Francois-Bernard. 'The UNESCO Courier'. Online. Available at www.huyghe.fr/ (accessed 26 May 2014).

International Court of Justice. 'Press Releases: Whaling in the Antarctic (Australia V. Japan: New Zealand Intervening)'. Online. Available at www.icj-cij.org/docket/index.php? (accessed 19 May 2014).

Kalas, Peggy Rodgers. 'International Environmental Dispute Resolution and the Need for Access by Non-State Entities'. *Colorado Journal of International Environmental Law and Policy* 12, No. 2 (2001): 191–244.

Latour, Bruno. *We Have Never Been Modern*. Cambridge, Mass.: Harvard University Press, 1991.

Latour, Bruno. *Pandora's Hope: Essays on the Reality of Science Studies*. Cambridge, MA: Harvard University Press, 1999.

Latour, Bruno and Woolgar, Steve. *Laboratory Life: The Construction of Scientific Facts*. Princeton: Princeton University Press, 2013 (1979).

Lovelock, James. *The Vanishing Face of Gaia*. New York: Basic Books, 2009.

Margulis, Lynn and Sagan, Dorion. *Dazzle Gradually: Reflections on the Nature of Nature*. White River Junction, VT: Chelsea Green Publishing, 2007.

Marshall, Alan. *The Unity of Nature: Wholeness and Disintegration in Ecology and Science*. London: Imperial College Press, 2002.

McIntyre, Owen. 'The Proceduralisation and Growing Maturity of International Water Law: Case Concerning Pulp Mills on the River Uruguay (Argentina V Uruguay), International Court of Justice, 20 April 2010'. *Journal of Environmental Law* 22, No. 3 (2010): 475–497.

McKibben, Bill. *The End of Nature*. New York: Random House, 1989.

Morton, Tim. *Ecological Thought*. Cambridge, Mass.: Harvard University Press, 2010.

Murphy, Sean. 'Does the World Need a New International Environmental Court?'. *George Washington Journal of International Law and Economics* 32 (2000): 333–350.

Paulson, W. 'Michel Serres's Utopia of Language'" *Configurations* 8 (200): 215–228.

Pavoni, Riccardo and Samuele, Linda E. 'Environmental Rights, Sustainable Development, and Investor-State Case Law: A Critical Appraisal'. In *Human Rights in International Investment Law and Arbitration*, edited by P. Dupuy, F. Francioni and E-U. Petersmann. Oxford: Oxford University Press, 2009: 525–556.

Permanent Court of Arbitration. 'Optional Rules for Arbitration of Disputes Relating to Natural Resources and/or the Environment'. The Hague: Permanent Court of Arbitration, 2001. Online. Available at www.pca-cpa.org/showfile.asp?fil_id=42 (accessed 26 May 2014).

Permanent Court of the Environment. 'Environmental Dispute Resolution'. Permanent Court of the Environment: The Hague, 2006. Online. Available at www.pca-cpa.org/showpage.asp?pag_id=1058 (accessed 6 August 2014).

Permanent Court of Arbitration. *In the Arbitration Regarding the Iron Rhine ('Izeren Rijn') Railway (Belgium V Netherlands)*. The Hague: PCA Award Series, T.M.C. Asser Press, 2007.

Permanent Court of Arbitration. *Case Concerning the Auditing of Account between the Kingdom of the Netherlands and the French Republic Pursuant to the Additional Protocol of 25 September 1991 to the Convention of 3 December 1976 on the Protection of the Rhine against Pollution by Chlorides*. The Hague: PCA Award Series, T.M.C. Asser Press, 2008.

Pinkard, Terry. *Hegel's Naturalism: Mind, Nature, and the Final End of Life*. Oxford: Oxford University Press, 2013.

Rockström, J., Steffen, W., Noone, K., Persson, III, A., Chapin, F.S., Lambin, E. and Lenton, T.M. 'Planetary Boundaries: Exploring the Safe Operating Space for Humanity'. *Ecology and Society* 14, No. 2 (2009a). Online. Available at www.ecologyandsociety.org/vol14/iss2/art32/ / (accessed 4 August 2014).

Rockström, Johan, Steffen, Will, Noone, Kevin, Persson, Åsa, Chapin, F. Stewart, Lambin, Eric F. and Lenton, Timothy M. 'A Safe Operating Space for Humanity'. *Nature Climate Change* 461 (2009b): 472–475.

Salman Salman. 'International Water Disputes: A New Breed of Claims, Claimants, and Settlement Institutions'. *Water International* 31, No. 1 (2006): 2–11.

Sands, Philippe. 'International Environmental Litigation and Its Future'. *University of Richmond Law Review* 32 (1999): 1619–1637.

Sands, Philippe. 'Litigating Environmental Disputes: Courts, Tribunals and the Progressive

Development of International Environmental Law [Contribution to the Liber Amicorum of Judge Thomas Menash – 2007]'. In *OECD Global Forum on International Investment*. Paris: OECD, 2008.

Sands, Philippe. 'Foreword – on Being 40: A Celebration of "Should Trees Have Standing?"'. *Journal of Human Rights and the Environment* 3, No. Special Issue (2012): 3.

Schlosberg, David. *Defining Environmental Justice: Theories, Movements, and Nature*. Oxford: Oxford University Press, 2009.

Serres, Michel. *Les Cinq Sens*. Paris: Grasset, 1985.

Serres, Michel. *The Natural Contract*. Trans. Elizabeth MacArthur and William Paulson. Ann Arbor: University of Michigan Press 1995.

Serres, Michel. 'Revisiting the Natural Contract'. In *Institute of the Humanities at Simon Fraser University*, edited by Anne-Marie Feenberg-Dibon. Burnaby, BC: Simon Fraser University, 2006.

Serres, Michel. *The Parasite*. Trans. Lawrence Schehr. Minneapolis: University of Minnesota Press, 2007a (1980).

Serres, Michel. 'A Return to the Natural Contract'. In *Making Peace with the Earth: What Future for the Human Species and the Planet?*, edited by Jerome Binde. USA: UNESCO and Berghahn Books, 2007b: 129–137.

Serres, Michel. *Malfeasance: Appropriation through Pollution?* Trans. A-M. Feenberg-Dipon. Paris: Le Pommier, 2008.

Serres, Michel. *Biogea*. Trans. M. Randolph Burks. Minneapolis: University of Minnesota Press, 2012.

Serres, Michel and Latour, Bruno. *Conversations on Science, Culture and Time*. Ann Arbor: University of Michigan Press, 1995.

Steffen, Will, Crutzen, Paul J. and McNeill, John R. 'The Anthropocene: Are Humans Now Overwhelming the Great Forces of Nature?'. *Ambio* 36, No. 8 (2007): 614–621.

Stephens, Tim. 'The Limits of International Adjudication in International Environmental Law: Another Perspective on the Southern Bluefin Tuna Case'. *The International Journal Of Marine And Coastal Law* 19, No. 2 (2004): 177–197.

Stephens, Tim. 'Multiple International Courts and the "Fragmentation" of International Environmental Law'. *Australian Yearbook of International Law* 25 (2006): 227–271.

Stephens, Tim. *International Courts and Environmental Protection*. New York: Cambridge University Press, 2009.

Stone, C. *Should Trees Have Standing?: Law, Morality, and the Environment*. Third edn. New York: Oxford University Press, 2010.

The Earth Charter Initiative. 'Values and Principles to Foster a Sustainable Future'. Earth Charter Associates. Online. Available at http://earthcharterinaction.org/content/pages/Read-the-Charter.html (accessed 20 May 2014).

United States. 'Restrictions on Imports of Tuna'. GATT Doc DS2/R, 1991.

United States. 'Restrictions on Imports of Tuna'. GATT Doc DS29/R, 1994.

United States. 'Import Prohibition of Certain Shrimp and Shrimp Products'. WTO Doc WT/DS58/R: Report of the Panel, Report of the Appellate Body, Shrimp-Turtle I Appellate Body Report, 1998.

World Trade Organization. 'Environmental Disputes in GATT/WTO'. WTO. Online. Available at www.wto.org/english/tratop_e/envir_e/edis00_e.htm (accessed 22 May 2014).

Zalasiewicz, Jan, Williams, Mark, Steffen, Will and Crutzen, Paul. 'The New World of the Anthropocene'. *Environmental Science and Technology* 44 (2010): 2228–2231.

13 Climate justice and the distribution of rights to emit carbon

Brendan Mackey and Nicole Rogers[1]

Introduction

Most people accept that the climate change problem is real and a matter of concern,[2] even though it resides largely outside their everyday experiences. Yet public debate on climate change, the impacts of global warming, what may or may not happen, and who is or is not to blame, remains more of a cacophony than a symphony. Vested interests compete with public good advocates for popular support and the political will needed to either prevent or bring about the required rapid and substantive changes in policy.

The scientific consensus, which is evidence based and not to be mistaken for the bargaining and trade-offs associated with normal social consensus, is that warming of the climate system is unequivocal and it is extremely likely that human influence has been the dominant cause of the observed warming since the mid-twentieth century.[3] Climate change is now primarily the consequence of humans burning fossil fuel, in particular coal, oil and natural gas, for energy, thereby releasing carbon dioxide into the atmosphere more rapidly than natural processes can remove it. Emissions from deforestation and degradation are also significant. The result is an increase in the quantity or stock of carbon dioxide in the atmosphere, which in turn leads to global warming and climatic disruption. The solution is to decrease fossil emissions in order to stabilize the atmospheric stock of carbon dioxide and thus avoid an unacceptable degree of climate change. If we wish to avoid the catastrophic consequences of runaway climate change for future generations of people and other species, this current generation must collectively take urgent action to achieve the requisite deep cuts in greenhouse gas emissions from all sources.

A developing discourse on the nature and requirements of climate justice is increasingly playing a role in shaping international negotiations and public policy. In the context of climate change adaptation, a prominent climate justice issue concerns the fate of people whose homes on small islands or otherwise low-lying coastal areas are becoming uninhabitable due to sea level rise. We are witnessing the first attempts at litigation instigated by such communities and individuals displaced by climate change. The Inuit village of Kivalina, which will soon have to be abandoned as a consequence of erosion caused by the melting of sea ice, mounted an unsuccessful lawsuit in public nuisance against various oil, power and gas companies. The suit was dismissed by the United States District Court and an appeal to the Ninth Circuit Court of Appeals was unsuccessful on the basis that the claim was non-justiciable and displaced by legislation. In 2013, the United States Supreme Court refused to hear the case. In New Zealand, Kiribati citizen Ioane Teitiota unsuccessfully sought to claim refugee status under New Zealand law, arguing that Kiribati is rapidly becoming uninhabitable due to climate change impacts. A deciding factor for the judge was the absence of persecution as required under the 1951 *Convention relating to the Status of Refugees*.[4] The case highlighted the deficiencies of existing international refugee law in its application to climate change refugees.

Generally, the outcome of such cases suggests that existing domestic legal frameworks cannot provide climate justice. The plight of those dispossessed by climate change cannot be ignored in the context of climate justice. For the purposes of this chapter, however, our focus will be on the climate justice issues which arise in the context of mitigation. Many different kinds of justice are relevant to international negotiations on climate change mitigation. Ethical issues in climate change policy debates have been raised in terms of economic cost arguments against mitigation, limitations to economic valuation of future costs and benefits, the relevance of scientific uncertainty and the application of the precautionary principle, foreknowledge and the duty to act, the setting of mitigation targets and national emissions allocations, and responsibilities for loss and damage and the costs of adaptation.[5] To date, however, the ethical dimensions of these issues have been sidelined in both treaty negotiations and public discourse.

The climate change problem requires a globally coordinated solution among all the world's nations, as the cumulated stock of greenhouse gases in the atmosphere must be addressed and every country will be affected. We must find solutions which are not only practical but also just, or at least sufficiently just, for all parties, namely national governments. Solutions must be practical as existing energy needs must be met; people need energy for light, cooking and heating or cooling homes and business, and economies need energy for manufacturing and transportation. Alternative energy sources can meet these energy needs[6] but they must be turned on in step with fossil fuel sources being turned off. Solutions must be just because there is great disparity between nations in their contribution to the problem, their access to fossil fuel and alternative energy sources, their level of poverty and what is needed to provide a decent standard of living for their citizens, and their socio-economic and technological capacities and abilities to adapt to the now unavoidable harmful impacts of a rapidly changing climate.

What kinds of justice are needed for climate justice?

The climate change problem is sufficiently complex to encompass multiple kinds of justice. Here we focus on the different kinds of justice relevant to climate change and in particular the mitigation challenge: reducing greenhouse gas emissions to a level that avoids dangerous climate change.

Consequential justice

In some important respects, climate ethics are not normal ethics. The climate change problem is the result of the unintended consequences of actions which are in themselves seemingly morally neutral or positive. Greenhouse gas emissions result from burning energy when parents drive their children to school or a factory produces steel to be used in construction of a hospital. We are all complicit in the generation of greenhouse gas emissions and hence we all contribute to climate change. This complicity has been compared to Hannah Arendt's notion of the 'banality of evil',[7] which she used to describe the conduct of law-abiding Nazi bureaucrats during the Holocaust. Commentators have pointed out that 'perhaps all individuals within the modern industrial world carry out a banal evil against the environment simply by going to work, sitting in their offices and living in homes attached to a power grid'.[8]

The problem is compounded by the fact that the impact of our activities is, thus far, largely invisible. The harm from climate change is removed in space and time from the underlying causal actions. The further we look into the future, the greater are the prospects for harmful impacts. As documented by the Intergovernmental Panel on Climate Change (IPCC), these include rising sea levels; changing patterns of rainfall; an increase in the frequency and intensity of climate-related extremes, such as heatwaves, droughts, floods, cyclones and wildfires; and increased heat-related mortality and the distribution of vector-borne diseases. Differences in vulnerability and exposure arise from non-climatic factors and development inequalities. Climate-related hazards exacerbate other stressors, often with negative outcomes for livelihoods, especially for people living in poverty.[9]

Climate justice is, at its core, concerned with consequential justice: the harmful consequences of climate change for humans, especially for those communities who are most vulnerable and at risk. It shares this in common with environmental justice issues more generally. Consequential justice can be served when climate change harm is avoided or minimized, when the harmed are compensated, or when the perpetrators are held responsible for their actions. This interpretation is related to the philosophical concept of consequentialism: whether an act is morally right depends on whether it causes good or harm to others as calculated by maximizing utility for the greatest number of people.[10]

In the context of climate change mitigation negotiations, we need to consider what might constitute good outcomes or consequences. Our main concern is to avoid the primary consequence of dangerous levels of climate change, which will occur if the international community fails to address the mitigation challenge. The international community has agreed, based on scientific advice from the IPCC, that global warming should be limited to below 2 °C.[11] Business-as-usual scenarios project that global temperatures could increase by 5 °C by the end of this century, and up to 12 °C by the close of 2200, with dire consequences for the human species. There is ultimately no escape if we fail to mitigate greenhouse gases; all nations and all people will have to contend with ever-increasing climatic disruption.

A secondary consequence is the potential for harm from mitigation measures. There is currently a strong positive relationship between fossil fuel energy use, gross domestic product (GDP) and standard of living, including life expectancy.[12] Mitigation measures could damage the economy of developing countries, thus restricting their capacity to address poverty and provide a decent standard of living for their population. There are other indirect consequences which need to be considered here, including avoiding so-called perverse outcomes: unintended harmful outcomes with respect to other valued things. In implementing a mitigation agreement, some proposals for actions to reduce greenhouse gas emissions might have harmful effects in other areas, such as accelerating the loss of biodiversity or reducing food security.[13] For example, carbon offset projects managed through the Clean Development Mechanism, which was created under Article 12 of the Kyoto Protocol, are designed as a mitigation initiative but the creation of tree plantations in development countries as carbon offsets has led to loss of biodiversity and pollution of waterways with agrichemicals.[14]

Procedural justice

Procedural justice is concerned with the fairness and the transparency of the processes by which decisions are made. This is also called procedural fairness or due process. An important component of procedural justice is the inclusion of those affected by decisions in the decision-making process.[15] This normally applies to individuals but the concept can be extended to nations in the context of international climate change negotiations.

Under the United Nations Framework Convention on Climate Change (UNFCCC), negotiations are in progress to develop a new international climate change agreement that will cover all countries. The new agreement will be adopted in 2015, at the Paris climate conference, and implemented from 2020. It will take the form of a protocol with legal force applicable to all state parties. The 2015 agreement negotiating process is endeavouring to bring together the current patchwork of binding and non-binding arrangements under the United Nations climate convention into a single comprehensive regime. The European Union, a few other European countries and Australia have agreed to join a legally binding second period of the Kyoto Protocol[16] which runs until 2020, while over 70 other countries, both developed and developing, have made different types of non-binding commitments to reduce, or limit the growth in, their greenhouse gas emissions.[17]

There is widespread concern that no substantive agreement will emerge in 2015 and that the outcome of the negotiations will be voluntary emission reduction commitments which fall short of the reductions needed to limit global warming to the 2 °C target. If the world community fails to reach a substantive agreement in 2015, it is quite possible that the political will to achieve mitigation through such United Nations negotiations will evaporate. Some people hold the view that it is not possible to achieve consensus among state parties, that a multilateral approach should be abandoned, and that a 'pragmatic' attitude should prevail which enables ad hoc agreements, including bilateral and regional clusters, to be conducted outside the UNFCCC process. The main arguments in favour of abandoning the UNFCCC processes are that they are proving intractable, are unlikely to deliver concrete mitigation outcomes, and given that only a small number of countries are responsible for most of the emissions,[18] negotiations could more fruitfully proceed amongst these countries.

At the end of 2013, in the wake of Typhoon Haiyan, the climate change negotiator from the Philippines at the COP19 talks in Warsaw enacted a powerful performative expression of disenchantment with the lack of progress in the UNFCC negotiations, announcing his intention to adopt the Gandhian strategy of a hunger strike for the duration of the talks until ‘a meaningful outcome is in sight’. He wept as he pleaded for ‘drastic action now to ensure that we prevent a future where super typhoons become a way of life’.[19]

Although some parties have expressed dissatisfaction with the negotiation process as currently conducted, there are considerable risks and disadvantages in the abandonment of formal multilateral negotiations, as noted by Lawrence Solum:[20]

> We can easily rationalize the sacrifice of procedural justice from a consequentialist perspective: the measurable marginal benefits of participation-less procedure may exceed the marginal costs. In the end, however, these rationalizations ring hollow. Procedure without justice sacrifices legitimacy. Law without legitimacy can only guide action through force and fear. Procedure without participation may command obedience, but it cannot win principled allegiance. When we sacrifice procedural justice on the altar of substantive advantage, we risk a very great evil. But when we regard ourselves as bound by the principles of procedural justice, we produce a very great good – we give citizens a principled reason to respect the outcomes of civil process.

Multilateral environmental agreements such as the UNFCCC act like legally independent organizations with autonomous institutional arrangements usually comprising a conference of the parties (CoP) with decision-making powers, a secretariat, and one or more specialist subsidiary bodies.[21] These mechanisms provide opportunities for all nations and, to the extent that their governments are representative, all people access to the decision-making process. If parties choose to abandon the UNFCCC process, they no longer have access to UNFCCC's institutional arrangements and decision-making processes; this approach could well lead to the exclusion of the less powerful and most vulnerable states, and those with the least adaptive capacity, from the negotiation process.

Intergenerational justice and earth justice

We have already highlighted some of the intragenerational issues associated with climate change, including the domination of international negotiations by powerful, high-emitting nations and the inequitable distribution of current climate change impacts such that the poorer countries are experiencing the most severe impacts. The intergenerational issues raised by climate change are even more compelling. The climate change problem is going to be with us for a long time. The issue is not whether there will be any climate change, but by how much the climate is and will be disrupted. Even if we stopped greenhouse gas emissions immediately, the climate system will continue to be disrupted for millennia.[22] If we fail to mitigate, Earth's climate will be pushed into an unimaginable state with global warming of +12 °C by the end of the next century. If we succeed in limiting global warming to 2 °C, the harm will be constrained and the worst impacts avoided.

While climate change impacts are now evident, it is apparent that the prospects for harm to humans and nature increase dramatically when we look forward into a future of unrestrained climate change. It is our children and future generations who will bear the burden of the climatic disruption which we are now causing. This has been poignantly expressed by the group of United States teenagers and children who in 2011 initiated lawsuits and petitions against various governments and government authorities in the United States; they have argued that the atmosphere forms part of the public trust and that governments have an obligation to protect it for present and future generations. These young people have expressed in court documents their sense of personal deprivation and their very real anxiety and concern about the impact of climate change on their futures.[23]

The ethical principle of intergenerational equity emerged in the context of international dialogue around sustainable development. The definition provided in the Bruntland Commission report *Our Common Future*[24] is commonly cited:

> Sustainable development is development that meets the needs of the present without compromising the ability of future generations to meet their own needs.

The extraordinary projections of the long-term negative impacts of climate change require much more than consideration of questions of equitable ability to meet undefined needs. Intergenerational justice imposes on us a duty to deliver future generations a planetary climate that is within the range of natural variability under which the human species evolved and contemporary societies and civilizations have flourished. This process will require transformational changes in our sources of energy, technologies, modes of production and lifestyles. It will probably require a fundamental reshaping of our definition of 'the good life' and acceptance of both limits to growth and the importance of steady-state economies.

It is not only the well-being of future generations of people that is at risk. The health and survival of other species and entire ecosystems is also threatened as the rate of climate change exceeds natural adaptive capacities, leading to mass species extinction and loss of valuable ecosystem services.[25] We can also consider, therefore, as an extension of intergenerational justice, the need for Earth justice: the well-being of the greater community of life and the integrity of the Earth system. A philosophical basis to Earth justice was provided by Hans Jonas:[26] if we accept that life is better than non-life, it follows that we must be concerned for the quality of life lived. This ethical proposition also underscores the sense of universal responsibility that many people feel is now warranted: to extend the community for which we are morally responsible to include all people, future generations, and other species with whom we share Earth as home. This ethic of universal responsibility based on respect and care for all life is the foundation of the *Earth Charter*, a civil society declaration of ethical values and principles for a more just, sustainable and peaceful world.[27]

Intergenerational and earth justice require nations to consider the long-term consequences of their negotiations. Current governments must meet the costs of making the extensive changes necessary to reduce emissions while the benefits will largely accrue to future generations. National governments must place the needs of future generations and other species ahead of short-term national self-interest. Yet, national governments operate under the constraints of short-term political cycles and are subject to pressure from powerful corporations with a vested interest in maintaining the status quo. Author Ian McEwan has observed that 'we are shaped by our history and biology to frame our plans within the short-term, within the scale of a single lifetime; in democracies, governments and electorates collude in tight cycles of promise and gratification'.[28] The political reality is that governments will not formulate and implement such a radical policy agenda without a broad base of public support and a transformational shift in public consciousness.

Taking effective action to prevent runaway climate change will require an unprecedented level of cooperation between the world's nations. We can expect economic factors to increasingly influence the political landscape when the financial benefits of avoiding climate change begin to outweigh the measurable costs of projected impacts and there is an economic case for early action.[29] It remains to be seen, however, if in the absence of a universal ethic of care[30] the world's nations will be prepared to incur the costs needed now for benefits that will potentially flow to people in the future. This is particularly the case if an adequate political response requires more than lifestyle sacrifices and involves the curtailment of what are currently seen as fundamental rights in modern societies: the right to produce and consume and the right to freedom of movement, including the right to catch airplanes for recreational and work purposes. Profound cultural changes are necessary in order to generate the political will needed to meet the mitigation challenge.

Deontological justice

Another relevant form of justice to consider here is deontological justice, which is what most people mean by what is 'right': duties based on specific ethical principles framed as commandments, imperatives or moral laws.[31] Ethical principles do not prescribe right behaviours; rather, they provide guidance as to what is right or wrong in relation to specific decisions. Article 3 of the UNFCCC details principles that the parties agreed to use to guide their actions in achieving the objective of the convention[32] and implementing its provisions. The principles articulated in Article 3 include the parties' common but differentiated responsibilities and respective capabilities, their rights to sustainable development, the special needs of poor countries, and use of the precautionary principle. As argued by John Rawls in his theory of justice, there is a need for society to be organized around fair principles of cooperation in a way that people are prepared to accept.[33] The use of these principles by the state parties in their negotiations will help to ensure that important issues of justice are considered.[34]

The world community, as comprised by the 194 national governments and the 1 regional economic integration organization which are parties to the UNFCCC, have been locked in treaty negotiations now for 22 years since the UNFCCC was opened for signature on 9 May 1992. The annual UNFCCC conference of the parties involves a complex agenda which addresses, amongst other matters, issues of mitigation, adaptation, finance and technology. However, mitigation is the fundamental issue in relation to which all other matters are contingent. OECD nations have become wealthy and continue to get wealthy from causing climate change; the poor countries which are least responsible for climate change will be the most vulnerable to climate change impacts; developing countries and 'economies in transition' need economic growth to alleviate poverty. The BRICS nations (Brazil, Russia, India, China and South Africa) and MINT nations (Mexico, Indonesia, Nigeria and Turkey) are, however, now an essential part of the mitigation problem and its solution.[35] We urgently need approaches to mitigation negotiations which offer more than a token acknowledgement of the principles and different dimensions of justice.

Distributive justice

According to Thomas Aquinas, distributive justice concerns the way in which collective goods and responsibilities are 'fairly apportioned among people who stand in a social community'.[36] Distributive justice is a major theme in climate justice debates and encompasses a myriad of interrelated issues in UNFCCC negotiations, as noted by Emanuele Campiglio:[37]

> Agreement must be sought among states who differ in their stage of development, prospective costs of unmitigated climate change, costs of mitigation and adaptation, and, most importantly, in terms of their perceived historical responsibility and ability to pay. Indeed, the clear distinction between developed and developing regions and the issues of fairness that this inevitably gives rise to, are the main factors holding back the attainment of a common agreement on emissions reduction and burden sharing.... In a nutshell given the asymmetric nature of global climate change and the issues of fairness and historical responsibility that this implies, I take the view that

> climate change mitigation is fundamentally a development problem and has to be linked to equity considerations.

A pivotal distributive justice issue in UNFCCC negotiations is how permissible carbon emissions are to be allocated among nations. The IPCC has calculated that in order to limit global warming to 2 °C only around 1,000 billion tonnes of carbon dioxide can be emitted this century; this is equivalent to about 33 years of current annual anthropogenic emissions.[38] This amount (1,000 billion tonnes) is referred to as the permissible emissions, the global carbon budget or, as we like to call it, the 'carbon pie'. Given this, in negotiating an effective 2015 agreement, nations have to agree on what constitutes a fair apportioning of the global carbon budget and what principle or principles are used to allocate the permissible carbon emissions.

At least three principles have been proposed for allocating emissions.[39] The first is simply based on the status quo: emissions are frozen at existing levels and every nation has the right to its current level of emissions. The second uses a per capita allocation whereby each nation gets a slice of the carbon pie based on its population at a specific time. The third is called redistributive where the carbon pie is allocated in order to achieve specific social justice aims, such as ensuring the economic development of the poorest countries is not impeded. There is no ethical justification for the status quo approach as it simply reflects pragmatic acceptance of the current distribution of wealth and technology. Distributive justice would not be served were it to be adopted as the guiding principle for distributing the carbon budget pie.

The per capita approach is based explicitly on the ethical principle that each human being has equal rights as stated in Article 1 of the *Universal Declaration of Human Rights*:

> All human beings are born free and equal in dignity and rights. They are endowed with reason and conscience and should act towards one another in a spirit of brotherhood.

It follows that each human has equal rights to the ecosystem services provided by the global commons, in this case the carbon absorbing capacity of the Earth system.

The redistributive approach has ethical appeal but comes with certain risks. Goals set by appeals to retributive justice, which require punishment of those most responsible for climate change, or development justice, which support more emissions on an ongoing basis from developing countries, could 'blow out' the carbon budget: there will be more emissions allocated than is permissible if we are to limit global warming to less than 2 °C. Unlike normal problems where there is flexibility in the goal being negotiated, the carbon pie cannot be baked bigger, nor can we bake more pies. There is only one Earth with physical boundaries within which we have to operate.[40]

The issue of development justice warrants further scrutiny as it is central to climate change negotiations. Developed countries are responsible for 52 per cent of the additional greenhouse gases that have accumulated in the atmosphere due to humans burning fossil fuel and land use, with the United States, EU-28, Japan, Canada, Australia and New Zealand responsible for around 42 per cent of these.[41] The developing countries are responsible for 48 per cent. As noted, 2 of the top 3 and 7 of the top 20 carbon dioxide emitting countries in 2010 were BRICS/MINT nations. Yet the burden of poverty falls on these and other developing countries, including China and India.[42] There will continue to be conflict between the goals of emission reduction and poverty alleviation while economic development is coupled with fossil fuel energy use.

Contraction and convergence

One approach to framing the mitigation negotiations is called 'Contraction and Convergence'.[43] If implemented, this approach would, in the words of its originator, Aubrey Meyer, yield 'climate justice without vengeance'.[44] We use the term 'vengeance' here in the sense of retributive justice against those nations most responsible for climate change on behalf of those which did not cause the problem but which will suffer the most. The latter includes poor and largely undeveloped countries; within such countries, the sense of injustice is palpable. As Robert Aisi, who represents Papua New Guinea in the United Nations, stated to the United Nations General Assembly on behalf of the Pacific island countries: 'We are likely to become the victims of a phenomenon to which we have contributed very little and of which we can do very little to halt'.[45]

Contraction and Convergence provides a framework for the international mitigation negotiations which focuses attention on key questions. 'Contraction' refers to the steady reduction in global emissions to a safe level. 'Convergence' refers to each nation's per capita emissions converging to the same annual rate at an agreed date. The first key question is the size of the global carbon budget. This decision sets the total amount of permissible emissions which are to be allocated among the world's nations.[46] The second question concerns the time frame over which global emissions will be reduced to the agreed level: for example, the period up to 2080. The permissible emissions are then allocated to each country on a per capita basis, which could be calculated based on their current population.

As it would not be practical for the world community to continue to emit greenhouse gases at the current rate until the global carbon budget is exhausted, emissions need to be steadily decreased each year to enable a transition from fossil fuel to alternative energy sources, in a way which minimizes economic harm and allows for the necessary sustainable development. The next question therefore is to agree upon the year at which each nation's annual per capita emissions become equal. There is currently great disparity in per capita emissions, with per capita emissions for the group of high-income countries almost ten times that of low-income countries. Therefore, for the period up to the time of convergence, there will be a steady reduction in carbon emissions for countries currently with high per capita emissions and increased emissions allowed for nations currently with low per capita emissions, until the entitlements of all countries converge to the same rate. After convergence has been achieved, all nations will reduce their emissions at the same per capita rate until the global carbon budget is expended at the agreed end point in time. If considered desirable, the world community could establish a parallel trade in per capita carbon allocations whereby countries sell their unused allocations to countries which struggle to meet their continuously reducing emission allocations. The earlier the date set for convergence, the greater the rate at which wealthy countries have to decrease the emissions, and the more demand there would be for emission allocation credits.

No consensus has emerged among experts or decision-makers as to which is the optimal allocation principle. Those who advocate the Contraction and Convergence approach acknowledge that there is a potential tension between policies which prioritize the need to avoid future climate change and those directed towards alleviation of poverty. Contraction and Convergence is a pragmatic approach reflecting the reality that no allocation principle can deliver a perfectly just outcome with respect to all forms of justice and the burdens and responsibilities of both past and future emissions. Its supporters also argue, correctly, that the greatest injustice will result from a failure on the part of the world community to mitigate emissions. With such an outcome there will be no winners and everyone, especially the poor, will suffer in the long term.

Conclusion

Will the world's nations deliver a just solution to the climate change mitigation challenge? History provides ample evidence that we should remain cynical about the role of ethics in international relations. Nations tend to respect ethical values and accept ethical principles only to the extent that such values and principles are useful and convenient without presenting a challenge to national sovereignty.[47] International relations continue to operate under the shadow of the ongoing assumption of 'war readiness'.[48]

Climate justice demands that those responsible for the problem should fix it and help those who will be worst affected adapt to the now unavoidable impacts of a human-forced future climate. If we ignore the nuances of climate justice, however, and seek perfect justice in all its manifestations, we risk failing to reduce greenhouse gas emissions and limit global warming to below 2 °C. The consequences of runaway climate change will be dire for future generations and the poorest will suffer the most. We cannot allow the urge for retribution to trump the need to avoid and minimize long-term climate change impacts. Nor can we expect climate change negotiations to solve all the world's development challenges. Appropriately implemented mitigation policies and actions can help alleviate poverty. The root causes of poverty, however, lie elsewhere.

Cases

Ioane Teitiota v. The Chief Executive of the Ministry of Business Innovation and Employment (2013) NZHC 3125.

Notes

1 We are grateful for insightful advice and comment from Ron Engel on matters of ethics, philosophy and their application to environmental justice issues, which greatly improved this chapter. Thanks also to Rakhyun Kim for discussions on the use of principles in the UNFCCC.
2 Reser *et al*. 2012: 245.
3 Stocker *et al*. (eds.) 2013: 1535. Note that the IPCC term ‘extremely likely’ equates to an assessed likelihood of an outcome of 95–100 per cent.
4 *Ioane Teitiota v. The Chief Executive of the Ministry of Business Innovation and Employment* (2013) NZHC 3125 at [63].
5 Brown 2013; World Commission on the Ethics of Scientific Knowledge and Technology 2010.
6 See, for instance, the Energy Research Institute, ‘Zero Carbon Australia 2020 Stationary Energy Plan, an Initiative of Beyond Zero Emissions’, University of Melbourne.
7 Arendt 1963.
8 Kochi and Ordan 2008: 1–21.
9 Intergovernmental Panel on Climate Change 2014b.
10 Sinnott-Armstrong 2014.
11 United Nations 2010. Part Two: Action taken by the Conference of the Parties at its fifteenth session. Decisions adopted by the Conference of the Parties.
12 Intergovernmental Panel on Climate Change 2014a, Fig. 5.13.
13 C. Palm *et al*. 2010: 19661–19666.
14 Beder 2007: 16–17.
15 Solum 2004: 181–322.
16 As documented on the UNFCCC website:

> The Kyoto Protocol is an international agreement linked to the United Nations Framework Convention on Climate Change, which commits its Parties by setting internationally binding emission reduction targets. During the first commitment period, 37 industrialized countries and the European Community committed to reduce GHG emissions to an average of five percent against 1990 levels.
>
> (United Nations 1997.)

17 Details here sourced from: European Commission, ‘Climate Action – the 2015 International Agreement’.
18 The top 10 countries ranked in terms of carbon dioxide emissions in 2010 were: China (first); USA; India; Russian Federation; Japan; Germany; Islamic Republic of Iran; Republic of Korea; Canada; United Kingdom. They accounted for 64 per cent of emissions that year. The next 10 countries account for a further 12 per cent. Source: The World Bank, ‘Co_2 Emissions’, The World Bank.
19 Goyette 2013.
20 Solum 2004: 181–322.
21 Churchill and Ulfstein 2000: 623–659.
22 Mackey *et al*. 2013: 552–557.
23 See a discussion of these lawsuits in Rogers 2013.
24 United Nations 1987.
25 The IPPC concluded that there are high risks of extensive biodiversity loss with associated loss of ecosystem goods and services with around 3 °C additional warming (see Intergovernmental Panel on Climate Change 2014a, Addendum, ‘Summary for Decision Makers, Assessment Box SPM.1, Human Interference with the Climate System’).
26 Jonas 1987.
27 Mackey 2005: 63–68. And for further details on the Earth Charter document see www.earthcharter.org.

28 McEwan 2008: 36.
29 Garnaut 2011; Stern 2006.
30 Boff 2008.
31 Alexander and Moore 2012.
32 United Nations 1992, Article 2, Objective. The ultimate objective of this Convention and any related legal instruments that the Conference of the Parties may adopt is to achieve, in accordance with the relevant provisions of the Convention, stabilization of greenhouse gas concentrations in the atmosphere at a level that would prevent dangerous anthropogenic interference with the climate system. Such a level should be achieved within a time frame sufficient to allow ecosystems to adapt naturally to climate change, to ensure that food production is not threatened and to enable economic development to proceed in a sustainable manner.
33 Richardson 2005.
34 Interestingly, Article 3 on Principles was included in the operative part of the convention text rather than the preamble. For further interpretation of Article 3 see Bodanskyt 1993.
35 Among the top 20 carbon dioxide emitting nations in 2010 were: China, India, Russia, South Africa, Mexico, Indonesia and Brazil. Source: The World Bank, 'CO_2 Emissions'.
36 Fieser 2012.
37 Campiglio 2012.
38 Global Carbon Project, 'Global Carbon Budget 2013'.
39 Posner and Sunstein 2008.
40 Rockström *et al.* 2009: 32.
41 Accumulated anthropogenic emissions 1850–2010. Source: den Elzen *et al.* 2013: 397–412.
42 South Asia has 31 per cent and sub-Saharan Africa has 48.5 per cent of their population living on less than $1.25 per day. Source: The World Bank, 'Poverty and Equity Data', URL appears in references.
43 Meyer 2000.
44 Aubrey Meyer is founder and director of the Global Commons Institute. The phrase 'Climate justice without vengeance' is the banner subtitle of GCI's website where details of Contraction and Convergence are comprehensively documented at www.gci.org.uk/.
45 Aisi 2007: 65–66.
46 As noted, if we want to limit global warming to below 2 °C then the global carbon budget is about 1,000 billion tonnes of carbon dioxide. The world community, however, could decide to allow global warming to increase to a higher level, such as 3 °C, in which case more emissions would be permitted and the global carbon budget pie would be larger.
47 Dower 1998; Machiavelli 1979 (1531).
48 Hobbes 1651.

References

Aisi, R. 'Facing Extinction. Climate Change and the Threat to Pacific Island Countries'. *Reform* 65 (2007): 65–66.

Alexander, Larry and Moore, Michael. 'Deontological Ethics'. In *The Stanford Encyclopedia of Philosophy*, edited by Edward N. Zalta. Stanford, CA: Stanford University, 2012. Online. Available at http://plato.stanford.edu/archives/win2012/entries/ethics-deontological/ (accessed 12 May 2014).

Arendt, H. *Eichmann in Jerusalem. A Report on the Banality of Evil*. London: Faber and Faber, 1963.

Beder, S. 'Carbon Offsets Are Not Sustainable'. *Green*, 2007, 16–17.

Bodanskyt, D. 'The United Nations Framework Convention on Climate Change: A Commentary'. *Yale Journal of International Law* 18 (1993): 451–558.

Boff, L. *Essential Care: An Ethics of Human Nature*. Waco, TX: Baylor University Press, 2008.

Brown, D.A. *Climate Change Ethics: Navigating the Perfect Moral Storm*. London: Earthscan/Routledge, 2013.

Campiglio, E. 'Who Should Pay for Climate? The Effect of Burden-Sharing Mechanisms on Abatement Policies and Technological Transfers'. Centre for Climate Change Economics and Policy Working Paper 114: Centre for Climate Change Economics, 2012.

Churchill, R.R. and G. Ulfstein, G. 'Autonomous Institutional Arrangements in Multilateral Environmental Agreements: A Little-Noticed Phenomenon in International Law'. *American Journal of International Law* 94 (2000): 623–659.

Dower, N. *World Ethics: The New Agenda*. Edinburgh: Edinburgh University Press, 1998.

Elzen, M.G.J. den, Olivier, J.G.J., Höhne, N. and Janssens-Maenhout, G. 'Countries' Contributions to Climate Change: Effect of Accounting for All Greenhouse Gases, Recent Trends, Basic Needs and Technological Progress'. *Climatic Change* 121 (2013): 397–412.

Energy Research Institute. 'Zero Carbon Australia 2020 Stationary Energy Plan, an Initiative of Beyond Zero Emissions'. Melbourne: University of Melbourne. Online. Available at http://bze.org.au/zero-carbon-australia/stationary-energy-plan (accessed 12 May 2014).

European Commission. 'Climate Action – the 2015 International Agreement'. European Commission. Online. Available at http://ec.europa.eu/clima/policies/international/negotiations/future/documentation_en.htm (accessed 5 August 2014).

Fieser, J. 'Thomas Aquinas'. In *The Internet Encyclopedia of Philosophy*, 2012. Online. Available at www.iep.utm.edu/ (accessed 12 May 2014).

Garnaut, R. *The Garnaut Review 2011: Australia in the Global Response to Climate Change*. Cambridge: Cambridge University Press, 2011.

Global Carbon Project. 'Global Carbon Budget 2013'. Online. Available at www.globalcarbonproject.org/carbonbudget/index.htm (accessed 12 May 2014).

Goyette, Braden 'Philippines Climate Negotiator Makes Emotional Plea at Cop19, Vows Hunger Strike'. The *Huffington Post*, 12 November 2013.

Hobbes, T. *Leviathan*. Cambridge, MA: Cambridge University Press, 1651.

Intergovernmental Panel on Climate Change. *5th Assessment Report Climate Change 2014: Mitigation of Climate Change*. Working Group III IPCC, 2014a. Online. Available at https://www.ipcc.ch/report/ar5/wg1/ (accessed 12 May 2014).

Intergovernmental Panel on Climate Change. *Climate Change 2014: Impacts, Adaptation, and Vulnerability Summary for Policymakers*. Working Group II IPPC, 2014b. Online. Available at www.ipcc.ch/report/ar5/wg2/ (accessed 6 August 2014).

Jonas, H. *The Imperative of Responsibility: In Search of an Ethics for the Technological Age*. Chicago: University of Chicago Press, 1987.

Kochi, T. and Ordan, N. 'An Argument for the Global Suicide of Humanity'. *Borderlands e-journal* 3 (2008): 1–21. Online. Available at www.borderlands.net.au/issues/ (accessed 12 may 2014).

Machiavelli, N. 'Discourses'. Trans. P. Bondanelli and M. Musa. In *The Portable Machiavelli*, edited by P. Bondanelli and M. Musa. Harmondsworth, UK: Penguin Books, 1979 (1531).

Mackey, B.G. 'The Earth Charter and Ecological Integrity – a Commitment to Life on Earth'. In *The Earth Charter in Action*, edited by P. Corcoran. Amsterdam: Royal Tropical Institute (KIT) Publishers, 2005: 63–68.

Mackey, B., Prentice, I.C., Steffen, W., House, J.I., Lindenmayer, D., Keith, H. and Berry, S. 'Untangling the confusion around land carbon science and climate change mitigation policy', *Nature Climate Change* 3 (2013): 552–557.

McEwan, I. 'The Hot Breath of Civilisation'. *The Sydney Morning Herald*, 8–9 March 2008: 36.

Meyer, A. *Contraction & Convergence: The Global Solution to Climate Change*. Schumacher Briefings. Vol. 5, Totnes, Devon: Green Books for the Schumacher Society, 2000.

Palm, C., Smukler, S.M., Sullivan, C.C., Mutuo, P.K., Nyadzi, G.I. and Walsh, M.G. 'Identifying Potential Synergies and Trade-Offs for Meeting Food Security and Climate Change Objectives in Sub-Saharan Africa'. *Proceedings of the National Academy of Sciences of the United States of America* 107 (2010): 1661–1666.

Posner, P.A. and Sunstein, C.R. *The Harvard Project on International Climate Agreements: Discussion Paper 08–04*. Cambridge, MA: Harvard University, 2008.

Reser, J.P., Bradley, G.L., Glendon, A.J., Ellul, M.C. and Callaghan, R. *Public Risk Perceptions, Understandings, and Responses to Climate Change and Natural Disasters in Australia, 2010 and 2011*. Gold Coast City, QLD: National Climate Change Adaptation Research Facility, 2012. Online. Available at www.nccarf.edu.au/publications/public-risk-perceptions-second-survey (accessed 12 May 2014).

Richardson, R.H. 'John Rawls'. In *The Internet Encyclopedia of Philosophy*, edited by James Fiesner and Bradley Dowden, 2005. Online. Available at www.iep.utm.edu/ (Accessed 12 May 2014).

Rockström, J., Steffen, W., Noone, K., Persson, III, A., Chapin, F.S., Lambin, E. and Lenton, T.M. 'Planetary Boundaries: Exploring the Safe Operating Space for Humanity'. *Ecology and Society* 14 (2009): 32.

Rogers, N. 'Climate Change Litigation and the Awfulness of Lawfulness'. *Alternative Law Journal* 20 (2013): 22–24.

Sinnott-Armstrong, Walter. 'Consequentialism'. In *The Encyclopedia of Philosophy*, edited by Edward N. Zalta. Stanford, CA: Stanford University, 2014. Online. Available at http://plato.stanford.edu/entries/consequentialism/ (accessed 12 May 2014).

Solum, L.B. 'Procedural Justice'. *Southern Californian Law Review* 78 (2004): 181–222.

Stern, N. *Stern Review on the Economics of Climate Change*. Cambridge: Cambridge University Press, 2006. Online. Available at http://webarchive.nationalarchives.gov.uk/+/http:/www.hm-treasury.gov.uk/sternreview_index.htm (accessed 4 August 2014).

Stocker, T.F., Qin, D., Plattner, G.-K., Tignor, M., Allen, S.K., Boschung, J. and Nauels, A., (eds). *Climate Change 2013: The Physical Science Basis. Contribution of Working Group I to the Fifth Assessment Report of the Intergovernmental Panel on Climate Change*. Cambridge: Cambridge University Press, 2013.

The World Bank. 'CO_2 Emissions'. Online. Available at http://data.worldbank.org/indicator/EN.ATM.CO2E.KT (accessed 12 May 2014).

The World Bank. 'Poverty and Equity Data'. Online. Available at http://data.worldbank.org/topic/poverty (accessed 12 May 2014).

United Nations. 'Report of the World Commission on Environment and Development: Our Common Future'. Annex to document A/42/427 1987.

United Nations. 'Framework Convention on Climate Change'. FCCC/INFORMAL/84 GE.05–62220 (E) 200705, 1992.

United Nations. 'Kyoto Protocol to the United Nations Framework Convention on Climate Change'. UN Doc FCCC/CP/1997/7/Add.1, 10 December 1997.

United Nations. 'Report of the Conference of the Parties on Its Fifteenth Session, Held in Copenhagen 7–19 December 2009'. FCCC/CP/2009/11/Add.1, 30 March 2010.

World Commission on the Ethics of Scientific Knowledge and Technology. *The Ethical Implications of Global Climate Change*. Paris: United Nations Educational, Scientific and Cultural Organization, 2010.

14 Nuclear power and human security

Lessons from the Fukushima Daiichi nuclear power plant accident

Yasunobu Sato

Introduction

On 6 August 1945, the first nuclear weapon, an atomic bomb, was dropped over the heads of people in Hiroshima. It killed an estimated 150,000 people, most of whom were civilians, women and children, instantly and in the following months. On 9 August 1945, a second bomb purportedly killed about 80,000 individuals in Nagasaki. Survivors are suffering from the radioactivity released by the explosion of the atomic bombs even now. At the sixty-eighth anniversary of the bombings in 2013, 286,818 persons were listed as deceased as a result of the Hiroshima bomb and 162,083 persons in Nagasaki according to records published by the local governments of Hiroshima and Nagasaki.

No nation or person was incriminated for these unprecedented, inhuman and human-made disasters, nor was any person blamed. Under a special law, the Japanese government has been assisting survivors (though not compensating them) with treatment of the diseases caused by the radioactivity. Eligibility for treatment has expanded as a consequence of numerous revisions of laws, though in general, eligibility for various allowances is limited.[1] A number of people are currently engaged in legal action in order to be officially designated as eligible victims. The length of time since the bombings has made it more difficult for these litigants to prove that the blasts caused their illnesses.

There is no international legal regime for the assistance and compensation of survivors of a nuclear attack. No compensation for damages by the US government or the Japanese government can be expected. No criminal sanction can be imposed, even though it can be argued that the Hiroshima and Nagasaki bombings constituted genocide, or, at least, a crime against humanity.

In 1996, upon a request by the World Health Organization that had been endorsed by the United Nations General Assembly, the International Court of Justice (ICJ) announced its advisory opinion on the legality of use of nuclear weapons:[2]

> [T]he threat or use of nuclear weapons would generally be contrary to the rules of international law applicable in armed conflict, and in particular the principles and rules of humanitarian law. However, in view of the current state of international law, and of the elements of fact at its disposal, the

> Court cannot conclude definitively whether the threat or use of nuclear weapons would be lawful or unlawful in an extreme circumstance of self-defense, in which the very survival of a State would be at stake.

Astonishingly, despite the Japanese people's strong interest in abolishing nuclear weapons, the Japanese government abstained from voting in favour of the UN General Assembly's resolution, referring the question of the legality of the use of nuclear weapons to the ICJ. It is probable that the Japanese government considered the likely negative US reaction to such a position, since Japan is now under the 'nuclear umbrella' of the United States.[3]

International efforts in support of nuclear disarmament seem to have advanced slowly but steadily since the so-called cold war. Since human security issues have assumed a higher importance on the UN agenda, the nuclear disarmament argument has become more persuasive.[4] However, the justification of nuclear weapons for national security purposes by deterring a nuclear attack by another state has led to endless competition in the development and deployment of more and more advanced nuclear arms, and that, in turn, has created more serious security risks all over the world. This security dilemma has created a vicious circle. With the conclusion of the cold war, this curse should have been lifted and the world should have become safer. That did not take place. Instead, the dangers of nuclear power has been disguised within the seemingly benign faces of nuclear power plants. Ironically, this risk became real for Japan as a result of a major power plant accident categorized at the highest level by IATA.

In this chapter, I argue that the absence of an effective international legal regime for the assistance and compensation of victims of the Hiroshima and Nagasaki bombings has meant that the victims of the disastrous meltdown of the Fukushima Daiichi power plant in 2012 have had no international legal recourse for their complaints.

The nuclear meltdown

During the cold war, in the 1950s, Japan developed a nuclear power industry with the assistance of the US, importing nuclear power plants from that country. The Japanese government justified this development as a peaceful means of nuclear power. Since then, Japan itself has developed nuclear technology by constructing more than 50 nuclear power plants all over Japan. This is the third highest number of nuclear power plants after the US and France.

Japan has also developed nuclear fuel reproducing plants to reuse nuclear waste and try to operate faster breeder reactors. These projects have been justified as a dream technology, recycling nuclear energy by saving uranium, which has to be imported. As a country with insufficient natural resources, in particular oil and gas, Japan has had a strong desire to establish a nuclear recycling industry.

This industry, however, produces plutonium, which is much more dangerous than uranium and can be used to produce a nuclear bomb. Thus, such an industry is highly controlled and monitored by the International Atomic Energy Agency

(IAEA). Japan is the only country that does not have nuclear weapons and is allowed to possess such nuclear technology, since Japan has been trusted as a country without the ambition of building nuclear armaments. Nevertheless, it cannot be denied that Japan has been promoting nuclear technology with the intention of using it for strategic purposes. Japan has the technology and material to manufacture nuclear armaments. It is argued the nuclear power plants exist in Japan in support of her national interest for military advantage – a hidden agenda that is seemingly backed by the US–Japan Securty Treaty which supports the development of a global nuclear strategy.

On 11 March 2011 (14:46:23 Japan time), a 9.0 magnitude earthquake struck Japan's northeast coastal region facing the Pacific Ocean. This catalytic event caused three disasters in Japan, the Asian region and beyond. These included: the destruction of houses and buildings; the destruction of villages and towns by an ensuing tsunami (the large run-up reached heights exceeding 39 metres); and serious radioactive contamination caused by the meltdown of the Fukushima Daiichi nuclear power plant.[5]

The Fukushima Daiichi plant was built in 1966. The US company General Electric (GE) manufactured its reactors – the oldest model reactors in Japan. The tsunami is understood to have destroyed its emergency power generators, which were stored underground.[6] The safety system developed for the US-made plant model was not suited to the Japanese context. This is because the US plants were designed to withstand damage by tornados, which seldom happen in Japan. In Japan, earthquakes and ensuing tsunamis are a greater risk. The adaptation of safety systems to Japanese conditions does not appear to have been seriously considered at the time.

Normally, product liability rules would be applicable in such a case, since the nuclear facilities were designed defectively, and were highly dangerous and risky. Strict liability should have been borne by the manufacturer. To the contrary, in fact, Japanese law and international law provides immunity for manufacturers from any legal liability. Thus, GE enjoys this immunity and is not legally liable for any damage caused by the accident nor has the company received any claim against it. How can such immunity be justified? We should examine the background to this accident and its repercussions so that a contemporary international refime for access to justice in the even of a nuclear incident can be developed.

What happened in Fukushima, Japan?

According to the Fukushima prefectural government, the number of Fukushima residents evacuated was more than 160,000. As of 6 August 2013, the number of evacuees was 148,617. As of 4 July 2013, 53,227 evacuees remained outside the Fukushima prefecture.[7]

The meltdown of the Fukushima Daiichi nuclear power plant prompted many foreign governments to advise their citizens to evacuate from Tokyo and even from Japan.[8] A substantial number of Japanese families, even those who lived outside the Fukushima prefecture, left for the western part of Japan due to fears of radioactivity affecting their children.[9] Various parts of Japan were contaminated by radioactive leaks due to specific climate conditions, such as wind and rain, and geographic features, such as mountains and rivers. Even in Tokyo and nearby regions, highly contaminated spots ('hot spots') were found. While no deaths or serious health effects from the radioactivity have yet been reported, the lessons from Hiroshima and Nagasaki indicate that illnesses and disease caused by radioactivity may take considerable time to manifest. Any delay in this regard does not render the damage less worthy of compensation.

Indeed, by March 2013 (the second anniversary of the disaster) 789 people, mostly hospitalized aged patients, had died due to lack of medical support or stress caused by the emergency evacuation.[10] The amount of radioactive material released from the hydrogen explosions that occurred in the Fukushima plant is understood to be as much as 168 times greater than that of the atomic bomb dropped on Hiroshima.

Four major investigations of the accident took place. On 2 June 2012, the Independent Investigation Commission on the Fukushima Daiichi Nuclear Accident published its Research Investigation Report.[11] Tokyo Electric Power Company (TEPCO), the operator of the plant, released its own report on 20 June 2012.[12] The National Diet of Japan published the report of its Fukushima Nuclear Accident Investigation Commission on 5 July 2012.[13] Then on 23 July 2012, the Japanese Government's Investigation Committee on the Accident at the Fukushima Nuclear Power Stations of Tokyo Electric Company issued its Investigation Report.[14] Three of the four reports (all except the TEPCO report) concluded that the accident was caused by the negligence of TEPCO. The National Diet's report described the accident as 'Made-in-Japan' – an accident caused by aspects of Japan's industrial culture, a point I return to below.

Access to criminal justice

On 1 August 2012, the Public Prosecutors' Offices in Tokyo, Fukushima and Kanazawa received criminal complaints: 1,300 people accused 33 TEPCO senior officials and Japanese regulatory officials of professional negligence resulting in death and injury pursuant to the Criminal Code, and violation of the Nuclear Reactor Regulation Law as well as the Act for the Punishment of Crime Caused by Pollution Harmful to Human Health. The Tokyo Public Prosecutor's Office announced on 9 September 2013 that all complaints were dismissed. However, even if these people are found guilty, the maximum sentence under the Criminal Code is only five years imprisonment or a 1 million yen fine. The maximum sentence under the Act and special laws which facilitate prosecution of such an unprecedented case is similar.

As in the case of the Tokyo Public Prosecutor's Office mentioned above, it would be extremely difficult to find these senior officials liable for negligence: arguably an earthquake and tsunami are not foreseeable, and their individual roles were not within the relevant chain of command. Surprisingly, there is no special offence applicable to this extremely dangerous industry. People convicted of dangerous or negligent driving can receive higher penalties.

It is argued that the extremely high risks associated with nuclear activity require the introduction of an aggravated offence to punish negligence. It is the writer's opinion that this type of crime has not been introduced because to do so would involve a political admission that nuclear incidents of this nature are possible. In the international context, the logic hold as no international crime due to a nuclear accident has been seriously argued. No action in the criminal justice sphere whether in the domestic or international arena is expected in the near future.

Access to civil justice

Significant compensation pay-outs are expected. TEPCO, as the nuclear reactor operator, is liable for damages and is obliged to provide them under the Nuclear Damage Compensation Law. The manufacturer, GE in this case, is, however, immune from any responsibility. TEPCO, as a joint-stock company, could be bankrupted, and its liability limited under company law. However, the Japanese government intervened to support TEPCO (Art. 16 (1)) and will therefore assist TEPCO in providing compensation. In fact, on 27 June 2012, TEPCO was substantially nationalized. Nuclear power operators are now required to have a contract of insurance for an accident up to JPY120 billion, and are liable without fault and limit under the law in the event of an accident.[15]

The Nuclear Damage Claim Dispute Resolution Center was established by the Ministry of Education, Culture, Sports, Science and Technology (Mext) as a special alternative dispute resolution (ADR) centre, under the auspices of the Japan Federation of Bar Associations in August 2011.[16] Since it commenced operation on 1 September, until 2 August 2013, the Center has received more than 10,078 cases. Among these, 7,188 cases have been completed. Additionally, the number of mass litigations related to the nuclear power plant's accident stands at 5,537 as at February 2014.[17] Most of the evacuees who are living in temporary housing in other cities and towns have not been compensated. TEPCO has insisted that compensation should be for temporary hardship; however, the damage to the lives of evacuees is incalculable and ongoing. A recent announcement by the Dispute Resolution Committee revealed that the average compensation paid by TEPCO was 90 million yen per four-member household and 45.1 million yen per single household who resided in an area categorized as difficult to return to.

The government has accelerated cleaning of the radioactive materials, but intermediate brokers are reported to have corruptly deducted significant amounts of money that was set aside for the remuneration of workers involved in the cleaning. The cleaning work itself is very difficult and tiring. Negligent work is often reported. It is also widely reported that the government budget for rehabilitation and reconstruction of Tohoku has been overwhelmingly misappropriated for unrelated public services. Abuse and manipulation of the clean-up and public works funding by people taking advantage of the confusion in the post-disaster environment cannot be denied, even in Japan. The neediest people cannot access justice easily.

Japanese culture as a cause of the accident?

As mentioned previously, the National Diet's report on the Fukushima disaster concluded that the accident was 'Made-in-Japan'. Use of this phrase was intended to point out that elements of the Japanese 'Iron Triangle' culture were responsible. The Iron Triangle is an informal system of interdependent relationships among industry, bureaucrats and Liberal Democratic Party politicians (the ruling party for more than half a century) associated with the command economy created by the Japanese after the Second World War, which led to rapid economic growth. This industrial culture created a 'Nuclear Power Village',[18] characterized by a closed, community-oriented collectivist industrial culture that acts in favour of vested interests and excludes opposing viewpoints. It was alleged that the nuclear power industry, bureaucrats, politicians, academics, experts and judges have colluded with each other to avoid taking responsibility for nuclear safety. As a result, safety risks increased. While it is true that Japan's unique governance practices could contribute to such a fragile safety system, there are also universal or global elements explained by world-systems or dependency theory at play.

The Fukushima prefecture, which is in the Tohoku (north-eastern) region of Japan, is a poor, marginalized and underdeveloped area. To convince people concerned about safety risks to accept these dangerous plants, the 'Myth of Absolute Safety' was used to overcome sensitivity lingering from the awful experiences in the aftermath of Hiroshima and Nagasaki. 'Nimby' ('not in my backyard') politics also operated in this context, as marginalized areas of Japan are exploited to house risky industries. In addition, the Japanese regulatory body responsible for nuclear safety was practically controlled by TEPCO (so-called regulatory capture) as it had considerable expertise that the regulator did not possess. The so-called 'Myth of Absolute Safety' was constructed so that any sound criticism or even the slightest doubt on safety was taboo and marginalised. Blame can also be attributed to the academy which contributed to the dogma in return for sizable research grants.

Moral hazard and governance as common issues in the nuclear industry

As for the root causes of the accident, Ramseyer[19] points out universal elements as follows:

1 Private company's moral hazard by corporate law due to limited liability – no incentive to avoid damage beyond the corporate assets.
2 Government's democratic governance issues on progressive taxation – majority voters prefer low utility rates and do not care for damages incurred

to be covered by increased taxation to compensate beyond the company's assets and insurance.

Thus, unless the world takes lessons from Fukushima, similar nuclear accidents may happen in other advanced market economies.

The purpose of Article 1 of the Nuclear Damage Compensation Law in Japan is to promote the sound development of the nuclear power industry and the protection of victims. Its fundamental objective is promotion of the nuclear power industry through victim compensation. The safety of the people, that is human security, is secondary. Article 3 provides immunity for Extraordinary Major Natural Disasters or Social Upheavals. TEPCO has not invoked this immunity, but the immunity clause may well have been weighed in consideration when TEPCO conducted its cost–benefit calculations for safety. As discussed, Article 4 of the law provides immunity from liability for manufacturers, which blocks any possibility of seeking compensation from GE, the manufacturer of the reactors that exploded in Fukushima. So who is accountable and responsible for safety?

In Japan, the regulatory body was controlled by the Ministry of Economy and Industry, which promotes the nuclear power industry and the Ministry of Education, Culture, Sports, Science and Technology, which also promotes this technology. The dual ministerial control was confusing and contributed to the problem as no single department had clear oversight.

Thus, a new regulation agency was set up under the Ministry of Environment after the accident, though still under the control of the government. Even if the independent body regulated the nuclear power industry, there would remain concerns about regulatory capture. Unfortunately, in Japan, the regulatory bodies and the electric companies collude with each other and have supported each other for a long period. TEPCO often seconded their staff to the regulator to provide technical support. It was a part of the 'Nuclear Power Village'. It has since been revealed that the newly established regulatory agency has leaked internal information to TEPCO.

Access to justice under international law

Nuclear damage compensation

As for international rules on compensation for nuclear damages, the OECD-based Paris-Brussels Convention on Third Party Liability was adopted in 1960 and entered into force in 1968. The Vienna Convention on Civil Liability was adopted by the International Atomic Energy Agency (IAEA) in 1997 and entered into force in 2003. Also, the US-led Convention on Supplementary Compensation for Nuclear Damage (CSC) was adopted in 1997, though it has not yet come into force.[20] If Japan accedes, the Convention will enter into force immediately.

Japan is not a signatory to any of these treaties, though Japan is now considering accession to the CSC since it limits the liability of manufacturers of nuclear technology. This step would protect Japan's economic interest as a country that promotes the export of nuclear power plant technology. In fact, the Vietnamese government has urged the Japanese government to explore its nuclear expertise even after the Fukushima disaster. The prime minister of Vietnam claims that from the experience of the accident, the Japan-made plant would be the safest in the world. Using the same logic, Prime Minister Shinzo Abe and his government have been active in the sale of nuclear power plant technology worldwide, even though many of the suspended plants in Japan have not yet resumed operation.[21]

The CSC also limits the jurisdiction of damages claims exclusively to the country in which the accident takes place. This is a desirable outcome for Japan, as it would immunize Japan from extraterritorial claims for damages. In addition, the CSC enables sharing of the damages among member countries. Thus, international law supports and promotes nuclear power by limiting the availability of compensation for victims and is not directed to the advancement of human security.

Contemporary international law does not seem to ensure sufficient international access to justice for victims of nuclear power plant accidents. Rather, it has been developed to restrict it in order to promote the nuclear power industry worldwide. Compensation for damages is regulated for this purpose under international law. Human security for people suffering the effect of nuclear incidents is a secondary concern. Human sacrifice is premised as a necessary cost for the development of the nuclear industry. The primary goal of international laws on compensation for nuclear damage is to minimize the burden of states in order to develop the nuclear power industry.

Environmental law relating to nuclear accidents, and nuclear safety law

An estimated 13,000 tons of radioactive contaminated water had been produced by the Fukushima meltdown by April 2011. Under international law, however, there is no more than territorial responsibility. Article 192 of UN Convention on the Law of the Sea (ratified by Japan in 1996) provides for the duty to preserve the environment in general, but it imposes no concrete obligations. The London International Maritime Organization (IMO) prohibits dumping, but only from vessels. There is no international law to govern the contamination caused by the Fukushima accident even if other countries suffer from this contamination.[22]

The Early Notification Convention and Convention on Assistance were adopted after the Chernobyl accident in 1986. The Convention on Nuclear Safety was adopted in 1994 and in force by 1996. Japan ratified it in 1995. As of April 2014, 77 countries, including all major nuclear states, were signatories. The Convention is the cornerstone of the international legal framework on nuclear safety as it is the first legally binding international instrument. These treaties recommend a 'Three-S-Approach' to nuclear energy, 'safety – security – safeguarding'. In 2006, the International Atomic Energy Agency adopted 'Ten Fundamental Safety Principles' drawn from this earlier international law.

However, the Convention contains no concrete obligations. A 'soft' approach to achieving their objectives was adopted. They are so-called incentive conventions.[23] The 'enforcing instrument' is just the peer review exercised by the contracting parties at the review meetings. The instruments are demonstrably too soft and ineffective.[24]

It does not, however, stipulate detailed safety standards and rather fundamental safety principles for land-based nuclear power plants.[25] The so-called Three-S-Approach to nuclear energy requesting 'safety – security – safeguarding' was based on comprehensive international legal grounds.[26]

As explained, controlling the growth in nuclear power plants is not irrelevant to proliferation concerns relating to nuclear weapons. Although President Obama made a historic speech on abolishing nuclear weapons in Prague on 5 April 2009 and was awarded a Nobel Peace Prize, the real practice has not moved forward. Rather, US policy appears to support the advance of nuclear militarization through its support of nuclear power plant construction by its allies. Nuclear power plant construction and the associated issue of non-proliferation of nuclear weapons are global issues that require action through access to international justice.

Implications for human security as ethics and governance

There is little hard law for access to international justice for human security to protect from nuclear threat. Nevertheless, some soft laws are emerging. The UN Guiding Principles on Internal Displacement,[27] which were adopted by the UN Commission on Human Rights in 1998 and by a UN General Assembly Resolution in 2004, can be applied to the displaced people from the nuclear disaster in Fukushima. The principles apply to people who are internally displaced by a natural disaster which triggers a human-made disaster. There is no international instrument to protect people who cross national borders though. The human security idea should address this ethical gap in our global age. As for private sector engagement, the UN Global Compact is now promoting responsibility for human rights and environmental issues, although nuclear threat is not directly mentioned.

Global governance based on the 'Precautionary Principle' due to the risk presented to all people and creatures by a nuclear disaster should be introduced, whether the nuclear damage is human-made or not – since we share a common ecology. The threat of nuclear accident is real. Kori nuclear power plant in Korea experienced an accident caused by human error in February 2012 and, alarmingly, the accident was hidden for a month. Human security must now become our paramount consideration.

The Fukushima incident has reminded us that we have not yet solved the problem of nuclear waste, which has the potential to cause harm for approximately 100,000 years. Notwithstanding this challenge, the construction of nuclear power plants is continuing worldwide. The cost and risk of nuclear waste appears ignored and forgotten, leaving future generations a huge burden and significant safety and security risks. No international law addresses these significant issues. Access to international justice for future generations should be seriously considered to prevent further humanitarian disasters such as the Fukushima disaster.

There is no hard international law like the Convention of Status of Refugees addressing the security of persons who cross national borders in the even of a disaster. The UN Global Compact engages the private sector and promotes corporate social responsibly for human rights and environmental issues but a nuclear threat is not specifically dealt with as yet. Similar to global warming, a nuclear threat could be addressed directly through market-based mechanisms as nuclear power is promoted as an alternative energy source replacing fossil fuel. Sooner or later, soft law will emerge to cover these limitations. Assisted by the UN Global Compact, ISO26000 has been adopted as a guidance document for a sustainable society covering human rights and environmental issues. The nuclear threat is a complex combination of human rights and environmental issues requiring redress through a global code of conduct.

Conclusion

The people in Hiroshima and Nagasaki were sacrificed not only for the war to be ended but also for the peace that followed. However, we are not free from the dangers posed by nuclear power. Nuclear power has been used for peaceful means. Fukushima has reminded the world of the significant threat of nuclear disaster. Despite criticisms based on the experience of Fukushima Daiichi a quarter century after the Chernobyl disaster, the number of the nuclear plants is still increasing and affecting more people worldwide.

Now we know its risk much more clearly than before and we can predict that accidents like the one at Fukushima will take place again at some point, we need to take steps to ensure that there is an international legal regime for justice and compensation, and reasonable access to it. A future nuclear disaster could be even more catastrophic than Fukushima, ignoring national borders and geographic demarcations as the radioactivity spreads by wind and water. We cannot ignore this threat any longer. We must take steps to ensure human security.

At present, we do not seem to be ready to face this reality. The international framework to address such transborder catastrophes is not well developed. Rather, the current regime seems to promote proliferation and dissemination of nuclear power without dealing with the issue of the disposal of nuclear waste.

Victims of the Fukushima meltdown are still suffering, and in the aftermath radioactive contaminated water is still leaking into the ground and the Pacific Ocean. The Japanese government admitted that it would take more than three decades to remedy. If Japan wants to sell its nuclear technology as safe, it should demonstrate that it has the technology to deal with accidents and waste. If it does not do so, then it is perpetuating the irresponsible myths of risk-free nuclear power. This poses a threat to human security, and the human security of future generations. Furthermore, in light of its history, Japan should take a leadership role in promoting an international legal framework and cooperation for human security in the face of nuclear threats, whether caused by weaponry or nuclear power.

For this purpose, the international legal framework for access to justice for victims of nuclear incidents must be strengthened. Justice in these matters is not just a matter of punishment and sufficient compensation but learning and applying lessons from history. A combination of criminal and civil justice instruments as well as the implementation of the IAEA 'Precautionary Principle' will need to be introduced to ensure a better global framework for nuclear safety.

Japan has promoted the human security concept for the last two decades since the United Nations Development Programme proposed it as a new development paradigm in its Human Development Report 1994. Is Japan's nuclear power policy consistent with its human security policy? In particular, how does Japan justify nuclear power plants all over the world without simultaneously ensuring that there are meaningful safety measures in place, and a suitable regulatory framework underpinning that safety? It is highly recommended that Japan's efforts for the development of an international legal regime to protect victims of nuclear disasters and the development of systems to ensure access to that new international regime should be supported. Its efforts to do so and its failure to do so should be the subject of continued examination.

Notes

1 *Hibakusha Engo Ho* (The Law concerning Atomic Bomb Survivors Relief) (adopted as of 16 December 1994 Law No. 117 and entered into force as of 1 July 1995 as amended through 24 June 2011 Law No. 74) replaced the previous laws, including the Law Concerning Medical Treatment of Atomic Bomb Survivors enacted in April 1957. At that time, more than 200,000 persons received certificates for such medical treatment by the government.

2 International Court of Justice 1996, para E.

3 Japan refused to sign a joint statement on the humanitarian consequences of nuclear weapons submitted to the NPT PrepCom by 74 other non-nuclear weapon countries on 24 April 2013. Ambassador Mori explained to NHK TV that it conflicted with the Japanese national security policy, as the US could use nuclear weapons to defend Japan. The joint statement read that the use of nuclear weapons must be prevented 'under any circumstances'. See Loretz 2013.

4 Nanda 2009: 335–337.

5 Details of the accident are discussed in Burns 2012.

6 Some scientists suspect that the generator was broken before the arrival of the tsunami. See Tanaka 2013.

7 See the Fukushima prefecture government's spreadsheet: www.pref.fukushima.jp/j/jishin-sokuhou1002.xls (accessed 6 August 2013). It also reported on 28 May 2013 that 29,148 children under the age of 18 were evacuated because of the earthquake and the nuclear accident. The number of displaced persons amounted to approximately 10 per cent of those who had lived in Fukushima prefecture before the earthquake. See 'Fukushima Nuclear Power Plant Meltdown: Evacuees Number', *Asahi Shimbun*, 15 May 2012.

8 The US government recommended that its citizens should evacuate from 50 miles

(80 km) from the Fukushima plant, while the Japanese government announced the evacuation of people living within 20 km of the plant. See Vastag *et al.* 2011.

9 For detailed data of the total forced migration immediately following the earthquake, see Anderson 2012.

10 See, 'Nuclear Crisis Deaths', *Tokyo Shimbun*, 11 March 2013.

11 See Independent Investigation Commission on the Fukushima Nuclear Accident 2014. According to the Norwegian Institute for Air Research, Fukushima released cesium at roughly twice the official Japanese Government figure. See Brumfliel 2014.

12 See Tokyo Electric Power Company 2012. Online.

13 See The National Diet of Japan 2012.

14 See Investigation Committee on the Accident at Fukushima Nuclear Power Stations of Tokyo Electric Power Company 2012.

15 For details, see Vasques-Maignan 2011.

16 Ideii 2012.

17 See Umeda 2013. In 2012, laws were enacted for the support of children and victims of the accident. In late 2013, a statute of limitations for damages was introduced. Claims were allowable for loss of assets, inability to work, and emotional damage. According to Feldman (2013) initially only those who were forced to evacuate were eligible to receive payments for emotional harm.

18 Kainuma 2011.

19 Ramseyer 2011.

20 Kuş 2011. Kuş discusses details of the legal instruments on nuclear safety and the third-party liability, which was developed after Chernobyl.

21 The former DPJ (Democratic Party of Japan) government announced that Japan should be free of dependence on nuclear power by the 2030s. But the DPJ was beaten by the LDP led by Mr Shinzo Abe, who was appointed prime minister again as the result of the House of Representative's election in December 2012. The LDP, which was responsible for the nuclear policy causing the accident, formed a government and has returned to its policy of promoting nuclear power in order to boost the Japanese economy. This policy has been adopted even though the safety risks caused by the Fukushima Daiichi meltdown have not yet been fully controlled. There have also been no further regulatory innovations designed to ensure the punishment of the perpetrators of the accident. This policy involves tacit acceptance of the myth of absolute safety.

22 On 6 August 2013, it was reported that highly radioactive water was seeping into the Pacific Ocean from the Fukushima Daiichi nuclear plant. Since the accident, highly radioactive water that is used to cool the reactors has been preserved in numerous tanks, but nobody knows how to dispose of such a huge amount of contaminated water. Thus the aftermath of the Fukushima accident has not yet been solved, it is still outstanding, and it is said that it will take more than 30 years to decommission the reactors. CBC News 2013.

23 Cavoski 2013: 368.

24 However, Pelzer argues that nuclear safety is becoming a 'collective responsibility', supported by the Convention. He also argues that criticism of the incentive approach neglects the reality of international life: Pelzer 2013: 71–72.

25 Kuş 2011: 17.

26 For details, see Endo 2009: 3–6.

27 UN Commission on Human Rights, 11 February 1998.

References

'573 Deaths Related to Nuclear Crisis'. *Daily Yomiuri*, 5 February 2012. Online. Available at www.asyura2.com/13/genpatu30/msg/719.html (accessed 14 May 2014).

Anderson, Chris C. 'Japan Earthquake Anniversary: Survivor Yoriko Miura Tells of Daughter's Death'. The *Huffington Post*, 9 March 2012.

Brumfliel, Geoff, 'Fallout forensics hike radiation toll: Global date on Fukushima challenge Japanese estimates'. Nature International Weekly Journal of Science, 26 October 2011. Online. Available at www.nature.com/news/fallout=forensics-hike-radiation-toll-1.9237 (accessed 2 October 2014).

Burns, Stephen G. 'Global Nuclear Energy Law Regulation Symposium: The Fukushima Daiichi Accident: Global Community Responds'. *Washington University Global Studies Law Review* 4, No. 4 (2012): 741–745.

Cavoski, Aleksandra. 'Revisiting the Convention on Nuclear Safety: Lessons Learned from the Fukushima Accident'. *Asian Journal of International Law* 3 (2013): 365–391.

CBC News. 'Fukushima Nuclear Plant Facing New Disaster'. The *Huffington Post* (Canada), 22 August 2013. Online. Available at www.huffingtonpost.ca/2013/08/23/fukushima-water-leaks_n_3797446.html (accessed 11 August 2014).

Endo, Tetsuya. *Countries Planning to Introduce Nuclear Power Generation and the 3ss: Making 3ss an International Standard.* ICNND research paper. Tokyo: Japan Institute of International Affairs Associated Research Centre of ICNND (International Commission on Nuclear Non-proliferation and Disarmament), 2009.

Feldman, Eric A. 'Fukushima: Castrophe, Compensation , and Justice in Japan'. *DePaul Law Review* 62 (2013): 325–356.

'Fukushima Nuclear Power Plant Meltdown: Evacuee Numbers'. *Asahi Shimbun*, 15 May 2012.

Ideii, Naoki. 'The Nuclear Damage Claim Dispute Resolution Center'. *JCAA Newsletter* 28 (2012): 1–4.

Independent Investigation Commission on the Fukushima Nuclear Accident. 'The Fukushima Daiichi Nuclear Power Station Disaster: Investigating the Myth and Reality'. Edited by Mindy Kay Bricker. London: Routledge, 2014.

International Court of Justice. 'Advisory Opinions'. In *Legality of the Threat or Use of Nuclear Weapons*. ICJ, 1996. Online. Available at www.icj-cij.org/docket/index.php?p1=3&p2=5&p3=-1&y=1996 (accessed 7 August 2014).

Investigation Committee on the Accident at Fukushima Nuclear Power Stations of Tokyo Electric Power Company. 'Final Report'. Tokyo: Government of Japan, 23 July 2012. Online. Available at www.cas.go.jp/jp/seisaku/icanps/eng/final-report.html (accessed 7 August 2014).

Kainuma, Hiroshi. *Fukushima Ron: Genshiryokumura Wa Naze Umareta No Ka* (*Fukushima Study: Why Was the Nuclear Power Village Born?*). Japan: Seidosh, 2011.

Kuş, Selma. 'International Nuclear Law in the 25 Years between Chernobyl and Fukushima and Beyond…'. *Nuclear Law Bulletin* 1 (2011): 8–25.

Loretz, John. 'Japan Admits the Obvious'. *International Physicians for the Prevention of Nuclear War*, 25 April 2013. Online. Available at http://peaceandhealthblog.com/2013/04/25/japan-admits-obvious (accessed 14 May 2014).

Nanda, Ved P. 'Nuclear Weapons, Human Security, and International Law'. *Denver Journal of International Law and Policy* 37, No. 3 (2009): 331–350.

'Nuclear Crisis Deaths'. *Tokyo Shimbun*, 11 March 2013.

Pelzer, Norbert. 'Safer Nuclear Energy through a Higher Degree of Internationalisation?: International Involvement Versus National Sovereignty'. *Nuclear Law Bulletin*, 2013.

Ramseyer, J. Mark. 'Why Power Companies Build Nuclear Reactors on Fault Lines: The Case of Japan'. In *Discussion Paper No. 698*. Cambridge, MA: Harvard Law School, 2011.

Tanaka, Mitsuhiko. 'Presentation by Former Nuclear Power Plant Designer and Member of the National Diet Investigation Commission on the Accident of the Fukushima Nuclear Plants'. In *The Truth of the Fukushima Nuclear Accident and the Myth of Nuclear Safety*. Komaba Campus in the University of Tokyo: University of Tokyo, 2013. Online. Available at http://hsp.c.u-tokyo.ac.jp/eng/others.html (accessed 14 May 2014).

The National Diet of Japan. *The Fukushima Nuclear Accident Independent Investigation Commission Report*. Tokyo: The National Diet of Japan, 2012. Online. Available at http://cryptome.org/2012/07/daiichi-naiic.pdf (accessed 7 August 2014).

Tokyo Electric Power Company. 'Fukushima Nuclear Accident Analysis Report'. Tokyo Electric Power Company, 20 June, 2012. Online. Available at www.tepco.co.jp/en/press/corp-com/release/2012/1205638_1870.html (accessed 14 May 2014).

Umeda, Sayuri. *Japan: Legal Responses to the Great East Japan Earthquake of 2011*. Washington DC: The Law Library of Congress, Global Legal Research Center, 2013.

UN Commission on Human Rights. 'Report of the Representative of the Secretary-General, Mr. Francis M. Deng, Submitted Pursuant to Commission Resolution 1997/39. Addendum: Guiding Principles on Internal Displacement', (E/CN.4/1998/53/Add.2), 11 February 1998. Online. Available at www.refworld.org/docid/3d4f95e11.html (accessed 12 August 2014).

Vasques-Maignan, Ximena. 'Fukushima: Liability and Compensation'. *Nuclear Law Bulletin* 2 (2011): 61–64.

Vastag, Brian, Maese, Rick and Fahrenthold, David A. 'U.S. Urges Americans within 50 Miles of Japanese Nuclear Plant to Evacuate; NRC Chief Outlines Dangerous Situation'. *The Washington Post*, 17 March 2011.

Index

Page numbers in *italics* denote tables

For Product Safety Concerns and Information please contact our EU
representative GPSR@taylorandfrancis.com
Taylor & Francis Verlag GmbH, Kaufingerstraße 24, 80331 München, Germany

www.ingramcontent.com/pod-product-compliance
Ingram Content Group UK Ltd.
Pitfield, Milton Keynes, MK11 3LW, UK
UKHW020013200926
475702UK00014B/1862

* 9 7 8 1 1 3 8 2 3 8 2 4 4 *